Administering the Co<del>lonizer</del>

Glen Peterson, *The Power of Words: Literacy and Revolution in South China, 1949-95*

Wing Chung Ng, *The Chinese in Vancouver, 1945-80: The Pursuit of Identity and Power*

Yijiang Ding, *Chinese Democracy after Tiananmen*

Diana Lary and Stephen MacKinnon, eds., *Scars of War: The Impact of Warfare on Modern China*

Eliza W.Y. Lee, ed., *Gender and Change in Hong Kong: Globalization, Postcolonialism, and Chinese Patriarchy*

Christopher A. Reed, *Gutenberg in Shanghai: Chinese Print Capitalism, 1876-1937*

James A. Flath, *The Cult of Happiness: Nianhua, Art, and History in Rural North China*

Erika E.S. Evasdottir, *Obedient Autonomy: Chinese Intellectuals and the Achievement of Orderly Life*

Hsiao-ting Lin, *Tibet and Nationalist China's Frontier: Intrigues and Ethnopolitics, 1928-49*

Xiaoping Cong, *Teachers' Schools and the Making of the Modern Chinese Nation-State, 1897-1937*

Diana Lary, ed., *The Chinese State at the Borders*

Norman Smith, *Resisting Manchukuo: Chinese Women Writers and the Japanese Occupation*

Hasan H. Karrar, *The New Silk Road Diplomacy: China's Central Asian Foreign Policy since the Cold War*

Richard King, ed., *Art in Turmoil: The Chinese Cultural Revolution, 1966-76*

Administering the Colonizer
Manchuria's Russians under Chinese Rule, 1918-29
Blaine R. Chiasson

UBCPress · Vancouver · Toronto

20 19 18 17 16 15 14 13 12 11 10   5 4 3 2 1

Printed in Canada with vegetable-based inks on FSC-certified ancient-forest-free paper (100% post-consumer recycled) that is processed chlorine- and acid-free.

Library and Archives Canada Cataloguing in Publication

Chiasson, Blaine R. (Blaine Roland), 1964-
   Administering the colonizer : Manchuria's Russians under Chinese rule, 1918-29 / Blaine R. Chiasson.

(Contemporary Chinese studies, ISSN 1206-9523)
Description based on Publisher data. This item is not in the LAC collection.
ISBN 978-0-7748-1656-4 (bound); 978-0-7748-1657-1 (pbk)

   1. Russians – China – Manchuria – History – 20th century. 2. Manchuria (China) – Ethnic relations – History – 20th century. 3. Harbin Shi (China) – Politics and government – 20th century. I. Title. II. Series: Contemporary Chinese studies

DS731.R9C55 2010   951'.840049171   C2010-903810-X

e-book ISBNs: 978-07748-1658-8(pdf); 978-0-7748-5923-3 (epub)

Canadä

UBC Press gratefully acknowledges the financial support for our publishing program of the Government of Canada (through the Canada Book Fund), the Canada Council for the Arts, and the British Columbia Arts Council.

This book has been published with the help of a grant from the Canadian Federation for the Humanities and Social Sciences, through the Aid to Scholarly Publications Programme, using funds provided by the Social Sciences and Humanities Research Council of Canada.

UBC Press
The University of British Columbia
2029 West Mall
Vancouver, BC V6T 1Z2
www.ubcpress.ca

To Washabuck and Cheticamp

"RUSSIANS ARE EASY TO MARRY, BUT IT IS HARD TO CHANGE THEIR CUSTOMS"

– *Title of Article in Chinese newspaper* Binjiang shibao *[Binjiang News] (Harbin), 2 February 1922*

DO NOT MAKE A *HOOCHA* [RUSSIAN NICKNAME FOR A CHINESE COOLIE] CITY OUT OF HARBIN!

– *Insult shouted during Harbin's 1922 municipal elections, "Unusual Fiasco in Municipal Elections,"* Zaria, *18 December 1922, NARA, RG 59, M329, Roll 100, File 893.102H/399, 17 January 1923*

OH, THOSE RUSSIANS ...

– *Boney M, "Rasputin,"* Nightflight to Venus, *1978*

Contents

Acknowledgments

Thanks first to my family, my parents, Roland and Elizabeth Chiasson, my brother, Mark, and my partner, Kevin Morrow, without whose love this monograph would not have been possible. I also thank my extended Macdonald and Chiasson families, the many uncles, aunts, cousins, and second-cousins, who have observed, with affection and exasperation over the decade, the progress of this book. I would have never written this without the influence of my supervisors, Timothy Brook and Olga Bakich, to whom I am very grateful for their guidance and rigorous criticism. Tim's cohort of students, in particular Ravi Vatheespera, Ruth Rempel, and Dot Tuer, from his amazing class in social theory, each have their own part here. From the University of Toronto I thank Michael Szonyi and André Schmid. Connie da Silva Borges, Jennifer Francisco, Tracy McDonald, Daniel Healy, Hilary Earl, and Carl Morey I remember with affection and gratitude. Friends such as Jeff Whynot, Glen Thomas, Terry Dawe, Sandra Hyde, Francisco deLago, and Catherine and Richard Tillman were a source of immense support. A very special thanks to my friend Kari Bronaugh who saw much of this book through its first incarnations.

I must also thank the inter-library loan staffs of the University of Toronto, McGill University, and Wilfrid Laurier University. Thanks also to the Wilfrid Laurier Research Office for their support in the preparation of this manuscript. My colleagues, indeed now friends, at the Wilfrid Laurier University history department have provided the support that has made it possible to complete this project. The staffs of the Jilin University Chinese Eastern Library Collection, the Jilin Provincial Archives, the Harbin Municipal Library, and the Hoover Institute were immensely helpful. Special thanks to Jay Carter for first showing me Harbin and for his careful reading of this manuscript. I wish three friends, Dinny Morrison, Janet Proctor, and Lynn Macfie, were still here so I could show them this book. Thanks especially to those who have read over this manuscript's many drafts – Olga, Deb van Ceder, Laraine Coates, Emily Andrew, Lesley Erickson, David Schimmelpenninck van der Oye, and Ronald Suleski – for their patience.

Perhaps all history is personal. Certainly I do not think I would have been attracted to this topic if it were not for having a family foothold among two displaced peoples, French Acadians and Hebridian Scots, each with their own languages, historical grievances, and long memories. Thanks to Lubie Chiasson, Agnes and Malcom Macdonald, and two of the places, among many, that I consider home.

Administering the Colonizer

Introduction:
Where Yellow Ruled White – Harbin, 1929

"It is little realized that in one city in the world the thing (Yellow Peril) is a fait accompli: the Oriental has ascended to the seats of power, is sitting there, and has been sitting there for some time. This city is Harbin, the only white city in the world run by yellows." So begins an article by Olive Gilbreath, "Where Yellow Rules White," published in the February 1929 edition of *Harper's Magazine.*[1] An American journalist and adventurer born in 1883, Gilbreath had travelled the Far East since 1914, witnessed the First World War and the Russian Revolution firsthand in St. Petersburg, and then fled Russia, as did many Russians, by heading east toward the Chinese republic. A sophisticated writer who during her travels in Europe and Asia had witnessed the extremes of human behaviour, Gilbreath was astonished by the northern Manchurian city of Harbin; its lifeline, the Chinese Eastern Railway (CER); and the "drama of changing peoples, of shifting social orders and races."[2] Located at the hub of two branches of the Trans-Siberian Railway's northern Manchurian shortcut, funded with Russian money, built with Chinese labour, and, prior to 1917, administered as a Russian concession, Harbin was by 1929 a city in which "the mass of the city is white, but the wires, the antennae that control it, are Chinese. The whole administration, in short, of this Russian city of eighty thousand is Chinese."[3] Gilbreath was one of many Anglo-American tourists and journalists who visited the northeastern Chinese city of Harbin in the decade between 1920 and 1930. As much as these foreign visitors were accustomed to the world and its diversity, they found (depending on their politics and racial prejudices) Harbin intriguing, unparalleled, and deeply shocking. Harbin, which was the railway and administrative centre of the newly founded Special District, was in its culture, architecture, and population a combination of two very different cultures and peoples: Russian and Chinese. Adding to the shock and generating a frisson of threatened racial hierarchies (which one can still feel when reading these articles today) was the fact that, unlike other great Chinese concession cities with large foreign populations, such as Shanghai or Hankou, the Russian population did not control the city and the concession. The Special District's administration was Chinese.

Although today Harbin is something of a provincial backwater, in the 1920s it was not only the hub city for the CER – which took passengers and freight north to the USSR, west to Europe, and south to Dalian and China proper – it was one of the few modern cities with the distinction of having been founded by two countries and two nationalities. Russians and Chinese had worked together under the CER's supervision to settle the city and its concession in the late nineteenth century. As the heart of this international rail network and the largest northern Manchurian city, Harbin was a vital commercial, administrative, and cultural centre that pulsed with a cosmopolitan energy that is very much absent from the present-day city. Prior to 1949 Harbin had, at most, 250,000 to 300,000 inhabitants; as many as 40,000 were Russians. Today, many people take the chaotic nature and the racial, linguistic, and cultural mix of vibrant multicultural cities for granted; such cities have become the background noise to our everyday lives. For Harbin's visitors in the 1920s – many of whom took for granted, especially in China, racial segregation and European superiority – the ease with which racial and cultural boundaries were crossed and flaunted in Harbin was unsettling.

What follows is a study of Gilbreath's "Chinese wires": the Chinese administration of the Special District of the Three Eastern Provinces [*dongsansheng tiebie qu*] (hereafter referred to as the Special District), created in 1920 to replace the Russian-controlled CER concession.[4] Replacement, however, is only half of the story. This study is equally concerned with how the Special District's new Chinese administrators crafted policies that would not only ensure Chinese supervision but also preserve the conditions that made the CER concession – and its successor, the Special District – one of republican China's most prosperous regions by securing the economic, cultural, and political rights of its stateless Russian settlers. This is a history of an administrative experiment in pragmatic accommodation that partially failed because of deeply held ideas of racial superiority on the part of Russians, lingering colonial resentment on the part of Chinese, and the power of national identity to shape all of these actors.

Although this book opens with Gilbreath's observations, this is not solely a story about foreign reaction to this administrative experiment. Most Anglo-European accounts posit the Special District as a cautionary tale of the fate awaiting all foreigners in China should extraterritoriality be abolished. In their decision to concentrate, embellish, or outright fabricate narratives of foreign exploitation, these sources ignored the policy successes pioneered by the Special District.

Nor is it a story about Russian Kharbin or Chinese Haerbin, for these narratives are often driven by national pride and a combination of colonial and postcolonial resentment. Like many émigré sources the world over, those of Manchuria's former Russian population are often infused with nostalgia and bitterness. For émigrés (forced out of China in the 1950s and thus doubly exiled) who sought to justify and defend Russian colonialism in northern Manchuria, the story of the Chinese administration's success is also the story of Russian decline and marginalization. Although foreign or Russian accounts tend to also celebrate Russian achievement and criticize the Chinese, contemporary Chinese histories of the Dongsansheng, written to secure for that region the Chinese past it never truly had, literally excise from the region's history Russian influence as well as the contributions of other nations and nationalities.

Instead, this book shows that Harbin's Chinese administration – along with its administrative parent, the Special District – was a localized response to the problem of asserting Chinese sovereignty in a former foreign concession, one greatly influenced by its Russian population and founding administrative model. The city and district's Chinese elite did not merely seek to imitate but also to create new opportunities for civic expression and good governance. The administrative form it pioneered was shaped equally by the two founding peoples and the conditions each faced to establish their national, cultural, and administrative presence in a regional frontier. Studies of the interaction between Chinese and foreign communities in Manchuria and China proper have stressed foreign-Chinese conflict and the emergence of a rather uncomplicated (read xenophobic) Chinese nationalism. In this book the focus is on Harbin's and the Special District's special conditions. The region was a frontier area recently occupied by China and therefore needed administrative policies based on compromise rather than conflict. Circumstances in the area encouraged a more flexible Chinese nationalism, one that allowed for considerable Russian influence. In essence, the goal of extending Chinese sovereignty in northern Manchuria was shaped by the presence of a large non-Chinese immigrant community that was essential to the region's economy and whose needs could not be ignored.

The administrative experiment also had a pedagogical function. The Special District's Chinese administration served as an important example of how Chinese sovereignty could be asserted over China's foreign concessions without threatening the political and property rights of the foreign settler community. However, the essentially colonialist nature of the Russian and Soviet presence in northern Manchuria and the resentment many Chinese felt toward the region's former colonial masters poisoned some aspects of the administrative experiment. Regional Chinese and Russian identities that influenced the policy of compromise clashed with national ideologies, both Russian and Chinese, that refused to accept an equal partnership. Despite the difficulties they encountered in the administration of the Russian community, the Chinese elite – which, like the Russian elite, consisted primarily of Chinese administrators and administrative personnel for the CER – used this opportunity to experiment with new forms of municipal and local governance and to expand the boundaries of civic participation.

Not all of the inhabitants of the Special District, especially some of the displaced Russian elite and the representatives and nationals of China's remaining concessionary powers, praised these administrative solutions. In newspaper and journal articles, memoirs and bitter diatribes, diplomatic dispatches and consular reports, and political tracts designed to inflame racial or political divisions, these critics derided the Special District's decade-long administrative experiment. By describing the Special District as a reversal of natural racial hierarchies, as the assertion of crude Chinese nationalism, and as a harbinger of doom for the whole edifice of treaty-backed foreign privilege in China, these accounts have shaped how historians view the region's history.

These narrators employed a variety of images – a Chinese merchant and his Russian wife, a Russian maid washing the windows of her Chinese employer's home, Russian bodyguards protecting wealthy Chinese clients, and Russian beggars on the streets of the now Chinese-controlled city of Harbin – to communicate that Harbin represented, for them, a world turned upside down. Nevertheless, one image dominated their stories – an image that Caucasian journalists writing for the treaty port press knew would provoke the strongest reaction from their readers. It was the image of a Chinese who not only held power over a white man or woman but whose power was also buttressed by a Chinese administration that had abolished extraterritoriality, the right of some nationalities to be outside of Chinese law. In short, the image represented fears about Caucasians being subjected to a Chinese-controlled administration. Foreign journalists such as Gilbreath, for instance, included images of Chinese policemen remonstrating or beating Russian men or women. "Now the traffic policeman, who puts up his hand at which the bearded *Jehu* stops short, has a yellow skin and slant eyes. If there is an altercation, the Russian will be slapped or beaten before a crowd and there is no redress. If he is arrested, it is the heavy hand of the yellow which hales him to the *yamen* and the judge he meets is yellow."[5] Some saw Harbin as the "grave of the white man's prestige" because "Caucasians are governed and bullied by Chinese officials and Chinese soldiers and policemen."[6] In the Special District, Chinese control over foreigners was seen as a portent "for nowhere in all the East – since the early days of Treaty Ports and extraterritorial privileges – have yellow men ever ruled over whites, with the power of arrest and punishment."[7]

During the 1920s these questions of extraterritoriality and imperialism moved to the forefront of Chinese-foreign relations, and the Special District was where anxieties about Chinese rule and the position of the white race in China were played out.[8] Harbin was portrayed as "the largest foreign community without rights, subject to the vagrancy's [sic] and eccentricities of Chinese law."[9] One English author, on the subject of the end of extraterritoriality, wrote that the Russians were

abominably treated by Chinese officials, beggared, leaderless and helpless in a strange land, were as meek and as long-suffering as cattle. Of this temper every Chinese coolie took delighted advantage, and knocking Russians about became a favorite Chinese sport throughout North China. Although small foreign communities in China supported thousands of these poor folks who could find no work, helped others to find employment and liberally patronized all manner of Russian charities, there was much inevitable suffering which the Chinese did virtually nothing to relieve but which they soon learned to aggravate, taking delight in humiliating and abusing these poor folk to their own imagined aggrandizement.[10]

The author could marshal no evidence to support this claim, but none was needed. The image was enough, and the warning was clear. The Chinese had their inspiration to take over all concessions "from their experience of taking over Russian areas and Russian Consulates, giving the Chinese officialdom much courage in pushing forward a policy of encroachment upon the treaties and which prompted the Chinese common people in many quarters to regard this surrender of the Russians to the Chinese as license to browbeat and abuse aliens."[11] Foreign correspondents were obsessed by the ongoing drama of the Russian princess as taxi dancer or the Chinese policeman who beat the Russian beggar. This obsession reflected the belief of foreigners in China that their continued prosperity and elevated social position rested solely on maintaining their extraterritorial status. For these reporters and their audience, the fate of China's Russian émigrés, as foreigners saw it, was a cautionary tale of the fate that awaited all foreigners should extraterritoriality disappear. Because they lack objectivity, foreign accounts of the Special District administration have limited usefulness.

It is therefore necessary to problematize contemporary European and Japanese treatment of the Harbin administration. Changes to Harbin's administration were linked in the treaty port press to the overthrow of the natural order and accepted conventions of work, race, and sexuality. Maurice Hindus wrote in 1928: "Since the change in government the old stigma of social inferiority has gone, there is no place in Harbin from which the Chinese are barred. They work together on the railroad; some wealthy Chinese have Russian servants. There are shared bandits gangs and intermarriage. A number of them (Russians) have become Chinese citizens. A host of Russian Émigrés has to win and hold the good will of the Chinese in order to earn a living."[12]

These images – of Russians labouring for Chinese or, more often than not, being subject to the power of Chinese – were reported as having been told to the authors or as hearsay. These stories should be read as examples of treaty port anxiety rather than the unconditional truth. Nevertheless, the stereotypes they perpetuate have influenced the historiography on Harbin and the Special District.

Russian histories and accounts of Harbin and the Special District are, quite simply, diverse; they reflect the complexity of the Russian community in Manchuria. The Russian community was split along class lines. Old Russian Harbin families, for instance, were economically secure and tended to monopolize the better jobs. They also tended to be politically and culturally conservative. Residents also distinguished themselves through the length of their residence: *starozhily* (old-timers) were differentiated from émigrés.[13] And they were divided along political and national lines – some chose to be Chinese citizens, some Soviet, and some remained stateless. Not only was Harbin the most cosmopolitan city under Chinese control (Shanghai was divided between Chinese, French, and Anglo-American administrations) during the 1920s, it was also the only city in the world in which communities representing Imperial Russia and the USSR worked and lived closely together. After 1924 the CER administration was divided between Soviet Russians and Chinese staff appointed by the Manchurian warlord government. According to Gilbreath, "The officials of the Chinese Eastern Railway represent Moscow, and whoever controls the Chinese Eastern Railway controls Harbin. But in population Harbin is White Russian, the stand of the Old Regime." In a fashionable riverside café, she continues, "a group of the Old Regime, the women marked by thin faces and fragile skulls, the men in well-cut suits," sit across the room from Soviet officials. Harbin's opera, clubs, and churches were full of French- and Russian-speaking émigrés, but if you attend an official CER dinner "you dine with Stalin." "In Russia, the Old Regime has ceased to exist in sufficient numbers to affect the scene. In Harbin, they sit side by side."[14] The tension that existed between the Soviet-appointed CER management, regular workers of varying political sympathies, recently arrived refugees, and Bolshevik workers who arrived after 1924 makes any attempt to write of a singular Russian position impossible.

Histories and memoirs written from the perspective of the Russian émigrés reveal that this segment of the population despised the Soviet Union and the post-1924 Sino-Soviet CER administration. Nevertheless, these works share the perspective that all that was good in North Manchuria was the result of Russian colonization. The Chinese, when they appear in these narratives, are portrayed either as good but submissive co-workers and servants or as tyrannical overlords who have to speak pidgin Russian so that Russians can communicate with them.

> Granny lived in Harbin for 54 years and did not know a word of Chinese! But she got on famously with the natives of the country, was adept at making sense of the atrocious pidgin lingo where the words and notions were neither Russian nor Chinese but perfectly understandable to both. Peasants fled to Harbin in droves, carrying in wicker baskets on yokes their old mothers, missies with tiny deformed feet and small children. And begged the Russians, on their knees, to save them. The Russians, they lived behind high, strong fences. In their yards they hid the refugees, gave them food and looked after them. How many lives were saved thanks to the right of extraterritoriality!'[15]

In these narratives, the Chinese are infantilized, the Russians are their saviours, and extraterritoriality is upheld as the foundation of foreign life in Manchuria.

Although contemporary documents from Harbin in the 1920s and 1930s point to a high degree of co-operation between Russians and Chinese, those Russians who chose to base their identity on cultural and national chauvinism have dominated émigré discourse. Insecurity, dislocation, and the ceaseless need for self-legitimization are hallmarks of every émigré population around the world, and these influences can be seen in Russian émigré memoirs on Manchuria. Harbin itself is often bathed in the perpetual light of a golden autumn as the last citadel of pre-war Russian culture in the world, a culture in which the Chinese again disappear. According to Viktor Petrov, "Harbin became, to all intents, a really free Russian town: a place where life continued as previously, in the old Russian way, a place of calm and contentment. As in old Russia, the deep solemn tones of the cathedral bell called the congregation to early morning service, and in the evening people crossed themselves once more as its measured tolling summoned them to mass."[16] Much of the memoir literature is either an overt or covert anti-Soviet exercise in nostalgia. Harbin before 1945 did witness a remarkable final flourishing of pre-revolutionary Russian culture. As a fully formed pre-revolutionary Russian community, Harbin was a refuge unlike any other Russian émigré community in the world. For most émigrés, Harbin was more than a refuge – it was home. These émigrés constructed a community to replace the one taken from them by the Russian Revolution. Once these Russians were forced to leave Manchuria, post 1949, their fragile community was extinguished, except in remembrance. These nostalgic memoirs are perhaps, as Olga Bakich hints, the coping mechanisms of a refugee community with no home other than their own memories. For many of these Harbiners, the past is either too painful to remember or one that must be defended against all detractors.[17] In either case, there is no place for the Chinese in Harbin.

Russian accounts write off the Chinese administration as an expression of narrow chauvinism at best or open persecution at worst. Intermarriage, the thousands of Russians who took Chinese citizenship, the Russians who worked daily with Chinese, who attended school with Chinese, or who lived in mixed neighbourhoods are not included in these memoirs. For Yaacov Liberman, growing up as a Russian Jew in Harbin meant defending that identity. In his memoirs, much like those of other Russian émigrés, he renders Harbin's Chinese invisible as a means of maintaining a Jewish identity:

> For us this existence (as Jews) outweighed the colossus (China) surrounding us, because our own lives were directed by an inner vision of communal integration. This integration was neither effected nor was affected by the local population and its problems ... As I grew older, I often wondered what the Chinese population was doing, while we continued to enjoy life in this city. The question continued to perplex me for many years. Hardly any Chinese youngsters shared our activities and the grown ups seemed to have moved out of sight in order to leave us, their guests, in total privacy.[18]

As in other memoirs, the Chinese disappeared. Yet they reappear when Liberman describes everyday life. His mother learned to speak Chinese. Most of the Chinese Liberman knew spoke Russian. His father worked in an import-export house that had extensive dealings with the Chinese administration and saw in the 1920s an increase in the number of Chinese employees. Chinese attended the Russian concerts and the CER Club. None of these observations were commented on as being unusual or out of the ordinary.

Soviet and post-Soviet Russian histories about Harbin and Manchuria reveal complex state interactions along a shared frontier and explore the dynamic of two nations seeking definition vis-à-vis each other. Histories from both eras, however, tend to exhibit a basic Russian chauvinism by claiming that positive developments in the region were due to Russian intervention. B.A. Romanov's *Russia in Manchuria* condemned the CER and the czarist Russian concession administrative project as imperialist infringements on Chinese sovereignty. Yet Romanov stressed Russian accomplishments in Manchuria and the taming of its wild frontier. The title of G.V. Melikhov's book *Manch'zhuriia: Dalekaia i blizkaia* (Manchuria: Far and Near) stresses not only Manchuria's regional distinctiveness but also Russia's historical links to the area. To paraphrase Melikhov's title, the region is – and yet is not – Russian. Both authors argue that Russians brought civilization and culture to the region and express resentment that the Chinese refuse to admit to the debt they owe Russia.[19] This is not to say that Russians do not have a claim on Harbin history. They do. But it is the possessive nature of that claim that continues to annoy both the Chinese, who did the hard labour, and the émigrés, whom the Soviet state abandoned and defamed and whom the new Russian republic would now reclaim. With the fall of the Soviet Union, a number of histories in addition to Melikhov's have been written about the Russian emigration, and there have been two significant conferences in Russia – one in Moscow and the other in Khabarovsk – on the subject of Harbin. At each conference it was the image of Russian Harbin and the accomplishments of Russians in Manchuria that predominated.[20]

This experiment in Chinese administration has also suffered from the fact that the Special District's political history does not fit the dominant historical narratives chosen by China's twentieth-century governments. During much of the period under consideration, China's national government was like a ball tossed from one warlord to another. Neither of two main political contenders in twentieth-century China – the rightist Nationalists and the Communists – can claim the region's innovations as their own intiative, and the disappearance of this administrative experiment from Chinese written history suggests that the compromises it entailed did not fit into either party's narratives of national or ideological triumph. In 1931 the Japanese conquered the region; in the 1940s the Soviet, Chinese Nationalist (Guomindang, GMD), and Communist armies all fought in Manchuria; and, from 1945 to 1949, the region was the principal battleground of the Chinese Civil War.

The attitude of members of Manchuria's Chinese elite toward their Russian neighbours in the 1920s is complex. Evidence from documents and the Chinese press suggests that there was no single Chinese response to Sino-Russian interaction. For instance, Chinese distinguished between the Russian and Soviet citizens of the Special District. In an exchange of letters between Zhang Zuolin, the warlord who governed Manchuria until his assassination in 1928, and Zhang Huanxiang, Special District police chief (no relation), Zhang Zuolin wrote about "our" Russians and the need to have these people and their skills on the Chinese side.[21] In Harbin's Chinese press, the Russian language was both criticized as a tool of imperial domination and praised as a means of getting ahead. Although Harbin's rising crime rate was blamed on poor Russian refugees conspiring with Chinese criminals, Chinese journalists acknowledged that Russians were driven into crime by economic circumstances and should be pitied and helped out of their plight. The compromise that was the Special District administration can be seen in the short-term solution, which was to hire additional Russian policeman but to teach them to speak Chinese.[22] The Russian elite was castigated for staging an opera that portrayed a servile Chinese character and for continuing to act as if the Russians were the dominant power in Manchuria by pretending to be the hosts instead of the guests. One fascinating article speculated that soaring rates of intermarriage between Chinese and Russians would produce a new civilization and race in Manchuria, one that combined the best elements of both races and cultures.[23]

Chinese histories published since 1949 tend to be written from a nationalist and Marxist perspective. A great effort has been made to establish a thousand-year history of the Chinese presence in Harbin – as if the Russian contribution were a recent aberration. Sun Zhengjia, for instance, writes: "To sum up, the historical culture of our city is one of great antiquity, continuity and variety, and it forms an important constituent part of the glorious and outstanding historical culture of the Chinese nation."[24] Histories written after 1949 also tend to blur the line between Marxism and nationalism. The Chinese Civil War is portrayed as a process both of national liberation and of cleansing Manchuria of its non-Chinese population and history.[25] Most Chinese accounts of Harbin history concentrate on the CER, and they emphasize Russian and Soviet economic and political imperialism.[26] This emphasis has the advantage of symbolically uniting the struggle against transnational capital with the struggle of the working Chinese against their Russian and Soviet oppressors. Officially sanctioned memoirs also stress national themes, although there are hints in descriptions of daily life that the two communities lived together in peace.[27] As for the experience of the Chinese who administered the Russian community and the two communities that worked and lived side by side – there is a gap. The few post-1949 works that mention the Chinese bourgeoisie who controlled the administration are caught between affirming that they defended China's sovereignty and asserting that they did so because of class interests.[28]

Certainly, China's experience with the Russian state, in its various incarnations, did not encourage the Chinese in general and the Manchurian Chinese in particular to explore the subtleties of the relationship. The formation of twentieth-century Chinese nationalism was concurrent with great power incursions on Chinese territory. Russia's occupation and detachment of the area now known as the Russian Far East – that is, its economic, cultural, and military penetration of China – has left feelings of deep resentment among many Chinese. Until recently, Chinese political centralism and a lingering animosity toward the Soviet Union/Russia have made it difficult for a regional historiography, a northeastern or Manchurian school of Chinese history so to speak, to express itself openly. However, there are signs that regional variations to standard Chinese nationalist histories are now being written. Although Ding Lianglun's "A Survey of Harbin's Russian Community, 1917-1931" presents its argument within a Marxist perspective, Ding acknowledges that after 1917, when the Russians had lost their privileged position, they saw the Chinese as equals. In a departure from other contemporary histories, Ding argues that both peoples had a hand in settling the region and that Harbin's political, cultural, and economic infrastructure owed much to Russian settlers.[29]

As a measure of change, in both history writing and Chinese views of their Russian neighbours, one can trace the evolution of Chinese names for Manchurian Russians. Texts from the republican era describe the Russians neutrally as White Russians *(bai-E)*, Russian sojourners or Russian nationals living abroad *(eqiao)*, or, sympathetically, as refugees *(nanmin)*. Many administrative texts describe them as *emin* (Russian settlers or immigrants), a term that carries a connotation of legitimate settlement. In contrast, the favourite term in texts published after 1949 is Russian bandit *(efei)*. Since the relaxation of Russo-Chinese tensions, the term *emin* has come back into use. By focusing on an identity based on settlement rather than on politics or temporary residence, some Chinese historians are beginning to acknowledge the contribution of Russians to the Chinese northeast.[30]

Harbin's origins continue to divide contemporary Harbiners. In 1994 the *Haerbin shizhi* (Harbin City Gazetteer) published a series of articles on how best to commemorate the upcoming centenary of the 1898 railway contact that led to the founding of the city. Most authors expressed caution about or did not believe that the CER should be linked to the foundation of the city. One article, titled "The Day of the Establishment of the Administration Should Be the Commemoration Day of the City," stated that 1920, the year the Special District was created, not 1898, should be designated as the real foundation of the city.[31] Presumably, a truly Chinese Harbin came into existence only at the moment the Chinese assumed administrative control of the city. One Chinese article, however, did make a case for 1898. The author Wei Guozhong argued, in Thomas Lahusen's words, that those who think that attributing the foundation of the city to the CER strikes a blow to China's dignity are narrow minded. Wei invokes the "secret treaty" of 1896, of which he says that it was, after all, signed by two sovereign nations and based on a common investment, that most of those who worked on the construction were Chinese, and that all foreigners were not necessarily aggressors and criminals. He adds: an independent nation that has confidence in itself must not be afraid to acknowledge the positive contribution of foreigners in its history.[32]

Aside from a few Chinese authors such as Wei who are willing to acknowledge Manchuria's multinational origins, however, this brief administrative experiment has no place in existing Chinese national or ideological narratives.

Until recently, the Special District and Harbin were subjects that likewise drew little comment in a Western historiographal tradition that looked to southern China, the nineteenth century, the crisis of extraterritoriality, and the development of Chinese nationalism for their paradigms of Sino-foreign relations. In this context, *Western historiography* is used to designate non-Russian works. This is not a judgment on the cultural place of Russia in the world but rather a convenient historiographical distinction that reinforces the point that the Russian approach to the Special District and Harbin differs from those of Western sources.

John King Fairbank's *Trade and Diplomacy on the China Coast* was an early attempt to categorize Sino-foreign interaction at the administrative level. Fairbank argues that Western contact led to a metamorphosis within Chinese institutions. The West destroyed the old Chinese political and cultural framework, and the Chinese elite was forced to remake itself and its political system. The result was an institutional, administrative, and intellectual Chinese-Western hybrid that Fairbank called "synergy." Leaving aside the dated conceit that Western interaction was the engine of historical change, Fairbank's speculations about synergy, a theory that he argued was beneficial to both parties and responsible for economic and political adaptation, offer a theory that suits this study of the Special District in the 1920s.[33]

In his work "Treaty Ports and China's Modernization," Rhoads Murphey continues Fairbank's theme by speculating on how Chinese and foreign elites were both transformed through their interaction. He characterizes the Chinese elite as a self-regulating society that took advantage of central government weakness to assert an administrative autonomy influenced by foreign economic and political institutions. This characterization fits with the elite's efforts to make the district's administration Chinese largely through trial and error and the Russian model it had inherited.[34] Nevertheless, there are limitations to Murphey's argument. When he states that the treaty ports were not Asian but belonged more to a "modernizing and supranational world than to the particular cultures and economies whose economic peripheries they occupied," he reveals that his argument is based on the Western assumption of European action and Asian reaction.[35] This argument shares a fundamental assumption with the modernization school and its critics – namely, that Asia can only imitate the West or isolate itself to achieve a more authentic form of development. This approach to the Special District places more emphasis on the foreignness and Asianness of the two partners and less on their common administrative problems.

The Fairbank thesis has also been attacked by a few scholars who argue that it echoes modernization theory and justifies imperialism.[36] These China-centred scholars argue that the synergy thesis has an intellectual foundation based on the concept of a stagnate China awoken by interaction with the West. These scholars, in contrast, argue that China must be understood within the context of Chinese history.[37] Indeed, in the 1960s and 1970s, when debates about imperialism left the classrooms and entered the streets, the trend was to de-emphasize the China coast, concessions, and Chinese-foreign interaction. This early debate on Sino-foreign interaction was driven by political and ideological concerns and took as its first principle state-on-state interaction on the China coast. It did not comment on regional administrative variations such as those in Manchuria. As political ideologies have faded and as starkly coloured colonial paradigms have turned to the varied hues of postcolonial theory, it is possible to adopt an integrated and nuanced approach to this episode in the history of Manchuria's administration. Histories of Chinese-foreign and centre-periphery interaction need not be informed solely by the question of whose nation and civilization will prevail.

Many studies of Chinese municipal government have influenced this book, and they share two common themes: the creation of new public spaces and the opportunities for civic participation outside of national control that emerged at moments when the national government was weak. These studies are geographically specific – all focus on southern cities. Maryruth Coleman's study of Nanjing, David Buck's book on Jinan, and David Strand's book on Beijing all examine municipal government as a means for creating a new form of public space in China's cities. Each of these studies concludes that post-imperial elites rose to the challenge of creating new municipal governments and encouraging civic participation. In both Nanjing and Jinan, foreign models were used as a foundation for these new polities. Strand comments that the growing interest in Beijing municipal politics throughout the 1920s was due to a long tradition of guilds and native-place associations and that municipal politics built upon this foundation.[38] Each study concludes, however, that the power and scope of these municipal governments were restricted because of their collaboration and co-optation by the Guomindang, which refused to allow autonomous political structures.[39] In contrast, the Special District obtained sovereignty over a foreign concession in 1920, well before most southern concessions were turned over to Chinese control, and it remained independent until 1932. (Twenty of China's thirty-three concessions would be turned over to Chinese control before 1937, the majority in the mid-1920s and early 1930s. Although the GMD flag was raised over Harbin in 1928, the GMD did not interfere as it did in southern China.

Geographically, the study of concessions, treaty ports, and municipal governance has been dominated by work on southern China, particularly Shanghai and, to a lesser extent, Hong Kong. This is because southern China is considered a site of political and social change, in contrast to the conservatism of the north.[40] Of the two cities, Shanghai has been the most studied. A sprawling, chaotic, multi-ethnic metropolis, Shanghai has captured both the Chinese and non-Chinese imagination, and numerous memoirs on pre-1949 Shanghai have shaped secondary research on this city. The relative ease with which scholars gain access to Shanghai's archives and the availability of primary and secondary sources in English and French have generated a number of studies of the city's municipal government and the relations between the Chinese and non-Chinese communities. Although they claim to be studies of Chinese-foreign interaction, these academic studies focus exclusively on one community or nationality rather then on interactions between groups. Multi-ethnic Shanghai was in fact three cities in one, and the separate communities rarely interacted. In this respect, Harbin offers a better example of true Sino-foreign interaction.

In his work on the Chinese Shanghai Municipal Council, Christian Henriot argues that the Anglo-American and French city councils of Shanghai were the models for Chinese municipal government. Henriot agrees with Strand, Coleman, and Buck that the creation of the city council represented the appearance in China of a new form of public space. Henriot also agrees with a point made in other concession studies – that GMD politics shaped and controlled local politics and ultimately restricted municipal governance.[41] Although they focus only on southern cities, the findings of studies such as Henriot's have been universally applied to all Chinese cities of the 1920s.

Robert Bickers' article "Shanghailanders: The Formation and Identity of the British Settler Community in Shanghai, 1843-1937" is the one work that examines how the experiences of a settler community shaped the formation of a foreign identity. Bickers argues that historians of empire have ignored the history of the British diaspora in Shanghai. His observation that China's settler communities "have been difficult to define and their particularities and problems lost in the wider accounts of the progress of Sino-British relations" is tailor-made for the Russian settler community of China's northeast.[42] He concludes that the economic, racial, and political identity of the English settler community was tied to the maintenance of municipal and judicial privileges in Shanghai and that the struggle to retain these privileges shaped British relations with the Chinese community. In Harbin and the CER concession, the

Russian settler community's identity was linked to the maintenance of that community's privileges, and the real and imagined Chinese threat to those privileges determined the Russian response to Chinese administration.

One Chinese historian has attempted to tell the story of the Russian community in Shanghai. Wang Zhicheng's *Shanghai e-qiaoshi* (A history of the Russian émigré community in Shanghai) is a pioneering work that captures the scope of Shanghai's Russian experience. However, Wang's book is essentially a catalogue of Russian societies, newspapers, and organizations that has little analytical content of the Russian community's cultural or political impact on Shanghai. Wang's history is not a political history of the Sino-Russian relationship because, unlike in Harbin, the Russians were never a strong imperial presence in Shanghai.[43] Hong Kong is the other popular subject in studies on the Sino-foreign administrative experience. In *Hong Kong in Chinese History*, Jung-Fang Tsai argues that the initial colonial relationship of submission and domination determined all future interactions between the English and their Chinese subjects. Tsai counters a school of English triumphalism that sought to disguise the coercive nature of the original colonial relationship.[44]

There have been two recent substantial contributions to the small field of Harbin studies. David Wolff's *To the Harbin Station: The Liberal Alternative in Russian Manchuria, 1898-1914* concentrates on the foundation and early years of Russian-controlled Harbin. Wolff's work has been crucial to establishing Harbin as a valid subject of study, and his book on the city's and the concession's foundations has served to untangle a complicated narrative. Wolff must also be commended for his work in the archives of both founding nations, which has made it clear that it is impossible to study Harbin and the CER government from only one perspective. Wolff's principal claim is that Russian Harbin was a liberal alternative to the more autocratic Russian motherland, which he convincingly bases on the fact that Harbin's city government – the Municipal Council – enfranchised women, Jews, and Chinese.[45] From the perspective of nineteenth-century Imperial Russian history, Harbin appears to have been a more liberal polity. When it is viewed from a pre-1919 Chinese perspective, however, the concession's civic administration was dominated and controlled by the CER and motivated by the need to maintain Russian power in the face of the concession's Chinese majority. After 1919, using the Russian administration as a model, the Chinese would extend the franchise.

James Carter's book *Creating a Chinese Harbin: Nationalism in an International City, 1916-1932* examines the creation of nationalism, an education system, and national symbols in the postcolonial context of 1920s Harbin. By focusing on the Chinese elite, Carter's insightful study uncovers the tension between the goals of achieving sovereignty in a region once controlled by others and the shaping of Chinese nationalism within a regional and multiethnic context.[46] Nevertheless, the key Chinese players in Carter's work are largely outside the Special District's administration, a situation that reflects their espousal of a Chinese nationalism aimed at excluding the Russians. If the administration itself is studied, a much more pragmatic policy, one conditioned also by the demands of administering a multinational government, is revealed.

Carter's conclusion – that because Chinese nationalism in Harbin was weak, China had to compromise with both the USSR and Japan – provides an interesting contrast to the one presented in Rana Mitter's *The Manchurian Myth: Nationalism, Resistance, and Collaboration in Modern China*. Mitter argues that the Manchurian elite gave little resistance to Japanese invasion because their ideas about nation, state, and national identity differed from those of the inhabitants of central China. Manchurian Chinese elites' pliable policy vis-à-vis the invading Japanese confounded the southern Chinese, who had clear national goals of active resistance. Mitter's work points to a regional understanding of Chinese nationalism, one in which the Dongsansheng did not share the south's dogmatic nationalism.[47] This same pliable sense of national identity can also be detected in policies crafted for the region's Russian population in the 1920s.

Manchuria, except as a focus of Japanese imperialism, has received little attention from historians even though in the 1920s the region was the most technologically developed part of China. It had the fastest-growing population, the most developed transportation infrastructure, and the highest rate of urbanization. Despite the seemingly transitory nature of the Special District, its history as an administrative solution – to ruling a large foreign population and asserting Chinese sovereignty – deserves our attention, not only because it complicates our understanding of Chinese nationalism but also because the Special District is an important example of an early solution to problems that dominate the history of many societies today: the settlement of refugees, the collective administration of diverse populations, and the search for a common civic identity in a multicultural context. Although the experience was shaped by the colonialist enterprise that created the Russian CER concession, the Chinese elite used this experience to reformulate ideas about civic participation and nationalism. They would do this earlier than elites in the south and outside the context of GMD politics. In terms of Sino-foreign relations, the influence of foreign ideas on Chinese administration, civic participation, and concepts of citizenship, Manchuria was as important, if not more so, than Shanghai and Hong Kong. Although it draws on questions asked in and responds to the limitations of studies that focus on southern China, this history of the Special District administration goes beyond the southern school of Sino-foreign relations. The Special District was an administrative region in which, in Prasenjit Duara's words, "the tensions between minorities, the border areas and nationalism, at the moment nationalism coalesces" were in full view.[48] National histories written from the perspective of the centre have wiped out these ambiguities. This book restores them.

Railway Frontier:
North Manchuria before 1917

It is said that the Chinese Eastern Railway (CER) concession and its hub city, Harbin, was founded in 1898. The use of the passive voice is deliberate, for the concession's origin is a controversial and contested subject. Chinese sources written after 1949 stress the continuity of Asian settlement in the region of what was then northern Manchuria, while Russian sources point out that the area that became Harbin was relatively uninhabited and contained only a few dilapidated huts and an unused distillery.[1] Although both Russia and China have a stake in establishing that they were the first to occupy the territory before 1890, it is probably local tribes that have the best original claim to northern Manchuria. Unfortunately, like tribal peoples the world over whose homes would become prime real estate, those in Manchuria, having no papers and no national identity to back claims, were swept away in the competition between two nations and two competing frontier colonial projects.

Nevertheless, just as it is impossible to deny that Russia's establishment of the CER concession began the process of large-scale industrial development that transformed northern Manchuria, it is impossible to deny that the Chinese provided the people and the muscle that made this transformation possible. The story will therefore begin with the Russian half of the concession's two founding peoples. Chinese documents written prior to 1949 readily acknowledge the Russian fact in northern Manchuria. For instance, one article from 1929 credits the Russians with building the settlement that became Harbin on a "barren land, empty of people," while Harbin's city guide freely admitted in 1931 that Harbin and the Special District would not exist were it not for the Russians.[2]

The Imperial Russian Finance Ministry created the CER railway concession. The principal justification for running this branch line of the Trans-Siberian Railway through a foreign country was that it would serve as a time- and money-saving shortcut. By building a line through northern China's relatively flat land to Vladivostok, the CER would enable the Trans-Siberian Railway to avoid the twisted Amur River that formed the border between the

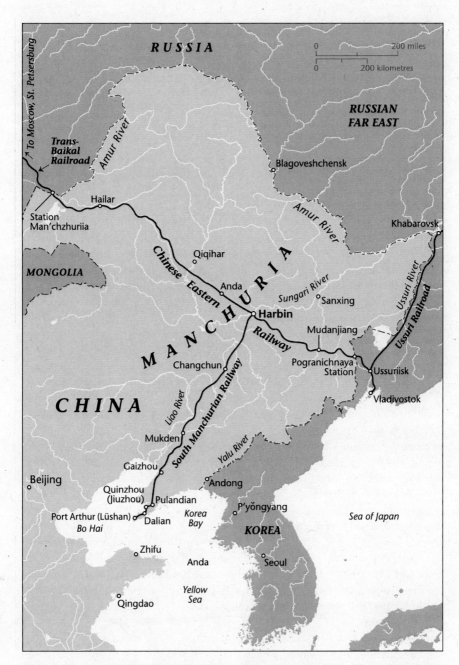

Manchuria, the Chinese Eastern Railway, and the South Manchurian Railway, c. 1901 | Source: David Wolff, *To the Harbin Station: The Liberal Alternative in Russian Manchuria, 1848-1914* (Stanford: Stanford University Press, 1999), xivii.

two countries.[3] Behind this rather bland and pragmatic justification, there were other imperial dreams and foreign policy anxieties that motivated the Russian government's Manchurian project.

For the Russian government, the creation of the CER concession embodied Imperial Russia's contradictory regional policies in the Far East: peaceful economic penetration and direct military domination. Although the CER was administered as a separate company, the concession was a vehicle for Russian economic penetration of northern Manchuria, just as the Trans-Siberian Railway served a similar purpose in the Russian Far East. Colonization and economic development of the largely uninhabited Russian Far East was subsidized by the construction of the Trans-Siberian Railway, in accord with a policy laid down by the builder of both railroads, Sergei Witte. Charismatic and intelligent, Witte controlled the Finance Ministry, which endorsed his policy of government intervention to jump start the Russian economy. Witte saw the creation of the CER concession as a way for Russia to establish an economic foothold in Manchuria, an area rich in natural resources that could be developed for Russia's benefit. The soil produced "amazing and magnificent crops." Wild fruit trees and wild flowers – especially "lilies of the valley, violets, and tulips" – grew in abundance. The hills contained tigers and boars, and the plains teemed with pheasants, partridges, hares, and quail – "capital sport for all."[4] The more temperate climate opened up the possibility that the area could become a breadbasket for the agriculturally challenged Russian Far East. In Witte's own words, the railway was Russia's "peaceful economic penetration" of the region.[5]

Russian administration of the Far East was relatively new. The area had only been detached from the Chinese sphere of influence and given to Russia by the Treaty of Aigun in 1858 and the Treaty of Peking in 1860. Russia had been expanding continuously since the seventeenth century and had extensive experience in bringing new territories under its control. The Russian Far East, however, was far from central Russia. The Russian population of the area was miniscule and, despite attempts to increase the numbers of Orthodox Russians (as opposed to indigenous populations or Chinese or Korean immigrants), the Russian population remained small. The soil and climate of the region did not meet the expectations of the Russian government, and central Russian agriculture was not suitable for the new territories. Because Russian settlers were reluctant to adapt their diet and agricultural production to local conditions, food had to be imported from central Russia. Similarly, the non-Russian population of the area was growing rapidly and was dependent on foodstuffs imported from China.

In addition to these practical considerations, there was anxiety that other countries would take control of the region if Russia did not. In particular, both Japan and China were held up as potential competitors who, as Asiatics, were better adapted to control the region. Nevertheless, rapid expansion of the European sphere of influence in Asia also acted as a catalyst to Russian imperial pretensions. The creation of the CER concession was therefore both a means for Russia to expand its influence in China and a buffer zone between the vulnerable Russian Far East and other countries that could threaten the region.

At the level of national ideology, there was a sense that Russia had a special mission in Asia, a mission that was fuelled by the debate, which dated from the reign of Peter the Great, within Russia's governing and intellectual elite on the nature of the country's national identity. Was Russia a European or an Asiatic power? Late nineteenth-century Russian nationalists took up this debate and synthesized the concepts of a unique Slavic civilization with the idea that Russia had a special tie to Asia. According to this theory, the West was soulless and materialistic. Only Russia, equipped with European learning yet possessed of a national essence that was more Asian than European, could save Asia.[6] Russia, in their opinion, had a special role in Asia. It acted as a bridge between East and West by developing China but preserving it from Western materialism.

Russia's domestic and foreign policy along its border with China was, therefore, shaped by a number of factors: a negligible Russian colonial presence, fear of Chinese economic and demographic competition, fear of another country competing with Russia for the region, and Russia's prestige and mission in Asia. A more vigorous defence of the border region by Qing China might have taken the air out of some of Russia's grand Manchurian pretensions; however, the Chinese political imagination had not yet fully incorporated Manchuria. In addition, the Chinese government had limited resources, and those it did have were taxed by the payment of indemnities and the costs of late Qing institutional reforms.

For the Russian builders of the Trans-Siberian Railway, the Manchurian landscape was particularly well suited for a railroad because it was relatively flat and uninhabited. The CER's raison d'être as a shortcut for the Trans-Siberian Railway enabled the Russian transcontinental railway to avoid a circuitous route along the Russo-Chinese border. The CER was, however, always much more than a simple business concern. Railways are both a rationale and a means for creating ordered, administered landscapes. The straight line of the tracks heralds the arrival of civilization and modernity in a previously untamed landscape. Railroads and railroad colonialism have played a crucial role in the subjugation and settlement of North and South America, Australia, and Africa. In Russia, railroads were crucial to the settlement of Siberia and the Russian Far East and the creation of a Russian presence in what would become Russian Central Asia. The CER would be the means and the end, the alpha and omega, of Russian colonialism in Manchuria.

The Sino-Russian dispute over the railway centred on the CER's exact nature and purpose – commercial enterprise or instrument of Russian colonization? The railway had been created in the wake of the First Sino-Japanese war, when the Japanese government demanded the entire Liaodong peninsula. Russia, hoping to prevent the interference of another country in

Manchuria, co-operated with Germany and France to force Japan to relinquish its claim to the area. Although the Imperial Russian Foreign Ministry had presented itself to the Chinese government as a friend, it pressed for compensation in the form of a railway concession in return for deflecting Japanese designs from the region. The Russian government had been planning a cross-country railroad for a number of years and seized this opportunity to extend the line into Chinese territory. It was not entirely an illogical decision: a route across the northeast would avoid the need to lay track though the Amur border region. By building through Chinese territory from Chita to Vladivostok, a distance of 1,529 kilometres, the total length of the Trans-Siberian Railway was reduced by 913 kilometres.[7] In the opinion of Russian officials, the "Chinese Eastern Railway may be compared to an enormous bridge which through Manchuria spanned two Russian shores and was to serve the requirements of Russian transit."[8]

Negotiations for the CER's construction were conducted by Count Witte and a Chinese envoy, Li Hongzhang. As a respected Qing official, Li had advanced China's so-called self-strengthening movement and helped develop a modern naval, transportation, and military infrastructure. As Qing China's most prominent foreign officer, Li had also been responsible for negotiations after the Sino-Japanese War.[9] Li had experience with the Russians and was sympathetic to transportation infrastructure projects. He also knew firsthand the threat Japan posed to Manchuria. During negotiations for the Treaty of Shimonoseki in 1895, Li promised the Russian minister to Beijing, Count Artur Pavlovich Cassini, military and communications rights in Manchuria if Japan was forced from its postwar claims to the Liaodong peninsula. Pressure was applied, and Japan withdrew its claim to the peninsula as part of the compensation package. When he was dispatched to Moscow in 1895 to attend the coronation of Nicholas II, Li resumed talks with Count Witte, who reminded Li that Russia had fulfilled its part of the bargain.

Writers inspired by Chinese nationalism from the 1920s onward have accused Li of letting the Russian wolf into Chinese territory. In his defence, the policy of using Russia to discourage Japanese aggression was one that circulated in the highest Chinese circles.[10] The Qing Empire had little administrative presence in northern Manchuria and would not begin its colonization project until after the 1900 Boxer Rebellion. These government officials were not deluded and knew that Russia had ulterior motives; however, they believed that the Japanese threat was more significant.

> But Russia does not want Japan to be strong, and Japan's invasion of our
> Three Eastern Provinces makes Russia even more jealous. Thus, by the Sino-
> Japanese peace treaty we had already ceded Liaotung [sic] to Japan, but
> Russia, France, and Germany compelled her to return it to China. Is Russia
> doing this especially for us? She is, at the same time, working for herself.
> If we take this opportunity to establish close relations with her, for mutual

assistance, and also give her some concessions, Russia will be surely glad to comply.[11]

Russia was also a known quantity to the recently founded Zongli Yamen, the Foreign Ministry, and China had had treaty relationships with the Russian Empire for over 250 years. By the late nineteenth century, Imperial Russia, the best known of the barbarian powers, was perceived as being less rapacious than the other foreign powers, a perception that necessitated forgetting Russia's acquisition of Qing territory in the late nineteenth century.

> Now if we wish to make a treaty, and to have a bond for mutual assistance, naturally Russia is most convenient for us, because England uses commerce to absorb the profits of China, France uses religion to entice the Chinese people, Germany has no common territorial boundary with us, and the United States does not like to interfere in others' military affairs. It is difficult for all of these neighbours to discuss an alliance with us. It is known that Russia, as China's neighbour, has kept treaty agreements with us for more than two hundred years, and that she has never embarked on hostilities; she is different from other countries who have frequently resorted to warfare with us. Moreover her behavior is grand and generous, and cannot be compared to that of the Europeans. For example, in the church case at Tianjin in 1870, in which all the countries were busy making a clamor, Russia did not participate, and in the treaties over Ili (1879 and 1881) our nation completely refused and then modified the eighteen articles, and Russia generously consented. This time she has demanded the return of the territory of Liaotung [sic] for us; although she did it for the sake of the general situation in the East; yet China has already received the benefit.[12]

Chinese negotiators went to great lengths to delineate the functions and scope of the new railway so that the enterprise did not impinge on Chinese sovereignty. In the secret Sino-Russian treaty of alliance, signed June 1896, Russia and China pledged to come to each other's assistance in the event of a Japanese attack. Article 4 of this agreement defined the CER as a mixed military-business enterprise.

> In order to facilitate the access of the Russian land troops to the menaced points, and to ensure their means of subsistence, the Chinese government consents to the construction of a railway line across the Chinese provinces of the Amour [sic] and of Guirin [sic] in the direction of Vladivostok. The junction of this railway with the Russian railway shall not serve as a pretext for any encroachment on Chinese territory nor for any infringement of the rights of the sovereignty of his Majesty the Emperor of China. The construction and exploitation of this railway shall be accorded to the Russo-Chinese Bank, and the clauses of the Contract which shall be concluded for this purpose shall be

duly discussed between the Chinese minister in St. Petersburg and the Russo-Chinese Bank.[13]

Despite the military origins of the CER, the Chinese government insisted that the railway should function as a commercial enterprise by forbidding the Russian government any direct control over the CER. The Chinese reinforced this position by demanding that both Chinese and Russians manage the company. The Russo-Chinese Bank, chartered in December 1895, would be the legal body charged with the Russian half of the co-administration of the railway.[14] On 8 September 1896, the construction contract between the Russo-Chinese Bank and the Chinese government was signed; French was used as the language of final arbitration. The Russo-Chinese Bank's position as the main signatory to the agreement, rather than the Russian government, emphasized the Chinese government's position that the concession was solely a commercial enterprise co-administered by the bank and the Chinese government. Article 1 stipulated that the Chinese Eastern Railway Company, organized by the Russo-Chinese Bank, would construct and operate the railway. Therefore, the Russian government was twice removed from the railway's administration.

Article 6 of the treaty would have the greatest influence on later Sino-Russian administrative disputes:

> The lands actually necessary for the construction, operation, and protection
> of the line, as also the lands in the vicinity of the line necessary for procuring
> sand, stone, lime, etc. will be turned over to the Company freely, if these
> lands are the property of the State: if they belong to individuals, they will be
> turned over to the Company either upon a single payment or upon an annual
> rental to the proprietors, at current prices. The lands belonging to the
> Company will be exempt from all land taxes.
>   The company will have the absolute and exclusive right of
> administration of its lands. (La Société aura la droit absolu et exclusif de
> l'adminstration de ses terrains.)[15]

Article 6 clearly states that the lands turned over to the CER were to be used for commercial purposes only. In the Chinese translation, the word employed for administration is *jingli. Jingli* is understood as the administration of a business, unlike the word *guanli*, which means political administration.[16] There are additional differences between the Chinese, Russian, and French texts. According to historian Olga Bakich, the Chinese text reads as follows: "All leased land used by the company is exempt from land taxation and to be managed by the said company single-handedly." In both the Russian and French texts, the sentence is broken into two and reads, "The lands belonging to the company would be exempt from taxation. The company is granted the absolute and exclusive right of administration of land."[17] A reading of the second version allowed the CER to avoid paying taxes to the Chinese administration and permitted it to tax and administer land within the concession. This outcome was not in accordance with the Chinese government's wish for the railway to remain only a railway. When the contract had been signed in Berlin, the Chinese had read both the Russian and the Chinese versions, which were close in meaning, but did not see the French translation. They had not been told that the French translation was the legally binding version.[18]

So the Chinese were not aware that the contract's French translation was binding in the event of a dispute, and the word *administration* in the French text was interpreted as meaning full territorial administration. The exact nature of the CER's relationship to its leased lands was also unclear. In Russian the term used was *polosa otchuzhdeniia* (zone of alienation), and the Russians would disingenuously argue that the land had been alienated administratively but not politically from China. Russian actions, however, revealed that the CER zone was, in their opinion, Russian territory. From 1898 onward, the Chinese argued that the contract specified a simple right-of-way for a railway, a business enterprise, but did not provide for an accompanying administrative privilege.[19]

French and Russian interpretations of the contract were not the only factors that limited Chinese sovereignty – a number of other measures ensured Russian control within the CER zone. For instance, although the CER's lands were exempt from Chinese taxation, those living on them were subject to a tax levied and collected by the railway administration.[20] Because the CER's gauge was identical to that of the Trans-Siberian Railway and different from that of the Chinese, it was difficult for the CER to be used within the Chinese railway system.[21] The Imperial Russian government also guaranteed its control over the enterprise by announcing the public sale of the stock on the morning of the day they were to be sold. Not unexpectedly, when few buyers came forward, the Russian Finance Ministry purchased 25 percent of the stock with an option to buy the remainder, an option that was exercised after the 1900 Boxer Rebellion, when the ministry increased its share to 53 percent. All of these actions flouted the spirit of the original contract, which designated the CER a private company, not a Russian government concern.[22]

Chinese authority was vested in the largely ceremonial position of the Chinese-appointed president, who resided in Beijing and was removed from the CER's daily concerns. The president was to "see particularly to the scrupulous fulfillment of the obligations of the Bank and of the Railway Company toward the Chinese government; he will furthermore be responsible for the relations of the Bank and the Railway Company with the Chinese government and the central and local authorities."[23] What little supervisory power the Chinese had was limited further by the fact that the position remained vacant between 1900 and 1920: there was not even a limited Chinese voice to mediate between the CER's administration and Chinese central and local authorities.[24] True authority was vested in the Russian vice-president, also known as the general manager, CER head, or chief engineer (the title most used among Russians. For the sake of clarity I will use "chief engineer"). Buried in subsections 18 and 19 of the CER statutes – which were published four months after the signed contract and, therefore, kept from Chinese revisal – were statutes that gave the vice-president real power over the CER. Although the president was a Chinese government appointee, the vice-president was chosen by the CER board from among its own members – that is, from the Russian-dominated board. The statutes ensured that control over the CER and its concession would rest in Russian hands.[25]

Some statutes did reaffirm China's sovereignty by explaining that "offences, litigation etc. on the territory of the Chinese Eastern Railway shall be dealt with by local authorities, Chinese and Russian, on the basis of existing treaties."[26] Russian and Chinese authorities appeared to have equal power, but article 8 of the contract extended and secured Russian authority. "The Chinese Government has undertaken to adapt measures for securing the safety of the railway and of all employed on it from any extraneous attacks. *The preservation of law and order on the lands assigned to the railway and its appurtenances shall be confided to police agents appointed by the company.*"[27] Russian control agencies would thereafter control day-to-day police jurisdiction in the concession. Finally, through article 16 the Russian government removed any doubt that the CER was a simple commercial enterprise. In this article the Russian government, through the Finance Ministry, guaranteed that it would subsidize the CER, "should the gross receipts of the railway prove insufficient for defraying the working expenses," as was the case between 1898 and 1919, when the Russian government directly subsidized the CER's operations.[28]

In 1897, following discussions between Britain and Russia about their respective Chinese spheres of influence, Russia was granted Manchuria. Russia seized the tip of the Liaodong peninsula in December 1897 on the pretext of protecting the area from Germany. In January the government began to evict Chinese from the peninsula and killed those who resisted. In March it formally demanded the two Liaodong peninsula harbours – Dalian and Lüshun. The Chinese government at first resisted, but agreed to negotiate after the Russian government threatened to seize the territory by force.

On 27 March 1898, the Chinese Foreign Ministry and the Russian government signed a separate twenty-five-year lease for Russian possession of the Liaodong peninsula. Although article 1 once again specified that the agreement did not violate the sovereign rights of the Chinese emperor, the lease went further in articulating and extending Russian power. The newly leased area was divided into two sections. The first ran from the ports of Dalian and Lüshun to just north of Pulandian Station. The entire military and civil administration in this area was given over "to the Russian authorities and will be concentrated in the hands of one person who however shall not have the title of Governor or governor-general."[29] Presumably, this was a small concession to the Chinese, who wished to maintain the appearance of nominal control. In the neutral zone, which ran from Pulandian Station to Gaizhou, the civil administration was left in the hands of the Chinese. The Russians controlled the military, however, and Chinese troops were only admitted with Russia's permission.[30] An addendum allowed for a token Chinese administration in the city of Quinzhou, located in the first area.[31] Control by the CER and, by extension, Russia had been extended southward to the tip of the peninsula. Russia had already broken two promises made during negotiations for the CER's construction, namely, not to build the railway through areas already populated by Chinese and not to extend the CER south of the city of Changchun.

In 1900 northern China, and to a lesser extent Manchuria, was racked by the Boxer Rebellion, a rebellion that had its origins in an anti-Qing, religiously inspired peasant ideology. It was triggered by drought, an economic depression in the Grand Canal region, missionary activity, and poor harvests in Shandong Province. After forging an alliance with the Qing court in the summer of 1900, the Boxers spread across northern China, attacking foreigners and the Chinese associated with them. The rebellion's influence was, therefore, most significant in the northern region surrounding the capital city of Beijing. In Manchuria the uprising produced isolated attacks on the Russian-owned railways, a siege of Harbin, and a general feeling of panic among Russian settlers in Manchuria.[32]

After the Rebellion, as part of the multinational force that invaded Qing China, Russian forces usurped the administrative functions of the Chinese in Manchuria and Russian administrators assumed the duties of local administrators.[33] Before the Boxer Rebellion, the Russians had been militarily and administratively quarantined to the boundaries of the CER concession. In November 1900, however, Russia pressured Qing representatives to sign an agreement that allowed Russia to assume all military and administrative power in Manchuria. The final provision stated that Russian supervision would end only when Russia determined that order had been restored; therefore, the possibility of Russian withdrawal was unlikely.[34] Russian troops continued to patrol Manchuria until they were forced – by pressure from Japan, England, and France – to withdraw in 1902. Despite this pressure, many Russian troops remained; they simply exchanged the uniform of the Russian army for that of the CER guards.

Following the Boxer Rebellion, czarist judicial control over the concession was extended by an imperial decree. The construction of the CER had "attracted a great number of Russians to the line of the railway, which passes through the territories of China, where our subjects, by virtue of the treaties concluded between the Imperial government and the government of the Bogdokhan [Qing emperor], have the right of being judged in accordance to Russian laws."[35] By this decree, any case that involved a Russian was to be tried by a Russian court. The decree contravened CER statues that stipulated that only cases in which both parties were Russian nationals were subject to extraterritorial procedure. In addition, CER concession courts were placed under the jurisdiction of the governor general of the Amur region and the district courts of Vladivostok and Chita.[36] The CER was not, originally, supposed to have a separate judicial system (as did some of the foreign concessions to the south). The Chinese government reserved for itself the right to police and administer justice within the concession. Through a complex net of overlapping treaties, the administration of justice in the CER concession, located in another country and *de jure* a commercial enterprise, had become part of the Russian provincial court system. In 1901 Russia forced the province of Heilongjiang (at that time a province north of the Songhua River [*Sungari* in Russian]) to build its railway bureau in Harbin – that is, outside of the provincial boundaries – to control one of the few remaining Chinese administrative offices left in northern Manchuria. The railroad bureaus were created to function as a liaison between the CER and the Chinese administration. Now, the Harbin railroad bureau, nominally independent, was funded by the CER, which also appointed the Chinese staff. Bureau officials were selected by the Chinese, but they were appointed only with the permission of the CER general manager.[37] The CER constructed and furnished all bureaus in its zone and paid all salaries.[38] Bureau officials, now located within the Russian concession, were to examine all cases of interest to the CER that involved "interpreters, servants, artisans and ordinary labourers in the railway service, persons supplying materials, contractors for work of various kinds, and finally of all Chinese residing in the territory of the railway."[39] In other words, all Chinese in the railway zone were now under the jurisdiction of an institution controlled by the CER. The bureau examined all serious violations of Russian *and* Chinese law in the concession. A special official of the bureau could settle less serious affairs that did not constitute an infringement of Chinese law on the spot by agreement with the district engineer, a CER official.[40]

The amount of money spent on the creation of Russian economic and administrative structures in the Russian Far East and Manchuria reveals the area's importance to the Russian government – an importance that placed it beyond the constraints of sound fiscal policy. Between 1897 and 1902, the average annual deficit of the government of the Russian Far East was 171 million rubles. The total expenses for the Russian Far East and the CER in these years was more than one billion rubles, a figure that almost exceeded the entire state budget for 1903. The railway's commercial activities covered only 10 percent of its costs; 90 percent of the CER's income came in the form of a direct subsidy from the Russian government.[41]

In 1903 the CER zone was placed under a Russian viceroy of the Far East, whose power was not restricted by Russian ministerial ties: the viceroy answered to the czar alone. The viceroy was given the supreme authority "regarding the maintenance of order and security in the localities appropriated for the benefit of the Chinese Eastern Railway."[42] The new viceroy, Admiral Evgenii Alekseev, supported Russian annexation of the Chinese northeast and immediately placed the CER concession under his personal control. Alekseev also planned to appoint a general commissar to supervise each of the Russian military commissars that had been appointed since 1900 to the three Chinese provincial governments. The commissar was to take all measures to obtain the broadest guarantee of [Russia's] political and commercial interest in Manchuria ... He [the commissar] has full influence over Chinese officials, their appointment and administration; [he] gathers information on the taxable resource of the region and their expenditure; [he] encourages just and humane judicial procedures, communicating to the Chinese people the principles of humanity and respect for Russia."[43]

The 1903 creation of the Russian viceroy of the Far East, under whose administrative purview the CER concession fell, was a clear signal that Russia was moving from the realm of peaceful economic penetration to direct control of the Far East and Manchuria. Within the context of Imperial Russian administration, the creation of the viceroyalty, a geographical area under the direct control of a viceroy who was appointed by and answerable only to the czar, was an administrative practice used to further Russian colonization. Viceroyalties such as the Viceroy of Poland or the Viceroy of the Caucasus had traditionally been created in areas that were ethnically and culturally non-Russian and believed to be in danger of slipping out of Russian control. Therefore, the viceroyalty was a temporary administrative solution to the problem of establishing Russian power in non-Russian areas. Once an area was deemed sufficiently "Russified," it was incorporated into the regular Russian administrative system.

The appointment of a viceroy of the Far East, whose powers included the final say in administrative matters within the CER concession zone, that is, in a foreign country, sent a clear signal that Russia considered the administration of this Chinese area to be within the sphere of Russian national interests.

> The Imperial Lieutenant of the Far East is invested with the supreme
> power in respect of civil administration over those provinces (Pri-Amur on
> the Russian side, Kuantung on the Chinese) and is independent of different
> ministries. He is also given the supreme authority regarding the maintenance
> of order and security in the localities appropriated for the benefit of the
> Chinese Eastern Railway. Due care and protection in regard to the interests
> and wants of Russian subjects in the neighbouring territories outside of the
> border of the Imperial Lieutenancy are also confided to him.[44]

The appointment of Admiral Alekseev to the position also sent a clear message. Alekseev was a strong Slavic nationalist who believed that Russia had a special mission in Asia and that domination of the region should be pursued not only by economic but also by military means. He strongly advocated the annexation of Manchuria by Russia. His bellicose attitude undermined Witte's policy of peaceful economic domination and helped provoke the Russo-Japanese War of 1905.

Opinion differed among the czarist ministers as to the wisdom of annexing Manchuria. Along with Alekseev, General Andrei Y. Matynov, the commander of the Russo-Chinese border, declared in 1910 that the "idea of eventual annexation of North Manchuria [had] permeated Russian thinking for years."[45] Among the czarist ministers, both the minister of war and the foreign minister endorsed annexation.[46] Even Prime Minister V.N. Kokovstov, who was considered a moderate, said in 1910 that Russia should acquire Manchuria in the future.[47] The Russian Council of Ministers echoed his conclusion and left open the possibility of direct military intervention: "So far as Northern Manchuria is concerned, the Ministerial Council regards annexation as dangerous at the present moment, but it is of the opinion that the trend of events may force Russia to this step. All Ministries must therefore be guided by the consideration that our stipulated privileges in Northern Manchuria must be maintained to permit eventually an annexation at some future date. The Ministerial Council sanctions the measures proposed by the Minister of Foreign Affairs to exert pressure on China. In case of necessity however there must be no shrinking from forceful measures."[48] By 1905, Russia, through its legal control of the CER zone, through its military and administrative control of Manchuria, had severely constrained Chinese sovereignty in what British envoy Sir Claude MacDonald called the "Russian province of Manchuria."[49]

Following the loss of the CER's southern branch to Japan in 1905, Russia was forced to rethink its policy for the Far East. Before the Russo-Japanese War, Russia followed an openly expansionist policy, and the czar's ministers debated annexation. This policy alarmed the Japanese government and provoked war between the two Manchurian competitors. The Russian government was then forced to play a more careful game. In turn, the Chinese government began to aggressively increase the Chinese state's administrative presence in Manchuria to counter Russian and Japanese claims. To break Russia's exclusive sphere of influence, China opened up sixteen towns to foreign business. Some were located very close to the CER zone, and the closest, Fujiadian, adjoined it.[50] In addition, beginning in 1907, China began to harmonize Manchuria's administrative structure with that of the Chinese heartland to emphasize that the area was politically Chinese.

The CER could no longer depend on Russian imperial largesse to survive financially. Russia's defeat by Japan had been very costly. In addition to the estimated one billion rubles that St. Petersburg paid to the viceroy and the CER between 1897 and 1902, the Russo-Japanese War had cost Russia 6.6 billion rubles and over four hundred thousand dead or wounded.[51] Russia had also undergone the 1905 Revolution, which caused it to be politically preoccupied with the Russian heartland. Subsidies to the CER would be curtailed but not abolished, and a new Russian mission in northern Manchuria – one that emphasized commerce and colonization to make the concession pay – was necessary.

Russia began by imposing new tariffs. Prior to 1905, the CER had introduced punitive tariffs, which encouraged rail traffic south to Changchun and toward the then Russian-controlled port of Dalian. This did not pay because Manchurian trade normally went from west to east or from south to north. The Russian government could, however, be counted on to subsidize the railway. Not so after 1905. Responding to declining subsidies and the need to develop sound business practices, the CER set privileged rates for traffic moving eastward from Harbin to Vladivostok and set prohibitive rates for goods going south to the Chinese-controlled city of Changchun, which now served as the connection to the Japanese-owned South Manchurian Railway, the railway created out of the CER's southern route, which Russia lost to Japan after 1905.[52]

Although the CER was supposed to give up its administrative role per the post-1905 settlement, Russian administrative and military control over the CER concession was maintained. The Russian vice-president, or chief engineer, remained at the top of the CER hierarchy. Prior to 1920, General Dmitrii Horvath a distant relative of the czar, held this position. Horvath's powers, not only over the regular administration of the CER's business affairs but also over the CER's governmental and administrative functions, were absolute. His responsibilities were divided into two equal spheres – railway affairs and civil administration – that were reflected in the CER's principal departments: (1) General Communications and Explorations, (2) Diplomatic (for dealing with Chinese officials), (3) General Secretariat, (4) CER guards, (5) Military Railway Brigade, (6) Military Transportation, (7) Judicial, (8) Commercial, (9) Financial, (10) Land Office, (11) Medical, (12) Meteorological, (13) Mining, (14) Supplies, (15) Repairs and Construction of Tracks, (16) Mechanical, (17) Traffic, (18) Telegraph, (19) Postal, (20) Motive Power, (21) Technical, (22) Land Administration (Harbin), (23) Local Commercial, (24) Steamship, and (25) the Civil Department.[53] In addition, Horvath also supervised six separate Russian government offices: the Manchurian Military Forces; its military court, the Russian Frontier Circuit Court; the Post Office; the Telegraph Office; and the Russian Consulate. The predominance of control enterprises among the Russian government offices indicates that the Russian mission in North Manchuria was as much about control, of its own population as well as the Chinese, as it was about development.

Russian civil administration in the concession was vested in the CER's Civil Department, which was a unique department not only within the CER's administrative organization but also among all other railway administrations in Russia proper. Of all the Russian-owned railways, only the CER had a civil department, established on the czar's order.[54] The Civil Department functioned as a colonial civil administrative body whose head was one rank below the CER head and reported directly, and only, to him. Within Imperial Russia's ranking system, the rank of the chief of the CER's Civil Department was equal to that of a Russian provincial governor. The position in the ranking system indicated the importance that the Russian government accorded to the post.[55] A list of the Civil Department's sub-departments illustrates its administrative scope: (1) Police, (2) Medical, (3) Veterinary, (4) Passport, (5) Land, (6) Education, (7) Religion, (8) Construction, (9) Meteorology, (10) Building Maintenance, (11) Department for Relations with Chinese Officials, and (12) Prisons.[56]

The 1905 Russian Revolution had been motivated partly by a desire for representative government in Russia, including a new national assembly, the Duma, and more independent municipal governments. Following the revolution, administrative practices in the CER concession were brought into line with Russian norms, including the creation of municipal governments. (The creation of Russian self-government in the CER zone paralleled the creation of the Duma. The Duma's role was also purely consultative, and it exercised very little power. The czar, like the CER general manager, retained the right of veto.) Because Russia had lost its dominant role in Manchuria and could no longer rely on a military presence alone to establish a secure Russian presence in the region, Russian control was linked to the creation of administrative structures modelled on Russian local administration. The decision to create municipal administrations in the CER concession was made in 1907 and culminated in 1909 with an accord on municipal self-government. Many of the Civil Department's duties were transferred to the new municipal governments, but the CER's general manager was invested with final veto power over any decisions taken by these municipal governments. The CER continued to function as a quasi-colonial regional government until 1920, when many of its administrative functions were taken over by the Chinese government.

The CER Civil Department therefore oversaw the CER concession between 1898 and 1909. The powers of this department, and the general manager who oversaw it, were truly comprehensive. It functioned, as CER head Horvath wrote, as "a state mechanism in miniature."[57] City and town administration, the police, medical and sanitary matters, the press, approval of any construction, passport control, education, and the Russian Orthodox Church were all under the CER Civil Department's control. The germ of the new municipal government was a twelve-member city commission that Horvath ordered Harbin's homeowners and leaseholders, both Russian and Chinese, to elect in November 1903 to aid the CER in the task of governing Harbin. Because of the revolution, however, the commission achieved little beyond taxing Harbin's residents. The amount collected (592,000 rubles between September 1905 and February 1907), when compared to the amount the CER Civil Department spent on administration (1,390,000 rubles), demonstrated two things to the CER: civil administration was very expensive, but the cost could be partially, if not completely, turned over to Harbin's ratepayers.[58]

Despite Witte's policy of peaceful penetration, Harbin and its concession became as much a military as a civilian or commercial outpost. From 1900 to 1905, the city was the headquarters of the Russian occupying army. When soldiers were converted into paid CER employees, Harbin became home to the CER guards. Between 1905 and 1908, Harbin was, in turn, transformed from a military to a civilian centre. The CER lifted martial law in the concession in 1906, and the first Russian consulate was established that year. Significantly, there had been no Russian consul in the zone to this point because it was considered part of the Russian Empire. Both of these changes signalled a turn away from establishing legitimacy through military authority toward building legitimacy on modern civil administration. The Russian Chamber of Commerce was established in 1907, and in 1908 the Russian Civil Administration for the zone was created.[59]

Municipal administration in the concession was complicated further by interministerial rivalries within the Russian government.[60] When the CER was built, it was controlled by Sergei Witte and his Finance Ministry. However, the Russian Foreign Ministry, jealous of Witte's separate kingdom, argued that because the concession was outside Russia's borders, the Foreign Ministry should also have a say in its affairs. After Witte's fall in 1903, the two ministries divided the CER between them. The Finance Ministry, no longer the nation-building enterprise it had been under Witte's tenure, was determined to economize.[61] Given that the ministry was no longer responsible for the concession's foreign policy, it pursued the cost-cutting measure of creating local governments. In October 1907 the Finance Ministry's representative, in Harbin on an inspection tour, met with Horvath and Harbin's leading residents to discuss proposals for municipal government. One month later, in December 1907, the first city statutes, based on Russian municipal regulations, were published.

In a private protest to the Russian Finance Ministry, the Russian Foreign Ministry argued that establishing municipal governments in foreign countries was outside the Finance Ministry's jurisdiction (the issue of the project's basic illegality was not discussed). For the sake of unity, however, the Foreign Ministry publicly supported the Finance Ministry.[62] By dividing the supervision of the concession between the two ministries, the Russian government ensured that it could bury international protests by citing bureaucratic rivalry. In response to protests from the Chinese government and Harbin foreign consuls, that creating a Russian-controlled municipal government in a concession established purely for commercial purposes was illegal, the Foreign Ministry replied that it understood their concerns but the project belonged to the Finance Ministry. The Finance Ministry, however, could not respond to protests from outside Russia.[63] Although they protected the Finance Ministry's actions, officials in the Foreign Ministry never accepted the municipal agreement and characterized the system by which the CER, not the Chinese administration, controlled municipal self-government as "not to their taste."[64]

Seeing that Russia and the CER were determined to create municipal governments in the CER zone, the Chinese government conceded to the plan in an attempt to save face and insert some Chinese control into the system. In April

1909 representatives of the CER and the Chinese Foreign Affairs Department signed a preliminary agreement on CER concession municipal government. Dong Shien, the daoyin (circuit intendant) of Binjiang County, and Horvath were to meet at a future date to work out the final settlement. Dong had begun his administrative career as daoyin in 1908. He counted the CER's Russian administrators as his friends and was familiar with Russian administrative practices.[65] The daoyin wanted Harbin and the other six stations that would receive municipal governments to become international settlements, a development that would limit Russian power by placing the CER stations under multiple jurisdictions. The daoyin was supported by all the foreign consuls, particularly the consul from the United States, because they were worried about exclusive Russian control of the region. Horvath publicly declared his support for the proposal; in the meantime, as a temporary solution, he created a Russian-style municipal administration.[66] The proposal to allow all powers equal access to Manchuria – the famous open-door policy – was later dropped, and the final agreement on municipal governments, which was signed in August 1909, was identical to the one signed three months earlier. Horvath insisted that he, rather than a representative of the Russian government, sign the text.[67]

Article 1 acknowledged Chinese sovereignty within the CER concession, but article 2 effectively limited it. China, the article stated, could take any measures to protect its sovereignty, and neither the CER administration nor the municipal governments could oppose it, so long "as the said measures are not in contravention of the contracts concluded with the CER company."[68] Because the contract gave the CER the power to determine a contravention, article 2 effectively gave the CER sovereignty within the concession. Article 15 placed the CER in control of municipal councils. All important questions concerning the public interest or municipal finances in the concession were to be turned over, after discussion by the municipal assemblies, for approval by the CER's Chinese president and the CER's board of directors.[69] Given that a Chinese president had not been appointed since 1900, the CER's Russian board of directors had the final veto over municipal affairs. The agreement also stated that municipal governments would be established in important commercial centres, that all concession inhabitants were to enjoy the same rights and were subject to the same obligations (which bound the Chinese to Russian administrative and judicial control), and that all members who owned property or paid a fixed amount of rent had the right to vote.[70] In reality, however, the Chinese franchise would be severely restricted.

The CER's control over municipal government was enhanced by two sets of regulations published in 1909.[71] Taken together, these regulations completed the CER's domination of the concession's municipal politics. The first set of fifteen regulations explained the relationship between municipal government and the CER's Civil Department. Article 1 stated that municipal government existed because of the Civil Department ("the department determines the right of municipal government to exist") and gave that department the right to supervise all municipal activities. Article 2 empowered the Civil Department to participate in discussions on public funds and the right to increase or decrease those funds. Article 9 gave the Civil Department the right to deny or approve any motions passed by the municipal assemblies, and article 16 gave the department the right to place delegates in municipal assemblies, either as chairmen or as members of the election committees.[72]

A second set of regulations concerned the powers of the CER's board of directors. Article 1 gave the board the right to determine the legality of all actions taken by the municipal assemblies and councils. Article 3 gave the CER directors the power to change land classifications from public to private, thereby returning land to direct CER control.[73] Article 7 gave the board the right to check the allotment of land for public use, and article 8 stated that the CER board could supervise any construction. Article 12 allowed the board to approve or deny any council motion, while article 14 gave the board the power to supervise any controversies between the municipal administrations and the railway.[74] The importance of this article was not lost on the Chinese. The author of the introduction to a Chinese-language history on Harbin's municipal government wrote that the CER "completely abandoned the principle of local government and instead used the autocratic Tsarist regulations. They did this in the beautiful name of autonomy but with the secret method of aggression."[75]

Other factors tempered Chinese sovereignty. The first was a 1910 decree by the Russian Senate that stated that the CER was legally an extension of Siberia,[76] while the second was the right of the CER head or board to veto any decision made by the Municipal Council. This power was unique within China's foreign controlled concessions, where power was customarily vested in the consul. However, Horvath insisted. The 1909 agreement would not be signed unless Horvath himself, in his capacity as CER manager, had this power.[77] Horvath also attempted to temporarily combine the position of consul and CER general manager, a development that had been expressly forbidden by the 1898 CER agreement. When pressed by the American consul to provide a rationale for the proposed change, the Russian ambassador to Beijing, J. Korostovetz, responded: "In the days when Russia looked upon Harbin as an integral part of the Empire ... all the administrative machinery of a Russian city in the way of courts, police and public officers had been established in Harbin, so that the duties of a consular officer had been reduced to a minimum, and his presence or absence did not materially affect the transaction of international relations, which were, for the time being, rather facilitated than otherwise by merging into one office those of the general manager of the railway and consul-general."[78] In other words, there was no need for a consul in an area that the Russian government considered to be Russian. Although its administration now fell under the title of municipal self-government, the CER remained firmly in control of concession city government.

The CER's crucial and extensive supervisory role mirrored city government within the Russian Empire itself. Self-governing bodies had been created in both the towns and countryside as part of Alexander II's Great Reforms. The Russian municipal regulations were initially relatively liberal. The 1870 City Statute provided for elected municipal organs in 423 towns of the empire and, within the limits of the authority granted to them, these bodies were allowed to operate independently. However, after the assassination of Alexander II, the new czar, Alexander III, authorized a return to strict autocratic control. The 1870 statute was watered down, and the state was given broad powers to enact martial law and suspend elected city government. In 1892 the autocracy enacted a new city statute that limited the franchise to those who owned several thousand rubles worth of property and allowed the local czarist administration to veto the election of council members. A new level of bureaucracy, the Special Office for City Affairs, was created to review all city council decisions. City councils did have many responsibilities, but municipal law "permitted many restrictions on their work."[79] Therefore, rather than the municipal governments of Harbin and the CER concessions being examples of Russian liberalism outside of Russia, the relationship between the CER and the councils under its control was identical to the relationship between the Russian Imperial government and Russia's few elected municipal governments. Rather then being bastions of independent and participatory politics, the municipal governments in Imperial Russia and its quasi CER colony were mere facades of participation.

Municipal government in Harbin was two-tiered. Its legislative body, the Municipal Assembly, had sixty members who were elected by local residents. All inhabitants who owned property in Harbin worth not less than 500 rubles or paid annual taxes of at least 10 rubles were permitted, regardless of nationality, to vote for members of the assembly.[80] Three assembly members were Chinese and appointed by the Chinese Chamber of Commerce. They were observers only – they had no vote and were assigned a Russian supervisor "with a view to familiarizing them with their duties."[81] The Municipal Assembly's duties were to estimate expenses, fix taxation rates, and implement the city council's decisions. All Municipal Assembly decisions were forwarded to the CER general manager for approval,[82] and in the event the CER vetoed a decision, the matter was returned to the assembly for revision. If the matter passed with three-quarters approval, it was turned over to the Finance Ministry in St. Petersburg for a final decision.[83]

Executive power, such as it was, was vested in the Municipal Council, which had six, and later ten, members. The assembly elected three members of the council, and a chairman and two members were appointed by the CER. The council chairman was required to be a Russian subject. Municipal Council decisions were to be submitted to the local Chinese authorities as well as the CER manager for approval. Harbin's Municipal Council did not permit even the token presence of Chinese. In 1911 the Chinese Chamber of Commerce petitioned the council for the inclusion of the three Chinese nominated seats, as was provided for in article 13 of the municipal regulation.[84] The petition and the question of Chinese participation was left "to the future"; in the short term, the Chinese members were requested, as "delegates without vote," to attend council but not vote.[85] By council decision, Russian members were paid 4,200 rubles annually while the Chinese delegates were paid only 600 rubles per year.[86]

The concession's municipal councils were concerned with the ordinary details of city administration. According to the Harbin Municipal Council's 1911 report, the council dealt with street repair, the city hospital, farm animals within city limits, and the enforcement of stone and brick as proper building materials.[87] The council had a budget of 800,000 rubles, 616,300 of which were derived from municipal taxes.[88] The rest was provided by CER subsidy or loan. When asked for their opinion on these municipal changes, most Harbin residents replied negatively and cited their fear of higher taxes. Others questioned whether true representative government would ever come to be. In a pamphlet titled "On the Question of Mutual Relations between the CER Company and Harbin Russians," which was published by the Harbin Ratepayers' Association, Harbin's Russian citizens argued that because the CER completely controlled the concession, a municipal government would function only as another CER-controlled mechanism, albeit one that taxed residents for the privilege of having a facade of self-government.[89] Therefore, despite Wolff's claims that the 1905 Revolution would inaugurate a period of municipal liberalism, the reforms simply confirmed and extended the CER's powers of local administration and shifted its financial burden from the Imperial Russian Ministry of Finance onto the CER's taxpayers.

By 1917, on the eve of the momentous changes that would transform the concession, the Russian government was not doing anything unique in Manchuria. Foreign countries, using broadly defined extraterritorial powers, had created areas throughout China where Chinese did not exercise economic and political control. The manipulation of business contracts, the deliberate neglect of China's legal right to supervise the CER, the deliberate exclusion of Chinese through hiring and language policies, and the creation of a non-Chinese local administration under the control of the CER were colonial strategies to exercise power and create legitimacy that were employed by other countries. What is remarkable is that, unlike concessions in which the rights conceded by China were acknowledged by the Chinese government as political rights, the contract for the CER concession was signed by China because it believed it was signing a business contract for a railway right-of-way and nothing more. By employing a flimsy interpretation of the word *administer,* the Russian government managed to erect an apparatus of commercial, military, and civilian control. The existence of this apparatus was then used to justify Russia's ongoing presence in the region and the CER's ongoing domination of the concession. The initial Russian goal of domination over the region did not disappear after its defeat by Japan in 1905. Instead, Russia's priorities in the CER zone shifted from direct military to direct commercial and administrative domination. Russia's aspirations prior to 1905 were overt; following the revolution of 1905, they were clothed in the guise of peace, order, and good government, all of which were under Russian control in the concession. The normality of Russian control – the sense that Russian control of the region was correct, modern, and natural – provided the intellectual and emotional superstructure for the post-1920 Russian-Chinese co-administration. Émigré and Soviet partners tried but could not truly share power with the Chinese.

The CER was not simply a jointly owned Sino-Russian railway company that happened to operate in China. Until 1920 joint co-management of the CER was a polite myth rarely discussed by either side. The Russians did not want to make the implicit explicit; the Chinese did not want to acknowledge that a Russian colony had been established in Manchuria. Nevertheless, presenting the CER as a simple tool of Russian colonialism disguises the complex relationship that existed between the Chinese and their Russian neighbours and glosses over the CER's role as both an employer and an instrument of local administration for Russians and Chinese alike. The CER's establishment and the controversy over the limits of its jurisdiction had a profound effect on the administrative landscape of the entire CER concession. The struggle over the railroad was not an issue of simple Russian versus Chinese control: it was, in essence, a microcosm of the entire Sino-Russian administrative experience in northern Manchuria and the struggle over the region's political identity. For Russians, the CER symbolized the Russian project of development – taming and settling *Man'chzhuriia*. And the idea persisted after the October Revolution of 1917, when the established Russian community used the CER's new role as a commercial enterprise to justify a continued Russian administrative presence in China. After 1920 Russia would take advantage of China's willingness to co-administer the CER to promote a Russian vision of northern Manchuria being directed and controlled by Russians. This brought Russia into direct conflict with China, which had envisioned a new equal relationship between the two owners. In this manner, the CER's colonial origins determined the antagonistic relationship between Chinese and Russians into the next decade. Even joint administration with the Soviet Union, which China turned to after the older Russian community blocked shared control, was tainted with, and inherited, the implicit colonialism of a Russian commercial and administrative enterprise that had no clear boundaries between economic and colonial control

The Russian government had built, maintained, and subsidized a commercial enterprise that was the raison d'être for establishing a complete Russian community in the northeast. Once built, the CER and the Russian community existed in a symbiotic and circular relationship – the Russian community was necessary to the continued well-being of the CER, and the CER was necessary to the well-being of the Russian community. The CER's essential meaning was contested from the beginning. For the Russians, the CER represented Russian imperial civilization making its way into the northern Chinese hinterland, for it brought with it progress and development. This definition of the CER was not political. Politics involved ugly and divisive disputes between parties. The CER was an objective force for progress.

The Chinese contested this definition of the CER from the beginning. In their opinion, the CER was built for the primary benefit of the Russian community. Its administrative pretensions were based on the shady interpretation of an unclear and biased contract. In the meantime, Russian culture, administration, and education became the norm for Harbin and the CER concession. While a coherent Russian government existed, the Chinese could not press their case. After 1920, however, the Chinese began to establish their own presence in the concession through pragmatic and conciliatory policies that acknowledged the CER's Russian origins and the importance of the Russian community to its continued functioning. However, the Chinese called for Chinese co-administration and the introduction of a Chinese managerial class. Most of all, the Chinese wanted to strip the CER of any political or administrative pretensions and make it a simple commercial enterprise.

The struggle between Russia and China reflected the inability of either side to define the CER. Any enterprise that has as its primary function the opening, taming, and development of an empty landscape will never be just another company. It will, in fact, represent the political, cultural, and moral values of the group in control. It was, therefore, impossible for China and Russia, despite the success of the CER as a commercial enterprise, to work together, for they differed on the fundamental meaning and intent of the enterprise they were co-administering. Co-operation was possible between northern Manchuria's two founding peoples, but it was achieved only when the Chinese began to reverse Russian colonial policies after 1917.

3

The Chinese Eastern Railway:
From Russian Concession to Chinese Special District

In 1923 the newly appointed Chinese president of the Chinese Eastern Railway (CER), Wang Jingchun, met with the American consul to set out the Chinese position on Russia's use of the 1898 contract to establish administrative and political control over the CER concession.[1] Wang argued that the CER's, and by extension the Russian government's, policies were colonialist and that China had never accepted the Russian position that the administration was politically neutral and that China had willingly given up its sovereignty: "The Chinese point to the presence of a very large Russian population along the line of the Chinese Eastern Railway, domiciled on land acquired by the Railway through the measures described above. It is claimed by the Chinese that the Railway thus openly acted as the agent of the Russian Government in an attempt to colonize a portion of Northern Manchuria with a Russian population, and they assent that not only is there no evidence in any document that the Chinese Government understood this to be the aim when the contract of 1898 was negotiated."[2]

Wang's position was consistent with that of Chinese representatives from 1896 onward. Not only did the Chinese oppose Russian attempts to build a virtual colony in northern Manchuria, they also responded to this project by reinforcing Chinese administration in the region. Like Imperial Russia, the Qing Empire and its successor, the Republic of China, would use these administrative innovations to accomplish two aims: making Manchuria politically, administratively, and demographically Chinese and using Russian administrative examples to frame Chinese policy.

Nevertheless, to view the creation of Chinese administration in northern Manchuria as only a simple response to Russian incursion does not acknowledge the complex process by which globalized capital and power politics were refashioning Qing China and czarist Russia. China and Russia were both multicultural and multi-ethnic empires that had developed a variety of flexible political and cultural approaches to the heterogeneous peoples and cultures they ruled. In the late nineteenth century, both were undergoing internal political transformations to meet challenges posed by the developed world, particularly unqualified sovereignty within internationally recognized borders. The Russian conquest and colonization of the Russian Far East and the Chinese political and demographic transformation and incorporation of Manchuria were both responses to the centralizing, state-driven demand for resources, markets, and capital and the desire to fill in "empty," politically ambiguous frontiers on imperial borders.

For China, the rush to sinify the frontiers – a late nineteenth-century process that had more to do with the imposition of a centralizing state (and its acceptance by peoples with clearly defined national identities) than it did with the older idea of spreading Chinese culture – was a project that gained relevance because it was associated with dynastic and national survival. From the 1850s onward, the Qing Empire had seen foreign powers nibble away at its rich southern coasts. The political and economic incursions increased, in number and scope, at the century's end, when world powers decided the Qing Empire was unable to defend its empire and scrambled to establish their own spheres of influence before the empire fell. The Russian penetration of northern Manchuria; Japan's significant expenditures to secure southern Manchuria; and ever-present American, French, and English interests in the region were only one small part of a political drama being played out across China. Qing China's political incorporation of Manchuria was part of a national strategy to secure a geographical region that most Chinese were rapidly coming to view as not part of the Qing empire but, rather, of the Chinese state and nation. At the same time, the administrative solutions to the problem of extending Chinese sovereignty in Manchuria were conditioned by Manchuria's traditional political exclusion from the Chinese body politic and the pragmatic and open nature of the Chinese administrators who settled there.

On 31 October 1905, the Qing government opened the Binjiang County Office in Fujiadian, which was adjacent to Harbin, thereby establishing Chinese local government on the very edge of Russian administration. Not coincidentaly, the Qing government allowed Binjiang County and Fujiadian to be opened as an international port. The act was designed to attract non-Russian investment to the region, which, in turn, would dilute Russia's illegal claims to exclusive and special rights to the region.[3] This initiative was part of a larger late-Qing project to modernize China's government to meet the threat of Russian imperial power, for the Qing Empire, rather than Imperial Russia, would determine who could trade in northern Manchuria. In particular, this initiative was one of many aimed at replacing the northeast's ambiguous identity as a Manchu homeland – one that left unanswered the question of whether the region was Chinese – with three Chinese provinces that, legally, would be no different than the provinces of the Chinese interior.

Dongsansheng, or the Three Northeastern Provinces, had only recently been designated as part of China proper. Before 1900, the region, as the homeland of the Qing Dynasty, had been closed to Han colonization and had been administered separately as a part of the Qing imperial household. Chinese settlement was banned, then restricted to southern Manchuria. In the minds of many Chinese, the region was not Chinese, as the Central Provinces were; however, Russian and Japanese interest in the region had convinced the Qing government that full administrative control had to be extended over the region.

The establishment of Chinese offices across Manchuria followed the 1905 Russo-Japanese War. The seemingly unstoppable Russian Empire had been humiliated by Japan. Although rightly suspicious of Japan, and still itself smarting from a defeat at the hands of the Japanese in 1895, the Qing Dynasty was encouraged to action by the spectacle of a fellow Asian power defeating Russia. From 1905 onward, Russia would have competition in Manchuria, and the Qing Dynasty would use this revival to its advantage by pressing forward Qing claims to Manchuria and framing those claims in the context of the Chinese state rather than of Manchuria as the Qing homeland. The Qing were perhaps also chastened by the violence of the 1905 war – nearly two hundred thousand Japanese, Russian, and Chinese had died – and decided that the establishment of a strong Chinese presence in Manchuria would prevent the outbreak of future hostilities. More specific Chinese administrative reforms were introduced in 1907. Manchuria was divided into three distinct provinces – Jilin, Liaoning, and Heilongjiang – and the region's military governorship was abolished, signalling that the area was to be ruled by a civil administration. A system of provincial governments, headed by a governor in each province and a governor general for the entire region, was introduced on a trial basis,[4] and the entire region was opened to Chinese settlement, which the Qing government actively encouraged. No longer would the area have a distinct and separate administrative identity. The Qing, like the Russians, began the process of settling and making good their claim to Manchuria. Ironically, the CER, built as an instrument of Russian economic and demographic colonization, served as the means by which the Chinese populated the area and came to rapidly outnumber the Russians.

The creation of Railway Foreign Affairs Bureaus in the provinces of Jilin and Heilongjiang was another means by which the Chinese ensured greater control over local affairs in areas where the Russians were extending their influence. The purpose of the bureaus was to supervise settled Russians and representatives of the Russian government to ensure that all concession agreements were strictly adhered to and that Russia was not, by stealth, increasing its power in Manchuria. Staffed with Russian-speaking Chinese administrators, these offices acted as training schools in the art of administration. Many of the Chinese officials who moved into the Chinese-controlled Special District Administration that replaced the CER concession after 1920 received their training in the bureaus. Branch offices were built in every CER station. As well, each province had a bureau of foreign affairs, a judiciary, and an education department, all of which had staff who studied the Russian administration in the CER concession.[5] As Russia attempted to extend its power, the Chinese offices and bureaus advised Beijing on how best to counter Russian measures. For example, between 1904 and 1907, during preparations to create Russian municipal governments in the CER concession, the governor of Heilongjiang Province sent proposals to Beijing that had been submitted to him by the railway bureaus on how best to extend Chinese jurisdiction in the province and use the legal system to prevent an extension of Russian power.[6] Since the Qing government could only protest, and not prevent, the establishment of these Russian municipal governments, Heilongjiang's governor proposed, with the bureau's assistance, a number of measures to restrict Russian power. A Chinese presence was increased through the appointment of a Chinese official to the Harbin mixed court. Chinese imperial customs were established in Harbin and other concession communities to clarify the boundaries of the Russian-controlled area and to prevent Russia from treating all of northern Manchuria to Russian customs. Finally, Chinese troops were posted at Harbin, and the rule that required Russians travelling outside of the concession zone to carry passports was enforced.[7] All of these measures asserted Qing, and Chinese, sovereign rights within the context of creeping Russian colonialism.

The Qing government insisted that several Chinese provincial offices be represented in Harbin as a means of establishing that Harbin was Chinese and not Russian. These offices – diplomatic bureaus in Jilin and Heilongjiang, the Jilin Forest and Tax Station, and the Chinese military command – had mixed success in establishing Chinese sovereignty. The diplomatic bureaus, which were located in Harbin under Russian supervision rather than in the Chinese-administered city of Fujiadian, were gradually pulled into the CER's orbit. Created to adjudicate disputes between Chinese labourers and their Russian bosses, facilitate Chinese-CER relations, and uphold Chinese sovereignty, the diplomatic bureaus were reduced to quasi-Russian posts through the CER's power to finance and appoint officials to these offices.[8] Nevertheless, like the railway bureaus, the diplomatic bureaus became a finishing school for future Chinese administrators in the Special District.

Chinese authorities vigorously protested the creation of Russian city government in Harbin and other CER stations. In 1907 Manchuria's governor general lodged a protest with the Russian authorities after receiving a copy of the proposed municipal regulations. His protest rested on four points: (1) the regulations transformed Russians into local administrators, (2) political authority thus passed to the Russians, (3) the policy infringed on Chinese authority, and (4) Russians were illegally assuming the authority to issue and impose taxes.[9] When the new municipal government attempted to tax concession residents, Chinese and foreigners alike refused to pay. When the municipal governments, with the assistance of the CER police, responded on 21 February 1908 by forcibly closing Chinese businesses and shops, harassing their owners, pulling down their signs, and placing guards to prevent persons from conducting business, the Chinese authorities advised the Chinese not to pay.

When Spanish and German merchants in Harbin protested the municipal tax collection, it was suspended.

Chinese authorities were aware that Russian taxation in their territory set a precedent for the further erosion of Chinese sovereignty: "[Although] the effort of Russians to impose taxes on the Chinese at Harbin appears to be a small matter, it really affects the whole question of the open door in Manchuria, for if the Russian ownership of the North Manchurian railway (CER) confers the rights of territorial administration the same will apply in the South Manchurian railway zone and China's sovereignty will be minimal."[10]

The municipal government again began collecting taxes in July 1909 and all shops, Russian and Chinese, closed in protest. When a final agreement was negotiated with the Chinese government and when the taxes were paid two days later, the shops reopened.[11] The governor general, in a 1909 speech, revealed that the Chinese government was determined to salvage some face from the imposition of Russian local government over the concession: "The conclusion of the late agreement [preliminary agreement] regarding the Municipal administration of Harbin proves still more that in regard to international questions, we are fair, and respect the rights of others. I sincerely hope that the detailed regulations of the Municipal Council will be drawn up amicably and that will be a great improvement."[12] At a separate meeting with the Chinese Chamber of Commerce, the governor general had likewise urged merchants to pay the taxes and, pragmatically, to make the best of it.[13]

In 1909, under Chinese pressure, the Russian Embassy summarized its position on the municipal dispute. The CER concession, it argued, differed from other treaty ports because, according to article 6 of the 1898 contract, the company had full administrative power over the concession. These powers were not considered political powers because the company's activities in the concession were those of a lessor under a private agreement. According to the Russians, the contract clearly indicated that the CER had territorial control and administrative power. All of these principles were reaffirmed in the 1909 agreement.[14] Not surprisingly, the Chinese government did not accept the interpretation that China had given Russia administrative control over Manchuria in 1898 and had reconfirmed that control in 1909. The Chinese Foreign Ministry argued that article 1 of the 1898 contract stated that the Chinese government had only engaged the Russo-Chinese Bank as a commercial enterprise, and article 6, in China's opinion, gave the CER control only over the construction of stations, telegraph lines, and engineering work. The company's full commercial powers extended only to territory needed for the railway. This would remain China's national, regional, and local position on the question of municipal government in the concession for the next twenty years.[15]

After the fall of the Qing Dynasty in 1911, Manchuria came under the control of the regional warlord Zhang Zuolin (1875-1928); although it was nominally part of the Chinese republic, it functioned in reality as a separate state.

Zhang began his career, like many other warlords, in the Qing imperial army. He was allied with Yuan Shikai (1859-1916), the head of the Qing's northern army and the man who assumed the presidency of the Republic of China after the fall of the Qing. Yuan managed to keep together an uneasy coalition of provincial military leaders, but this coalition fractured after his death in 1916. China entered a period sometimes referred to as the warlord era, during which military leaders fought one another for control of the state. This period, reviled as the absolute low point of China's century-long crisis, would herald a period of relative growth and prosperity for Manchuria.

Manchuria had benefitted from two decades of industrial development by the Russians in the north and the Japanese in the south. The Japanese owned and operated the South Manchurian Railway (SMR), which had been created from the southern CER branch taken from the Russians in 1905. The SMR was operated in the same economic and colonial context as the CER in the north, but while the Japanese extended the SMR's colonial jurisdiction from 1905 onwards, the overt Russian colonial project ended in 1920. Because Russian and Japanese investments had spurred Chinese investment, Manchuria was home not only to the administrative structure built by the Qing but also to many Chinese entrepreneurs and millions of new settlers.

Zhang Zuolin continued this policy of developing Manchuria in opposition to Japan and the USSR, and he adopted policies to modernize Manchuria's administration and promote economic development. Although Zhang cast himself as a Chinese nationalist throughout his career, as someone who was dedicated to reuniting China, his actions were those of an independent regional governor dedicated to preserving Manchuria's relative independence from the rump national government located in Beijing. Zhang was a political acrobat, balanced between Japan and the USSR, and he sometimes worked with the Beijing government, especially when he was attempting to take over northern China and establish himself as the national government. At the same time, he worked to maximize Manchuria's options.

Zhang is generally portrayed as a ruthless warlord, and there have been few attempts to examine him outside the context of his military exploits.[16] His administrative reform of the Special District and Harbin was part of his bid to limit the control of the USSR and to create an alternative to the Japanese-dominated administration of southern Manchuria. In this regard, his relations with the Russian community, and the CER, in the region were crucial. The Special District administration would give Zhang, on the one hand, the opportunity to create a buffer against Japanese presumptions in northern China and, on the other, access to the expertise and talents of Russian subjects who were now under his protection.

Nevertheless, the Chinese authorities had to be content with limited influence in the CER concession, where Russian power was still paramount. It was only after the Russian revolutions, beginning in 1917, that Chinese authorities could begin the process of taking over the CER concession and establishing full political control. The administrative solution was the Special District, which was created piecemeal as Russian power in the concession disintegrated. Following the dissolution of Imperial Russia, the Chinese government seized the chance to assert Chinese sovereignty in the CER concession by creating the Special District of the Three Eastern Provinces, which left most of the Russian institutions intact but inserted a new Chinese supervisory class. These innovations were a response to Manchuria's Russian-dominated administration and population, but they also fulfilled many goals of Chinese administrative reform in the region. The changes established a Chinese administrative presence in Manchuria; however, the nature of these administrative changes is also important. Manchuria was being divided and administered, not as the homeland of the ruling dynasty, but as an integral part of the Chinese state.

Not surprisingly, given the importance of control institutions to the maintenance of Russian power, the disintegration of the Russian police and military was the first step by which the CER concession was transformed into the Chinese-controlled Special District. Both Russian and consular sources deemed the transfer of concessionary police and military to Chinese control illegal. However, the Chinese police was formed in response to calls not only from the Chinese but also from the Russian and consular communities and the establishment of the force was carried out at the opportune moment by Chinese authorities, who were equally concerned about legality and Chinese control.

In 1919 the Binjiang police chief, Zhang Nanzhao, included his memoirs of the takeover of Harbin's Russian police and militia in *Haerbin zhinan* (Guide to Harbin). Zhang Nanzhao's memoirs reveal that Dmitrii Horvath and the Chinese authorities were in close contact from 1917 to 1919. On 1 November 1917, in a telegram sent to Jilin, Zhang described political disturbances in Harbin. In October, the Harbin Council of Workers and Soldiers (Bolshevik) had organized a Committee of Public Safety and tried to take over the CER.[17] The organization was led by the Bolshevik Liuqin (Russian Martem'ian Nikitich Riutin), who had formed his own military patrol and was organizing daily demonstrations.[18] Police and guards with the CER were unable to control the situation because many of their number sympathized with and had joined the Bolsheviks.[19] Because the number of Binjiang police was small, Jilin authorities permitted Zhang to recruit another 240 troops to guard Harbin's train station and CER headquarters.[20] They had no power, however, to interfere in concession affairs. When the Chinese troops entered Harbin proper, CER police allowed them to take up guard duties. It was the first time the Chinese police had entered the concession unchallenged and was a covert recognition that the Russians were no longer capable of keeping order.

On 5 December 1917, fighting between Bolsheviks and the Russian militia resulted in the destruction and closure of all downtown shops. Indignant

Chinese and Russian shopkeepers lodged complaints with the CER and Binjiang authorities. In December 1917, when Harbin's Bolsheviks announced their intention to overthrow the CER head, Horvath, and take over the concession, the consuls urged Horvath to remove the police from the CER's control and end the "rule of robbery, murder and rape at Harbin."[21] The Russian consul, no longer trusting his own Russian guards, retreated to the safety of the Jilin Railway Bureau, where the consular archive was being protected by the Chinese.[22] Horvath, in an interview with Daoyin Dong Shien, admitted that the CER police and guards were no longer capable of keeping public order. In response – through a series of telegrams between Shenyang, Changchun, and Jilin – the daoyin made preparations to protect the concession with Russian soldiers under Chinese supervision. At this point, the Chinese police were co-operating with the Russian police; however, within the concession, Russian police still had jurisdiction.[23]

On 15 December 1917, after a meeting between Daoyin Dong Shien and provincial and national military figures in Changchun, the Chinese authorities, using the takeover of the concession's control apparatus as an opportunity to assume Chinese sovereignty, announced a new plan. Dong admitted that this, legally, was a controversial move because, according to the original contract, Russia had been given the right to police the area. But he explained that the provincial and national authorities were exploring a loophole – the position of Chinese CER president, which had not been filled since the Boxer Rebellion. If a new Chinese president could be found, he would have the power to effect the change.[24] However, general manager Horvath was still in charge. In an interview with Horvath, the CER guards chief, Zhang Nanzhao (Binjiang police chief), Daoyin Dong Shien, and five newly appointed Chinese officers entrusted with pacifying Harbin, the Chinese pressed the general manager to provide a date after which he could re-establish control. Horvath replied that he had been in contact with the Bolshevik Liuqin and had urged him to respect Chinese law. Horvath was positioning himself as the mediator between Liuqin and the Chinese; in a final veiled threat, he expressed the hope that China would not push him into any "negative actions."[25]

At the same time, Horvath admitted that he no longer had the power to control the Bolshevik Party, and the CER guards chief admitted that he could not vouch for the loyalty of his troops. Horvath suggested expelling the Bolshevik troops and their sympathizers, but Dong Shien pointed out that the troops (along with their weapons), if dismissed, would probably join the Bolsheviks. When Dong suggested that Chinese troops should supervise the disarming of the Bolsheviks, Horvath disagreed and, when pressed, said he would solve the problem in two or three days.[26] In the meantime, the daoyin increased the number of Chinese police and soldiers, and Horvath agreed with the order on the condition that the Chinese troops be limited in number.

In a telegram to his superiors, Daoyin Dong reported that Horvath, with his long career in China, was as cunning "as a snake" and was trying to maintain his power by any means necessary. According to the telegram although the intendant wanted to expel Horvath, his superiors had decided against it. In Zhang Nanzhao's opinion, they had missed a "golden chance." The telegram also reveals that the authorities were cautious and did not want to provoke a crisis. Instead, in a subsequent telegram, they advocated a strong show of force accompanied by negotiations with the Bolsheviks. In the meantime, the Chinese waited to see whether disarming the Bolsheviks had produced any results.[27] The Chinese authorities took the initiative and negotiated with CER Bolsheviks, but the Russian Bolshevick Liuqin was unwilling to give up his plan to take over the railway. On 23 December 1917, Liuqin tried to seize the Harbin armoury but was prevented by Chinese troops. The Chinese authorities then gave Horvath an ultimatum – either solve the problem or Chinese troops would disarm the Bolsheviks and expel them from the territory. The general manager reluctantly agreed, but he would not allow CER guards to be disarmed. However, on 25 December he agreed to place his guards under the control of the Chinese. The Bolsheviks were to be disarmed and sent back to Russia. The same day, made aware of the plan, Liuqin tried to seize the CER. Chinese troops moved quickly to protect Horvath's home and office and every important building in Harbin. The next day Liuqin and his troops were surrounded and disarmed. On 26 December Chinese troops were ordered to disarm the 559 and 618 Railway Brigades. At Harbin's railway bridge, the Russian troops opened fire and the Chinese returned it. Two Russians were killed. The Russians surrendered, and within ten minutes the fighting was over.[28] Disarmed and broken into small groups, Russian troops were deposited on the Russian side of the border. Their weapons and barracks became Chinese property.

Once the problem of armed Bolshevik insurrection in the concession was solved, the daoyin was ordered by telegram from Beijing to disarm the Russian police and replace them with Chinese officers. The daoyin's superiors assured him that national officials were working to have the CER contract redrawn to permit a full complement of Chinese police.[29] Initially, Horvath refused to allow an independent Chinese police force and would only permit, as a compromise, the establishment of a commercial police. According to the author of one Russian source, the Chinese insisted on having the adjective *Chinese* added to the title – the Harbin Chinese Commercial Police – to establish that the new force was Chinese.[30] The commercial police were merely a step toward the ultimate objective of assuming all police powers. This was made clear to Horvath during a meeting on 11 January 1918 – the Chinese would be satisfied with nothing less than control of all concession policing. Horvath sidestepped the issue when he replied that he had no opinion on China's capacity to police the district but that he was worried that language difficulties may affect its ability to do so. Horvath also retreated to the standard position that the CER was only a business concern; therefore, police and guards had no political power and posed no threat to the Chinese.[31]

On 31 December 1917, Daoyin Dong decided that the Chinese and Russian police would work together and hired translators to smooth the transition. The re-organization process continued into February 1918, when the first temporary Harbin police bureau was formed. Neither the Bolsheviks nor Horvath acquiesced to these changes, and on 28 February, the police, responding to a tip about a Bolshevik uprising, surrounded all of Harbin's public buildings. Horvath had organized the resistance to Chinese control by hiring three thousand Chinese soldiers. When police headquarters ordered the force to dissolve, Horvath responded by creating quasi-military groups with names such as the Far East Fighters and the Save Russia Association that were made up of one thousand former Russian soldiers. In an attempt to take over the Russian Far East and the concession, Horvath declared martial law in the concession on 9 May. The Chinese police reacted with caution. On 16 May the murder of a Russian Bolshevik teacher by Horvath's troops provoked a general strike. By way of an apology, Horvath paid for the funeral and for the coffin's transportation to Russia. His actions calmed the situation, but on the 17 May a union leader, son of a prominent Harbin newspaper editor (in Chinese, Tumake, in English, Cherniavskii) was killed. Accounts of his death differ, but according to Zhang's diary, he was kidnapped by rogue CER guards, perhaps Horvath's, and murdered.[32] According to a Japanese source in the American consular records, Cherniavskii was murdered after he had mocked a church service for dead Russian officers and had claimed that the Chinese police were encouraging Bolshevik activity in order to destabilize the CER administration.[33] The basis of these allegations was the Chinese authorities' suppression of the CER militia after the first murder and the fact that the Harbin Bolshevik Party was able to function while the same party in Vladivostok had been shut down.[34] Cheriavskii's death caused a riot in Harbin that was put down by the Chinese police.[35]

Although the CER guards and the joint Chinese-Russian police force worked together uneasily in 1918 and 1919, Horvath had co-operated in bad faith. In August 1919 the general manager secretly asked the British consulate for five thousand rifles and some machine guns to help bring the CER guards completely under Russian control.[36] At the same time, he prepared to assume complete control of not only the CER concession but also the entire Russian Far East.[37] However, Horvath, without the might of the Russian Empire behind him, no longer controlled the dominant force in the concession. Control over the CER guards and the concession was slipping out of his hands and into those of the Chinese, a process that was confirmed by two events. At the end of January 1920, the CER guards went on strike because of the poor quality of their uniforms.[38] At the same time, a letter circulated by the consuls acknowledged Horvath's inability to control the situation by calling on the Chinese authorities to expel all armed Russian political groups.[39]

Responding to the consuls in February 1920, the Chinese government informed them that it intended to replace the Russian police and courts and impose a true co-administration on the CER.[40] On 28 February, realizing he had no other option, Horvath allowed the daoyin to have a joint deployment of Chinese and Russian troops.[41] Two weeks later, Chinese troops under Zhang Huanxiang, head of the CER guards and governor of the Special District after 1924, occupied CER guard headquarters, police stations, and arsenals and disarmed all police and guards. Notices posted across Harbin acknowledged the political context in which the takeover was taking place: "China declares that all political power in Harbin, which is a part of China, has been regained. All Chinese and foreigners at Harbin should return to their former occupations. The Chinese police will maintain the order of the city and protect the citizens while anyone who creates a disturbance will be punished according to Chinese law."[42] By 15 June 1920, the disarming of the CER guards had been completed, and policing was taken over by the Chinese administration. Three hundred Russian police, judged to be politically unreliable, were deported from the Special District to the newly created Soviet Union.[43]

The three-year process by which China gradually gained control over the concession's police and military demonstrated that China was capable of bringing order to the concession. It also showed that Horvath would resist any Chinese attempts to overturn Russian control and that he would have to be removed before further changes could be made. As the process of extending Chinese control over the CER concession security forces unfolded, Binjiang's Chinese administrators realized that they would have to prepare not only for Horvath's eventual resignation but also for the possibility that the entire Russian state-sponsored administrative apparatus would disappear. This was not a cause for celebration, the Binjiang intendant wrote, for the Chinese were completely unprepared to take on an administrative task of this sort. Not only would the Chinese be responsible for the enormously complex CER commercial and administrative apparatus within the concession, they would also have to contend with the fact that the apparatus was completely Russian and came with a Russian civilian population that, because of refugees, was beginning to number in the hundreds of thousands.[44]

At some point between 1918, when the first Chinese police appeared on Harbin's streets, and 1920, when the idea of a special area that combined Chinese supervision with "a goodly number of foreign supervisors" was first recorded,[45] it was decided that the answer lay in substituting Chinese supervision for the former colonial power of the CER. The solution recognized the distinct multi-ethnic nature of the CER concession and retained as much of the administrative talents of the founding Russian population as possible.

In 1920, by order of the president of the Republic of China, Russian extraterritoriality was revoked. Russians and their property now came under the protection of the Chinese state. On 31 October 1921, the Chinese government replaced the CER concession with the Special District of the Three Eastern Provinces. Although the proclamation's scope was limited – it established

Chinese control over the Russian court system, police, and municipal governments – it signalled the beginning of China's administrative experiment.[46] The Special District would become a dual project – to establish and extend Chinese sovereignty, on the one hand, and to maintain the district's economic viability through the preservation of the Russian population and Russian administrative staff, on the other.

This project satisfied many agendas. The creation of a special district kept intact those structures that had so successfully transformed Manchuria. It enabled the Chinese to detach the CER from its administrative duties and Russian political context but retain the trained personnel that the Special District and railway needed in order to function. The CER could be placed on a secure commercial footing under true Sino-Russian co-administration. Meanwhile, all of the CER's auxiliary administrative functions – policing, the courts, municipal government, and education – could be placed under Chinese supervision but retain their personnel and institutional memory. Chinese managers and workers could be introduced and trained within the system. The local foreign population, which was essential to the continued functioning of the district, would be satisfied that the system had been left intact. The cause of Chinese sovereignty would be promoted, and the district could illustrate to foreigners that the Chinese could administer a foreign community.

The CER concession had been an administrative measure designed to achieve Imperial Russia's goal to economically, politically, socially, and culturally dominate Manchuria within the context of an existing concession or treaty system that granted to foreign powers extensive economic and political autonomy in China. It had perhaps also been a means of detaching the region from Chinese control and integrating it into the Russian Empire. For the Chinese, the Special District was also a means to an end – control of an important economic and political region dominated by a non-Chinese population. In this context, the creation of the Special District fell within the tradition of Chinese administrative control of non-Chinese areas. Following the fall of the Qing Dynasty, the new republic grappled with the problem of promoting Han Chinese nationalism and maintaining the multi-ethnic Qing Empire as it attempted to stifle non-Chinese minority national movements. Special districts were an administrative compromise that still asserted the superiority of Han developmental modernity over primitive minorities.[47] The creation of special districts in minority areas such as Tibet, southwest China, and Qinghai Province between 1911 and 1920 was a response to minorities' demands for greater autonomy and a republican correction of what were perceived to be lax Qing administrative practices that left far too much control in the hands of minority leaders. The Qing, as a dynasty accustomed to ruling subject peoples according to its norms of leadership, had been content to leave most administrative, religious, educational, and economic practices with minority leaders and organizations. The Qing demanded that minority institutions or leaders acknowledge the Qing as their rulers and did their utmost to appear to the minorities or their representatives as rulers within the minorities' traditions. Thus, the Qing emperors appeared to the Tibetans as Tibetan Buddhist leaders, to the Mongolians as Mongolian rulers, and so on. Republican administrators found this practice objectionable because it promoted administrative, religious, social, economic, and educational practices that they considered pre-modern obstacles to minority development. The creation of special districts answered minorities' demands for special consideration, a favour that fulfilled the long-standing traditions of the now-defunct Qing Dynasty, but ensured more pervasive administrative control in these regions. Chinese supervisors were appointed to every administrative level within the special districts and were urged to modernize archaic minority practices. The Han Chinese state, following a revolution in the name of Han nationalism, circumscribed further revolution among minorities by allowing them a degree of self-administration in Han-controlled special districts.

The creation of the Special District from the boundaries of the CER concession is a little known example of a Chinese administrative innovation designed to extend and enhance Chinese control and ideologically justify Chinese rule by pragmatically ensuring minority co-operation in areas where the Chinese were a demographic or economic minority. The Special District of the three northern provinces was different, however, because the region had only recently registered itself in the Chinese political imagination as Chinese and the area's two dominant populations were of equal vintage – neither could claim a long-standing presence in the region. Furthermore, it was impossible for the Chinese to portray the Russians and Russia's presence in the region as pre-modern, because the CER concession itself was the epitome of Western imperial economic penetration. For the Chinese elite, the concession's municipal governments, its significant economic investment, its modern educational institutions, and its well-laid-out cities and towns all represented the last word in modern administration, albeit in a colonial context. The Chinese would graft Chinese projects of modernity and the recovery of sovereignty onto the former concession in order to associate its new administration with Russian modernity.

Although the Special District was established by a national mandate from Beijing, the details of its organization were left to regional, provincial, and municipal elites. This strategy reflected the fact that regional leaders, in this case Zhang Zuolin, had taken over when the initial promise of republican unity gave way to warlord rule. Given Zhang Zuolin's overwhelming power, one could downplay the national government's role in the Special District, but this would be a mistake, for Beijing remained a significant player. It confirmed all appointments made by the Manchurian government and gave advice on particular administrative problems, especially municipal government and legal reforms. The administration of the Special District, therefore, involved a degree of regional and national co-operation in the warlord period that is rarely acknowledged.

The Special District administration was the district's general administrative supervisory office: it co-ordinated administrative reforms, it was a clearing house for information on new administrative practices, and it disseminated information on the district to interested foreign and Chinese parties. The Special District's principal mandate was to separate the formerly entwined political and economic powers of the CER and allocate them to proper spheres in the Chinese administration. To do so, the district administration asserted that the CER had been a colonial government that contravened the original railway treaties. It immediately reformed areas, such as the CER company and the former concession's police and court systems, in which Chinese supervision was either weak or absent. Other areas – for example, education, municipal government, and language policy – were dealt with at a later stage. This strategy reflects the pragmatism of Chinese administrators, who did not want to disrupt the district and potentially destabilize the region, and their recognition that the interests of the Russian population would have to be considered.

The district's Harbin office supervised all aspects of government and governance. It acted as a complete local government by taking on powers normally reserved for national, provincial, and regional administrations. The Special District existed as a zone of administrative experimentation within the regular Chinese regional government. This fact, combined with the complete trust that the warlord Zhang Zuolin placed in the district, gave the Special District administrative freedom to work out solutions to the task of ruling the local Russian community. The Special District, therefore, was typical of early Chinese administrative attempts to secure Chinese control over minority areas but unique in the degree to which it co-operated with Russian administrators and retained Russian institutions. The local Chinese elite respected what their Russian neighbours had created in Chinese territory, but they wanted it to be under Chinese control.

The solution also prevented nasty competition that could potentially have killed the Manchurian goose. Beijing and Shenyang were both eyeing the CER concession. The concession straddled the provinces of Heilongjiang and Jilin, each of which wanted control over the concession, which was the richest part of northern Manchuria. Creating the Special District preserved concession boundaries and the concession's income-generating potential without placing the area under one particular provincial jurisdiction. It was Shenyang, specifically Zhang Zuolin, who reaped the benefits of China's careful hands-off policy in the Special District. Letters from Zhang to Special District staff indicate that Zhang was, in fact, one of the solution's architects.[48] By 1922, China and the Soviet Union had already begun to discuss the possible co-administration of the CER. By initiating administrative reforms in the Special District, Zhang denied the USSR the possibility of regaining an administrative role within the former concession.

Zhang was also acting in the spirit of the Qing and republican governments by actively encouraging Chinese migration to Manchuria to develop the region and offset Russian and Japanese imperial pretensions. Zhang's administration established a Colonization and Development Plan in 1923, which encouraged labourers from central China to settle in Manchuria for longer than the harvest season by providing government-owned land, funds for the construction of a house, and rent reductions for the first three years.[49]

If the district's inspiration was national or provincial, the policy's success was due to regional administrators such as Li Jiaao (Li Lanzhou), former Chinese consul to Vladivostok, first Binjiang daoyin, first Special District chief justice, and fluent Russian speaker who was later to work in the Special District courts and on the CER board; Dong Shien, Binjiang intendant and friend of Russian administrators; Ma Zhongjun, a member of the Railway Negotiation Bureau, future vice-head of the Special District's Municipal Administration Bureau and future Harbin mayor who protected the interests of the Russian population; and Li Xiaogen, who had been educated in Harbin's Russian schools, served in the Jilin Foreign Affairs Bureau, and was appointed to represent the district on Harbin's Municipal Council. Li Xiaogen was the beneficiary of the CER's policy of sending Chinese boys to Russian schools to create a comprador class. Instead of working in the railway administration, most were hired by the newly created Manchurian Chinese administration because of their Russian language and cultural skills. Li later became a member of the Russian-dominated Harbin Municipal Council and an advocate for municipal reform in the Special District.[50]

These men, who were either raised in the district or pursued careers there after immigration, were all Chinese nationalists and strong supporters of the district. Their nationalism did not preclude their adopting a modern foreign-built and foreign-staffed commercial and administrative apparatus with relatively few changes. Because Russians and Chinese had settled the area simultaneously, the problem was not that the Russians had built administrative and economic institutions (institutions the Chinese admired) but the colonial context under which these institutions had been developed. In central China, foreigners and their concessions were settled in areas of centuries-long Chinese habitation. In China proper a nationalist, anti-foreign Chinese citizen could position him- or herself, albeit with difficulty in places like Shanghai, outside of the foreign-built and foreign-administered structures of central and coastal China. These concessions, despite their size and importance, remained tiny foreign specks in a Chinese sea. In northern Manchuria, by contrast, a Chinese man or woman living in the CER concession, or next to it, could do nothing to avoid interacting with Russian power, for it defined commercial, administrative, and territorial rule in the region.

The prolonged and bitter rights-recovery movements that were common in the concessions of central and coastal China were also relatively absent in the Special District, with the exception of protests against Japan in the late 1920s. Between the Opium Wars of the 1840s and 1942, the year that the extraterritorial system ended, the Chinese engaged in a protracted battle to recover sovereignty and erase the shame of foreign-dominated concessions. Facing this nationalist Chinese challenge, foreign concessions and their mother countries summoned the full panoply of military, legal, commercial, and political power in the defence of foreign privilege. For foreigners who lived in China, it was a losing battle. Time, changing ideologies on the usefulness of direct imperial control, and demographic changes guaranteed that the mother countries would eventually tire of defending a handful of missionaries, settlers, and treaty-port imperialists and become more interested in negotiating directly with a coherent Chinese national government to protect foreign access to the mythical Chinese market. The treaty ports would eventually be abandoned and, in the meantime, personal relations between Chinese and foreigners were often ruined.

Not so in Manchuria, where overnight the Russians went from being colonial administrators to stateless refugees. The state power Russians could have mustered to defend their position was gone. Even worse, the new state that replaced the Russian Empire rejected the refugees and their values. In Manchuria, Russians became, for some Chinese, objects of pity; for most Chinese, however, they became unarmed Russian neighbours. The Russian Revolution had reversed the conditions of colonial domination that continued in the remaining Southern Chinese concessions, creating intense animosity between the foreign and Chinese populations living there. In contrast, Manchurian Chinese took the opportunity to step back from a resentful national position and respond to their former colonizers with pragmatic solutions, magnanimity, partnership, and even friendship. The Special District was the result.

Although the Special District was established in 1921, its executive branch was not established until 8 December 1922.[51] The executive and its head, the chief administrator of the Special District (hereafter referred to as district head), united the Special District's disparate activities. That the district head's rank equalled that of the governors of Jilin and Heilongjiang reveals the importance that both the national and provincial governments accorded to the office.[52] In September 1923 the Special District was given full administrative independence, equal to a province, and reorganized into three departments: general, administrative, and educational-industrial.[53] The district head had extensive powers and answered only to Zhang Zuolin. He acted as a liaison between Shenyang and the Russian population and did "his utmost to communicate through the local press the intentions and decisions of the Special Area," to have articles on Chinese affairs translated and disseminated in Russian and other languages, and to educate the local population on the Special District's work.[54]

The first head of the Special District, Song Xiaolu (1920-22), was not a notable administrator, and his replacement, Wang Jingchun (1922), was preoccupied with his duties as CER president. On 2 December 1922, Zhu Qinglan became the head. A native of Sichuan, Zhu was described as a "fine looking man with a clean record" who after the 1911 Revolution became the military and then civil governor of Heilongjiang. These appointments were followed by a position as civil governor of Guangdong.[55] Zhu's career mirrored that of his two successors – each of the three chief administrators was a military man with extensive administrative experience. Each man's administrative outlook resembled that of Zhang Zuolin. Zhu was described as being interested in progressive enterprises, and he took a "great interest in the suffering of the Russian refuges." He founded the International Society for the Protection of Refugees, which lobbied the Chinese commercial class for funds and carried on extensive charity work.[56]

Zhu was replaced in 1924 by General Zhang Huanxiang (no relation to Zhang Zuolin), who held the position until 1929, when he was replaced following the CER Sino-Soviet crisis. Zhang had reorganized the CER guards and police prior to the creation of the Special District, and during the 1924 CER land department conflict he headed the CER police, providing police escorts to CER offices to obtain documents, and managed to ease tensions and avoid the outbreak of violence. Unlike Zhu, General Zhang was well regarded by the consular body.[57] When Zhang retired in November 1929, he was replaced by General Zhang Qinghui (no relation), former head of the police and the administrator responsible for merging the Russian and Chinese police forces to produce a bilingual and bicultural force.

The Chinese staff of the Special District's executive offices was largely local. Many had begun their careers in Binjiang offices or were self-made businessmen. Some of them, as children, had been placed by the CER in Russian homes and sent to Harbin's Russian schools. These men, among them Li Xiaogen, were intended to be middlemen between the Russian and the Chinese populations. By the 1920s, these young men had made use of their bicultural education to become bureaucrats in the new special district.[58] In the years prior to 1919, members of this Harbin Chinese elite were keenly aware that they lived under the administrative control of a foreign power in their own country. In the words of one Chinese businessperson who spoke in 1922 about the fact that Chinese were shut out of municipal elections, "Society has certain standards. These rights and privileges come with duties and responsibilities. But these four words have been exhausted. For many years, the Chinese businessmen have had the responsibilities without the rights. It is nonsense that the Russians hold this power in their hands, trying to turn this into their country when China is now a republic."[59] It is significant that the speaker not only recognized the Chinese right to representation in municipal politics but also the duties and responsibilities that accompanied that right. Already conditioned by a political system in which he could not participate, this businessman had absorbed the lessons of municipal politics. The Chinese had seized control of the CER concession and created the Special District to preserve what they perceived to be the region's most valuable assets – its modern infrastructure and the Russians who managed it. Chinese administrators – trained in railway bureaus, diplomatic offices, or the Binjiang administration – were placed in supervisory positions because they were familiar with Russian administration. However, before the Chinese could effect change in the CER company itself or at the level of municipal politics and the limited franchise, it was necessary to monopolize the district's security institutions – the police, the courts, and the prisons – to build Chinese control on a foundation of Chinese power.

4

Securing the Special District:
Police, Courts, and Prisons

"The most memorable sight in the East today is not Yokohama struggling up from the ashes or the modern stone buildings of Shanghai or Tokio. It is in North Manchuria – a Chinese policeman beating a white driver."[1] This image, more than any other, dominated Western accounts of the Special District during the 1920s. It was used to illustrate Manchuria's new racial hierarchy and the fate of foreigners in China without extraterritoriality. In this often-repeated scenario, Chinese police are represented as being, by nature, excessively violent, while the Russians are portrayed as their powerless victims. As a rhetorical device, this metaphor held a great deal of power; however, the reality was quite different. Many police in Harbin and the Special District were Russians who had either been retained from the previous force or employed by the Chinese after 1920. There were few documented incidents of inter-ethnic violence, and those that were documented cannot be matched to any journalistic accounts of Russians being brutalized by the Chinese police. Compared to Chinese and Western cities, and especially to Manchuria under Japanese control, the Special District in the 1920s was well policed.

The Special District was an administrative response and challenge to foreign extraterritoriality, the state of being subject only to the laws of one's own country rather than the country where one happens to reside. During the Qing Empire, a number of powers acquired extraterritorial status for their subjects by arguing that foreigners should only be subject to the supervision of their own governments, through consuls, because of "uncivilized" Chinese policing and judicial practices. By the 1920s, patriotic Chinese were challenging the concept of extraterritoriality in China's treaty ports, and the legal practice had come to symbolize China's humiliation and loss of sovereignty. Foreigners living in China believed extraterritoriality was the only means by which their property and persons could be protected from what they considered to be corrupt and arbitrary Chinese administrations. The only way that China could prove that foreigners would be safe and their rights protected was to demonstrate that China could rule a non-Chinese population that did not have the benefit of extraterritoriality. This gave the Special District administration, especially its policing and legal components, a particular pedagogic quality for Chinese and non-Chinese alike. For China, the Special District was a means of adapting a foreign administrative model to a situation in which Chinese and non-Chinese lived together. For non-Chinese, the Special District demonstrated that China could not only protect foreigners but also improve on the model it had inherited to benefit all residents. The Special District's police and judicial reforms have been described as the application of Chinese nationalism. Like all nationalist histories, however, this nationalist paradigm does not show that the Special District's police, courts, and penal system were influenced not only by nationalism but also by the region's dual cultural heritage.

The Special District's control institutions, the courts and the police, had their origins as Russian institutions that had played an important role in the establishment and justification of colonial power in the Chinese Eastern Railway (CER) concession. The police and the courts, the means by which Russian power was exercised by the CER company over the concession's Chinese and Russian populations, were as much a part of the CER's public face as were Harbin's Cathedral of St. Nicholas and its other fine European buildings. For Chinese inhabitants, regardless of whether they were told by a Russian police officer to stay out of Harbin's parks or brought to court for the nonpayment of a Russian municipal tax, the police were a point of contact with the Russian administration. Nevertheless, to view the post-1920 takeover as simply nationalist-inspired revenge is to reduce it to the righteous triumph of one nation and state over another.

The story of the Special District's police, courts, and penal system, like the history of the entire region, is infinitely complex. The Special District was a frontier society built, according to its Chinese and Russian elites, to civilize a wild region in the name of commerce and the Chinese and Russian states. To members of the Chinese establishment, the district's police and courts were the best examples of modern control institutions under Chinese supervision. Although the Chinese elite replaced Russian with Chinese control, it also sought an accommodation to ensure the smooth transition of power and the continued functioning of the CER concession. Some Chinese elites would claim that this accommodation was charity and emphasize the fine manner in which they had protected the Russian population under their control. The dominant Chinese discourses, however, were pragmatic and emphasized equality. They claimed that Special District institutions were based on Russian institutions and tailored to suit the needs of the influential Russian population, which was not composed of sojourners but immigrants who deserved equal treatment.

The process of absorbing the former CER Russian police and creating a dual Chinese-Russian police force illustrates the means by which the Special District accommodated the Russian population. A multi-ethnic force was necessary, not only because of the large Russian population but also because of criminality within the Russian community (a subject, because it did not show foreigners in China in a positive light, that was not often touched upon in the foreign and Russian-language press). The police force was not an institutional expression of the need for the Chinese to dominate the Russians as the Chinese themselves had been dominated. Rather, administrators of the Special District sought to provide a modern security force tailored to the unique needs of a multi-ethnic population.

Article 8 of the 1898 contract between the Chinese government and the Russo-Chinese (later Russo-Asiatic) Bank established the Russian police. The article – on the maintenance of security and order on the railway – stipulated: "The Chinese government has undertaken to adopt measures for securing the safety of the Railway, and of all employed on it, against any extraneous attack. The preservation of law and order on the lands assigned to the Railway and its appurtenances shall be confined to police agents appointed by the Company. The Company shall for this purpose draw up and establish police regulations."[2] Police were divided into three types: the railway police, usually referred to as CER guards, the secret police, and the regular police. Russian CER guards were formed when the CER was being built. The first Russian police department, whose officers were primarily of Cossack origin, was created for the entire concession in 1903. In 1908 the regular police force was supplemented by a secret police, whose primary task was to supervise the Russian population for political crimes but who also hired Chinese to spy on military targets.[3] The police forces had much power but little training. The American consul wrote, "[They could] arrest for breach of the peace and violation of public order. An act of public indecorum is a breach of the peace. The police of the railway administration are for the most part a rough and ignorant class. They are not paid to think and do not think; they know enough to carry out an order with severity but not with discrimination."[4]

Legally, concession police activities were restricted to the concession and its Russian inhabitants. According to the 1898 agreement, Chinese suspects were to be turned immediately over to the railway bureaus. The Railway Guard's official duties – guarding railway platforms and stations – were restricted to railway territory. In practice, however, the Russian authorities extended police powers outside of these boundaries. Registered by the Russian police and given a special identification, in essence a passport, Chinese in the CER concession were described as "immigrants in their own country."[5] Chinese police from the adjoining Chinese-controlled city of Fujiadian in Binjiang County were routinely stopped, searched, and disarmed. The distinctions between regular and railway forces were often blurred, as in 1909 when the Harbin Municipal Council called on the CER guards to settle the tax strike on the part of Russian and Chinese merchants. The same guards broke up a legal meeting of 250 shopkeepers and forced the merchants to pay the tax.[6] Harbin's police did not restrict themselves to CER territory. In February 1911, for instance, Russian troops invaded Fujiadian to suppress, by force, Chinese anti-Qing groups who supported the 1911 Chinese Revolution and who had called for the abolition of the CER concession.[7]

Using the elliptical language commonly employed to explain Russian administrative power in Manchuria, Dmitrii Horvath explained why Russian police found it necessary to go beyond what was legally permitted by the original agreements:

> In reality the institution that possessed more actual rights than anyone in the leased territory was the CER company itself, which from the moment it started its activity began to exercise administrative and police functions, first of all in respect to its own employees and subsequently over the population which had settled in its territory. This administrative activity being desirable with no protest on the part of the population of the territory or on the part of the local Chinese authorities and that gradually both became accustomed to the idea that the company possessed the rights of civil administration of the territory.[8]

In contradiction of Horvath's claim, Chinese and foreign consuls protested Russia's assumption that it could police Harbin and the Special District. The US consul reported that the practice made Harbin a "virtual Russian colony." When the US consul proposed a "municipally based or Chinese controlled" police force, the Russian administration responded by removing the US consulate's police protection.[9]

Although Russians and some foreigners later claimed that Harbin under Russian administration had been a well-policed city, the quality of Harbin's Russian forces was very poor. In 1908 the *New York Times* reported that in Harbin, "governed and administrated by a private railway company," residents feared for their lives and few left their homes after dark. The Russian police were conspicuous by their absence, and the Chinese town of Fujiadian, the *Times* pointed out, was much better administered and policed.[10]

The disintegration of the Russian police forces after 1917 (see Chapter 2), struck at the heart of Russian power in the CER concession. On 28 December 1917, Binjiang County daoyin, Dong Shien, was ordered by Beijing to disarm the Russian police and replace them with Chinese soldiers. He was assured that the CER contract would be redrawn to permit the establishment of a Chinese-controlled police force.[11] Unbeknownst to Horvath, Binjiang's administration had decided in December 1917 that Chinese and Russian police would work together under a Chinese-controlled force. The city was divided into four districts, and five hundred new police, Chinese and Russian, were hired. In his inaugural speech to the force, Dong made reference to Chinese nationalism, pragmatic solutions to Harbin's multi-ethnic reality, and the example a Chinese-controlled police would set for other concessions. He emphasized that China was not usurping the CER's rights – it was reassuming rights long ago abandoned by the Chinese republic. He stressed that Harbin's unique position as a frontier city with two founding peoples and nations came with the responsibility to set an example for China and the world. "In Harbin Russians and Chinese live together. It is not like central China. The responsibility of the police is to maintain public order and safety. This task is also a national problem, for if we do something wrong it will be an excuse for foreigners to make trouble. There may be hardships and difficult situations, but if we lose the right to police (ourselves) we only have ourselves to blame."[12] Dong acknowledged that the problems of foreign control in Harbin and its concession were unlike those of southern China. The region was one in which both Chinese and Russians had pioneered the frontier. Although the region was politically Chinese, the administrative infrastructure was Russian, as was a good portion of the population. And these peoples' rights could not be ignored. Finally, a policy of pragmatic compromise would demonstrate to other foreigners that the Chinese could not only police themselves well, they could also protect a foreign population under Chinese control. It was up to the Chinese themselves to demonstrate that they were capable of the task.

There was some question as to whether the Chinese would accept the new regime and Dong Shien stressed that the new situation would be difficult for the Russian population. "Bad Chinese citizens and businessmen have relied on foreigners to do their dirty work. When Chinese police discipline them the Chinese will not be able to do what they please. These Chinese should be treated according to the police regulations. For the foreigners it is better not to use too much force, it is better to use peaceful and strategic methods, to move them by our good will so that they will gradually become persuaded."[13]

Precise instructions that clarified the scope of these new police powers arrived on 21 February 1918 from Shenyang. In the case of altercations between Chinese and foreigners, the police were to investigate and transfer the case to the police station or the Harbin Railway Bureau. Disputes between foreigners were turned over to Russian police, who were now under Chinese control. Disputes between Chinese that did not concern the CER were taken to the police station and the courts; if it was proven that they did concern the CER, they were turned over to the railway bureaus. Assistance from the military could be requested, but force on the military's part could not be used.[14] On 1 April 1918, a language school was established to teach colloquial Chinese to Russian police officers, and at a conference on the new joint force held the following month, the former head of the Russian police agreed that every Russian officer would carry identification in both Russian and Chinese. In addition, the two nationalities within the police force, which shared the same rights and obligations, would salute each other to show friendship. Chinese colleagues were urged to turn over disputes between Russians to Russian police; however, if no Russian police were available, the Chinese police had the right to sort it out themselves. When the Chinese police were unsure of procedure, they were required to ask the Russian police for assistance.[15] It is clear that as the Shenyang and Harbin governments took on the burden of policing the new Special District, they wanted the new police force to treat all of the district's inhabitants in a fair and equitable fashion. Differences in the two peoples' legal cultures were respected by the decision to retain as much as possible each people's linguistic, procedural, and legal norms.

The new Chinese security force was divided into three parts: a force of CER guards under Zhang Huanxiang's direct control; the CER Police; and the Special District Police, which was still temporarily funded by the CER. The last two police forces were under the direction of Wen Yingxing, an English-speaking West Point graduate noted for his honesty and simple life and for fostering good relations with both Chinese and Russian officers.[16] After 1923, during the municipal reorganization, the two police forces were separated, and Police Chief Wen Yingxing remained head of the CER police.[17]

The principal difference between the CER guards and the CER police was their jurisdictions. The guards patrolled stations and worked closely with the Russian-trained staff. They were responsible for on-train security and for protecting "all employees of the Railway, regardless of nationality. They were instructed to avoid clashes with the Russian employees, show correctness in all relations with Russians along with moderation and friendliness."[18] CER police duties were CER affairs outside of the railway's precincts, and in the smaller stations the CER police acted as the municipal police.[19] The new Chinese regulations created ten CER guard districts – four for Harbin and six along the line. In Harbin, acknowledging that the Russian community was still paramount, the Chinese appointed Russians as the director and vice-director of the district. In the other six districts, directors could be and were Russian, but the vice-director was Chinese.[20] Both foreign and Chinese commentators agreed that the CER guards were a much better organized and effective force than their predecessors had been.[21]

The hiring practices of the CER guards and the CER police immediately led to a conflict that prefigured later ethic and racial tensions over the staffing of the new Special District administration. The CER guards – under their Chinese director, Zhang Huanxiang – were a mixed Sino-Russian force. The CER police, by contrast, were still predominately Russian and under the control of the new general manager, Boris Ostroumoff. Ostroumoff, hired in 1920 by the recently formed CER board to replace the aristocratic and autocratic Dmitrii Horvath, was a former Russian government administrator from Siberia. Ostroumoff had built his career advancing the goal of Russian settlement in the Far East, and fled, like many of Siberia's administrative class, for China.[22] He was an excellent administrator who was committed to leading the newly depoliticized and, in theory, racially integrated railway into its new role as a regional economic engine and profit-making enterprise. His sympathies, however, lay with the former Russian regime. Ostroumoff was committed to preserving the CER in case a non-Communist government reconstituted itself in Russia. Ostroumoff also saw the railway as a means of supporting the

Russian community, an idea that was very much in keeping with the railway's former colonial mandate. Ostroumoff therefore promoted and hired Russians at the expense of Chinese, a policy that would eventually earn him the hostility of the Chinese CER board members and his eventual dismissal.

Most of the CER Police were Russians inherited from the former system. Few Chinese were hired because Ostroumoff believed the Chinese, as a people, lacked the necessary skills.[23] By contrast, the CER Guards, who were not under Ostroumoff's direct control, hired Chinese to replace recently disarmed and expelled Russians. Because employment in the CER Guards and Police included a food and housing allowance, hundreds of unemployed Russians applied. It is clear that Ostroumoff viewed the hiring of Russians over Chinese as a means of supporting the growing numbers of unemployed refugees entering the Special District. This policy matched Ostroumoff's management of CER's resources in general, but it was immediately criticized by the new Chinese board. Chinese board members complained that the CER Police occupied all of the barracks housing of the former guards and that the police's ethnic composition had not changed.[24] In response, CER President Wang Jingchun froze further Russian employment in the CER police and cited the need for parity.[25] Russian CER Police were paid 700 to 800 rubles a year, a salary that was much higher than that received by the Chinese police. This prompted a suggestion by the Chinese to reduce Russian salaries.[26] Perhaps as a way to threaten Ostroumoff with Russian layoffs within the CER Police ranks, Chief Wen Yingxing of the Special District Police suggested replacing Russians with Chinese who would be paid a half salary to economize.[27] As a compromise, salaries and benefits for Chinese CER Police were increased, existing Russian personnel were retained, and more Chinese were added to the already large CER police. By 1928, the year before the outbreak of hostilities between China and the Soviet Union over the CER, the company was paying 3,500,000 rubles for the CER Guards and Police.[28] The CER Guards alone numbered 3,356 men.[29]

Both forces were kept busy. There were 163 recorded assaults in 1921, and 95 in the first half of 1922. During their first two years, Chinese CER Guards and Police and Russian engineers clashed, especially over the issue of free travel for police. Perhaps with an eye to centralizing power and removing the CER Police from the control of Ostroumoff and future Soviet co-administrators, the CER Police were placed under the Special District head in 1923. The change reduced tension between Chinese soldiers and the CER's Russian employees.[30]

Funding for the Special District's security apparatus was a controversial administrative topic. Prior to 1920 all security expenses, railway or municipal, were met by the CER and backed by Russian government subsidies. When the three branches were placed under Chinese control, it was estimated that one million rubles were needed to finance the force – half the funds would be provided by the Chinese government, half would be provided by the CER. Initially, the Chinese government's share was provided by the Russian share of the Boxer indemnity fund. Because of the growing rift between Zhang Zuolin and Beijing, however, the Chinese government discontinued the subsidy after 1920. Zhang began to pay the subsidy directly from his own budget.[31] The CER continued to pay 360,000 rubles annually for the forces. The sum was equal to the tax monies received by the company for their Harbin land but was much less than the two million rubles that were once provided directly by the Russian Finance Ministry.[32] Nevertheless, costs increased. By 1922, the CER had contributed a total of 1,553,617 rubles to the three forces and another 150,000 rubles for buildings.[33]

Zhang Zuolin had alienated funding from both national and provincial sources by refusing the requests of the Jilin and Heilongjiang provincial governments to place the CER Guards and police under their control. Hoping to keep the Special District (and its control institutions) under his direct supervision, Zhang Zuolin claimed that the Jilin and Heilongjiang governments would tamper with his policy of retaining and employing Russian police. If he wished, Zhang could have forced the two provincial governments to pay. His unwillingness to force the issue is a testament to his administrative skills and his desire to protect the Special District. In lieu of the provincial funds, the Special District had to increase CER and Special District taxes. The decision was bitterly resented and was reported on extensively in the consular press.[34] A police tax, or duty of 7 rubles for each grain car travelling on the railway, produced 850,000 rubles annually. The tax became so important a source of funding that police in outlying stations delayed trains for nonpayment. Railway Police received 1.5 to 2 million rubles a year from direct taxation. The Special District police received 240,000 rubles from taxes in 1920 and 540,000 rubles from taxes in 1923.[35] Another police tax, which was a source of émigré complaints, was the registration tax levied on all documents, papers, and passports needed to establish either nationality or residency in the Special District. One Russian newspaper estimated that the registration tax brought in annual revenues of 500,000 rubles, while the passport tax brought in another 200,000 rubles.[36]

Under the Ostroumoff administration, the CER complained about the high cost of security but paid the bill. Because so many of the security personnel were Russian, funding not only paid their salaries but supported their housing, education, and health care. High security costs, therefore, directly benefitted the émigré community. Under the Sino-Soviet co-administration, the Soviet directors were much less inclined to keep these émigrés on the CER payroll.[37] In 1924 Soviet board members cited the high proportion of police to railroad employees on the CER in comparison to several English railways and asked for a 30 percent reduction in the CER security budget.[38] Police Chief Wen Yingxing defended his Russian and Chinese CER guards by explaining that security for English and Manchurian railways could not be compared. In response, the new Soviet chief engineer, A.N. Ivanov, tried, without warning, to fire five hundred Russian CER police. His initiative was ostensibly a cost-cutting measure, but the plan to replace these men with Soviet officers at comparable salaries indicates that his true goal was to replace Russians with dubious loyalty to the USSR with true believers.[39] Police Chief Wen Yingxing fought for the dismissed Russian officers. In a consular interview, Wen argued that the dismissals were invalid. He singled out his Russian employees for praise and encouraged them to become Chinese citizens as a means of avoiding dismissal on the grounds of nationality.[40] Not anxious to exchange émigré Russians for Red Russians, Chief Wen and the Special District appealed to Zhang Zuolin, who ordered the Soviet CER board members to cease threatening Russian guards and police.[41] The issue was dropped.

The third component of the Chinese-controlled security forces in the Special District was the Special District Police, which was under the control of municipal governments and found in larger stations like Harbin. Although the Special District Police had been under Chinese control since April 1920 – when the Russian municipal police forces exchanged their Russian uniforms for Chinese, provoking a foreign resident to comment that although the uniforms were "neither good looking nor effective," Harbin was quiet for the first time in several years.[42] Foreign observers commented extensively on Russian police in Chinese uniform.[43] In Harbin alone there were 168 Russians working on the police force in 1923. The majority (111) were patrol police, which is not surprising given the need for Russian-speaking police on Harbin's Russian-speaking streets. In Harbin's suburbs, where Chinese and Russians lived together, there were fewer Russian police, although the Special District mandated that a minimum of one Russian police officer be hired for each suburb.[44] Within Harbin, sixteen police supervisors were ethnic Russians.[45]

Not surprisingly, in the first months of the Chinese administration, there were a number of incidents between the newly formed Chinese police, the Russian police, and the Russian population. Former Russian police who entered the Chinese force to retain their jobs and homes often found their orders contradicted by Chinese colleagues, and Russians in general had difficulty treating the Chinese as both equals and superiors. Between April and August 1920, there were forty incidents of violence between individual Russians and Chinese police officers. Many of these were between CER employees and Chinese who, as police, had the right to ride the railway for free. This privilege had not been a problem when the force was predominantly Russian. Once the force was blended, however, Russian engineers resented carrying Chinese police free of charge. A crisis was provoked by CER general manager Ivanov in November 1925 when he forbade CER guards and police from riding without paying directly and claimed that the Special District owed 11 million rubles to the CER. A brigade of CER guards seized the trains in January 1926, and Ivanov shut down the line. In response, Zhang Zuolin arrested Ivanov on 21 January 1926. In the post-1929 settlement, it was agreed that this bill would be paid from China's share of the CER's profit.[46] There were some unsubstantiated claims that

Chinese were seizing Russian property illegally, and in one case a Chinese police officer, taking advantage of his position, entered a theatre without paying and beat the Russian owner who attempted to make him pay.[47]

In keeping with their commitment to accommodate the Russian population, the Special District's administrators stressed police education in the district's two languages and cultures. The first joint Chinese-Russian class of sixty CER guards and Special District Police graduated in 1920 from a temporary police academy, and a second class of two hundred was enrolled in 1921.[48] A formal police academy, managed jointly by the Special District education department and the district police department, was founded in Harbin in 1922, and the CER police were given their own school, funded by the CER. Chinese and Russian police were taught each other's language and examined for language proficiency.[49] In his speech to the graduating class, Chief Wen emphasized the national and international importance of the CER and its function as a lynchpin of the local economy. He stressed that police had to be disciplined and should learn both spoken and written Russian as a part of their duty to keep public and social order.[50]

Not content to create a bilingual and bicultural police force, the Special District police pioneered new domestic security technology. Every home in Harbin had to have a triangle signal lamp outside its door, and the lucrative contract for the production of these lamps went to a Russian-owned company.[51] The lamps formed part of a warning system for fires and robberies. The signal connected each home to the police station. Residents pressed once in the case of robbery and twice in the case of fire. Each signal owner, in turn, pressed his or her signal upon hearing that of a neighbour. Because of the inconvenience and the expense, the first installation failed. "With the approach of winter and its evildoers," however, the system became mandatory, and poor residents were given a free installation at the district's expense.[52] In addition, thirty-nine guardhouses were erected across Harbin, and each was connected by telephone to the central police station. The system garnered for Harbin a mention in the American journal *The Special Police Weekly.*[53]

The joint force also employed role-playing. In one case, two plainclothes officers, one Russian and one Chinese, were sent out disguised as bandits to provide other officers with on-the-job training. Their description was circulated to the police with the intent to test their vigilance. One of the disguised officers was captured, but the capture of a real bandit of some importance and a cache of weapons was an unexpected bonus.[54] In 1924, ten sergeants and forty police were sent to Port Arthur for forty-five days of practical training in patrolling, census taking, policing, and street traffic control.[55]

As time passed, the Special District demonstrated its support of the Russian population by replacing retired or dismissed Russians – for instance, a Russian parole officer dismissed for untrustworthiness, another fired for not reporting captured drugs, and another who lost his identification – with other Russians.[56] Some Chinese, especially those with knowledge of the Russian language and experience in working closely with Russians, were rapidly promoted to higher positions. Adolescents who had been former assistants – or boys, as they were known by Russian railway employees – were singled out for police training because of their experience.[57] All off this highlights the immediate task of the new police administration: to create a modern, trained force tailored to the bicultural conditions of the Special District. Great care was put into the recruitment of Russian-speaking Chinese police and vice versa. The result was a dual-language and dual-race police force at every station of the line, which was much admired by sympathetic foreign visitors. The fluent Russian-speaking Chinese policeman at Station Man'chzhuriia who informed American author Maurice Hindus that the songbird he wanted was not for sale by its elderly owner "because this bird brings him luck," was just one such example.[58]

Beyond keeping public order and preventing crime, Special District police had numerous duties, ranging from population registration, tax collection, press censorship, and dog catching.[59] Special District Police were very active in the 1923 CER land controversy. Officers were posted at all CER Land Department offices and accompanied Chinese officials transferring deeds to the Chinese Land Bureau. Although there was frequent comment on the presence of the Chinese police, there were no recorded cases of violence. Police were also responsible for press censorship. On 27 July 1922, for instance, the CER's *Far Eastern News* was closed by police for printing articles that were critical of a fundraising lottery controlled by Zhang Zuolin.[60] Much censorship of the press was directed against leftist publications because the police carried out the Special District's political work. Censored publications could petition the Special District to resume publication, as did the editor of the leftist paper *Molva*, whose paper had been shut down for spreading Communist propaganda and insulting the English king.[61] In 1928, undoubtedly because it was a Soviet-controlled organization, the police raided the CER's Association of Russian Teachers and seized its publication, *The Educator*. Another means of controlling the press involved enforcing the regulation requiring the names of all Special District newspapers and journals to appear on lease agreements.[62] The Soviet paper *Tribuna*, which printed articles critical of the Special District police, was repeatedly closed in this way. A number of bookstalls patronized by Harbin's students were also closed for selling "communistic" literature that caused demonstrations that, interestingly, did not condemn the police but rather "reactionary teachers" who directed police to the stalls. The booksellers were later released on bonds paid by students.[63] In turn, the police censored émigré publications, especially during periods of tension between the émigré and Soviet communities. During the 1924 Sino-Soviet negotiations, an émigré editor approached Special District police to establish a Chinese-Russian cultural association. The police refused the application because they feared the association would become a front for émigré politics.[64]

The police were also accused of using so-called special taxes to fleece the foreign community. These taxes covered the Special District's entertainment and cultural activities. The Special District police kept a list of all theatres, clubs, cinemas, and dance halls, which were required to pay a tax designated for policing. This list included a combined charity and Red Cross office that rented its premises to an amateur theatre. The police continued to pester the charity for the tax, even though several inspections had shown that it was indeed a charity. When the head of the office was threatened with imprisonment, the US consul intervened and ended the matter.[65] All cabarets and performances of nude dancing in the Special District were likewise vetted by the police, and artists criticized the imposition as unduly controlling. Unfortunately, no details about the vetting process survive.[66] The Special District police were also responsible for registering cinemas and censoring films.[67] The popularity of Russian, foreign, and Chinese films meant that cinemas made a great deal of money; however, the cinemas often refused to pay the special entertainment tax. The police considered banning cinemas in the Special District because of non-compliance, but they realized a ban would be both impractical and impossible. Instead, in an effort to strictly enforce the regulations, all cinemas were listed with their owner's names on registration papers. The buildings were inspected, films were registered, the number of seats in the cinema could not be altered, and police had the right of entrance to inspect cinemas and the films they showed.[68] This was undoubtedly the source of many altercations between police and cinema owners, particularly when police took advantage of the law to watch free films.

The police performed several tasks for the Special District and the municipal government.[69] For instance, the police were responsible for traffic regulation. In some Harbin neighbourhoods, police forbade the use of rickshaws and restricted the streets to automobiles or Russian horse-drawn carriages. These practices may have indicated a preference for the modern over the traditional (and demeaning). In other areas, however, some three thousand rickshaws were permitted to improve traffic circulation and Chinese employment. Russian police in particular were assigned traffic duty in the city's busiest sections. When one unfortunate was struck by a vehicle, his gun was stolen by a Russian bandit.[70] Police were also responsible for collecting vehicle taxes and for testing and issuing driver's permits. The taxes were a good source of revenue because Harbin had the fourth largest number of motor vehicles in China, after Shanghai, Beijing, and Tianjin. Not all attempts at taxation were successful, however. In June 1921 a marine police tax was announced, but it was cancelled by December because of complaints from Russian and Chinese businessmen in Harbin.[71]

Security prior to 1920 had as its main function the registration of the concession's population. All Russians were required to have passports, and all Chinese had to be registered. However, pre-war passport registration was haphazard at best, and it was fairly easy to slip across the border.[72] After 1921 the right to issue passports was taken from the CER and given to the Special District police, who imported the *baojia* system of registration, which had been employed in Binjiang since 1915. The system was a traditional form of Chinese population control and surveillance by which families were organized into brigades of ten to police one another. In 1918 the system was extended to Chinese living in the Special District but not to Russians, whose movements were controlled through passport regulations. The Chinese press gave different reasons for the increased regulation of passports. Some claimed that it was a means of deporting Russians who could not find work and a way to weed out bad Russians if instability in the Soviet Union translated into political conflict in Manchuria. Others cited Chinese nationalism and saw the registration of Russian émigrés as a means of showing "who is the guest and who is the host" in the Special District.[73] The majority of articles, however, cited the protection of Russian political refugees as the principal reason for passport reform.[74]

The elaboration and enforcement of passport regulations by the Special District and its police was seen as a great imposition by members of the Russian and foreign communities, who were unaccustomed to having limits placed on their movements. In 1926 the US consul complained that he had been forced to show his passport when he left Harbin.[75] The foreign community accused the Special District of using passport regulations to increase revenue and harass foreigners. The Chinese, however, viewed the Special District as a sensitive region that needed special controls. Located only a few hours by train from the Russian border and home to a very large population of refugees, subject to the political machinations of a dozen political parties and under the watchful eye of Japan, the Special District and its population needed to be regulated and registered carefully. General Zhang Huangxing, head of the CER guards, told the press that Chinese authorities, because of turmoil in the Soviet Union, could not permit the "indiscriminate flow of refugees into the country."[76] All refugees were fed and sheltered by the Special District, but those without a visa from Vladivostok's Chinese consulate were returned. Handled by a special brigade of Russian-speaking police, the returnees were permitted to choose their destination and were not forced to return to places where they felt unsafe.[77] Registration of Russians began in 1920, when all Russians who were not already Chinese citizens and all other foreigners were instructed to register with the police or the Jilin diplomatic bureau within two days of their arrival in the Special District. A passport was required. If a passport was not available (which was often the case with refugees), two photos and a fee of two yuan was required to create a Special District registration card. In addition, all Russians who had resided in the district before 1920 and all homeowners were required to register with the police.[78] The registration card listed the individual's name, age, address, and occupation. At a later date, the card included the person's official rank or title, father's name, education, religion, and health status. For stateless Russians travelling within China, special internal passports were required. These applications were very detailed; they included name, address, age, date, place of birth, and citizenship and listed any relatives in China or the Soviet Union.[79] Originally, there was no expiration dates on registration permits. In April 1922, however, Beijing cancelled all passports. The order was not implemented in the Special District until July, and those requiring new permits were given one year to obtain them. With the exception of the very young, permits for stateless persons were renewed annually.[80]

The result was that July saw queues of five to six hundred Russians daily, along with tedious paperwork. Special District police were dispatched to outlying stations to register refugees. The required two yuan registration fee was waived for those who were over sixty or too poor to pay.[81] Police efforts to crack down on registration halted the free flow of people and foodstuffs that the governments of the Russian Far East considered essential for survival across the Sino-Russian border. When the Amur provincial government asked Zhang Zuolin's government to reconsider these new measures in 1923, the Special District stood firm. Only Russians with a job and a letter from a Russian committee in Harbin or a guarantee from a Chinese businessman were permitted to stay. Russians arriving from the Soviet Union required a letter from the Chinese consulate or a prominent Russian citizen. Once in China, the immigrants' papers were examined for forgeries before they were given registration documents.[82]

Those émigrés who chose to become naturalized Chinese citizens were treated no differently from ordinary Chinese: "Even if their color and clothes are different we treat them the same."[83] Issued regular Chinese passports, which indicated their émigré origins,[84] these Russians were invited to become Chinese citizens. All citizenship decisions were made at the Special District level. To expedite the process, Special District police were given the right to process citizenship papers for families of naturalized Chinese Russians. Despite these precautions, refugees did enter the Special District illegally and did disappear into the Russian community.[85] In September 1925 the police were ordered to search hostels, boarding houses, and shops for illegal Russian immigrants. Several Russian criminals had hidden or were being protected in Harbin's many hostels.[86] The police were reminded to pursue their task of registering émigrés and to keep an eye out for unregistered weapons. Russian police were warned to be extra vigilant and cautioned to not allow pity or sympathy to get in the way of their duties.[87]

After the creation of the Chinese-Soviet CER co-administration in 1924, émigré members of the police force shared with their new Chinese supervisors a dislike for the Soviets, and many émigré police officers were openly hostile to the new Sino-Soviet co-administration. The Soviets, in turn, perceived émigré officers to be a threat. In 1924, during negotiations over joint

CER administration, the Soviets asked that Special District Russian police be fired and the Soviet consul be given control over all ethnic Russians. The Special District protected its Russian officers, and the Chinese negotiators firmly denied both requests.[88] The incident was one of many in which the Special District protected its Russian officers. In October 1924, after China recognized the Soviet Union, Chief Wang gathered his Russian employees to reassure them that their positions would be secure even if they applied for Soviet citizenship. In the Special District's opinion citizenship was a personal matter and would not affect their positions. Both categories of Russians, Soviet and non-Soviet, were allowed to work as Special District police.[89] After the 1929 CER crisis, the Soviet consul demanded the dismissal of all émigré police serving in Harbin and the Special District. The Special District Police Association, responding to pressure from the Soviet CER co-administration, sent out a warning to Russian police naturalized as Chinese citizens that anyone "failing to discharge their duties in a conscientious and straightforward manner would be discharged and deported." The warning did not pertain to ethnicity or national origin – only failure to perform one's duty would be grounds for dismissal.[90]

Russian police were charged with the supervision of their own émigré associations. In 1929 the police were told to dissolve any Special District émigré associations, prohibit their meetings, and arrest any émigrés engaging in anti-Soviet activity.[91] All public meetings had been subject to police approval since 1920. The organization's name, address, meeting place, agenda, and the number of people in attendance were recorded, and permission to hold the meeting was required three days in advance.[92] In 1925 the police chief increased regulations for police supervision of public meetings because of conflict between émigré and Soviet Russians. The new Soviet CER co-administration attempted to use these powers of supervision to break up émigré associations. However, there is no evidence that the administration actually targeted émigré associations. Instead, on 14 March 1929, the police broke up Russian and Chinese Communist activities at the CER club on the grounds that they defamed the fifth anniversary of Sun Yat-sen's death, and during the 1930 Russian October Revolution anniversary celebrations, Russian and Chinese police patrolled the Soviet festivities to ensure that no overt acts of propaganda took place.[93]

Because of the fine training received by the Special District police, the district's residents petitioned to have police stations built in their neighbourhoods.[94] By 1929, Harbin, in the words of one reporter, was a "model of order and cleanliness," and the Chinese police, who "fearlessly enforce order," were greatly appreciated by its residents. Police vigilance and high standards were attributed to the bi-ethnic nature of the police force. More vigorous law enforcement in the European sections of Harbin, the reporter explained, reflected the European population and higher police standards, which had been passed on to Chinese partners. Fujiadian police, by contrast, were singled out for retaining bad Chinese habits: "Although efficient, [they] adjust themselves to the more easy-going conceptions of life."[95]

As was the case with law enforcement, the CER concession's judicial system was based on the principle of Russian extraterritoriality and had been established in 1858 by article 7 of the Treaty of Tientsin:

> No lawsuit between Russian and Chinese subjects in places open to commerce shall be brought into court and decided by the Chinese authorities otherwise than together with the Russian consul or the person who represents the authority of the Russian government at such a place. In case of Russian subjects accused of having committed a crime or an offence, they shall be tried according to Russian laws. Equally shall Chinese subjects, for every offense or crime against the life or property of Russian subjects, be tried and punished according to the laws of their country. Russian subjects who have penetrated into the interior of China and have there committed any crime or offense, shall be brought either to the frontier or to one of the open ports, where there is a Russian consul, in order to be tried and punished according to Russian laws.[96]

Extraterritoriality gave Russians the right to be tried according to Russian law and acknowledged the right of the Chinese to be tried under their own system. But, as occurred with policing, the Chinese were gradually brought under the purview of the Russian judicial system. This was accomplished through the railway bureaus, institutions created and funded by the CER to mediate disputes between the CER and the Chinese population and to act as a liaison between the CER and Chinese authorities. From the outset, these bureaus were fully under the control of the CER. The railway could therefore extend its power over the concession's Chinese residents.

In the first agreement between the CER and the Jilin Railway Bureau, which was signed in 1899, all criminal cases in Jilin Province, regardless of whether these cases "directly or indirectly touch[ed] the interests of the CER," were settled by Chinese bureau members who were appointed and paid by the CER and who consulted with their Russian co-workers. Cases of murder, theft, and adultery committed by unskilled labourers were settled on the spot by Chinese authorities according to Chinese law, but all cases had to be reported to the bureau, which had the right to re-examine any case.[97] A second agreement signed in 1901 enhanced the bureau's powers and literally brought all Chinese in the concession under CER control. All matters touching on the CER's interests that involved Chinese CER employees now fell under CER jurisdiction, including "all other Chinese subjects, whether merchants, artisans, domestic servants and other Chinese, temporarily or permanently residing in the Concession Zone of the railway, even if the nature of their occupation does not have any direct relation to the Railway."[98] This article applied to "Chinese and to Manchus and Mongols living in Kirin (Jilin) province."[99]

A final agreement signed in 1902 clarified the powers of the railway bureaus and the CER's Russian head and expanded the bureau's jurisdiction beyond the concession's boundaries to include all of Heilongjiang Province. All legal cases in the concession now had to be submitted to a railway bureau for examination; in addition, articles 3 through 6 gave the head, or his representative, the power to decide any legal case anywhere in the province.[100] According to Horvath, the bureaus functioned in a fairer manner than Chinese institutions: "The justice and impartiality that reigned in the bureaus as well as the speedy decision of cases, which distinguished them, to their advantage, from the Chinese yamen [chanceries], won the confidence of the local population and it often happened that natives who had no connection with the railway and lived outside its territory brought their cases to the bureaus."[101]

Each of these agreements was signed during the aggressive Russian intervention that followed the 1900 Boxer Rebellion and greatly reduced the application of Chinese law in Jilin and Heilongjiang provinces. All cases now deemed important to the CER (the decision was reserved for the Russian authorities) could be transferred to the company's courts. Any Chinese, regardless of whether they were employed by the CER or resided permanently in the zone were subject to Russian law. The bureaus literally had the power of life and death over them since "they could inflict such extreme punishments as penal service and capital punishment."[102]

The Imperial Russian government used judicial administration to extend formal and informal authority over Manchuria. In a secret order from the Russian Senate – dated 1901 and sent to the Finance, Foreign Affairs, and Justice ministries – all Manchuria was placed under the jurisdiction of Amur's governor general. Courts under the supervision of the Finance and Justice ministries were opened along the CER line and in Port Arthur to deal with affairs within their jurisdiction and to advance the cause of the Russian Empire.[103] These courts did not simply administer justice – they were, as the minister of war, Alexei N. Kuropatkin, said in 1903, "to act as did the courts in Turkmenistan" (a former Russian protectorate settled by means of a Russian railway and eventually annexed into the Russian Empire). Therefore, the Russian-controlled court system was conceived as a front line of Russian colonialism and a precursor to annexation.[104]

Why did Chinese authorities allow Chinese sovereignty to be limited beyond foreign extraterritoriality? According to a Russian source, ordinary extraterritoriality was no longer "in harmony with the present state of affairs" because Manchuria was occupied by Russia following the Boxer Rebellion. When the first agreement had been signed in 1898, it conformed more or less to the dictates of extraterritoriality – resident Chinese were not under Russian control. After 1900, however, the Russian army took over Manchuria and did not leave until 1904, primarily because of considerable foreign pressure. In 1901 Russia concluded a secret agreement that placed all Chinese police and troops in Manchuria under the Russian army's supervision. Only Russians could be retained as advisors.[105] Even after the army's evacuation, a large number of Russian troops were converted to CER guards and remained in the area to take over the region's administration. Horvath justified these developments by claiming that the Chinese were grateful because "they [the Chinese] felt their own [guards] inadequate to guard."[106] Therefore, by 1902 Chinese provincial authorities were in no position to resist Russian demands for an extension of their jurisdiction over Chinese nationals in Manchuria.

Control was established not only over Chinese in the concession, other foreigners also fell under the CER's jurisdiction. The consuls protested vehemently that the concession was a business venture and that the CER was assuming the position of a colonial power. (This was the same argument made by the Chinese authorities after 1920.) George Rea, an American who visited Harbin in 1909, wrote that, legally, Harbin was "distinctly a Russian city as though located on the Volga. The same obnoxious laws were implanted and enforced." A foreigner was required to carry a passport and could only establish a business "provided he sign[ed] a document binding himself to faithfully observe all the obnoxious binding Russian regulations and failing in which, at any time, his property could be forfeited and all his buildings demolished at the will of the railway manager." Rea was clearly aghast at the degree to which the fabled open-door policy had been flouted, when he wrote: "No white man could tolerate such impositions on his rights and no consul for a moment dare to witness or endorse such a document, which recognized absolute Russian jurisdiction."[107]

There were eleven courts in total in the CER concession. All were staffed by Russians, and stations with no court were served by a travelling circuit court. The final court of appeal was the Province of Irkutsk's High Court in Russia proper.[108] Although the courts claimed jurisdiction over Chinese nationals, this claim was accepted neither by the Chinese government nor by the foreign consuls. Chinese who were summoned before the CER courts often failed to appear, and the Chinese authorities did not recognize the legality of these summonses.[109] Chinese had a number of other criticisms concerning the CER courts. They claimed that the concession was a haven for Russian criminals who fled to the concession because it was beyond the reach of China's legal system. In 1912, for example, a Russian who had robbed and murdered several Chinese shopkeepers in the Russian Far East moved to the concession to avoid punishment.[110] They also claimed that Russians who committed serious crimes against Chinese used extraterritoriality to avoid justice altogether. A Russian who murdered seven Chinese men in the concession, for example, was extradited to Russia by Harbin's High Court and set free.[111] Before 1920, the Chinese accused, Russians could literally get away with murder in the CER concession.

On 23 October 1920, the president of the Republic of China abolished the extraterritorial rights of all Russian subjects living in China. The order was a significant first blow to Russia's sense of superiority and power; it was also an essential step in the assumption of Chinese control over the police and the judicial system. By the same order, the Russian consul's power to review all court cases involving Russians and Chinese complainants was also cancelled.[112] Although the formal end to the Russian courts began with this presidential mandate, preparations for the takeover had been underway since September 1920.[113] Zhang Zuolin had closed Harbin's Imperial Russian consulate on 27 September, when the Russian consul announced that he would turn over to the Chinese all legal affairs.[114] Tentative plans for a Chinese takeover had also been set out in a report prepared by a foreign advisor to the Chinese government, John Ferguson, who urged the Chinese to reorganize all of the CER's control institutions under Chinese control. Ferguson advised the Chinese to create tribunals to try civil and criminal cases and argued that although these should be under Chinese control, a "good proportion of foreign elements" should be included. The police organizations and territorial administration should be Chinese, and the CER "should give up all exterior evidence of being Russian."[115]

The Binjiang County administration supervised the judicial takeover, and timing was of the essence because the Russian Revolution presented the perfect opportunity to establish Chinese control. According to the county's daoyin, Dong Shien, who would later become head of the Special District's Municipal Administration Bureau, the Chinese assumption of administrative privilege was a precaution in case "the dead ash flamed" – that is, in case a strong Russian power re-emerged.[116] Master of the metaphor, Dong urged his fellow Binjiang administrators not to underestimate the Russians, who were like a powerful insect "with one hundred legs." Although Russian power was, in his words, "dead, the corpse was not yet stiff."[117]

Although the establishment of Chinese control over the courts and police was well co-ordinated among local, provincial, and national authorities, it was also achieved through trial and error. There were, however, a few basic principles. From the beginning, as was revealed in a series of telegrams that articulated the vision of the Chinese-controlled judiciary, Chinese authorities planned to retain significant Russian legal precedents and legal staff in their reformed system. The Russian courts, which were renamed Public Safety Courts, would have appointed judges "who know every country's language and legal system." Russians could continue as lawyers, and a law school was to be founded to teach Russian and Chinese law. The costs of the reforms were to be split among the provinces of Heilongjiang and Jilin and the CER.[118] Not all Chinese administrators immediately shared this vision of a dual legal system. Jilin's chief military officer, General Bao Guiqing, who had helped to create the district's Chinese police, initially argued (alongside Heilongjiang's chief military officer) for the immediate imposition of a wholly Chinese legal system. Yet Bao also raised questions about the applicability of a purely Chinese solution. According to Bao, the two peoples had different legal cultures, there were few bilingual employees, and the financial and social costs (in terms of the disruption to the concession) of implementing a Chinese system would be prohibitive. Because of the two countries' different national customs and the large

Russian population, Bao eventually decided it would be impossible to impose a Chinese system. Members of Binjiang's Legal Department agreed. They argued that because the legal system was purely Russian, it would be impossible to impose a Chinese system. In addition, the new Chinese CER president, Wang Jingchun, reported that the CER could not fund the reorganized courts because it was battered and debt-ridden. Wang argued, moreover, that if the Chinese wished to establish the CER as a business venture alone, the links between the railway and judicial administration should be cut.[119] Nevertheless, to leave the Russian system intact would simply encourage the other treaty powers to believe that the Chinese were incapable of self-government.

General Bao pointed out that the concession court's budget, originally supplied by the Russian government through the CER, was very generous and that the Russian judges enjoyed a high standard of living. These judges, he believed, should be retained at their previous salaries to ensure continuity and high-quality service. Bao was also persuaded that a policy of retaining most of the Russian staff would be best, and he suggested that Russia's Boxer indemnity payments be used to fund the Special District's courts, a suggestion that was adopted.[120]

On 2 October Binjiang's Legal Department appointed Zhang Yipeng, a graduate of Harbin's Russian schools who was familiar with both countries' legal codes, to co-ordinate the takeover of the Russian courts and to act as a liaison between the Russians and the two provincial authorities so that "the lives and property of the peaceful immigrants" and China's sovereignty could be protected.[121] Zhang, who had successfully negotiated with the Russian consul for the handover of that office's power to the Chinese, took up his position on 10 October and found the personnel of Harbin's courts, understandably, excited but also supportive.[122] He recommended that the existing legal system be retained and additional Russian judges and lawyers hired. He also urged that law classes be conducted in the two languages to train a new pool of specialists in both legal traditions. Both the Binjiang and Beijing legal departments agreed and advanced funds. In addition, Zhang borrowed 200,000 yuan on the strength of the national government's promise to advance him the money formerly paid into the Russian Boxer indemnity.[123]

Although the process of assuming Chinese control was difficult, it was not impossible. Russian objections often had little to do with national pride and more to do with the country's precarious financial position. Zhang appointed one Mr. Yin, who was formally appointed on 16 October 1920 by Zhang Yipeng to head the Special District preparatory court, to take over the Harbin High Court.[124] This was done on 5 October, when Yin requested all files and ordered that Chinese law be applied to all future cases. Russian staff members were not adverse to applying Chinese law but refused to hand over the files until Yin guaranteed their employment. Yin then closed Harbin's courts; in response, its Russian lawyers and judges announced a boycott of the new administration, and their challenge was encouraged by the foreign consuls.

Because the Russian translators hired by Yin had no legal training, Yin engaged a Russian lawyer, whose name (transliterated from Russian to Chinese) was Fugotou, to negotiate with the Russian staff on the administration's behalf. After twenty days of Fugotou's dubious negotiating skills, the Russian staff of Harbin's three largest courts, forty persons in total, announced a strike and refused to work with Russians and Chinese brought in to clear backlogged cases until their positions were guaranteed. Yin stepped in on 27 October, when he received permission from the Binjiang Legal Department to retain the former employees at full pay. But the final settlement was delayed for two days when Russian judges demanded that their former salaries, which ranged from 400 to 500 yuan, remain the same. The judges eventually settled for 300 hundred yuan, but the secretarial staff held out for their wages, housing, fuel, allowance, and salaries to be in Chinese dollars – not the rapidly devaluing Russian ruble. Although Yin conceded that the Russian staff were invaluable to the court, the staff had to accept a salary reduction in exchange for the housing and fuel allowance. Those who did not accept these conditions were dismissed and replaced by new bilingual employees.[125] What is notable in this exchange is that the Russian employees did not hold out for the sanctity of Russian law and, indeed, offered no resistance to the courts' application of Chinese law. Resistance was organized around issues more fundamental to survival in a rapidly deteriorating atmosphere – employment, wages, food, and housing. Because of this exchange, the Chinese realized that a wholesale attempt to impose Chinese law would be impossible without the co-operation of the Russian employees.

Every court on the line endured the same long series of negotiations. Although a draft of court regulations was prepared by 13 November 1920, a final settlement with the employees was not achieved until 10 December. To economize, the eleven courts were reduced to six – three in Harbin and three in the largest stations (Man'chzhuriia, Hailar, and Hengtaohotze), which represented the eastern, western, and southern branches of the railway. Yin retained as many employees as possible from the closed courts and used them to replace staff who had either resigned or retired. On 30 October 1920, the Chinese government officially confirmed what the Manchurian authorities had begun by authorizing the creation of a Special District High Court to supervise the aforementioned six courts. Appeals were heard by the District Court and then the High Court. The Supreme Court in Beijing served as the court of final appeal. In addition, a Chinese court was established in Fujiadian to deal with cases between Chinese and cases between Chinese and foreigners with extraterritoriality.[126]

The principal change to court procedure was the elimination of the preliminary examination by court officials. The procedure was not part of the Chinese system; however, in the Chinese courts, the procurator performed the same function – he examined witnesses, authorized searches, and ensured that judgments were properly executed. As the Special District's representatives,

Special District procurators had the additional responsibility of ensuring that all regulations were followed. One can judge the importance accorded to the procurator from the fact that, according to the regulations, they could be hired and fired only by the High Court.[127]

Each court had its own procurator, and Russian lawyers registered with the Chinese Ministry of Justice were permitted to fill the position. Ordinance 1186, which allowed all foreign lawyers in China to practise law, was promulgated on 28 December 1920, the same date as the creation of the Special District. Its goal was to allow Russian lawyers to continue to work – but only within the district and with a certificate issued by the Special District Legal Department.[128] Russian lawyers were originally only permitted to take cases that involved Russians and other foreigners, but this regulation was amended in response to an English national who wanted to bring a case to the Special District court. The Legal Department agreed that cases involving foreigners (that is non-Russians) should be allowed in court and advised the new courts to be flexible. Cases concerning only Chinese subjects were handled by Binjiang courts, an order confirmed by Beijing in January 1921.[129]

Another significant change from the former system was a prohibition on lawyers communicating directly with judges. Under the old system, Russian lawyers had had free access to judges, and some Binjiang lawyers "had picked up this bad habit." The Legal Department was afraid that lawyers would unduly sway judges through the communication of feelings and emotion. In the Legal Department's opinion, a lawyer's goal was venial: winning cases by any means possible. All lawyers, Chinese and Russian, were therefore forbidden to communicate with judges outside of the courtroom during the course of a trial.[130] There were sixteen Russian lawyers registered in December 1921, but their number had increased to thirty-eight (of sixty-eight lawyers, including Chinese) by 1923. Russian lawyers also joined the Society of Chinese Advocates, which became a bicultural and biracial institution in the Special District. Formed in 1921, the society's council had eight members who were drawn from both the Chinese and Russian communities.[131] By 1926, ninety-two Russians and thirty-six Chinese were registered. (The Harbin branch had its own uniform, a black toga similar to that worn by lawyers in the West.) Russian lawyers did have their own specific problems. For instance, because Chinese lawyers could communicate more fluently in court, they got the lion's share of the business. In 1922 the Russian lawyers were permitted to form their own association so they could lobby on their own behalf.[132]

In keeping with the decision to retain Russian influence in the Special District judicial system, Russian advisors were appointed to the High Court and to each of the two district courts. They were dispatched, when needed, to outlying stations and reported directly to the Special District Legal Department. As consultants on the Special District's behalf, these advisors were allowed to discuss case details with the judge and procurator, check files and demand information, attend trials, and demand that the plaintiff, defendant, and witnesses answer questions. In addition, advisors could give judges their legal opinion before judgment, mediate for those they believed had been illegally arrested, and enter prisons in which foreigners were held. However, the advisors were not independent judicial actors – they had to reveal all case details to the procurators.[133]

In addition to the advisors, a Russian legal consultant, chosen from the staff of the cancelled courts, was appointed to each of the remaining six courts. Aside from explaining points of Russian law, the consultants had no voice in the courts' decisions.[134] Qualifications were defined broadly by the national government to allow the maximum number of Chinese and Russian counsellors to be hired. In general, legal consultants were to be "familiar with Russian conditions ... versed in law, and engaged for three years in diplomatic affairs in the Three Northeastern Provinces." In addition, they were to be "well versed in the Russian language, spoken and written, and [were] qualified to sit for the judicial examinations." Finally, they were to be "persons who made a study of law and political science in the universities of Europe and America and who [had] certificates of graduation."[135] Within the Special District, these national regulations were amended with the district's particular Russian characteristics in mind. According to district regulations, a consultant should be hired on the basis of his knowledge of "existing or abolished Russian law, Russian habits, Russian religion, and other Russian regulations, orders and systems." As consultants, they would submit a signed report on the facts of the case to the district. They could ask for trial details but were not privy to sensitive material.[136] Translators (called *dragomen* in the Special District) and clerks charged with documents were to be bilingual (either Russian and Chinese or Chinese and another language) and were to have some demonstrable legal knowledge, to be determined by an examination set by the Special District Legal Department and with a required pass of 60 percent.

Translators could not accept outside fees or bribes and had to translate documents truthfully, without adding their own ideas. They were to avoid influencing cases. All translations were double-checked, and other fees were carefully laid out. Translating Chinese to Russian or another language cost forty cents a line for a civil case and eight cents a line for a criminal case. Translating Russian or another language into Chinese cost ten cents per line for civil cases and fifty cents per line for criminal cases. Simply copying Chinese documents cost ten cents per one hundred characters, while copying Russian cost three cents per line. A standard size of paper was specified, and if a Chinese document did not reach the required one hundred lines, the fee for one hundred lines was still charged and a receipt in Chinese and Russian issued.[137] The necessity of translating everything into Chinese was to the advantage of Chinese-speaking lawyers, and their fees were higher than those of Russian lawyers. Sensitive to criticism of excessive fees, especially for multiple documents, the Legal Department called for greater attention to what fees were charged and made receipts mandatory. The Legal Department admitted that should the fee abuses reported in Harbin's press be true, foreigners would have an excuse to interfere in the Special District. The courts would be at fault, and restitution would be necessary. The Legal Department advised that all fees be posted in both languages outside each court and procurator's office.[138]

Chinese was the Special District courts' principal language of business because "it demonstrates our [Chinese] sovereignty, and acknowledges who the owner of the country is and who is not."[139] All files, notices, and so on used Chinese. Any affairs concerning the Russian community were to be bilingual, in text and speech. Any cases concerning Russians used Chinese as the main language but required a Russian translator. In cases where the meaning of Russian and Chinese was disputed, the Chinese language was used as the standard.[140] In the first months of the transition, the rapid switch from Russian to Chinese law without a group of competent bilingual officials caused many difficulties. For instance, in one case a Russian accused of breaking a window was charged, by a Chinese-speaking judge working with a bad translation, with the murder of "Mr. Window."[141] Institutions with no parallel in the Chinese system – the Chancery Court, the Department for the Registration of Societies and Unions, and the Russian notaries – were simply absorbed intact into the Special District. Their employees were placed on the Chinese payroll, and Chinese co-supervisors were appointed to both supervise and learn the daily business. All of these measures demonstrate that instead of implementing forced sinification, the courts became truly Sino-Russian as the Russian judicial system was adapted to Chinese control.[142]

Of particular and immediate concern was a backlog of thousands of cases that had to be cleared. Given the need to expeditiously process these cases, the regulations for the settlement of old Russian cases were quite generous. A special office, the Office for Clearing Russian Cases, was established for civil and criminal cases. That this office was headed by the judge for the district's two highest courts indicates its importance. For civil cases, Chinese law was used; for criminal cases, the new Chinese criminal law code was employed. However, because Russian law was more lenient in some cases, the Russian code was preferred. The possibility of revising the Chinese law to account for Russian law was acknowledged in regulation 14. Political crimes were abolished and all political prisoners who had been imprisoned under the Russian administration were freed.[143] The backlog of cases was enormous because Russian courts had not functioned at full capacity since 1914. Between 1 December 1920 and 1 December 1921, over 2,960 civil and 1,409 criminal cases were decided, and some of "the most inequitable and ludicrous decisions were the result of the over-hasty assertion of Chinese sovereignty."[144] Chinese judges were likely lenient because Russians whose cases had been tried under the previous system requested retrials.[145]

According to the Chinese, who made extensive comments, the Russians were a litigious people much given to using the courts. For example, Russians registered all kinds of property, ranging from land to goods worth only a few yuan. Public notary offices were therefore busy and made a great deal of money. The creation of a special notary for the registration of household property in the Special District was a Chinese innovation to serve the Russian constituency.[146] To prevent superfluous lawsuits, the district courts paid close attention to property contracts and urged Russians immigrants to correctly register their land. To deal with the growing number of Russian small claims, a Chamber of Reconciliation, in effect a small claims court for cases not exceeding 1,000 yuan, was created and staffed by three judges. Its services were free of charge, and both parties were bound by its decisions.[147] According to one Chinese author, Harbin's Russian population, noted for its heavy use of credit (more than half of Russian immigrants bought essential goods on credit, often at a high price), ran up large debts at Harbin's stores. They frequently had to be taken to court for payment. The insolvency of the Russian community was confirmed by a Special District order that required Russians, but not Chinese, who wished to leave the district to obtain a certificate from the police that certified their status as debt-free.[148] Courts frequently intervened in debtor's cases and garnisheed wages. For instance, a Russian member of the former Municipal Council was made to pay 20 yuan per month to pay down a debt of 300 yuan. And these small claims courts were not merely punitive. A Russian shopkeeper, for instance, was taken to court by the Harbin Finance Committee for nonpayment of his lease to the former Harbin municipal government. The lease monies owed were 1,340 yuan, but the investigation revealed that the shopkeeper possessed insufficient assets to pay. Instead of putting him into bankruptcy, which would force him to lose his livelihood, the court proposed that the shopkeeper pay only 50 yuan per month (to a total of 750 yuan). Although the consuls claimed that the court was prejudiced against Russians, in this case it accepted a loss to preserve the livelihood of a Russian citizen.[149]

When it came to choosing between the Russian or Chinese legal codes, the district was flexible. The Chinese Foreign Ministry explained to the diplomatic corps in October 1920 that "the judicial authority of the Russian courts ceases [to exist] but Russian cases shall be guided by Russian law [except] in conflict with Chinese law. Possible persons expert in Russian law may be employed as advisors to the law courts. It will be evident to the representatives of the powers that the Chinese government is making every provision to safeguard the rights of Russians."[150] Because a new Chinese legal code was not introduced until 1929, judges applied foreign case law in trials that involved foreigners and for all cases that had no equivalent in Chinese law, in other words, pre-revolutionary Russian law and Chinese law were applied when needed.[151] Despite criticisms – one observer noted that many problems were beyond the Chinese judges' control – even "the most skeptical foreigners admitted" that the judges "sought faithfully to apply" the new codes and laws.[152]

From the beginning, Chinese authorities struggled to implement the new system. There were national implications to the creation of the Special District's hybrid legal system. Although the courts applied Chinese criminal law, capital crimes presented a particular problem because Russian law permitted executions, which were forbidden except under certain circumstances by the Chinese code. In early October 1921, the Heilongjiang daoyin, Sun Lieshan, asked both Beijing and the Special District's Legal Department how to prosecute a Russian accused of murdering a Chinese. Under the former system, he explained, capital crimes had been transferred to the Irkutsk High Court. The Special District's first reply confirmed that the Russian criminal was to be tried according to Chinese law. The second, dated more than a month later, after the Special District had consulted with the National Ministry of Justice, emphasized that the death penalty was not to be used against foreigners and requested that the central government revise the law on executions.[153]

The Special District took particular care to choose judges who could function in a dual legal system. The first Special District High Court Judge was Li Jiaao, also known as Li Lanzhou. Li, born in Jiangsu, had worked as a Binjiang daoyin, had been a Chinese consul to Vladivostok, and had served in the Jilin Railway Bureau before his court appointment. Married to a Russian and fluent in Russian, Li brought to the position much experience with Russians and the Russian administration. Referred to in both Chinese and Russian sources as a Chinese patriot and one of the district's best officials, Li was especially liked by members of the Russian community, who described him as "the best Chinese official in China" because he placed a high priority on Russian affairs.[154] Li was replaced by a Japanese-educated judge, Wang Jiabao, from the Jilin High Court. Wang's limited experience with the Russian community was the subject of much criticism, and he was replaced by Li Xiaogen after only two years because of his limited appeal. Li, born in 1897, was a native of Shenyang who had studied Russian in Harbin's schools. His career is indicative of the trajectory of the district's Chinese administration. After graduating from Harbin Russian Commercial School in 1920, he served on the Harbin Commission for Foreign Affairs and studied at Harbin's law school, where he received his LLB in 1925. In addition to his court duties, he was appointed a member of Harbin's Municipal Council and assistant to the mayor. He became director of the Harbin education department in 1926, a member of the CER board in 1927, and acting president of the board in 1930. He spoke both Russian and English and was popular among Harbin's Russian population.[155]

Consuls did not believe that the first translations of the law codes into Chinese and Russian were a success. In the opinion of the American consul, George Hanson, although the Russian code was the basis of the Special District's legal code, enough Chinese law had been added to render the code difficult to use. The quality of the judiciary also received much attention. Most of the judges who transferred from Chinese courts, Hanson wrote, were elderly and had insufficient training in modern legal affairs. Even graduates of Chinese and Japanese law schools lacked "the slightest conception of the theory, history or philosophy of law" and did not, according to Hanson, understand their own laws. The judges believed themselves to be infallible, Hanson wrote, and refused to listen to the "just and well-based observations of the Russian attorney"; they resorted to "ironical smiles, contemptuous silences or even provocations." Their salaries, which ranged from 250 to 600 rubles a year, were small and went unpaid for months on end. Judges, appointed by the national government in Beijing, were subject to dismissal by Zhang Zuolin and disappeared and reappeared without cause or explanation. Hanson criticized the regulation that prevented judges from conversing privately with lawyers and meeting with them socially. Although some Russian lawyers successfully gained access by "breaking into the offices of the judges and procurators," they were told to submit their requests in writing. Chinese lawyers were also forbidden access to the judges, "although there is no doubt that meetings between Chinese lawyers and judges often take place secretly." Lawyers, Hanson wrote, were treated by the judges as if they were "little better than ... servant[s]." In court the judges began with the assumption that the accused was guilty rather than innocent. Hanson also claimed that expert opinion was rarely called upon, but when the courts used medical testimony, he criticized them for showing a prejudice against Russian doctors.[156]

Hanson maintained that the pre-Revolutionary Harbin courts had been of a very high quality. (Although none of the consuls held very high opinions of the Chinese administration, Hanson stands out for the vehemence of his negative opinion.) His argument was based on notions about a hierarchy of civilizations and peoples: "The Russians feel the Chinese, recognizing on the one hand their own backwardness and the abyss that separates them from the cultured and educated Russians, and on the other hand desiring to emphasize their newly awakened nationalism, completely ignore the principles of Justice and Humanity which are accepted by the entire civilized world."[157] This criticism was common because Harbin's foreign consuls, an unofficial court of final appeal for many Russians, tended to report failures rather than successes. The consuls also consciously used the Special District judicial administration as an example of the fate of foreigners under Chinese legal control. Although the opinion of the consuls was likely exaggerated, it is true that the legal transition suffered from a lack of experienced personnel, corruption, insufficient funding, racial tension, and nationalism.

A commission of Russian lawyers, somewhat less critical and less prone to using charged language, asked for more communication with the new courts, either in person or in writing, and suggested that the two legal codes be more widely disseminated. According to the commission, the European tradition of direct communication between judge and lawyer, which was alien to the Chinese, was a legal necessity. They asked to speak directly to judges or counsellors. The lawyers also criticized the courts for being inaccessible, both geographically and linguistically. The courts, they argued, were too remote for the rural population, and Russians could not make themselves adequately understood. Russian lawyers criticized the principle of guilty until proven innocent and the detention of both the plaintiff and the accused. They requested the presence of several judges for serious cases because these men were "called upon to judge a people with the customs and manners of which they are entirely unfamiliar," and they asked for more trained interpreters and a more active role for the Russian court advisors. Overall, however, the lawyers were very pleased that the Special District used "an extended application of Russian law [which made] the role of Russian lawyers indispensable."[158]

The same mix of criticism and praise is found in the article "The Fourth Anniversary of the Chinese Court," in which a Russian author comments on four years of strained" relations with the Russian population. The greatest problem, he writes, is the tendency of the Chinese judges to bend the law. Older judges, however, those with a close connection to Russian lawyers, "have learned to respect the law and its unquestionable authority."[159] The author closes with a plea to the courts to lower expenses and rid themselves of excessive formalities. This tendency to bend the law was the result of having to mediate between two legal codes. Given the power to choose between two codes, judges, procurators, and advisors – attempting to find a middle way between two codes – sometimes sacrificed consistency to expediency or the particularities of a case.

The Special District courts were also criticized for putting too many bureaucratic obstacles in the way of the Russian population. For instance, by order of the National Justice Ministry, do-it-yourself Russian lawsuits were forbidden. These lawsuits had been permitted under the Russian system, but according to Judge Li Jiaao, they often required two or three translations. These translations delayed cases for several days because Russians had to have their translated legal documents stamped by Chinese officials several times.[160] Court officials were urged to consider these difficulties when they judged Russian lawsuits.[161]

In contrast to these fairly negative observations, G.I. Gerts, a Russian lawyer who worked in the Special District courts for a decade, was almost uniformly supportive of the legal experiment. His observations of the system were written after Gerts had emigrated to the United States and was under no pressure to produce a positive account. Because language problems dominated the courts' early years, Gerts reported, translators were the key to the courts' eventual success. The best quality Russian translators were graduates of the Vladivostok Institute of Foreign Languages who had Chinese citizenship. Other Russian translators were generally trained either at the Russian Orthodox mission school in Beijing or in Harbin's Russian schools. Gerts notes that although the quality of translators was at first inconsistent, it improved over time and as translators' knowledge of the law increased. Gerts contended that a persistent language problem did exist, not between Chinese and Russian employees but between Chinese who spoke different dialects.

Gerts also praised judges for "carrying themselves decently and correctly," for treating lawyers well, and for not judging Chinese and Russian cases differently. Gerts many times defended Russians "against rich and powerful Chinese ... and there was no favoritism at the expense of justice, which was evident in the Japanese courts." According to Gerts, ethnic Chinese had no advantage in the Special District courts because judges treated Chinese citizens of all origins and Russians without citizenship equally. Sartorially, Gerts judged the Special District courts as the best he had worked in – all judges, procurators, and lawyers dressed in dignified black robes.

When the dual system was first created, trials often began and finished late because of technical difficulties. These difficulties, however, were eventually overcome, and the courts functioned according to normal hours. According to Gerts, judges made full use of their Russian advisors and often employed committees of lawyers and consultants to assist their judgments. Important cases were translated, published, and circulated in both languages to set precedents and educate Special District lawyers and judges. Family, inheritance, and civil law, which were generally based on Russian precedents, required the greatest number of Russian advisors. Gerts demonstrated the Chinese judiciary's sensitivity by disclosing the details of a paternity case in which a wealthy Chinese had refused to recognize a son by a Russian mistress. During the interrogation, the judge angrily pointed out the resemblance between the man and the boy and exclaimed that it was a shame that a man would deny his son because "sons were the pride and happiness of every father." The man, in acknowledgment of his paternity, insisted that the Russian woman enter his house as a concubine. Although this was permitted under Chinese law, the judge, citing Russian precedent and the fact that this custom did not exist in the Russian community, refused to comply and ordered the man to pay monthly support payments to the Russian mother.

Gerts admitted that Russian lawyers were disadvantaged in criminal trials. Chinese lawyers often gave long speeches, while Russian lawyers were forced to speak in short phrases to allow for translation. Consequently, many Russian lawyers, much like Gerts, worked only in civil law. However, in Gerts's opinion the weakest part of the system was the enforcement of civil law decisions. Punishment was turned over to another court division, and this slow process enabled criminals to hide assets and flee the district. Those punished with a jail sentence were required to pay some incarceration costs and, if unable, could be released. The enforcement division was staffed by Russians, who, according to Gerts, were particularly corrupt. Several were fired during his tenure. On the whole, however, Gerts judged the twelve-year experiment in a dual legal system to be a success. The Special District courts were noted for their separation of legislative and executive power, something that was unknown in other Chinese courts at that time. Punishments were lenient, and judges had great discretionary power to pardon individuals who showed good behaviour.[162]

A survey of Special District cases revealed a mixed collection of decisions.[163] Those who could used extraterritorial privilege to avoid the courts. In two separate cases, Russian merchants who were naturalized US citizens used their US passports to claim immunity from the local courts and to refuse to pay municipal taxes. Attempts by the courts to prosecute the merchants came to nothing because the US government had never recognized the right of the administration, Russian or Chinese, to tax foreigners.[164] The courts also granted clemency because of age. In 1923, for instance, a sensational murder trial involved a Russian boy of thirteen. Sent to a restaurant to collect boiling water, the boy had been attacked by a Chinese cook with whom he had argued. The youth threw a pot of boiling water at the cook in self-defence, and the cook died from his injuries. During the trial, the procurator pointed out that the boy had acknowledged his crime and was contrite. The boy's lawyer argued that his client had acted in self-defence and pointed to the age difference between the two men. The judge sentenced the boy to eighteen months in prison but commuted the sentence to parental supervision.[165] The courts also granted extenuating circumstances when a CER engineer, arrested after dancing madly in a stolen fur coat in front of a mirror in the hall of the Railway Club, was said to have turned to drink after eighteen years of the quiet life. The engineer had witnessed his daughter's accidental death. He was judged not guilty because of insanity and released from the court to his family.[166]

The most sensational case tried under the dual system was the trial of the "thirty-eight." On 27 May 1929 thirty-eight Soviets were seized and charged with disseminating illegal propaganda and undermining the Special District's authority. The raid – Special District police claimed they had interrupted a secret meeting of the local Communist Party – resulted in the confiscation of several partially burned documents that confirmed that the USSR was assisting the Chinese Communist Party with ideological work in the district. Among the thirty-eight arrested were representatives of the Russian Communist Party Executive Committee, which controlled the CER Union of Workmen, the Youth Union, the Young Bolshevik's Union, and the Women's Section.[167]

The trial, which was held between 2 and 15 October 1929, was documented thoroughly by both sides. It offers a window into the Special District's legal and police reforms and exposes their strengths and weaknesses. Some in the foreign press used the trial to support their argument that because the Special District, and by extension the entire Chinese administration, was incompetent, extraterritoriality should continue to be applied. To the Special District's administration, which had recently been under Guomindang supervision, the trial was a means of demonstrating the Chinese judiciary's effectiveness, Soviet perfidy, and the Special District's defence of Chinese nationalism. The trial also highlighted divisions between Soviet citizens and émigrés within the Russian community. As gangs of reds and whites squared off on Harbin's streets and the Soviet army manoeuvred into position just across the Sino-Soviet border, diplomats, journalists, and ordinary citizens flooded into the High Court of the Special District to witness the Chinese-controlled court prosecuting its most important case since its creation nine years earlier. The Chinese administration was well aware that the trial, like other measures taken by the Special

District in its jurisdiction over a large non-Chinese population, would be used to judge the district's capacity to rule in a modern and humane fashion. Zhang Huanxiang, who had by 1929 been promoted from Special District police chief to head of the entire administration, was especially concerned that perceived legal irregularities would be used to judge the Special District's judicial and police systems a failure. The Special District head was also worried because, beyond the obvious political drama, the trial would be the most public demonstration of how the Special District policed and tried non-Chinese individuals within a Chinese-controlled legal system.

The police had received word from its network of spies that a meeting would take place at the Soviet consulate on 27 May.[168] After a day of surveillance, Russian and Chinese police raided the consulate at 7:00 p.m., when the Soviets, alerted to the raid, were burning documents. Most of those arrested were found in the basement, across from the room where the documents were being burned. The police claimed it was a secret room, while the Soviets claimed it was a dining hall. Two of the detainees, the vice-consul (who could not be arrested and tried) and a CER worker, were caught in the act of burning documents. In a fourth room, a stove was filled with ash and a few burned documents.[169] The thirty-eight were held in Harbin's best prison for five months before the trial, and six Russian defence lawyers, all Soviet citizens, were retained. At their head was T.G.N. Minsky, who was well regarded, according to one of the Chinese judges, for his "legal knowledge and ability."[170] There were two Chinese judges and several interpreters, and the foreign and Chinese press were given full access to the proceedings. The trial itself was notable for the high degree of professionalism on both sides. Even though the defence lawyers claimed that they had had only four days to prepare for the trial, they managed to mount an effective defence. The procurator tried to prove that each accused had attended a secret meeting in the consulate. The defence lawyers did their best to demonstrate that each defendant had been at the consulate on legitimate business. Not one of the thirty-eight prisoners deviated from his or her alibi; all said they were at the consulate either to obtain visas or to meet friends who were doing so.

It is impossible to judge whether the accused were truly guilty or innocent, and the police never revealed the source of their tip concerning the alleged meeting. Certainly, the presence in the consulate of a number of Soviet citizens, each from a different station along the line (several of which had consulates that could have processed their visa applications), all active members of their individual unions, and all found in rooms other than the one in which visa business was transacted pointed to suspicious activity. The procurator also commented on the use of several hot wood-burning stoves on a warm spring evening. Despite claims to the contrary, each of the accused maintained his or her alibi and was well prepared to testify. When the accused were all found guilty, with sentences ranging from two to seven years' imprisonment, they "received the sentence[s] good-humoredly and a few of them laughed and joked when the verdict was announced." Perhaps they already knew that the Chinese authorities intended to deport them, as a letter from the Special District head had made clear, and that they would not have to serve time. The defence launched an appeal to the Shenyang Supreme Court, which upheld the Special District's decision. The prisoners were released according to the protocol of 3 December 1929 that ended the Sino-Soviet crisis.[171]

The defence lawyers appealed to what they claimed were breaches of the Chinese legal code. They were successful on several points, notably the court's refusal to produce the original documents that had been seized – only photographs and Chinese translations were admitted. The judge claimed that the originals were not needed because photographs of the burned documents were available, as were English and Chinese translations of the contents.[172] Even the Chinese worried that they would not carry off the trial. In a letter from the Special District head, Zhang Huanxiang, to the procurator, which was written on 15 August, Zhang referred to a telegram from Zhang Xueliang (Zhang Zuolin's son who had succeeded as regional leader after his father's assassination). Zhang Xueliang was worried that rumours about the trial's fairness would not reflect well on China and recommended that the defendants be deported rather than risk the public humiliation of a botched trial. Zhang Huanxiang advised the procurator to confer "with the President of the Higher Court in order that no material be given for criticism by foreigners" and hoped the trial would speedily conclude.[173] Both letters were used by the defence as evidence that the Special District court's verdict had been influenced by advice on the case's political importance. That the defence had access to these documents demonstrates that the Special District placed few impediments in the way of the Soviet defence team. The court could certainly be criticized for failing to produce the original documents. The letter between the Special District head and the procurator makes it clear that there was a close connection between the administration of justice and political goals in Manchuria. However, the letter also makes it clear that the Special District wanted the trial to proceed under the fairest possible circumstances.

The Special District also allowed the trial to proceed despite pressures put on it by the Soviet Union. While the thirty-eight were imprisoned, the USSR sent forces across the border twice. The most serious offence occurred at Man'chzhuriia Station on 2 October, the first day of the trial. Soviet planes bombed a number of Chinese and Russian émigré villages south of the Sino-Soviet frontier; several acts of sabotage occurred along the CER; and several prominent émigrés, including an important detective with the Chinese police force, were assassinated, presumably by Soviet agents. (Whether this was the same detective present at the raid is unknown.) Through the trial and the wide publication of the circumstances surrounding it, both sides fully explained their versions of events.[174] Although the trial was highly politicized and took place in the atmosphere of an impending Soviet invasion, the judges, procurator, and lawyers behaved with a high degree of professionalism and decorum. Each side kept to its own interpretation of events, and the Chinese court, beyond attempting to prove that the accused were engaging in illegal political activities designed to subvert the Special District and the Chinese state, did not use the event to advance other agendas.

The reform of the Special District's jails likewise demonstrated that Chinese administrators intended to establish Chinese rule over the CER concession by improving on the Russian institutions that had been left to them. Improvements were also made to please different audiences. Dominating the discourse on district penal reform was a concern for modernity and prisoner rehabilitation through reform of what were perceived to be brutal, pre-modern Russian jails. Penal reform was a means of demonstrating that the district could be both modern and administered by the Chinese. The Special District was following a national trend in prison reform, and the district conformed to its pedagogical and reformist principles.[175]

On 3 September 1920, the five Russian prisons were placed under the jurisdiction of the Special District's Legal Department. The department considered the prisons substandard because of their poor living conditions and because their administrators used torture and other extra-legal procedures.[176] Under the CER, prisons were subsidized with 130,000 gold rubles. During the transition, Chinese authorities asked the CER to continue its subsidy because these jails were "entirely filled with Russians."[177] Like the establishment of the Special District itself, creating a more humane prison system went beyond simply establishing Chinese control. The Special District authorities were conscious that the provision of well-administered Chinese prisons would prove that the Chinese were capable not only of ruling themselves but also of ruling others in a fair and humane fashion. The 200,000 yuan that the Special District set aside for the Russian prison system testified to the importance it accorded to penal reform, especially when all eleven Special District courts only received 100,000. The sum for prisons was increased to 484,000 yuan in 1922. Plans for penal reform were extensive, but the principal change was the renovation of Harbin's main prison to meet the standard of the model prison in Beijing. The Special District administration wanted to build a new prison for Harbin, but this was judged impossible in the short term. Instead, torture was banned, and regular procedures were established for the interrogation of suspects and the prosecution of criminal offences. A single translator who had worked in all five prisons was replaced by a translator for each prison. Even after four hundred criminals were deported to Russia, the district's prisons still held large numbers of convicted and non-convicted inmates. The Chinese official responsible for prisons urged the Special District to keep all staff of the former Russian prisons. The Russian staff was retained, and additional Chinese staff was hired. By 1926 the Special District Model Prison had two Chinese directors and nine Russian department heads.[178]

Harbin's detention centre in the suburb of Halaer, which housed 271 male prisoners and 29 female prisoners, was an immediate priority. Working conditions were poor – twenty guards lived in one big room, and only two other small rooms were set aside for employees. Twenty-five prisoners had to be removed to house prison employees, and the waiting room had to be converted into cells because of the growing prison population. The women's prison, an ordinary house connected to the male prison, was deemed unsuitable, and a new women's prison was constructed in the exercise yard. The prison in Halaer had originally had no workrooms or classrooms. Keeping with the reformist impulses of the Special District's administration, the second floor of the women's prison was converted into a combined classroom and chapel, and the original chapel became cells for another hundred prisoners. Since Halaer's prison did not have a priest and branch prisons had no chapels, every prison in the Special District hired priests to minister to the Russian prisoners. The Special District's administration reduced corporal punishment, banned torture, added job-training programs, offered religious instruction, and imposed lighter sentences. After a series of hunger strikes in March 1921, a Russian menu was added for those prisoners who would not eat Chinese food. Sentences were reduced for good behaviour, and in cases of minor crimes, the sentences were commuted after two years.[179]

Although there were persistent rumours in the press and consular reports that Russians were being tortured in the prisons, the American consul noted that the cases were not frequent. Other than some documented beatings during preliminary police investigations (for which the police were reprimanded) and reports of individuals held against their will, there were no documented cases of prisoners or suspects being tortured. In 1920 it was reported that two Russian subjects had been beaten with bamboo and that one Russian had appeared in court with his arms trussed behind his back. Chinese prisoners' arms were customarily bound with rope. In more serious cases, prisoners were bound with iron shackles around their legs. Russian prisoners objected to this treatment and were allowed to remain unshackled. The policy resulted in a few escapes (in 1924, for instance, twelve Russian prisoners overpowered their guard and escaped).[180]

For members of the consular corps, the very fact that a European could be incarcerated in a Chinese-controlled jail – however well managed – was grounds for an accusation of torture. "It must be stated that the procedure and the treatment accorded to those arrested persons amounts to practical torture, mental if not physical, to the average European and American."[181] This was an obvious double standard: the Chinese could tolerate torture, but European and American sensibilities were more delicate.

In contrast to the dominant negative foreign assessment of the district's penal reform, one consul complimented Harbin's prisons by noting that any American prisoners detained in them had had no complaints. Harbin prisons' high standards, he wrote, were due to the efforts of the former Russian warden.

He gave no credit to the Chinese authorities for having retained the Russian staff.[182] Special District jail conditions compared favourably to purely Chinese prisons, in which prisoners were expected to provide for their daily sustenance. That the prisoners themselves considered the Special District jails their best option became evident during the district's only other recorded prison riot, when Russian prisoners who were being held for repatriation to the Soviet Union rioted to protest the transfer.[183] The success of the Special District's penal system is also evident in the fact that not a single protest was lodged by the USSR on behalf of Harbin's Russian community until 1926, six years after the reform. In this period the Soviet consul made regular complaints to the Chinese administration on behalf of Russians holding Soviet passports and those registered as stateless.

Another case that demonstrates the Special District's commitment to humane conditions for imprisoned Russians was the confinement of some fifteen hundred Soviet prisoners during the 1929 CER crisis. The thirty-eight Soviet citizens captured during the raid on the consulate on 27 May were jailed in Harbin and well cared for, even though they complained of not being allowed to see their wives. Beginning on 1 August, following a number of incidents of sabotage by Soviet CER employees and Soviet troop movements on the border, the Special District began to detain hundreds of Soviet citizens and their families. The authorities had to quickly house and feed the detainees.[184] The first group of 240 men, women, and children was imprisoned in Old Harbin, a suburb, in a building formerly used as a railway club. Authorities were severely criticized for the poor treatment of this group, who were allegedly confined to a few rooms during a heat wave with only tea, bread, and tomatoes for sustenance. Because of these complaints, the Special District police transferred the detainees across the Songhua River to an abandoned district known as Sungbei. Sungbei, the site of a planned railway and urban expansion that did not come to pass, had brick buildings in fairly good condition that were quickly renovated. The site became a detention camp that housed 1,168 prisoners, 200 Chinese railway police guards, 600 carpenters, and a few prison officials and farmers.

Motivated by reported stories of cruelty and rumours about extra-judicial executions, the Special District granted journalists a day-long interview with detainees to show that Soviet prisoners were not being abused.[185] J.B. Powell, writing for a Shanghai paper, reported that the tales of cruelty and execution were false and had been circulated by Harbin's consuls. Prisoners did complain extensively about a poor and monotonous diet that consisted of tea, sugar, tomatoes, cucumbers, and two pounds of bread per prisoner per day. Chinese officials explained that improvements would occur once the kitchen was constructed. Spouses not detained were allowed to visit, and detainees were allowed to receive food packages. Powell noted that only two cases of serious illness had been reported and that a temporary hospital and dispensary with two doctors had been built on the site. Altercations and beatings by the Chinese guards were rare except in cases where prisoners refused to be confined after their exercise periods. The prisoners themselves confirmed that guards did have to use force to break up several fights among the prisoners. Although conditions were not perfect, the Soviet detainees were not subject to inhumane conditions. Indeed, when compared to the treatment of thousands of Chinese citizens living in the Russian Far East – citizens who experienced or witnessed forced expulsion, the confiscation of property, and murder – the treatment of these Soviet detainees appears even more laudable.[186]

Although the consuls initially supported the transfer of the security institutions – police, courts, and jails – from Russian to Chinese control, they soon expressed their displeasure at having Chinese in positions of authority. The American consul referred to Zhang Huanxing, Harbin's first police chief, as an autocrat who "delights in the thought and exercise of authority over the white man," although no proof to support this accusation was offered in the consul's report.[187] Police superintendents were criticized for not speaking Russian, for being ignorant of Russian ways and customs, and for having "a most elementary knowledge of their duties."[188] Harbin's low crime rate in contrast to that of American cities of the same size was not credited to the police, who, the American consul wrote, "usually go missing," but rather to the "depressed nature of the political situation." Evidently, criminals were too saddened by politics to commit crimes.[189]

To foreigners, Russian and non-Russian alike, the creation of the Special District police and judicial system had reversed the natural order in which Caucasians dominated Chinese. As Chinese nationalists in the south demanded the abolition of extraterritoriality throughout the 1920s, the foreign press singled out the Special District's police, judiciary, and jails as examples of life under the Chinese should extraterritoriality be abolished. It appeared that control institutions in the Special District existed solely to show whites what would happen under Chinese rule. Yet, despite her predilection for racial stereotypes, even Olive Gilbreath admitted that Harbin was well run and safe: "The traveler need no longer give Harbin a wide berth ... Is it possible this experiment here in the north suggests that, if once he could be extracted from the melee of rival warlords, the Chinese might not prove incapable of governing?" However, Gilbreath's praise is conditional. "Yes, cleanliness, law and order, and a good police force prevail – the cleanness, order and police of the East."[190] Nevertheless, Gilbreath provides no proof of the Russian population's mistreatment, and, like other critics, her evidence relied on hearsay. Even the accounts of police brutality in other sources were presented as possibilities: the Chinese police could beat their Russian charges – if they so wished.

China's foreign-owned press printed the most biased accounts of the experiment taking place in the Special District. In "Extraterritoriality in Harbin," an article published in the *Manchurian Daily News* (a Japanese-sponsored paper from Dalian) on the visit of the Commission on Extraterritoriality to Harbin, the author points out that the delegates were prevented from leaving Beijing because of the chaos in China. The author also makes a brief sneering reference to China's most public foe of extraterritoriality, C.T. Wang: "Hiding in the foreign concession in Tianjin, whence, secure in the knowledge that his hide is safe, under the protection of the foreign administration, he continues to advocate against foreign privilege." Harbin, the laboratory for foreigners under Chinese rule, is, according to the author, "the only place in China where a large foreign community without extraterritorial rights is being held to the vagaries and eccentricities of Chinese law."

The author singles outs the Special District police for particular criticism. The article declares without supporting evidence that Russians were picked up and charged for non-existent crimes, kidnapped with the co-operation of the police, and subjected to a number of petty rules and regulations. The author refers to Harbin's foreign consuls being "bombarded with petitions, appeals and requests from Russians" but admits "it is difficult to draw the line where truth begins and imagination ends, for while many of these grievances are without foundation, there are, on the other hand, a large number of legitimate kicks against the arbitrariness and inconsistencies of the Chinese authorities."[191]

Improvements made by the Special District to Russian courts and jails were likened to an elaborate Potemkin village: "The newly white washed jails and carefully arranged courts, stage settings elaborately contrived for their [the commission's] edification by the Chinese in the naïve hope that the strangers might be beguiled." The duplicity of Chinese officials and the intelligence of foreigners, who saw through these stage settings, was emphasized: "The commissioners studied them [the courts] gravely, concealing courteously such chagrin as they may have felt at the rather low estimate of their intelligence evidenced by the belief that they might be taken in thus easily." "But," one of the delegates remarked, "we are not such fools as that, and since then, the chief of the American delegates, Mr. Strawn, has told the Chinese frankly that the ponderous and imposing codes which the Chinese jurists had worked out painstakingly for the occasion were all very well as literature, but that he failed to see that they had any bearing on the situation as long as the laws contained therein were not enforced."[192] The passage was based on the commission's findings in Beijing – nothing in the article pertained to Harbin or the Special District. Subsequent articles repeated the same allegations, but added a plea for the continued protection of Japanese property in Manchuria.

Certain altercations between foreigners and Chinese were reported by the press because they exposed the fate of foreigners under Chinese rule. For example, the American vice-consul and his party, during a trip to Fujiadian, caused a rickshaw with its Chinese passenger to tip over. The rickshaw was slightly damaged. The American party, observing that no one was hurt, continued on its way. The party was stopped by the police and told to report to a police station. At the station, the rickshaw driver, who said he represented the people, demanded justice. The vice-consul responded that he was protected by treaty as a diplomat and an American, and he advised the rickshaw driver to lodge a formal complaint with the consulate. The rickshaw driver demanded compensation, and the vice-consul refused because compensation would violate extraterritoriality and American rights. In the end, a member of the party paid the driver three dollars.

This incident provoked outrage among members of the press over the abuse of treaty rights, the precarious nature of Chinese justice, and the issue of what would happen to foreigners under Chinese control. The response was far in excess of the incident's importance and the *China Weekly Review* commented sarcastically that the outrage to treaty rights was "just the sort of Chinese miscarriage of justice which Englishmen on the China coast delight in writing letters [about] to the *North China Daily News*," a dig at the newspaper known for editorials expressing foreign outrage.[193] Abuses of extraterritorial rights were found in the most banal incidents. In 1922, when a dog belonging to an American bit a Chinese newspaper seller, the newspaper seller kicked the dog, and the American beat the man, identified as Li Yu, at length. A crowd of fellow newspaper vendors surrounded the American, the police intervened, and the American was taken to the police station, where he paid one yuan to repair Li's pants.[194] This street fight was interpreted as an egregious blow to extraterritoriality.

Even though the police censored the press, charges of police brutality against the Russian population were reported in Harbin's Russian newspapers. These stories tend to follow the same narrative as other foreign accounts – a Russian or a group of Russians is attacked by hostile Chinese, the police are called, the police support the Chinese, and Russians are dispatched to the police station. In October 1923, for instance, a man identified as Wang, a Chinese merchant, harassed two Russian schoolgirls. When two adult Russians came to the children's aid, Wang and a crowd of Chinese beat the two Russians. The police, when summoned, beat the Russians and took the entire group, including Wang, to the police station. One Russian allegedly died after having been beaten with bamboo. The Russian press followed the story for several weeks, reporting on the "maddened Chinese rabble" and the "brutal outrage."[195] The Soviet consul made a compliant to Zhu Qinglan, Special District head, who promised to investigate the matter and punish the guilty.

Many Russians felt that they had been singled out by the Chinese police. In a letter passed by CER General Manager Ostroumoff to the American consul, a Russian complained that "the Russian revolution has put us under the authority of Chinese administrators; we are in their hands, with every year life becomes more difficult, every Chinese soldier, policeman has become the master and does whatever he likes without punishment. Violence surpasses all limits. Chinese soldiers, policemen at Utzimihe constantly seize my carts, spoil wood, the authorities do not give any assistance. On March 7th soldiers of the 8th regiment brought one hundred carts and took the remaining wood. I am compelled to address myself to consuls for protection, we Russians are doomed to perish in case the consular corps refuses."[196]

The Chinese authorities claimed in response that the Russians were treated the same as the Chinese. In 1923, for instance, during an outbreak of door handle thefts in Newtown, Harbin's best neighbourhood, a Chinese watchman caught a Chinese newspaper boy stealing his employer's door handles. The police were called, and the thief was taken in. But it was reported that the policeman had berated the watchman for protecting foreign property and for failing to act like a proper Chinese when he caused another Chinese to be apprehended.[197] In another instance, the *Russian Daily News* reported that an elderly Russian man of about seventy years had been dragged in front of the American Bar in Harbin – that is, in full view of the foreign community – and struck by a Chinese policeman. According to the anti-Chinese *Russian Daily News*, the Russian man, wearing "hardly any clothes," was also placed in a cart and kicked.[198]

Despite the claim by some Russians and most other foreigners that Russians were subject to the casual violence of their new Chinese patrons, little evidence exists to back these claims. Not so in the case of the beating of Professor Voiekov, one of the most extensively documented incidents of police violence against a Russian. Voiekov was the director of the Station Echo Experimental Farm and manager of the station's summer resort. According to the *Harbin Daily News*, on 8 July 1923 – during a period when attacks on CER experimental farms were at their height (see Chapter 6) – Voiekov and the police inspector arrived at Station Echo on the same train. Voiekov claimed that he saw the police inspector striking several children with his whip. When the children's mother intervened, the inspector "in a state of intoxication and generally known for his drunkenness," attempted to drag her to the police station.[199] Voiekov intervened "in a most discreet fashion" by showing his card and asking for the inspector's name.

> In reply to this the barbarian seized him [Voiekov] by the collar, struck him, and falling to the ground, sank his teeth in Mr. Voiekov's head. As soon as he went down, several bandits in the uniform of the 6th regiment jumped at him and began mercilessly to belabor him with whips, fists and feet, the officer biting him several times in the shoulder and arm. Mr. Voiekoff [sic] attempted to get up several times, but was repeatedly knocked down and beaten. The officer finally went mad and beat him on the head, and in a sudden frenzy began biting him in the neck and head, yelling derisively at him at the same time.[200]

The Harbin consuls and the Chinese authorities were contacted immediately, and four separate investigations – by the Harbin chief of police; by the Special District head, Zhu Qinglan; by the CER; and by representatives of

Russian members of the police force – were undertaken. Not surprisingly, Chinese and Russian witnesses gave contradictory testimony. It was determined that the police inspector had not been drunk and had only threatened the children with a whip. Voiekov testified that the inspector had beaten him with an iron bar, but other witnesses contradicted his testimony. A physical examination showed no evidence of injuries by either teeth or an iron bar. The police inspector's injuries showed that he had struck first with his whip and that Voiekov had returned the blows. Voiekov himself later testified that the inspector had not beaten the children. Despite evidence to the contrary, *The Harbin Daily News* characterized the Chinese policeman as a brute. In the end, both he and Voiekov were found guilty.[201]

Although the Special District reprimanded Li, the Russian press remained divided. Most reporters represented the incident as an example of Chinese police brutality, but one author argued that the émigré policy of turning to the consuls was self-defeating and urged them to put their trust in the Special District authorities who, like the Russians, wanted law and order.

> Somehow we cannot grasp facts, somehow we cannot make ourselves understand that the maintenance of order in Manchuria belongs and will belong to the Chinese authorities ... This means that the inhabitants of Echo must appeal to the Chinese authorities, who are, themselves, interested in the annihilation of disorder. There is no doubt that the authorities will look into the latter and punish those who are guilty ... China is endeavoring to gain an unquestioned place among cultured nations ... The Eastern provinces pride themselves with the belief that there exists greater order and justice here than elsewhere in China.[202]

These stories and cases reveal that racial tension existed on the streets of Harbin and the Special District and that when both Chinese and Russians felt aggrieved, they did not hesitate to express their anger or go to the police and authorities. These cases were often exaggerated in Harbin's Russian press, but it is remarkable that there were so few serious cases. That a large multiracial city would have relatively few documented cases of racial discord is a testimony to the skills of the Special District police force.

Harbin and the Special District had their fair share of crime, but there is little to no evidence that crimes were perpetuated by the Chinese police on the Russian population. Instead, the police did all in their power to fight and prevent crime. Most crimes that involved Russians occurred within the Russian community and were motivated by poverty. The *Jilin sheng baogao* (Jilin provincial reports) archive numerous cases in which jewellery and other small valuables easily transported from Russia were stolen. In one case, a Russian woman was robbed of her jewellery, rings and a gold bracelet, which were later recovered by Russian and Chinese police. In another, reported by a Russian policeman, a gang of six uniformed soldiers robbed different stations in the Special District. At one station, the thieves robbed two families of nineteen dollars, two watches, two gold bracelets, one gold bar, one pair of shoes, one fox fur, one alarm clock, and three pairs of earrings.[203] Robberies could be quite violent. For instance, a priest's wife was struck several times on the head with a barbell and then robbed. She died from her injuries.[204] In one case, three Russian assailants robbed a Russian man of thirteen dollars; in another, a Russian man was mugged for his boots. Although most crime was committed between or among Russians, mixed Russian-Chinese gangs did exist. In one reported case, a gang of Chinese armed with handguns, led by a Russian, kidnapped a Russian restaurant manager.[205] In another case that took place in April 1926, twenty-six Russian businessmen, who had been kidnapped by a group of Chinese and Russian bandits, were released after the police captured the bandits, their weapons, and 4,000 yuan.[206]

A case that involved the robbery of two Chinese clerks by armed Russian bandits showcased the talents of the mixed police force. When the police tracked the thieves to their hideout, the thieves escaped through the back exit. The Russian police called the station for a "squad of policemen and plain-clothes officers" and proceeded with a house-to-house search. When the thieves opened fire, one detective was injured and was rushed to hospital amid "an incessant exchange of firing." When a women rushed out of her house and said her son had been shot, the police stopped firing and, on the orders of their chief, laid siege to the home. At daybreak, when the police entered the home, they found the body of the boy, the bodies of two thieves who had committed suicide, and the ashes of the stolen bank notes.[207]

In general, the Chinese press did not demonize crime within the Russian community but instead cited a declining living standard as the reason some Russians turned to crime. They portrayed Russians as good people who were used to living well but who had been forced by circumstances to the margins of society:

> The Russians of Harbin, several years ago, had a very high standard of
> living. There is no comparison [to today], because they were once very rich.
> Because of the civil war only a few businessmen have remained; otherwise
> the Russians are homeless and have turned to crime and they are forced
> into robbery and murder, for instance, the recent example of three Russian
> bandits who robbed and looted. Recent forgeries are also the result of
> Russian crime. These were formerly good people who now live difficult
> lives, whose status is not equal [to what it was]. Their level of life must be
> improved or society will be damaged.[208]

Despite Harbin's size and the presence of a large refugee community, its crime rate was rather low, and Russian criminals were the minority. In 1925 there were 1,657 reported crimes; of the 3,098 suspects who were arrested, only 1,064 were foreigners. Similarly, in 1927 only 562 foreigners were involved in a total of 1,194 crimes and 2,460 arrests. By 1929, the number of foreigners involved in a total of 525 crimes and 1,047 arrests had fallen to 13.[209] Several conclusions can be drawn from these figures. The Special District's Russian population was, largely, gainfully employed and did not need to resort to crime, and Harbin was not the lawless city some made it out to be in the early 1920s. Instead, a picture emerges of a well-policed and rather safe city and this image is supported by most accounts in journal articles.

The Special District's control institutions were not perfect. Chinese administrators did not work from a set plan but instead improvised at opportune moments to establish Chinese sovereignty by using the tools and models of a former colonial power. Providing crime prevention, justice, and incarceration facilities to two different communities and adapting Chinese and Russian legal codes to suit them was a tremendous task. From the beginning, Chinese administrators had the best interests of the district's Russian and Chinese inhabitant's in mind. Russian law and much of the Russian court staff were retained, and there was a considerable increase in the number of Chinese judges, prosecutors, and clerical staff members between 1921 and 1929. By 1929, a complete Chinese civil and criminal code had been introduced and distributed in both Russian and Chinese. Even after the introduction of the code, Russian law continued to be applied in particular cases.[210] Despite the negative assessments of foreign consuls and some émigrés, the district's administration of justice and law enforcement functioned well and received a great deal of praise. It was a hybrid system that represented the pragmatic values of the Special District's administrators.

Accounts of legal reform in the Special District have been unduly prejudiced by foreign observers who saw in China's assumption of control over a foreign population only the possibility of abuse and terror. The Special District did not abuse its Russian and Chinese populations; instead, the administration transformed security institutions, improved and expanded the courts, reformed prisons, transformed the police into a mixed Chinese and Russian force, opened police schools, employed the most modern technology available, and did its best to ensure that the district was safe and secure. The district's administrators went out of their way to ensure that Russians were represented in security institutions and to protect "their" Russians from dismissal by Soviet co-administrators. The result was a region that, considering the variety of peoples it housed and the economic and political pressures placed on them, was secure and well policed.

5

Experiments in Co-Administering the Chinese Eastern Railway

In 1920, when the Chinese government and the Chinese Eastern Railway board renegotiated the terms of the company's management, the railway was at its lowest point. The line had never turned a profit, but this fact had been obscured by Russian subsidies. These subsidies had decreased after 1905 and disappeared altogether after 1917. During the First World War, much of the railway's rolling stock was transferred permanently to Russia. Regional trade ground to a halt, and goods were transported for little or no payment to Russia to support the war effort. All capital expenditures ceased, and necessary repairs went undone. Between 1917 and 1920, the concession was also racked with political instability. The CER was powerless to stop the troubles because much of the activity originated with its own employees.

Yet the Chinese still wanted the railway. It represented millions of Russian rubles in investment, unpaid fees to the Chinese government, and the fruit of Chinese labour. The CER was one of the most modern and well-equipped railways in China. It connected Manchuria with the Russian Far East, which had a hungry population and unlimited opportunities for business, and it traversed northern Manchuria, a territory whose resources were the most abundant in China. The CER was the key to unlocking regional development. It connected to the rich South Manchurian Railway, and the partnership promised to restore the traditional north-south pattern of the Manchurian economy. Finally, the CER was the centre of political, administrative, and economic life in the former concession; it was the source of all conflicted and contested agreements. Because of the CER's importance to the Special District, the newly appointed Chinese administrators first turned to the CER and its many departments to create a Chinese Special District.

The power vacuum that resulted from the Russian revolutions gave Chinese governments (the national and Manchurian warlord governments, represented by Beijing and Shenyang, respectively) the opportunity to reclaim political and economic power in the CER concession. To do so, they employed a two-pronged strategy. First, they would detach administrative functions from the CER and place them under a Chinese-controlled administration – the Special District of the Three Eastern Provinces. This would have the benefit of preserving the boundaries and Russian management of the previous concession, but both would be placed under Chinese supervision. Second, the Chinese national and regional governments would attempt to impose a true joint management on the newly reorganized CER by replacing its czarist manager with a man committed to making the company a viable and rational business and by appointing a number of Chinese vice-presidents to its various departments. The CER was to reinvent itself by stressing its role in developing the region for international investment.

Between 1920 and 1924, under this new managerial order, the Special District's Chinese and Russian elites lived in an uneasy peace. Nevertheless, the CER – under nominal Chinese control and with a new Russian general manager, Boris Ostroumoff – retained its Russian personnel, and Ostroumoff successfully resisted Chinese attempts to completely transform the company. Instead, the CER once again resumed its role as the guardian and patron of the Russian population and their modernizing development project within the Special District. Frustrated with what they perceived to be continued Russian colonial arrogance and resistance to the expansion of Chinese control over the CER and the Special District, the Chinese turned to the USSR. The Chinese used an accord with the Soviet Union to uproot the CER's old regime, but they did not realize that the Soviets had their own agenda, one motivated in equal parts by new ideological goals and old colonial projects. The Sino-Soviet agreement of 1924, meant to enhance Chinese control, in fact created a new set of problems as the Soviets set about reconstituting Russian power in the Special District. Despite the problems associated with their Soviet partners, the Chinese did use the Special District's creation to advance a more inclusive administrative vision, one based on the early Russian administrative model.

The first goal of the Chinese was the removal of the CER's head, who had continued to meddle in regional politics and who wanted to use the CER concession as a base to attack the newly founded USSR. General Manager Dmitrii Horvath was forced to step down as the head of the CER in the fall of 1920, and a joint committee of Chinese, Russian, and foreign interests, including the Inter-Allied Railway Commission, was established to supervise the CER's deteriorating physical plant. The Inter-Allied Railway Commission was established in 1919 to take over and supervise the railways of the Russian Far East, and the CER, as part of the Trans-Siberian Railway, fell under the commission's mandate. The commission's main function was to ensure the railway's continued operation, especially for the evacuation of foreign troops in Siberia, but it also served as a means of foreign intervention in the Russian Far East. Although it was potentially a rival with the Chinese for control of the CER, the commission had no authority to discipline CER staff, and its orders were executed through CER employees.[1] Although the Inter-Allied Railway Commission functioned as a body of appeal for Russians displeased with growing Chinese influence on the CER, it did not interfere in the day-to-day functioning of the railway.

As for the CER's administrative functions, both the Chinese and the commission agreed that the CER's political and administrative functions should be turned over to the Chinese. The commission recommended that the Chinese take over the police, the courts, municipal governments, and territorial administrations, recommendations that were carried out over the next few years. It also recommended that the CER give up all property that was not needed for the line's operation. Finally, the commission recommended that the CER "give up all exterior evidence of being Russian. Its regulations, accounts, notices, timetables should be published not only in Russian but in Chinese and in some European language other than Russian ... in a word, it should stop giving the public the impression that Northern Manchuria is a Russian Province."[2]

Early in 1920, after establishing control over Harbin's Russian police and troops and forcing Horvath out of the CER administration, the Chinese central government asked the Russo-Asiatic Bank to revise the CER contract to increase China's responsibility for the railroad. China argued that it was a full partner according to the original contract and that by virtue of the five million unpaid taels owed to the Chinese government, as per the original agreement, it was also a shareholder in the Russo-Asiatic Bank. The Chinese government argued that Russia was no longer in a position to guard the line and that China had already assumed responsibility for the maintenance of peace and order in the concession. The Russo-Asiatic Bank had few options: it had to negotiate with the Chinese government to maintain its claim to the CER or risk having China negotiate with the newly formed Soviet Union. On 2 October 1920, China and the Russo-Asiatic Bank signed an agreement by which the Chinese took over temporary supervision of the CER. Half of the ten-member board of directors would be Chinese (a quorum of seven was needed to transact all business). The position of CER president was restored to the Chinese, while the general manager continued to be a Russian national. Article 6 of the agreement addressed the main Chinese concern that the CER, in its former incarnation, had been used as a tool of Russian colonialism in North Manchuria: "The rights and obligations of the Company will herefoth be in every respect of a commercial character: every political activity and every political attribute will be absolutely forbidden to it. To this end, the Chinese Government reserves the right to prescribe restrictive measures of any character and at any time.[3] Article 6, for the next decade, remained the basis by which the Chinese challenged Russian control over some of the district's institutions. Through article 6, the CER was officially stripped of any political role.

This new era of Chinese co-administration over the CER also fulfilled international plans for the railroad. The Washington Naval Conference (1921-22) passed a resolution, approved by all participants but China, that it was "the responsibility of China for performance or non-performance of the obligations toward the foreign stockholders, bondholders and creditors of the Chinese Eastern Railway Company."[4] In other words, China was responsible for the railway but had no promise of ultimate control over it. One concession to the Chinese was the Inter-Allied Technical Board's appointment of fifty Chinese engineers to supervise the CER.

Ostroumoff was appointed as general manager of the CER because it was believed that he could help the company fulfill its new role as a rational, viable financial institution. Ostroumoff was a bureaucrat from the Russian Far East who had worked to create a strong Russian presence in that region through development, investment, and settlement. Ostroumoff brought these skills to his new position, and his past experiences conditioned his style of administration. Under Ostroumoff, the CER became a vehicle for the economic, cultural, and political preservation of the Russian settler community in northern Manchuria. The railway's investment was expanded into health resorts, factories, and experimental agricultural stations. The company's schools, housing stock, libraries, and research societies were refinanced and entered a period of great productivity. Largely successful, these changes were presented by the CER as a benefit to the general welfare of the Special District. However, these successes also laid Ostroumoff open to the charge that he was trying to recolonize the Special District in the name of progress and modernity and for the Russian community's benefit. The Russians – who were long used to operating in a context of complete Russian control and who tended to conflate the CER's and the Special District's interests with those of their own community – responded that these changes economically benefitted all inhabitants of the Special District.

When Ostroumoff assumed leadership of the CER, the company was a mess. The line had lost forty-five million dollars by 1905 (at 1905 rates), and it continued to operate at a deficit until the end of the First World War.[5] The CER's new role, as mandated by article 6, was designed to repudiate the company's original purpose (although this plan was not entirely successful). When Russia built the CER, the railway and its concession functioned in a classic colonial economic relationship with Russia: it was to produce cheap raw materials and consume finished Russian products. With this goal in mind, in 1908 the CER set inexpensive rates for traffic moving eastward from Harbin to Vladivostok and prohibitive rates for goods moving south to Changchun and the Japanese-owned South Manchurian Railway. Although Dalian, the terminal port for the South Manchurian Railway, was a logical destination for Manchuria's goods, CER rates made this option too expensive.[6] In addition, because the Imperial Russian government was primarily interested in the CER as a means of expanding a Russian political and military presence in northern Manchuria, it was willing to subsidize the CER concession and the Russian settler communities and allowed the concession to meet most of its economic needs within the surrounding region. Because of this rather passive attitude toward international trade with China through the CER concession, the Russian government put little effort into encouraging Russian trade in the northeast and was content to let the concession's needs be satisfied by the local Chinese economy. The 1908 tariff led the CER to consistently lose money, but its losses were made up through annual Russian government subsidies that averaged 4.7 million dollars between 1908 and 1914. Up to 1920, given the importance of Russia to the CER concession, Russian imports and exports into the CER concession were quite low. (This testifies to the strength of local trade and manufacturing, which satisfied most local needs.)

In 1914 these subsidies were cut,[7] and from 1917 to 1920 the CER's portion of local trade declined further. Railway cars went to Russia and did not return, resulting in a severe shortage of rolling stock for the CER. The remaining rolling stock was in very bad repair, and the CER's buildings had not been maintained since the outbreak of the war. In addition, the continued use of the defunct Romanoff ruble in the railway zone had set off a currency crisis. Because of Russian mercantilist policies, which required Russian trade to pass over Russian railways, 80 percent of the northeast's exports before 1914 had been shipped through Vladivostok. There was a brief respite in 1920, when the Inter-Allied Board intervened, a friendly government was established in Vladivostok, and through trade was restored. Once Vladivostok became the capital of the Republic of the Far East, with a Soviet puppet government in place, trade with the CER was restricted. Export trade shrank to 116 thousand tons.[8] In 1922 the USSR began the process of absorbing the republic, a process that was completed when the republic joined the USSR in 1924. For this reason, the CER made a southern route the principal focus of its economic policy.[9]

Under Ostroumoff, the CER focused on business and profit, albeit in a context of continued Russian supervision and with a view to benefitting the Russian community. The CER's Economic Department was reorganized and charged with studying the local economy and how the railway could better serve and enhance it. With both a Russian and Chinese staff, the department embarked on an investigation of economic conditions in the Special District and well outside its boundaries. The Economic Department established its agents within the local Chambers of Commerce, the region's commercial and agricultural societies, and private firms. The Economic Department collected extensive data on local economic conditions and published it in 1921 in the form of pamphlets and journals. Publication was initially in Russian only, but English, Chinese, and Japanese translations soon followed.[10]

In terms of overall economic improvement, the Chinese and Russians made a success of CER co-management by 1921. The Chinese president and the Chinese Bank of Communication were said to be "in complete harmony with their Russian colleagues," freight and passengers were being efficiently transported, and the joint administration was doing its best to build up the line.[11] According to the CER's new motto, the line not only carried freight, it created it. To this end, the CER Agricultural Department was reorganized to promote new forms of agriculture and animal husbandry, to cultivate and cross-fertilize suitable species, and to establish experimental farms at Harbin and at Echo and Anda stations. In addition, agricultural machinery was made available for lease, and dairy and cheese factories were established at five stations along the line. Veterinary inspection and forest concessions were promoted. As part of the new regime, the CER assisted local industries such as sugar beet farming and soya bean oil factories. Success was evident in the increased production of bean oil – from 96.7 tons in 1920 to 296.8 tons in 1923. Tariffs were revised to coincide with the economic rhythms of the region, which ran north to south instead of east to west. By 1923, the CER was carrying 2,762,000 tons of goods, 762,000 tons more than at its 1917 peak; however, this was paying freight, not subsidized wartime government transport. Passenger traffic increased through the CER's promotion of cheap fourth-class cars to carry the growing Chinese population. By 1923, passenger traffic had doubled.[12] The CER also made large investments in employee infrastructure. In keeping with the statement "the Chinese Eastern Railway follows not only commercial purposes but it has also enriched the country with a series of undertakings of cultural importance," schools, clubs and housing were improved and more medical facilities were built. But these improvements opened the CER to the accusation that these developments were for the benefit of the company's Russian workers.[13]

The reorganization was a financial success. After years of deficit financing and despite a general worldwide trade decline in the early 1920s and restricted trade with the USSR, the CER began to show a profit. In 1922, with the Soviet takeover of the rump Far Eastern Republic well underway, the Soviet government was still placing restrictions on foreign trade through the CER in the hope of forcing the Chinese government to replace the émigré co-administrator with Soviet-appointed managers. Consequently, busy cross-border trade, the CER's primary function, was prohibited. The decline in Sino-Soviet trade was made up for by a flourishing domestic trade driven by increasing numbers of Chinese and Russian immigrants and by Sino-Japanese trade through the port of Dalian. Harbin, boosted by expanded agricultural trade and processing centred on the soya bean, continued to post healthy economic increases throughout the 1920s. By 1924, the CER was showing an annual profit of four million dollars, a marked improvement from its annual deficit of three to five million dollars before 1920.[14]

Were the CER's policies colonialist? The answer depends on the observer. In the Russian administration's opinion, the CER was modernizing an economically backward region. In the words of one member of the Russian émigré-controlled board, the railway was necessary to the regional economy and settlement: "The CER was a necessary link in the great Siberian railroad to the ocean, while Manchuria was a waste and wild territory through which it was necessary to stride." Russian descriptions of Manchuria emphasized its emptiness, not its Chinese identity.[15] The new CER administration, in an opaque statement, did not deny the CER's colonial origins: "The railway, was, as formerly, considered as a colonizing enterprise, and, even as formerly, among its problems were included, in addition to the question of transit carriage, cooperation with Russian industry in the conquest of the Far Eastern market, for which reason it was regarded, on the one hand, essential not to assist in the development of a local industry in the sphere of influence of the road, and, on the other, to encourage the shipment of raw materials into the Russian frontier districts."[16]

The CER administration admitted that the CER *had once* carried an administrative component but justified this expansion of what had been an economic mandate as necessary for the creation of a regional government. "The latter [CER] disposed not only of extensive rights as a carrier, but also regards the administration of the railway concession zone, the operation of lands, timber and coal mining privileges, because not only must the railway proper be constructed across the wide wilderness of Manchuria, but all the necessities for the living condition of man needs to be created as well."[7] However, in the opinion of the CER's Russian administration, these necessities, once created, became neutral infrastructure, and the CER now acted as an impartial commercial organization.

In the opinion of the Chinese, the CER's Russian administration had acknowledged but not broken with its colonial past – they had merely reinvented it. The Chinese articulated their own vision of the CER, a vision of Chinese sovereignty, economic exploitation, and co-operation with the Russian population. In a letter from Zhang Huanxiang, who was then chief of the CER guards and future Special District head, to Zhang Zuolin, dated 11 September 1921, Zhang Huanxiang argued that the CER absolutely belonged to the Chinese. (As a regional power, Zhang Zuolin's government and its representatives spoke as representatives of the Chinese nation but acted in Manchuria's interests.) He proposed coordinating external and internal policy in the district to maximize Chinese gains. According to Zhang Huanxiang, the Soviet Russians remained a formidable enemy, and "all measures should be taken to neutralize their power." Nevertheless, Russian émigrés could run the railway for China and could be a source of support against the Soviet Union and Japan. The administrative solution Zhang was proposing would be implemented through the Special District's creation. The newly stateless Russians would be protected and left in their jobs, while the Chinese administration positioned itself as the ally of the Russian population and demonstrated to the other concession powers that China was capable of ruling foreign populations.[18]

Although Zhang Zuolin is commonly portrayed as a brutal and self-serving warlord, his policies for the CER and its former concession suggest a different conclusion. Zhang endorsed a policy of Chinese control, yet he allowed the Russian population to maintain a stake in the political and economic affairs of its home. Through the creation of the Special District and the CER co-administration, Zhang proved himself to be a competent administrator and leader who had a vision of the CER zone as an area of administrative experimentation. The CER's success between 1920 and 1924 also reflected

Zhang's willingness to support Ostroumoff. In this period, when Zhang's coffers were full and before he launched his expensive campaign to usurp China's national government, Zhang's vision corresponded with that of Ostroumoff's administration to the degree that they both thought the CER should be a viable business.[19]

Sino-Russian co-operation broke down over the issue of continued Russian domination and the perpetuation of a Russian vision for the CER. For all the success of the CER as a business venture, it was clear that Russians still held a predominant role in CER affairs. The Russian administration could not escape accusations that the railroad was still a private Russian concern. Russians continued to make up the majority of the workers – 75 percent according to one Chinese source – and all senior managers were Russian.[20] According to one Russian newspaper, Chinese made up 44 percent of the CER's employees in 1924, and they mostly held minor or junior positions.[21] Other accusations by the Chinese were aimed chiefly at what they saw as the Russian émigré board's intention to use the CER as a weapon to defame the USSR. According to the Chinese press, the administration was fomenting opposition against the USSR by using the CER to recruit followers for an anti-Bolshevik crusade.[22] The Chinese press in the Special District was not sympathetic to Bolshevism; its members were bothered that the Russian CER board was involving the company in politics. The Chinese stuck to their vision of the CER as a business venture only. The new Russian board, through the use of the railway to promote an anti-Bolshevik agenda, demonstrated its essential insensitivity to the Chinese accusation that the line, once used for political purposes by czarist Russia, was once again being politicized for Russian purposes.

The Chinese press was especially sensitive to the issue of whether Chinese and Russians received equal treatment under the new joint administration in areas such as access to education, clubs, and research institutes, and access to promotions, management positions, and job training. The number of Chinese versus Russian employees was scrutinized, and the quality of housing for the two groups was a topic for comment. For example, the Russian administration was said to discriminate against Chinese by unfairly moving Chinese residents from their homes and raising their rent. Russians who lived on the same street as Chinese paid lower rents and lived in better quality housing.[23]

Harbin's Chinese press was concerned that the railroad, nominally under Chinese-Russian control, had retained its Russian identity. According to one article, although the CER had been taken back by China, Russian remained the principal language of the railway and the Special District. The article's author concluded that the Chinese in the Special District did not pay enough attention to promoting Chinese as a language of business, education, and daily life.[24] One can draw several conclusions from this article and others like it. Russian continued to be the language of daily life in the Special District. Members of the district's Chinese population, as least those who were literate, were well aware of what we now recognize as one of the central issues in postcolonial contexts: the ability of the formerly subject population to define its own culture and language when the former colonial power's language and culture retains its economic and political strength.[25] The Russian population argued that the continued use of Russian was common sense, good business sense, and the easiest and most logical policy given the Special District's Russian character. The Chinese elite responded that only a few short years ago Chinese had not only been rarely used in official circles but also prohibited in business circles in northern Manchuria, a territory that was nominally Chinese. Because of what can be called the burden of colonial and national resentment, the Chinese elite chastised the Russians for their insensitivity, an insensitivity that some Chinese saw as a double insult given administrative measures designed to acknowledge the Special District's shared Sino-Russian heritage. However, the author of the article also acknowledged that many of the Chinese inhabitants of the Special District spoke Russian well enough that the question of which language would be dominant was, for most Chinese, not a high priority. The use of Russian, along with control of the Harbin Municipal Council and the CER and its institutions, would later be actively resisted as an instrument of Russian political control.

The CER's Russian administration also complained about its Chinese partners. The complaints revealed essential Russian prejudices that affected the relationship with Chinese partners. These complaints shared one common theme – the corruption and inefficiency of Chinese rule – and they were aimed at the consular community, which was observing the Special District experiment to determine how China would rule its settler communities if all extraterritorial rights were abolished. Unfortunately, these complaints provoked a strong negative reaction from the Chinese, for they struck at the heart of what the Chinese elite was most proud of – the creation of a modern, efficient Chinese-controlled administration. Russian complaints implicitly and explicitly contained the argument that continued economic success in the Special District depended on Russian supervision. Russians complained that the Chinese courts were less efficient than the Russian courts. Chinese troops transported on the CER were said to be surly, rude, and the cause of numerous incidents.

By August 1924 there were 145 unresolved cases of conflict between Russian CER employees and Chinese soldiers. Cases included insults delivered to the Russians that reveal a newfound confidence and fragile postcolonial nationalism among the Chinese. Chinese soldiers abused Russian railway staff with statements such as "you are here on our good graces" or "who will protect you now?" It was standard practice for soldiers to ride the line without paying, and their commanders were later charged. This had been common with Russian soldiers before 1918. Before that year, no incidents of violence were reported between Russian soldiers and Russian conductors. In 1918 Zhang Zuolin's administration negotiated with the CER for Chinese soldiers' passage to be billed to Shengyang.[26] Despite the fact that Chinese soldiers were allowed to ride without paying, Russian conductors tried to force them to pay, often earning a beating in return. Highlighting the Russians' perceived new sense of vulnerablity, CER train staff complained that not only were they chastised for incidents involving Chinese soldiers, but also, Russian staff were now arrested if a Chinese person was run over by a train – even if the person had committed suicide.[27] These racial insults, the Russian's protective attitude toward the CER, and the Chinese soldier's swagger all demonstrated the reversed political roles of the two peoples and revealed the continued struggle over the region's identity. As voiced by ordinary Chinese soldiers and Russian engineers, the complaints demonstrate that the Sino-Russian tussle over the region's identity was not restricted to the elites.

The degree to which the Russians had failed to reflect on their own changed circumstances, their Chinese partner's sensitivity to the railway's colonial origins, and Russia's place in modern China became evident in 1923 during the CER's twenty-fifth anniversary jubilee. Coming soon after the CER's reorganization and Chinese comments on Russian colonial attitudes, the event could have been an opportunity for both the Chinese and the Russians to reflect on their roles in the CER's foundation and administration. Instead, the jubilee reinforced the perception that the CER, and by extension the Special District, was a Russian project. The jubilee exhibit, arranged by the CER-funded and Russian-staffed Manchurian Research Society, presented an interesting window into the Russian elite's views on the role of the Chinese and the Russians in Manchuria's development. The exhibit positioned – in the manner of an anthropological presentation on primitive peoples – artifacts such as clothing, housing, and arts and crafts that represented Chinese traditional culture and the cultures of other indigenous peoples in one room. The other rooms – which included Russian exhibits and artifacts, models of the railway, and pictures of the new experimental farms and industries and their Russian staffs – represented modernity and the region's future. The Russian press, which could have used the occasion to reflect on how the two countries and peoples had interacted and developed the northeast, used the occasion to reinforce the CER's and the Special District's Russian identity and the Russian population's claims on the region's economy:

> However, it is not only by exhibitions and by material distinctions to old
> employees that this holiday should be observed. The Railway is an emblem
> of Russian genius. With the efforts of the Russian mind, and with Russian
> energy, this country, which had slept for centuries, was awakened but
> improved and made to blossom with material and cultural progress. The
> might of the Russian mind was shown through the combined efforts of
> hundreds of thousands of Russians. Bearing this in mind the Railway should
> erect a number of monuments which would serve as an inspiration to further

efforts on behalf of this country. The Russian population of the Railway Zone has the right to demand, in view of the fact that it is with its efforts that the railway has been placed in its present condition, that out of the budget of millions of rubles that the requirements of this population should be satisfied.[28]

During the celebrations there was some acknowledgement of Chinese participation in the CER, an acknowledgement limited to the consession that one of the languages of publication was Chinese.[29] This history of Harbin, published in both Russian and Chinese, contained a "narrative of some 690 pages [that] justified and glorified Russian work and achievements in building the CER and Harbin."[30] Four scholarships – in honour of the first president of the Railway, Hsu Ching-chin [sic], and the Russian head of construction, Alexander Yugovich – were established at Harbin's municipal primary school. The first stone of the new Russo-Chinese Technical Institute was laid. And two free beds were established in CER hospitals: one in Pristen, a neighbourhood in Harbin formerly administered by the Russians, for employees of the Harbin municipality and one in Fujiadian for the Chinese. Despite the appearance of parity, all of these activities took place in parts of Harbin that had a predominately European or Russian population. Harbin's Municipal Council, at this time still dominated by Russian members, featured prominently in all the activities. From opera at the Railway Club, to the singing of a Te Deum at the Russian cathedral, to dances in the municipal gardens, each event signalled that the jubilee was a Russian celebration.[31]

The jubilee celebrations made it apparent to those espousing Chinese sovereignty that the joint Chinese-Russian CER administration was not satisfactory. The CER was still principally a Russian company, and the success of efforts to make the CER more commercially viable was perceived, perhaps misperceived, by some Chinese board members as evidence of an effort to extend Russian influence. Although the police and the courts in the Special District had been taken over by the Chinese authorities, Harbin's Municipal Council continued to resist attempts both to extend the franchise to more Chinese and to officially designate the Chinese language an official language of municipal affairs.[32]

Nor were Russian members of the administration happy. They saw all Chinese efforts to recover sovereignty in the Special District as a threat to Russian influence. In a letter to John Stevens, former head of the Inter-Allied Railway Commission, Ostroumoff complained that CER workers "have to suffer such a trying and prolonged period of crisis, in connection with the ever increasing tendency of the local Chinese authorities, acting under instructions passed from Shenyang, to do away with even the concessionaire rights of the Railway."[33] Ostroumoff neglected to write that the elimination of the railway's concession rights and the CER's political role had been achieved through the 1920 accord and the revocation of Russia's extraterritorial status. Because the

Russians did not see their continued control of the CER's management and the development of the CER's assets for the benefit of the Russian community as having political meaning, Ostroumoff failed, or did not wish, to see the debate from the Chinese perspective. Instead of trying to reach a settlement within the confines of the Special District, the general manager saw Sino-Russian relations solely in the context of international treaty rights. This was a legal conflict from which China's Russians had been eliminated, a fact to which Ostroumoff alludes by trying to link the status of China's Russians to the remaining treaty powers through the argument that the problem "should be conjoined to the general problem of the powers in China."[34]

Talks between the Chinese government in Beijing, Zhang Zuolin's government in Shenyang, and the Soviet government in Moscow had been under way since 1920, but the Russian Civil War, the Allied intervention, and the unsettled nature of Soviet power in the Russian Far East prevented a resolution of the CER question and removed the USSR as a strong regional power. By 1924, these domestic conflicts had been settled in the USSR's favour, and the Soviet government was once more looking to extend its ideological and national power beyond its borders. Manchuria, as a traditional Russian sphere of influence and a rich economic prize, seemed a logical place to apply the argument that, according to international law, the USSR should be considered the heir to Imperial Russia's investment. The Soviets publicly proposed that, in return for the joint Chinese-Soviet administration of the CER, the commercial nature of the railroad would be reaffirmed and all political activity by the CER or its employees would be banned. The Soviets promised that Chinese and Russians would have full parity in terms of employment and responsibilities. In view of Ostroumoff's efforts to curry favour first with the consular powers and then with the Japanese (he even conducted secret talks with the Soviets), the promise of more Chinese control and the elimination of Ostroumoff was tempting.

Nevertheless, it was the promise of full and complete Chinese control over the CER that brought the Chinese to the negotiating table. Lev Karakhan, the Soviet foreign minister, held out the promise that China's recognition of the USSR would be followed by the railway's sale to China, as long as the Soviet Union could continue to transport goods over the line.[35] The prominent place given to redemption of the CER in the agreement on general principles suggests that this was, for the Chinese, the prime motivation. In 1919 the newly formed Soviet Union, for propaganda purposes, suggested it would be willing to give up all claims on the CER concession. The Soviets later retracted the offer because the CER, to which the Soviet Union had a legal claim, proved too tempting to renounce. In general, Soviet actions in Manchuria were intended to consolidate and extend Soviet influence. The Soviets backed away from the promise to return the CER once an agreement was signed.[36]

It was not at first apparent that the Soviets and the Chinese would, or could, come to an agreement. Instead of one Chinese partner there were two:

Beijing and Shenyang. Beijing had the advantage of being the national government, but, without Zhang Zuolin's co-operation, it had little power to enforce its mandate in Manchuria. Shenyang was the true local power; nevertheless, Zhang Zuolin needed the Beijing government to acquiesce to his demands regarding the USSR to preserve the pretense that Zhang was working within the context of the Chinese state. Zhang could make unilateral decisions to enforce his agenda, as he did in February 1924, when he ordered that the Songhua River – a river that flows past Harbin to connect to the Assuri and flow to Vladivostok – be closed to non-Chinese trade. This move was aimed at the CER Merchant Marine, which, as a joint Sino-Russian company, had been engaged in a lucrative international trade between Russia and China but, according to the 1898 contract, was to be used for procuring construction supplies only. Thus, the Chinese did have a contractual right to close the river to Russian trade; however, Zhang's true motivations in this matter are unclear. He obviously wanted to enforce Chinese sovereignty over the Songhua River, even at the cost of reduced trade with the Soviet Union. But perhaps he also wanted to send a message to the CER émigré board to remind it who was ultimately in control. The order to stop Soviet commercial traffic on the Songhua may have also been a response to the Soviet order to shut down the CER port at Egersheld, in Vladivostok. In November 1922, the Far Eastern Republic had seized the CER's docks, wharves, sidings, ships, and warehouses in protest against the CER's émigré-Chinese administration.[37]

Questions about economics, sovereignty, and politics brought all sides – Shenyang, Beijing, and Moscow – to the negotiating table. On 31 May 1924, the Agreement on the General Principles for the Settlement of Questions between the Republic of China and the USSR was signed in Beijing (hereafter referred to as the Beijing agreement).[38] It is important to note that this agreement was signed as a prologue to a more detailed agreement that was to follow six months later. The Beijing agreement was also signed only with Shenyang's permission, which was provisional. Therefore, the Beijing agreement was of a temporary nature and left much of the existing CER contractual language intact. Article 9 was devoted entirely to the CER. Subsection 1 dealt with the CER's ambiguous status and declared the railroad to be a purely commercial enterprise. All other matters "affecting the rights of the national and local Government of the Republic of China – such as judicial matters, matters relating to civil administration, military administration, police, municipal government, taxation and landed property (with the exception of lands needed by the said railway), shall be administered by the Chinese authorities."[39]

The meaning was clear. China was to have full sovereignty in all matters that did not concern the business of the CER. Subsections 1, 2 and 3 promised that the USSR would sell the railway to the Chinese following a future conference that would set the price and the conditions for redemption. In subsection 7, the two parties agreed that the original CER contract would remain valid until the future conference.[40] When the promised meeting failed to material-ize, the Soviets took advantage of the contract to press their agenda. The Chi-nese would once again find themselves in an unequal alliance with a difficult partner.

The provisional agreement for the management of the CER, signed in Beijing, was the agreement that laid out the principles by which the CER would be run. The principles appeared to concede equality. According to article 7, there would be absolute parity between the Russian and Chinese staff and the board of directors would comprise five Chinese and five Rus-sians. The president was to remain Chinese and the vice-president, or general manager, Russian (but now a Soviet citizen). A quorum of seven was needed to pass any decision. Article 4 stated that if a departmental manager was Chi-nese, the assistant was to be Russian and vice versa. What the provisional agreement did not address was the power of the Russian vice-president. The Chinese president remained a symbolic position with few real powers outside of calling the board to meetings. In the absence of a quorum, the vice-president's word remained law. These deviations from the meaning of joint control were to be dealt with during the November meeting, a meeting that was never convened. The result was a board that was divided and paralyzed and a company that was run by a Russian general manager who acted in any manner he saw fit.

Unknown to Wellington Koo, the Republic of China's representative who was responsible for the talks, representatives of the USSR had been negotiat-ing with Zhang Zuolin. In September 1924 they concluded the Agreement between the Government of the Autonomous Three Eastern Provinces of the Republic of China and the Government of the USSR (hereafter referred to as the Shenyang agreement. Article 6 of the Beijing agreement became article 1 of the Shenyang agreement. Zhang Zuolin placed the most importance on the CER's status as a business enterprise and on ensuring that local administra-tion should be completely in Chinese hands. Like the Beijing agreement, the Shenyang agreement specified that another conference would be held in four months' time to work out further details. Like the conference promised in the Beijing agreement, this conference was never held.[41] Until that conference came to pass, the 1896 contract, in which "the rights of the two governments arising out of this Contract which do not conflict with the present agreement and which do not prejudice China's right of sovereignty, were maintained," that is, the fundamental power structure of the CER, remained the same.[42] Par-ity between Chinese and Russian employees was acknowledged, but an article not found in the Beijing agreement was inserted into the Shenyang agreement. It read: "In carrying out the principle of equal representation the normal course of life and activities of the Railway shall be in no way interrupted or injured, that is to say, the employment of the people of both nationalities shall be in accordance with the experience, personal qualifications and fitness of the applicants."[43] Equal representation was not to disrupt the normal activities of the CER. Since normalcy was a standard set by the Russian general manager, the Russians had a convenient excuse to not hire additional Chinese employees. In article 5, which stated that each party promised not to conduct propaganda on the other's territory, the foundation of another Chinese-Soviet dispute was laid.

In an interview with CER General Manager, A.N. Ivanov, the newly appointed Soviet general manager clarified the Soviet employment strategy. Claiming that very few Chinese were capable of operating a railroad and that there were too few trained Chinese for the CER to operate effectively, Ivanov hinted that Russians would continue to dominate the CER. Although he qualified this by stating that Russians would not be the sole employees and that Russia could not treat China as it had done in the past, his meaning was clear. For the short term, at least, the CER would continue to be dominated by Russian employees.[44]

The Shenyang agreement, which in practice superseded the Beijing agreement, stated that China had the right to buy back the CER – not that such a purchase would take place in the immediate future.[45] Taken together, the two agreements placed a number of obstacles in the path of equal power for the Russian and Chinese partners. For any changes to be initiated, there would have to be agreement among a majority of board members. Because the board was split evenly between Chinese and Russians, such an agreement was impossible. In the event of an impasse, according to the 1896 contract, the Russian general manager would break the tie. Unsolved disagreements between board members had to be referred to the two governments, a practice that resulted in prolonged, lengthy, and ultimately fruitless diplomatic discussions that the Soviet CER managers exploited to pursue their program. Finally, there was the question of which government – Shenyang's or Beijing's – would represent China.

Why did Zhang Zuolin accept the Shenyang agreement? It confirmed his control over the Chinese share of the CER and gave him control over those Chinese appointed to the board. It reopened the CER's port at Vladivostok, and it gave Zhang Soviet recognition of his position as head of Manchuria. In return, however, the USSR regained partial control over the CER under the same conditions that had ensured Russian predominance in the past. Although the USSR claimed that it had found a peaceful and equitable solution to the problem of who owned the CER, the Shenyang agreement heralded an aggressive Soviet presence in Manchuria – in essence, it confirmed northern Manchuria as a Soviet sphere of influence. This new status quo was reflected in an immediate change in Soviet-Japanese relations. A new Russo-Japanese accord, signed in 1925, confirmed southern Manchuria as a Japanese sphere of influence and northern Manchuria as a Soviet sphere of influence.[46]

The transfer from émigré to Soviet co-administration was a solemn occasion for the Special District's émigré community. The occasion was marked on

1 January 1925 by the raising of the new CER flag at Harbin's railway station. The émigrés hated the new flag – a five-colour Chinese republican flag with the hammer and sickle displayed on the red stripe. In the Chinese speeches, "beautifully translated into Russian by Li Xiaogen," the Russians were praised for their contributions to building the railway, but there was no mention of the Russian state. The émigré witnesses interpreted the speech as a denial of Russia's claim to the line that represented the literal disappearance of Russia as a state.[47] Nor did the CER's new Chinese board herald a bright new day for Chinese control over the CER. Although the former Chinese president, Wang Jingchun, had shied away from confrontation with Russian board members, he had been knowledgeable about railway affairs.[48] By contrast, Bao Guiqing, the new CER president, did not grace Harbin with his presence for two years.[49] In the opinion of the CER police chief, the new Chinese members of the board were, at best, weak. The chief described one member as having only one talent: the ability to simultaneously drink four quarts of whiskey and write classical poetry. Another board member, the former Chinese consul to Vladivostok, was accused by a number of Chinese merchants of corruption. But he, at least, was a fluent Russian speaker. Other board members were described as Zhang Zuolin's personal appointees, men with limited ability to oppose Soviet members.[50] Thus, the new jointly managed CER was burdened with an inexperienced Chinese board.

Zhang Zuolin expected these appointees to the CER board to be loyal, and when he doubted this loyalty, he took action that was not always to the appointees' or the CER's advantage. The fate of Yang Cho, CER board member and head of the Audit Committee, demonstrated Zhang's ruthless nature. Yang, although of dubious honesty, was a skilled administrator and equally comfortable in the Chinese and Russian communities. Long under surveillance because of suspicion that Yang was spying for the Soviet side, Yang's home was searched by police on 3 January 1927. The next day he was relieved of his duties.[51] One day later, Yang was taken to an area near the Russian cemetery in Harbin and shot.[52] Yang had been raised in a Russian family as part of Horvath's plan to raise a bilingual comprador class sympathetic to Russian interests. He had studied at Harbin Russian Commercial School and spoke fluent Russian. He was described by the American consul as being young, ambitious, and "unscrupulous and carefully ingenious in plotting." Having ingratiated himself with Zhang Zuolin, Yang had started as a general member of the CER Revision Committee. Married to a Chinese woman and the protector of a Russian concubine, Yang had been accepted as one of their own by both the Chinese and Russian communities, and his death was mourned by the Russian family that had raised him.[53]

The 1924 Shenyang agreement complicated the Special District's unique dual culture by adding a large Soviet Russian population – twenty-eight thousand people according to one source.[54] The new ethnic mix was reflected in holidays celebrated in the Special District after 1924. Chinese holidays such as

Spring Festival (23 and 24 January) and Chinese Revolution Day (12 February) were celebrated alongside Orthodox Christmas (7 and 8 January), Russian Easter (15 and 16 April), and the Transfiguration of the Lord (10 August). The anniversary of the Soviet February Revolution (12 March) and Workman's Day (1 May) were also celebrated. October celebrations of the Russian Revolution, while not officially marked, were tolerated.[55]

The Soviet half of the CER administration quickly made its presence felt among the Russian and Chinese population. This was evident in the popular railway clubs of every station, where "old" anti-Bolshevik Manchurian Russians stared down the newly arrived Soviet citizens and their families in an atmosphere of icy tolerance. The new Soviet administration closed the Department of Religion at every station. The departments had formerly been kept open and funded as part of the Special District's commitment to preserving Russian culture. In the departments' place, the new administration opened a number of Soviet committees that were used to extend Communist influence.[56] Russian religious instruction was replaced by secular and political propaganda. The new Soviet groups included a Young Person's Department, which was divided into the Comsomols and the Young Pioneers. There was also a Women's Department and an Instructional Department to coordinate the dissemination of propaganda. All local committees and clubs were placed under the supervision of the Communist Party.[57] These clubs, subsidized by the CER, were almost exclusively Russian, and their formation broke the Shenyang agreement and the Special District's practice of avoiding political conflict by politicizing CER workers and using CER funds for the exclusive benefit of one national group and one ideology.

Before 1924, the CER's Russian and Chinese workers had been organized into one union that was anti-Bolshevik in orientation. Ivanov, CER general manager, ordered this non-partisan Russian-Chinese union closed and insisted that all workers be members of the official CER union, which was under Soviet direction. Alarmed by the possibility that their union would be converted into a society for Bolshevik propaganda, the CER workers complained to Zhu Qinglan, Special District head. They expressed their reluctance to join a union controlled by Soviet citizens. Members of the Special District's administration were also alarmed by the possibility of a Bolshevik union with influence over Chinese and Russian employees: not only would the union destabilize the fragile peace established in the district, it was also a flagrant breach of the 1924 accords and their promise to leave politics out of the new joint administration. In his protest to Ivanov, Zhu demonstrated that he was paying attention to the larger issue of the Special District's tradition of accommodating and seeing to the needs of its Russian citizens. He cited the union closure as an instance of Soviet meddling in local politics through the forced participation of émigré Russians in Soviet politics. Despite his complaint, the non-partisan union was disbanded, an action that demonstrated the power of the Russian general manager. The Chinese board members, however, assured workers that they were not required to join the new union and could maintain their previous union as an informal association.[58]

In a move calculated to offend the Special District's administration, Ivanov also dismissed Harbin's CER police without warning. These railway police, technically under the CER's jurisdiction but fulfilling the function of local police, were a joint Russian-Chinese force. The force's Russian component was almost entirely composed of émigré or Chinese passport holders. Nearly five hundred police officers were summarily dismissed, ostensibly to cut down on costs. The replacement of these officers with Soviets, however, revealed the true nature of the action.[59] Given that police reform had been a point of pride, this action struck at the heart of the Chinese administrative project in the Special District. The head of the CER police complained to Shenyang, and the five hundred men were rehired to demonstrate the Special District's commitment to its Russians.

Immediately after the joint Sino-Soviet board took control of the CER, citizenship and Chinese parity became an issue. The new Soviet Russian members of the board moved to eliminate émigré Russian workers and Russian workers who had taken out Soviet papers but who were considered ideologically suspect. According to a strictly legal interpretation of the Shenyang agreement, employment on the line was to be limited to Chinese and Soviet citizens. Many Russian CER workers had left open the question of their citizenship, and thousands had kept their Imperial Russian passports. Because the Special District and its Chinese administration had protected Russian property and jobs, most Russians in the Special District had chosen to leave the question of their statelessness open, although many took advantage of the Chinese government's revised citizenship regulations to become Chinese nationals. When the 1924 CER accords were announced, the Soviet consulate was deluged with applications from Russians who hoped that a Soviet passport would protect their jobs. These famous "Harbin radishes" (red on the outside, white on the inside) were the target of the new co-administration.[60]

According to the *Peking and Tientsin Times,* Harbin on the eve of Chinese-Soviet joint management was tense, and there was a fear of Red Terror in the city.[61] It was rumoured that all Russian employees who had not secured Soviet papers would be dismissed. This was not an insubstantial number: in 1924 Chinese citizens made up 44 percent of the CER's 19,800 employees, and over 900 of them were Russian nationals.[62] Chinese board members, attempting to calm Russian employees and exhibiting the spirit of compromise that the Special District was noted for, sent a request to the Shenyang and Beijing governments that any Russian employees slated for discharge because of the Shenyang agreement be made Chinese citizens. The Soviet board members, however, opposed the retention of these Russians as Chinese citizens and insisted that all émigré Russians be discharged because of their unsuitability. This request showed a complete disregard for the Chinese government's power to determine matters of nationality.[63] Almost immediately upon taking their new positions, the Soviet members showed that they had little regard for the fact that Russian workers who took Chinese citizenship were no longer legally under the USSR's jurisdiction.

In February 1925, in what must have been a tense meeting between Ivanov and Zhang Zuolin in Shenyang, Ivanov threatened to withhold Zhang's and Manchuria's portion of the CER's profits if Zhang did not agree to Ivanov's plan to rid the line of émigré Russians, including those with Chinese citizenship.[64] The discussion was not recorded, but it is likely that Zhang, who had protected the Russians under his jurisdiction in the past, informed Ivanov that Russians holding Chinese passports were no longer Ivanov's, or the USSR's, concern. On 9 April 1925, Ivanov issued Order no. 94 without consulting with the CER's Chinese president or the Chinese board members. This order, which reflected Ivanov and the Soviets' narrow interpretation of the 1924 accords, stated that employees who held neither Russian nor Chinese citizenship were to be dismissed. Stateless Russians who had not left by 31 May would be fired by 1 June. Not only did the new Soviet administrators wish to rid the line of employees without Soviet citizenship, they also wanted to judge the purity and loyalty of Soviet citizens by targeting Harbin "radishes." Those Russians who had previously obtained a receipt from the Soviet consul granting them the right to become Soviet citizens were told that the USSR had refused to accept them.[65] There was an immediate run on papers to obtain Chinese citizenship by receipt holders, as they were called.[66]

Chinese board members, the Special District administration, and the Shenyang government weighed in with their support for threatened Russian workers. In an interview with the *Harbin Daily News*, the Chinese CER vice-president stated the Chinese position: as émigrés, the Russians were prized for their skills; as Chinese citizens, they deserved full protection. "Chinese members of the board had never shown any partiality for the interests of the so-called 'whites' [stateless Russians] but wanted only the practical benefits they could bring. Employees who adopted Chinese citizenship were Chinese citizens and the board would protest this [firing of workers]." The vice-president qualified his statement: "This did not mean that Chinese citizenship would protect them if they were derelict in their duties. There had been two cases of dismissal from administration of persons who had adopted Chinese citizenship. The case would be investigated and if the dismissals had taken place because of citizenship, stern reckonings would be demanded."[67]

Chinese board members released a statement on 26 April that supported the Russian CER employees: "The Chinese members of the Board of Directors will always find it their duty to stand up for the problem of those employees whose work is useful to the railway regardless of their belonging to the Red or White camp."[68] The position of Chinese board members on Russian employees mirrored the position of the Special District's administrators – because Russians were necessary for the continued prosperity and functioning of the zone, their interests (in a context of Chinese control) should be protected. Those who chose to take Chinese citizenship became fully entitled, as citizens, to their government's protection.

In May 1925, after a complaint by Chinese administrators to Shenyang, Zhang Zuolin ordered all employees of Russian origin who had been dismissed to be reinstated and Order no. 94 to be cancelled. Ivanov dropped the order with the understanding that he was permitted to submit to the CER president a list of the Russians he wished to dismiss.[69] Presumably, the Chinese were not sufficiently strict in their dismissal of Russian employees because in March 1926 Ivanov began another campaign against both Chinese and Russian workers with Chinese passports, this time under the guise of a security measure to rid the CER of bandits. Zhang Zuolin disliked this renewed attempt to scapegoat Russians who had served him faithfully and to politicize what the Chinese believed to be a politically neutral business. He instructed Zhu Qinglan to make his position clear in a letter to Ivanov. In this letter, dated 13 April 1926, Zhu wrote: "In accordance with instructions of Marshall Chang Tso-Lin [sic] I have to notify you that the meaning of the word 'Bandit' is fully defined in the Chinese language. All persons who in one way or another come under this nomenclature are punished by the courts with all the vigorousness of the law, independent of their nationality. On Chinese soil there is no such thing as 'white bandits' or bandits in general, independent of colour, and never less could they ever be accepted as citizens of China [sic]. The above is stated for your information."[70]

For Ivanov's failure to rid the CER of émigré employees and Chinese passport holders, he was recalled to Moscow and replaced with Boris Emshanov.[71] The issue of ideologically doubtful Russian employees was raised once again in 1928. Emshanov submitted to the board a request for the dismissal of eight hundred Russian employees holding Chinese passports. When the Chinese head refused, Emshanov rallied Soviet employees to strike in support of his measure. There were deep tensions between the Soviet workers, hired more for their proficiency at Communist politics than railroad skills, and the Chinese workers of Chinese and Russian ethnicity who prided themselves on their skills.[72] When the dismissal list was submitted to Zhang Xueliang, the Manchurian leader responded that he would allow the dismissals to go ahead on the condition that an equal number of Soviet workers, known to be Soviet agents, be dismissed.[73] Emshanov dropped the request.[74]

Once again, the Chinese position was clear. Chinese citizens of Russian nationality were not bandits and should not to be dismissed without cause. The issue did not end there. Dismissals continued into 1929, when Emshanov fired over two hundred employees, including forty-six Russians who were naturalized Chinese citizens, without notifying the Chinese board. Emshanov, who said the Chinese were "meddling with his authority," ignored a protest filed by the Chinese board members. The dismissed Russians sent a complaint to Shenyang and were rehired during the 1929 Sino-Soviet dispute over the CER.[75] The Russian workers themselves refused to be passive victims of the new joint management. In 1927, during celebrations of the third anniversary of the Shenyang agreement, over two hundred Russian ex-employees, fired for "refusing to accept the Soviet regime," invaded CER headquarters.[76] Led by a Mr. Elehin, these workers demanded a severance allowance, which was theirs by contractual right and that others had received. These employees, some of whom had been in service to the CER for ten to twenty years, had received no compensation because of their anti-Bolshevik views. When their request met with no response, the workers invaded the CER headquarters and began a hunger strike. Both the Soviet-influenced Russian press, which was normally sympathetic to workers' issues, and the foreign press condemned and mocked the hunger strikers. By contrast, the Chinese press was sympathetic, and several Chinese CER board members stated that the workers should be rehired. After a meeting with the Chinese CER president, the hunger strikers were awarded 750,000 rubles in retirement allowances. Although the compensation had been opposed by the Soviet members, it was paid out because of pressure from the Chinese board members and Shenyang.[77]

In addition to supporting émigré CER workers, the Shenyang government simplified the process by which stateless Russians could obtain Chinese citizenship. All that was required was a clean police record, a reference letter, and the payment of a fee. The process was so simple that during the 1929 Sino-Soviet incident the office in charge of Chinese citizenship, which had simplified the process, refused to take any new applications. It admitted that the process was now so simple that even some Soviet spies had obtained Chinese passports.[78]

The Soviets revealed, through their insistence on breaking the Shenyang agreement and targeting Russians and Chinese citizens for dismissal, that they placed politics above the goal of maintaining a well-run railroad. The Chinese administration revealed that they intended to protect Chinese workers of both nationalities and stateless Russian workers. Rationales for this policy ran the gamut from self-interest to an assertion of Chinese sovereignty. The Chinese protected a pool of skilled workers whose skills were essential to the CER, and they protected a powerless group who, in turn, would be loyal to Chinese rule. The Chinese were also upholding the sanctity of Chinese citizenship – Chinese workers would not be dismissed in their own country for circumstances that had nothing to with their work record.

Between 1920 and 1929, the CER's transformation from a semi-colonial Russian enterprise to a railway co-administered by the Chinese and the Russian Soviets was an ongoing process. Designed to reverse the railway's ambiguous administrative role, one that had its origins in a legally questionable interpretation of the 1898 contract, the arrangement was supposed to establish the Chinese as true co-managers. Like the Special District itself, Chinese policies for the CER's reform were motivated by a spirit of co-operation rather than confrontation. Instead of imposing a single Chinese administration, the Chinese local and regional authorities knew that the transformation of the

CER into a viable business that could fulfill its original mandate to develop and modernize Manchuria required the co-operation of the line's Russian management and workers. In return for Russian skills, the Chinese authorities not only retained Russian employees but also maintained the social, religious, and educational structures of the Russian community in the Special District and offered its members Chinese citizenship to protect them. What the Chinese authorities demanded in return was loyalty.

This essentially pragmatic approach continued when the Chinese began to work with their Soviet co-administrators. When the émigré members of the CER board proved to be resistant to a vision of Chinese co-administration and chose, instead, to use the railway to preserve a Russian vision of Manchuria, the Chinese turned to the Soviet Union, which promised to end the railway's politicization. Once again, the Chinese administration chose pragmatic compromise over the application of a purely Chinese solution that would ignore the region's dual identity. Once again, the Chinese were disappointed – the USSR also used the railway to advance a renewed Russian colonial agenda in northern Manchuria. Although the administrative experiment ended during the 1929 Sino-Soviet war over the CER, its demise does not take away from the fact that the underlying foundation of administrative reform had been co-operation rather than aggressive Chinese nationalism. Nevertheless, both émigré and Soviet Russians resisted this pragmatic Chinese solution because it threatened Russian control over the district's principal economic and political institutions. A long and bitter dispute over land controlled and taxed by the CER, land that the Chinese considered superfluous to the railway's operation, would reveal the limits of this pragmatic policy.

6

Manchurian Landlords:
The Struggle over the Special District's Land

On 10 April 1924, Chinese farmers attacked the Chinese Eastern Railway (CER) experimental farm at Station Anda. Invading the recently built, modern dairy-processing facility that was the pride of the newly rationalized CER, Chinese farmers tore down barns, ripped up fields, and destroyed crops. Armed with hoes and axes, they chased away the farm's Russian staff, and they immediately began to erect homes and plant traditional crops. They either ignored or destroyed the labour-saving devices that had been common on the experimental farm. At the same time, in communities across the Special District, the CER's leaseholders were engaging in a rent strike to protest against competing Russian- and Chinese-controlled institutions that were arguing that rent monies should go to them alone. Throughout 1923 and 1924, control of the land in the Special District's towns and farms had become a controversial and divisive issue that threatened to destroy the fragile compromise that the Special District's administration had forged between the Russian and Chinese populations.

No one fights for something not worth fighting for. By 1923, the Special District's land represented some of the most valuable real estate in China. This valuable land was a by-product of Russian investment in northern Manchuria and represented what Historian David Wolff refers to as Russia's role as a Manchurian landlord.[1] This intense development occurred rapidly in the early nineteenth century. Visiting Harbin in 1904, Maurice Baring expected an American-style city to have grown up overnight. Harbin, however, had not yet reached its geographical limits, and its final growth spurt would come only with the 1905 Russo-Japanese War. What Baring saw from the railway station was "a sea of mud, thick swamps that did duty for roads, a few houses in the distance and a certain amount of scaffolding." Not impressed with the new city – he called Harbin a "great modern abortion" – Baring left immediately.[2] Significantly, he noted that there remained lots of room for expansion within the concession's boundaries because the Russian builders had planned and laid out territory far in excess of what was needed for a mere railway headquarters.

E.Kh. Nilus correctly links the acquisition of CER land with the right of administration: "By becoming a Manchurian landowner the CER was a step from becoming a Manchurian landlord. With the issuance of leases, the CER automatically took upon itself many new obligations to the tenants. This process swiftly converted the CER from a railroad to a multi-faceted colonial enterprise."[3] The CER itself readily admitted this point in its official report on the land controversy: "The CER must not be considered merely as a carrying enterprise, as its activities greatly exceed the limits of operating the Railway line only. It is also entrusted with the administration of a vast Concession zone, which is calculated not only for the requirements of the Railway and its enterprises, but also for the requirements of colonization."[4]

Originally, the CER was not a landlord – the land was classified as a right of way rather than as a concession. According to the first contract, station buildings and maintenance facilities would be built at a bulge in the zone of alienation at each station. This bulge of 540 acres was enlarged in Harbin between 1898 and 1902 with the addition of 6,574 acres that were "more appropriate for city planning than station building."[5] From 1900 to 1902, the CER, with Russian financial backing, also purchased an additional 8,168 acres. According to Wolff, the Chinese acquiesced to this purchase.[6] By 1911, the expropriation process was at an end, and the concession zone had reached its full size of 164,301 acres.

Control and development of the concession was the province of the CER's Land Department – a department that fell under the purview of the railway's administrative arm, the Civil Administration. Like the Civil Administration, the CER Land Department was charged with responsibilities – such as administering buildings, hotels, and maintenance yards – that exceeded the duties of an ordinary railroad land-management department. Within the CER concession, these types of activities accounted for only 56,098 acres, while 134 acres were given over to public institutions. The remaining 108,069 acres were leased on a long- or short-term basis to individuals and companies.[7] According to the CER, these non-railway lands were assets whose improvement added considerably to the CER's value. However, most investment in property development, other than in infrastructure, was the responsibility of the individual leaseholders. Funding for these improvements was provided by the Russo-Asiatic Bank, which legally owned the concession in partnership with the Chinese government. The CER, ostensibly a private company (that is, not a political body), therefore leased and then subleased lands through its Land Department, gave loans to develop these lands, received yearly lease payments, counted these developed properties as added value to the CER, and performed all administrative functions. In short, the Land Department was a model of colonial development. This assumption of privileges was challenged by Chinese and other foreigners alike. American, British, French, and Japanese observers protested that the CER, as a private company, had no right to tax or administer their citizens. As early as 1910, the American consul admitted that most land in the zone was held illegally because it was not used to meet the technical needs of the railway.[8]

Despite protests from consular powers, Russia's model of colonial development through investment in transportation infrastructure was used around the globe. Russia used it in Siberia and Central Asia. The same model was used by national and colonial governments to develop the western parts of Canada and the United States, and the same principle could be seen in the development of the great canal complexes of Panama and Suez. Both pre- and post-revolutionary CER boards therefore believed that their project was justified through modern development. In contrast, their Chinese partners, pointing to the unequal power relationship and a half-century of foreign aggression, saw the project as a colonial plot to deprive China of its sovereignty.[9]

In contrast to post-1949 histories of Harbin and the CER, Chinese sources from the 1920s and 1930s are quite emphatic about the Russian contribution to the foundation of Harbin. Unlike post-1949 texts, which reach back to the Jin Dynasty to find a "Chinese" presence in Harbin, all of the pre-Communist sources agree that Harbin would not have existed without the investment and planning of Russia and the CER. In the 1920s it was not Harbin's Russian origins that offended the Chinese, it was Russia's assumption of administrative control over land in the CER zone.[10] According to the Chinese, the CER Land Department and its activities constituted an illegal political administration. The Chinese did not deny the Russians the right to live in the Special District. Nor did they deny the CER the right to land it needed to maintain the company. What the Chinese did deny was the CER's right to decide who could live on, and the types of uses of, thousands of acres of land that were unnecessary for railway management. The Chinese saw the question of territorial control as a political and moral issue: the Russians and the CER may have had the contractual right to control land (although the Chinese would cast doubt on the legality of the original contracts), but they and the CER did not have the moral right to control the territory.

The issue of control, particularly how to define it, was at the heart of the conflict. The Chinese argued that territorial control and political administration were fused; the Russians countered that land administration had no political component. At first, the Russians argued that control of concession territory devolved naturally to Russia because of an administrative vacuum. Dmitrii Horvath, the first CER general manager, admitted that this was a shaky claim. Imperial Russia had declared in the Treaty of Portsmouth (1905) and in several other documents that no Russian Manchurian concession could restrict Chinese sovereignty. Article 3 of the treaty stated: "Japan and Russia promise to restore entirely and completely to the exclusive administration of China all portions of Manchuria now in the occupation of or under the control of the Japanese or Russian troops, except the territory affected by the lease of the Liaodong peninsula."[11] Horvath evaded the question of administrative legality by declaring in his memoirs that neither Russia and the CER nor the

Chinese government had the right to organize an administration within the concession zone. The argument was tenuous, given that the zone was within the boundaries of the Chinese state. According to Horvath, in the absence of an established legal right and considering the facts on the ground, the CER had the right to establish an administration over the land it controlled.[12]

From the time of the concession's founding, administrative rights were tied to administrative capability: only the Russian-controlled CER was capable of providing the administrative structure needed for the Russian investment to flourish. This argument flew in the face of international law, which protected the right of governments to organize administration within the sovereign boundaries of their states. It also ignored the existing Qing administration in Manchuria. However, Horvath's position was consistent with those of the Russian government and colonial administrations around the globe. Manchuria was described as a land that had been empty before the Russian government and the CER expended considerable sums to develop it. China, in the form of both its national and provincial governments, was represented as being incapable of providing the administrative structure necessary for the area's development. Manchurian development was also linked to the creation of a population whose development was connected to the establishment of private property. According to this circular logic, the CER's leaseholds were crucial to the creation of a settled population, which was necessary for economic growth. Economic growth, in turn, required the extension of more administrative duties to the CER. In addition, the CER's position as the primary Manchurian landlord was buttressed by a legal system dedicated to preserving the sanctity of private property and protecting the extraterritorial rights of foreigners in China.

Thus, according to the Russian argument, the simple act of signing a property lease within the concession was an acknowledgment of the CER's right to manage its lands and its rights as a governing body. According to Horvath, the CER's rights were not only confirmed by statute 6 of the 1896 contract and regulation 8 of the CER's regulations but also "by the fact that persons who leased land within the territory of the railway bound themselves to submit to all police and sanitary, architectural, commercial and other regulations issued by the administration of the railway." Horvath avoided the charges of directing a colonial enterprise by describing the establishment of the CER Land Department as not a political act. According to Horvath, the land regulations "were exclusively of a cultural nature and had chiefly in view such things as the maintenance of law and order, policing for the sake of safety, etc."[13] Horvath's argument was that the original 1896 agreement was not a state-to-state agreement: it was between a company, the CER, and the government of China. Since the CER could in no way be legally considered an extension of the Russian government, the CER's right to administer the land under its control was only the natural function of a business seeking to protect and enhance its investment. According to this argument, because the relationship between the

CER and the Chinese state was that of lessee and lessor, the company was free to impose any type of administration it wished within the concession. This argument overlooked that the CER was controlled and financed by the Russian government. The Chinese would return to this point repeatedly. For instance, in *Haerbin zhinan* (Guide to Harbin), published in 1922 by Harbin's Chinese Chamber of Commerce, the account of the CER's post-1896 territorial expansion is found in a section titled "The Facts about the Violation of Our Sovereignty," which emphasized the point that many Chinese believed that the CER held the land illegally.[14]

The CER and its Land Department made a great deal of money through the annual fees it charged leaseholders. Lease rates in Old Harbin, the first area opened to public purchase, were originally very low – one gold ruble per square foot, according to one source – but were raised to seventeen gold rubles per square foot during the building boom that accompanied the war in 1905. Within one year of Harbin's foundation, it was estimated that monies spent by individuals in construction totalled five million gold rubles. By 1909, land prices had risen to five gold rubles per square foot (after a drop following the 1905 war), and the CER had made three million gold rubles by leasing land.[15]

Even after the Russian Revolution and the recommendation that the CER divest itself of non-railway lands, receipts from land leases and taxes between January and April 1921 totalled 1,475,703 gold rubles, while the Land Department's expenditures for street maintenance and salaries totalled 337,304 gold rubles. Since expenditures for the entire municipal administration were only 81,420 gold rubles, this left a profit of 893,118 gold rubles for the Land Department, which rendered it the CER's highest-grossing department. In 1922, land revenues increased 120 percent to 1,965,922 gold rubles.[16] Disruption of train traffic through Russia during the Russian Revolution had made lease monies essential to the CER's operation.[17] Although the Chinese would claim that the principal issue was the recovery of sovereignty, the monies that came with controlling these lands must have played a part in the decision to take them over. Russians and foreigners claimed that the Chinese were motivated by greed alone, but the issues of sovereignty, control over funds, and control over the reinvestment of those funds (for the benefit of all residents) were entwined and of equal importance to the Chinese.

At the heart of the Russian defence of the Land Department was the claim that the railway had not made a profit because of the administrative work taken on by the company. At first glance, the numbers seem to support the Russian claim. Between 1902 and 1923, the Land Department received 11,669,968 gold rubles but spent 30,966,409 gold rubles. However, the Russian government subsidized the CER until 1917. After 1920, once the CER had been reorganized into a purely commercial enterprise, it began to turn a profit. Most of this profit, however, was reinvested in enterprises aimed at keeping the CER (and its Russian population) the dominant player in the northern Manchurian economy. Up to 1919, the year Boris Ostroumoff took over the

CER, the average Land Department profit was 1,408,796 gold rubles. From July 1920 to July 1923, profit increased to 3,919,422 gold rubles annually.[18] These monies were invested into numerous enterprises and public works that the Chinese felt benefitted only the Russian community. Russia's decision to invest the Land Department's profit was a significant factor in China's decision to wrest control of the department from the CER. Land designated as being within the public domain but within the limits of the CER stations was transferred to the control of the stations' newly formed municipal councils in 1909. According to municipal regulation 2, the CER retained control over any property transferred to the municipal councils; according to regulation 3, the CER, through the Land Department, had the right of final approval over the transfer of public land for other uses.[19] Therefore, although all structures such as streets, squares, gardens, and bridges were transferred to the municipal government, the CER retained final approval over their use.[20]

Private land – that is, land leased to individuals by the CER – was not placed under the municipal councils' control. All property taxes, whether on private or public land, continued to be collected by the CER Land Department and were forwarded to the municipal councils. This practice rendered the councils subject to the CER's supervision in financial matters. In Harbin, it was not enough to justify control over land by foreign privilege and treaty rights – foreign control over land had to be linked to its present and future value. According to the Russian and consular press, Chinese control of Harbin's land would bring a fall in values. The insult was not hard to miss: Chinese supervision and ownership meant low property values.[21]

As a landlord, the Land Department was occasionally callous in its treatment of both Chinese and Russian tenants, as was illustrated by the treatment of the Chinese residents of Zhengyang. Zhengyang was a neighbourhood west of Harbin's commercial district Pristan that adjoined the Songhua River. The Chinese claimed that they had lived there until 1907, when the Land Department moved them to a new, less safe location to develop Zhengyang as a Russian residential neighbourhood. Because their new home was prone to flooding, the Chinese asked to return to their old homes on what had become Zhengyang Street. The move was permitted, but the price of each lot was raised to 50 yuan per year, which was many times the original lease price. In 1918 the Land Department raised the annual lease to 100 yuan and informed the Chinese tenants that their tenancy was temporary rather than permanent. Because of the high price and temporary nature of the leases, Chinese families leased only four lots. In 1919 lot prices rose to 150 yuan, and Chinese residents were told they had to pay eight years in advance. Throughout this period, Russians living on Zhengyang Street paid an annual rent of 60 yuan per lot, with no time restriction on their leases and with no requirement to pay years in advance. Zhengyang's Chinese residents refused to pay their leases, and in their protest to the CER board and the Special District, they noted that the Land Department treated them differently than Russian residents and that "they [the Chinese] were taxpayers and residents and how can they [the CER Land Department] charge different prices for a mixed Chinese/Russian area." Not only were the Chinese ratepayers claiming that they had been victims of racial prejudice, they were also claiming their right, as municipal citizens, to equal treatment from the Russian-controlled Municipal Council. As tensions rose in 1923, the Land Department evicted Zhengyang's remaining Chinese residents (more than one hundred people) and demolished their homes. To add insult to injury, the Russian authorities rebuilt the homes to the more stringent Russian building code and charged the displaced residents demolition and rebuilding costs. In their petition to the Special District's administration, the Chinese residents played on a feeling of national humiliation, calling the incident "an affront to Chinese sovereignty."[22]

Rent strikes seem to have been quite common among both Russian and Chinese leaseholders on the eve of the Chinese takeover of the Land Department. Russians owed 781,581 gold rubles to the department, and Chinese owed another 1,257,968. One Land Department official claimed that rent strikes were a conspiracy on the part of the Chinese administration and, pointing to the black hand of Chinese interference, "that somebody had caused the population to believe that they were entitled to use the lands of the Railway gratis." Because Chinese were the majority of leaseholders in the Special District, Chinese were the majority of defaulters. But in their refusal to pay what many considered to be illegal taxes, the Chinese ratepayers were not only benefitting themselves, they were also acting as agents of Chinese sovereignty.[23]

Given the political and financial importance of the Land Department to the CER's status as a Russian-controlled company, it comes as little surprise that the Chinese eventually tried to detach most of the district's land from the CER to place it under the control of a Special District department. Administrative changes since 1920 had either reduced or eliminated Russian control over the Special District's military, police, and judiciary. Regionally, the Chinese governments, both national and provincial, had tried since 1905 to establish a Chinese fact in Manchuria through administration and colonization. According to rumours that circulated among Chinese bureaucrats and consular staff, the Chinese administration had planned from early 1923 (perhaps because of the controversy over Zhengyang Street) to detach schools, hospitals, and lands not needed for the railway's daily functioning from the CER's control.[24] The takeover of land deemed unnecessary to the CER was confirmed on 20 July 1923. In a series of telegrams, Zhang Zuolin and the Special District head, Zhu Qinglan, informed the CER president, Wang Jingchun, that by violating the 1920 agreement, which had limited the CER to a purely commercial role, the Land Department had violated Chinese sovereignty. Wang gave permission for the takeover of the Land Department to proceed on 1 August. Demonstrating the kind of quality leadership typically associated with the Chinese CER president, Wang then claimed that he suffered from nervous exhaustion and immediately left Harbin for Station Man'chzhuriia.[25]

The icon of St. Nicholas located in the main hall of Harbin's railway station. After the CER passed to joint Soviet-Chinese co-administration in 1924, the Soviets demanded the icon be removed. Citing the icon's popularity with Chinese and Russian travellers, the Chinese CER board members refused the request. I *Manchukuo: A Pictorial Record* (Tokyo: Asahi Shimbun, 1934), 226. Thanks to Dr. Olga Bakich for this information and the photo.

Realizing that the Land Department was under increased scrutiny by the Special District, the CER made an effort in the summer of 1923 to accommodate Chinese criticisms. In July, one month before the first attempt to seize the Land Department, some land alongside the tracks was given to the Chinese Buddhist Society for the construction of a temple. This was a small consolation to the Chinese members of the CER board, who had criticized the Russians for continuing to use CER funds to subsidize Russian churches.[26] Shenyang and the Special District administration did not oppose the Russian Orthodox Church, and they would continue to support it materially and protect it during the CER's period of joint Sino-Soviet administration. What Chinese members did oppose was using funds from a commercial enterprise for the religious benefit of the Russian community.

Despite the rumours, the announcement of the takeover at the end of July took all concerned parties by surprise.[27] Perhaps the Special District administration wanted to give the Russian board members no time to organize resistance. At the end of July, the Special District administration made public the following telegram from Zhang Zuolin: "The function of the Land Department under the administration of the CER violates the directive of the main administration [of the Special District] and is obviously in opposition to the main directive of the agreement [of 1920] in which was stated that the territorial rights completely belong to the local [Chinese] administration."[28] The order set out the Chinese position. Continued CER administration of lands not necessary for a railway was a political activity that violated article 6 of the revised CER contract (1920). In the future, "all privileges and obligations of the railway shall be kept strictly within the scope of commercial business and all political activities on its part shall be prohibited." The order assured foreign leaseholders that other agreements pertaining to their leases would remain in force and that Russian clerks would be invited to come to work for the new Special District Land Bureau (hereafter referred to as the Chinese Land Bureau).[29] The national government followed with a telegram on 1 August:

> The Chinese government, since it partly recovered political rights in the railway administration by agreement in 1920, has resented control by the railway of territory ceded to it and which includes a considerable portion of New Harbin with docks and factories besides large tracts of grazing lands.
>
> The Railway exercised the taxing right over this property, and the proceeds were to have been used for the upkeep of the railway property since the resources formerly drawn by the railway from the Imperial Treasury have been stopped.
>
> It is the government's contention that the railway's administration of affairs is outside the legitimate sphere of railroad enterprise and an infringement of the Government's sovereign rights.[30]

Naturally, the CER administration resisted this attempt to remove a lucrative and essential component of the railway. On 1 August 1923, under Zhang Zuolin's orders, Zhang Huanxiang, who was then head of the Special District police, attempted to seize the Land Department's offices. Zhang Huanxiang arrived at the Land Department with an armed guard and insisted on being shown the department's work. Although Nicholas L. Gondatti, the department's head, did not allow Zhang to shut down the department, Zhang did establish a "Chinese fact" in the Land Department by lounging insolently in Gondatti's chair.[31]

This may have been a reaction to Gondatti's Russian colonial past and his anti-Chinese attitude. N.L. Gondatti was a former governor general of Pri-Amur (1911-17), an explorer, and an anthropologist who had been instrumental in the creation of the Russian Far East. As leader of an expedition to exploit Siberia and the Far East for Russian settlement, and as Pri-Amur governor general, Gondatti had been noted for his xenophobic attitude to Chinese settlement in the Russian Far East. Arrested by the Soviets in 1917, he had made his way to the Special District, where he was appointed to the CER.[32]

Following Zhang Huanxiang's visit, the Land Department was reported to be a hive of activity.

There was unusual activity in the corridors of the building. The General Manager himself, members of the board, the consuls, not to speak of the ever-bustling Gondatti, rapidly moved from room to room, from floor to floor, issued instructions, conferring ...

Couriers from the Land Department were running all over the building, carrying in their hands whole mountains of piled up plans, maps, and all sorts of documents bearing upon land matters. They had only a few days ago been moved from the archives to the Land Department, and they were now rapidly returned to their old places. All of these were placed into two closets, one metal and one wooden, and locked.[33]

Once locked, the Land Department's archive was covered with the seals of the American, French, English, and Japanese consuls. Although the consuls claimed to be objective, they allied themselves with Russian board members, which compromised their position in the eyes of Chinese board members. The consuls questioned the seizure's legality on several points and suggested that such actions could be construed as an example of capricious warlord behaviour. In a carefully phrased statement to Shenyang, the consuls pointed out that Zhang Zuolin's actions, done without Beijing's permission (they ignored the fact that Beijing had confirmed Zhang's actions within twenty-four hours), could be seen in the same light as warlord Wu Peifu's attempt to seize the assets of Chinese-owned railway lines, notably the Beijing-Hankou line.[34] The consuls argued that such a major change in the CER's administration contravened the Washington Conference, and they wanted to know why the Special District's administration had not first approached the CER's board of directors. Answering for his patron, Zhu Qinglan, head of the Special District, replied pragmatically that the board, dominated by Russian members, would never have allowed such a measure to be passed and that the Washington Conference had confirmed that the CER was solely a commercial enterprise.[35] The consuls asked Zhu to delay seizing the Land Department until they had had time to consult with their ambassadors in Beijing. Zhu agreed.

On 6 August 1923, Zhu and the Binjiang daoyin met with Chinese and Russian CER board members to resolve the land issue. The Chinese focused on the Land Department's political role and the moral right of the Special District to control non-railway property. The daoyin placed the issue of the Land Department on the same plane as the abolition of the Russian police and law courts, that is, he placed the seizure in the domain of administrative rights. The Chinese argued that additional purchases of land after 1896 had violated the original contract and the 1920 agreement, which limited the CER's activities solely to business.

The Russians argued from a purely legal position. The question of the rights and duties of the Land Department, they argued, had been decided by the 1896 agreement and confirmed by the 1911 agreement, which allowed for the creation of municipal governments in the CER concession. According to the Russian board members, the present CER board had not been a party to those agreements, which had been negotiated between national governments. Therefore, the contracts could be changed only by the national governments. Because the issue of who represented Imperial Russia's stake in the CER was in question, nothing could be changed. The Chinese position was that the Land Department was a political institution. The Russians refused to accept this position and maintained their argument that the CER board had no right to change the Land Department. The CER's president, they argued, had overstepped his powers. The Chinese argued that the president, as a representative of the government of China, had the power to correct mistakes and infringements on Chinese sovereignty.[36]

The two sides could not have been farther apart. The Russian side relied on tort law when it argued that the original 1896 contract was a legal document that, given the absence of a clearly defined Russian state, remained the only foundation on which to conduct the Chinese-Russian relationship. Although the Russian side refused to discuss it, the 1920 contract renegotiation between the Chinese government and the Russo-Asiatic Bank, which represented the former Russian government, had specified that the CER was a business enterprise under the control of the Russo-Asiatic Bank. The Russian side referred only to the 1896 agreement, even though the legitimacy of Ostroumoff's CER administration had been based on the 1920 agreement. The Russians' critique of President Wang Jingchun's powers was equally tenuous, given that both Horvath and Ostroumoff had governed the CER autocratically.

The Chinese position was also tenuous. While the Russian position relied on shaky legal precedent, the Chinese made a moral argument that was powerfully persuasive but left them open to accusations of self-interest. The Special District, Zhang Zuolin's Manchurian government, and the national government had gone beyond the limits of the 1920 contract when they attempted to seize the Land Department. According to the Chinese, the CER had no right to lands beyond those needed for the daily operation of the line. In their opinion, certain activities – collecting lease monies, supervising building regulations, laying out suburbs and streets, and spending CER monies on the Russian community – were evidence of the Land Department's fundamentally political nature. Yet, as it was defined contractually, the Land Department (as a mere CER department) was to have no defined political role. The Russians' refusal to see their actions as having political meaning drove the Chinese to distraction.

On 11 August 1923, the consuls sent a telegram to the provincial and national Chinese governments declaring that the seizure was in violation of the spirit of the Washington Conference. The conference had decreed that concession and extraterritoriality rights in China would remain as they were, but all countries concerned would work toward the full resumption of Chinese sovereignty. However, because Great Britain, Japan, and France had opposed measures that would limit their range of action in China, no binding regulations backed up these platitudes. Thus, each side could invoke the spirit of the Washington Conference to defend or denounce concession privileges. In response to the telegram, Beijing wrote on 25 January 1924 that the spirit of the Washington Conference would not be broken by the takeover because only land not needed for the daily operation of the railway would be removed from the CER's control. The national government drew on two points to support its argument: (1) the Land Department would continue to administer property according to the original agreements, so long as those matters were of a commercial nature; and (2) the Special District had the right to take over properties not essential to the CER and would pay the company for those lands.[37]

In response to the consuls' protest, Zhang Zuolin formed a joint Russian-Chinese land commission to investigate how much land was needed to maintain the CER. The commission requested in November 1923 a complete list of the long-term and short-term leaseholders, the area of leased lots, the area of vacant lots, revenue receipts for 1921 and 1923, and a survey of the entire Special District. These were reasonable requests, but the CER's Russian board members and the consuls were convinced that the Chinese authorities were only interested in obtaining information to aid in the Special District's takeover. They complained that the commission was merely another method for the Chinese authorities to extract land from the CER.[38]

Work continued in the Land Department because the Chinese had not managed to halt its activity. On 4 August 1923, Police Chief Zhang Huanxiang had had to repeat his order that "all transfers of land were to be done exclusively through the newly formed Chinese Land Bureau. The Chinese Land Bureau would collect all taxes and lease monies and all complaints were to be passed on to the Chinese Land Bureau."[39] On 5 August the Chinese Land Bureau sent telegrams to every station on the line demanding that the railway (that is, the Land Department) cease taking payments for any leases or land transactions. This hard line on the part of the Chinese did not prevent the Land Department from continuing its work. By the end of August, the two sides had reached a stalemate, and the CER and Special District land offices were functioning simultaneously. The Chinese Land Bureau was registering title deeds from the Chinese and some Russians but not from foreigners, while the Land Department was not receiving any revenue.[40]

Despite stubborn resistance on the part of the Land Department and the foreign consuls, at no point did the Special District employ force. Its administrators preferred to rely on negotiation. On 6 August, Gondatti received a second visit from Chinese authorities wishing to acquaint themselves with the day-to-day functioning of the department. The Chinese requested permission to come daily to review the paperwork and asked that rooms be set aside to conduct their work. Gondatti, acting on Ostroumoff's orders, refused, and the Chinese left without incident. At Station Yaomen, the CER agent had to be warned three times to cease collecting rents, and his railway pass was eventually seized to prevent him from travelling to collect rents. Significantly, the documents in his possession pertaining to land leases were not seized.[41] Although the Chinese Land Bureau attached great importance to obtaining these documents, at no time did any Chinese officials use force to obtain documents under consular seal or documents in the outlying stations.

The Chinese Land Bureau ignored provocative actions on the part of the Land Department and concentrated on a policy of divide and rule. Russians and Chinese had taken advantage of the change in administration to occupy vacant lots at several stations. The Chinese Land Bureau informed them their residences would be made legal if they registered with the Special District. Orders sent by the Land Department to land agents and passed on to the local police (now firmly under the control of the Special District) to remove these squatters were ignored. Those who had built with the Land Department's permission were warned that their buildings would be demolished, but they were also told that if they registered with the Chinese Land Bureau they would be given full title. At Station Mangou on the southern line, the Chamber of Commerce had requested vacant lots for the construction of a school. Although the Land Department granted two lots, the Chamber of Commerce refused to take them up until the transfer was confirmed by the Chinese Land Bureau. That an elite institution such as the Chamber of Commerce would refuse CER land indicates that the Chinese Land Bureau had made its presence felt in the outlying stations.[42]

Beginning on 1 August, police and representatives of the new Chinese Land Bureau began to visit the Land Departments at each station. In a well-coordinated campaign on the part of the Chinese administration, every Land Department agent was informed that he could not collect rents, lease lands, or give building permits. Some agents actively resisted. V. Bunin at Station Pogranichnaya refused to obey the order without confirmation from the CER. At Station Hailar, the police had to post officers outside the Land Department office to prevent leaseholders from entering, and the CER agent at Station Hantachetze was detained for collecting rents, which were taken from him. At some stations, however, CER agents were invited to take up positions in the new Chinese Land Bureau. Many accepted the invitation.[43]

By October, the Chinese Land Bureau was registering leases in every station west and east of Harbin, and registration on the southern line began on 3 November. An energetic propaganda campaign by the Special Administration had prepared the way for the registration.[44] In a report from Gondatti to Ostroumoff, dated 17 October 1923, the head of the Land Department detailed the methods by which the Chinese Land Bureau had gained control of the leasing process. First, the local police at all stations failed to implement requests from Land Department officials. Second, the Special District put pressure on the Land Department by having former CER workers and armed escorts come to the CER offices to ask for documents relating to land tenure.

In several instances, police guards were left outside CER offices to prevent leaseholders from entering. And in two cases, representatives of the Special District, both Chinese and Russian, urged CER employees to come to work for the new department. Documents were never seized, nor were the CER agents threatened, other than by the implicit threat that they would soon be unemployed. Police and employees of the Special District retired after making their position known. Third, the Russian population was informed through an extensive propaganda campaign carried out in the Russian language over a two-year period of the change in administration. Russians were told that it would be in their best interest to register with the new land administration. It was stressed repeatedly that the new Chinese Land Bureau would not raise fees and that in some cases leaseholder fees would be lowered. In contrast, Chinese leaseholders were simply told they would face a heavy fine if they did not produce their documents and go immediately to the new registration office.

The Special District's terms were generous and amounted to little more than a transfer of the lease. According to regulations published in November 1923, lessees were required to bring their documents to the Chinese Land Bureau for registration at no charge. No changes were made to the conditions of the lease, and those leaseholders living in outlying stations were allowed to give their documents to agents of the local Special District office for verification rather than making a trip to Harbin. Clearly, the change from the CER Land Department to the Chinese Land Bureau entailed nothing more than a change in registration. Contrary to the consuls' accusations, there were no extra fees and no modified rules.[45]

The Chinese Land Bureau made no distinctions between Chinese, Russian, and other foreign lessees. This policy reflected a desire to retain the Russian population, which was essential to the district's functioning. In former Russian concessions in China proper, the new Chinese administrations were much less willing to compromise. For instance, land in the former Russian concessions at Hankou and Tianjin could be sold only to those who held Chinese citizenship.[46] By contrast, a lease in the Special District could be sold to a person or organization of any nationality.

Despite the Chinese Land Bureau's efforts, the CER was still leasing land in November 1923. The Special District had succeeded in bringing most Russian leaseholders in the outlying stations under its control. In Harbin, however, where the greatest concentration of Russian leaseholders lived, property owners actively resisted. According to the Chinese press, all of Harbin's foreign and most of its Russian leaseholders were still paying their leases to the Land Department in October. Police Chief Zhang had to republish the order that all land, other than that essential to the CER, be transferred to the Chinese Land Bureau.[47] The Russian strategy was to continue the work of the Land Department in the hope that the Chinese would become discouraged. Gondatti was quoted as saying that the Chinese were quick to act without thinking about "whether they were correct or not" and were easily discouraged by obstacles placed in their path. He believed it would only be a "matter of time before their will wore down."[48]

By 1924, consular deeds remained under seal, but the ability of the Land Department to do its job was extremely limited. Leaseholders were reluctant to pay their rent to the department because they feared they would have to pay it again to the Chinese Land Bureau. The department continued to pressure those who paid their leases to the Special District for money, and it refused requests to refund the money of those who wanted to transfer their leases to the Special District. In the village of Alexeyevka, lessees were under pressure from both sides. Leaseholders, many of whom had subcontracted their leases to Chinese farmers, were under pressure from the Special District to register and pay for their leases or risk losing their property. After the Land Department refused to reimburse their leases, the lessees, many of them Russian, and their Chinese tenants occupied the Land Department and had to be forcibly expelled.[49] The CER refused to refund the leases and told those concerned to complain to the Chinese Land Bureau.[50] At Station Hailar, a Chinese subject who had been sent by the police to the Land Department to get his money back was refused. When department employees advised leaseholders that land should be registered with the CER in case the railway was given back the right to full administration, those Russian CER employees who were caught disseminating false information were charged and taken to court.[51] In January 1924, the Chinese Land Bureau stated that persons spreading such rumours would be prosecuted and that the transfer of land to Chinese administration was final: there was no going back, because the land was in "Chinese territory and defended by Chinese police and Chinese courts."[52] In December 1924, the Special District warned that it was extending one last chance for leaseholders to register their documents without penalty. The notice stated that anyone found in the new year with documents from the Land Department would be subject to seizure and the loss of property on the grounds that they held invalid leases.[53]

The Special District brought several cases against Chinese leaseholders for the nonpayment of rent. Significantly, the Chinese-controlled courts decided that the matter could not be settled until the CER and the Chinese Land Bureau decided on a final settlement. The Special District surprisingly announced that the courts had not been authorized to "stop proceedings in connection with land disputes or to refuse the acceptance of such cases"; in effect, it refused to accept the jurisdiction of its own court.[54] Given resistance to the Special District, especially in Harbin and among the consular corps, the Chinese administration chose to avoid confrontation while talks were ongoing with Soviet representatives.

A consular note sent to Zhu Qinglan, the Special District head, in late January 1924 revealed that the two sides were still far apart in their interpretation of events. When Zhu asserted that the annulment of the administrative rights of the Land Department did not contradict agreements concerning the CER, the consuls responded that it was absolutely illegal. They referred to article 6 of the 1896 agreement, which gave the CER the absolute right of administration. In regard to article 6 of the 1920 agreement, which prohibited any political role for the CER, the foreign consuls said it referred to the CER and political activity in Russia and only "indirectly touched the question of reciprocal relations between the Railway and Chinese."[55]

The consuls maintained that full administrative authority had been given to the CER and thus the CER "fully answers to the customary right of China and the conditions ruling in Manchuria. It is necessary to keep in mind that China at first was unable to exercise in the Concession Zone any administrative functions." The consuls stated that China's sovereignty was inviolable but that the "pretension of administrative functions" had been ceded to the CER. The Chinese administration was only interested in taking them back "when it became possible to profit for its own support, from the means of the Railway." To Zhu's point that article 6 restricted the CER to a commercial function, the consuls responded that "the normal functioning of an enterprise such as the CER is quite out of the question if there does not exist administrative activity of the Railway, placed on a correct standing of its own." They argued that China's sovereignty was not threatened because "there can exist no Russian social institutions, nor Russian Government military forces."[56] The consuls adopted a narrow definition of *political* and ignored the fact that Russian (that is émigré) social institutions continued to exist in the Special District.

In reports to Washington, the American consul presented Chinese actions on the land question as being greedy and self-serving. In his opinion, the Chinese only wanted the CER because it had become a profitable enterprise.[57] He wrote that China was "utterly incapable of exercising any administrative functions over the railway" and in no way could article 6 of the 1920 contract be interpreted to suggest that the CER had abandoned its administrative rights in the Special District. By admitting that the CER functions were those of an administrative body, the consul and the ministers confirmed the Chinese view that administration was not politically neutral. However, the consul did not view the Chinese attempt to deprive the CER of its property as a real threat to Russian power. Echoing Gondatti's charge that the Chinese would soon give up their attempt, the American consul wrote that the Chinese were "content to take over the office" and leave the real work to the Russians.[58] Contentment in a supervisory role can also be read as a strategic move. The Chinese were unwilling to throw the Special District into chaos by eliminating all Russian staff and had admitted that there were still too few trained Chinese to fill positions in the Chinese Land Bureau. Nevertheless, the non-governmental Chinese elite at Harbin was not happy with the fashion in which the seizure was progressing and saw the continued opposition of the Russian board members as a strategy to buy more time. They believed that a strong Chinese voice was needed on the CER board and telegrammed President Wang to ask him to return immediately to Harbin. Wang said he was too ill; he claimed that he had asthma and had not slept for three months. In an interview with the *International*, a Chinese newspaper, Wang refused to accept any blame for the affair and urged all patriotic Chinese to give their full co-operation to the newly formed Special District Land Bureau.[59] As the Special District was extending the scope of its activities, the Chinese Land Bureau posted notice on 11 February 1925 that it would extend the registration of leases until 20 February, pending the outcome of two events: the lawsuit on the land question that the CER had brought before the Special District's highest court and the conclusion of the Sino-Soviet talks already underway in Shenyang.[60]

Police Chief Zhang Huanxiang's first attempt to take over the Land Department had been rebuffed, but it had proven to be a popular move among Harbin's Chinese elite. Receiving a delegation from the Chinese Chamber of Commerce, Zhang was congratulated on the takeover. But the delegates also demanded that all land in the Special District be turned over to Chinese control. The same delegation visited the consuls' offices to explain that the Chinese merchant community fully supported the Special District's taking over the Land Department.[61] Their memorandum, presented to the consular bodies by the Harbin Chamber of Commerce, let it be known that the Chinese understood that "the policy of the old Russian Government to colonize the zone of the Chinese Eastern Railway was an outrageous result of her imperial aggrandizement." Infringement on Chinese sovereignty was mentioned, and it was stated that unless the Land Department was taken, "the hereditary colonial policy of the Chinese Eastern Railway can never be abolished."[62] In the eyes of Harbin's Chinese elite, the CER's control over Harbin's land was *prima facie* a colonial project. There was, however, no call to expel the Russians – only to end what the elite perceived to be a continuation of the CER's original colonial policy. The Chamber of Commerce linked continued taxation and administration by the CER to a violation of Chinese sovereignty and a political act, but it stressed that no feelings of ill will were held toward individual Russians or other foreigners.[63]

The Chamber of Commerce's attitude was consistent with that of General Sun Lieshan, former Heilongjiang daoyin and now Jilin Province's top military officer. On the afternoon of 22 August 1922, during a conversation between Shenyang's consuls and General Sun, which the consuls described as "trying," Sun repeated the Chinese position: the Land Department represented an infringement on China's sovereignty and Ostroumoff's administration was colonialist because it had developed the CER to benefit "white" Russian interests.[64] The following day, Harbin's consuls took their argument to Manchurian warlord Zhang Zuolin, who admitted that Harbin officials had perhaps not gone about the seizure in the proper fashion but supported his bureaucrats' actions by agreeing that the Land Department's actions were in violation of Chinese sovereignty.[65] The opinion of the northern Chinese elite was consistent: the Russian-dominated CER had been a colonial body and the present railway administration continued to use the company to ensure Russia's domination of Manchuria. Indeed, many Chinese believed that the Russians were once more attempting to colonize the Special District through the establishment of auxiliary industries under the control of the CER, the extension of Russian education, and the creation of Russian-controlled experimental farms. Although the Russian CER board members and the consular bodies accused the Special District of planting and manipulating a discourse of Russian colonial exploitation in the Chinese press and among the Chinese elite, the accusation of Russian exploitation echoes strongly in Chinese sources. Regardless of whether the CER's Russian board members were self-consciously attempting to control the zone through the economy, many Chinese were convinced that this was the case.

During a visit by the American ambassador to the Special District, however, it became clear that the CER was using its profits for the sole benefit of the Russian community. The American minister to China, Jacob Schurman, paid a visit to Manchuria in late August 1923. The tour provided the American government with an opportunity to present its views on the takeover of the Land Department and the prospects for Russian-Chinese co-operation. Over the next twenty-one days, Schurman was met at every stop by members of the Chinese administration and the Russian and Chinese Chambers of Commerce, feted, presented with guards of honour, and showered with attention. At Changchun, Schurman was given the use of a private, first-class train, which was used to transport him along the entire length of the CER. At every opportunity, both sides sought out Schurman to present him with their side of the story. The Schurman visit therefore offers a window into how the Russians and Chinese perceived the issue of property control and, in a larger sense, how each side saw the other.

The first source of acrimony was the itinerary. Schurman was to go first to Harbin and then proceed immediately to the western section of the line, where he would stop at Station Man'chzhuriia to meet with CER President Wang, who resided there because of poor health. The itinerary, however, was changed so that Schurman would first see the eastern portion of the line. Chinese board members accused the Russians of making this change so they would have the first opportunity to impress their views on the land question on Schurman.[66]

Ostroumoff, along with several members of the CER board, accompanied Schurman. At each station, the same pattern was repeated – visits with noted Chinese and Russian citizens were followed by meetings with Chinese administrators and Russian employees. The particular amenities – hospitals, schools, railway clubs, and "considerable Russian settlements" – of each station were pointed out. At each station Ostroumoff noted that the CER "does everything in its power to conduce the well-being of its Russian employees."[67] And Station Shitouhedze struck the American party as being a typical Russian community: "a distinct Russian colonization process was in progress along this railway and it may be stated that a large part of the feeling against the Russians on the part of the Chinese is caused and directed against the Russian settlements."[68]

Chen Han, head of the CER's Audit Department, in a private conversation with Schurman, characterized the CER as a Russian government enterprise whose main objective was the colonization of Manchuria. The agreement of 1920 had clearly stated that the CER was to give up all pretensions of political power and act as a business enterprise only. According to Chen, however, the CER under Ostroumoff was continuing Imperial Russia's colonial enterprise in the Special District. Given Ostroumoff's career as a Siberian colonial bureaucrat, Chen's assessment is accurate. In Chen's opinion, the Chinese government had been very generous in allowing the Russian management to use the funds of the CER to meet the needs of the Russian population. Schurman heard the same opinion expressed at Station Pogranichnaya, where Chinese officials complained that Chinese who lived and traded on the Soviet side of the border were treated harshly and had unfair levies placed on them. By contrast, the Russian refugees were well treated by the CER, which provided free grain shipments for famine relief.[69]

Chen admitted that Ostroumoff was a skilled and talented administrator, but he contended that Ostroumoff had embarked on various enterprises that ranged from mining to experimental farming to manufacturing without consulting with his colleagues. In Chen's opinion, these enterprises were not appropriate for the CER; although they might make money in the future, in the short term, they were money losers. The result of Ostroumoff's policies was an overall loss of revenue for the CER, even though the line was turning a profit for the first time in its history. For example, at a factory that processed waste products from the CER's forests at Station Shitouhedze, Chen took Ambassador Schurman aside to explain that the factory, along with the mines and the experimental farms, was not commercially viable and that the CER should not be involved. He also told Schurman that the accounts for these new enterprises were not sent to the Audit Department, as was required by the CER's regulations.

In short, Chen believed that the Land Department did not profit the CER; through it, the CER continued to exercise expensive government functions, such as the collection of taxes, the proceeds of which were then spent on the Russian population. Chen connected the problem to Ostroumoff's and Gondatti's former experiences as colonial administrators in the Russian Far East. As former Russian government officials and bureaucrats who had once been amply funded by St. Petersburg, Ostroumoff and Gondatti were accustomed to formulating development plans that did not necessarily have profit as the final goal. "They considered only the beneficial result at which they were aiming," that is, the development and prosperity of the Russian population. In contrast, the Chinese government opposed expenditures on an "alien colony" within China.[70] Certainly, in Ostroumoff's opinion, caring for the Russian population was the CER's main task. At Station Pogranichnaya, when Schurman was inspecting a well-turned-out group of Russian schoolchildren, Ostroumoff remarked, "They were the reason for the activities of the Russian railway officials, i.e., to provide for the well-being of the rising generation along the Chinese Eastern Railway."[71]

Ultimately, Schurman put his support behind the protection of treaty privilege and expressed his position in a speech to both parties at the final banquet on his itinerary. The Chinese were disappointed. Special District Head Zhu Qinglan wrote Schurman and stated, "It is clearly stipulated in Article Six that the railway should occupy only the land needed by it, while article six of the supplementary agreement clearly provided for the prohibition of all political functions on the part of the railway. However, the railway has utilized the land occupied by it to lay out commercial towns for rentals and made preparations for such administrative functions as the government of municipalities and collection of taxes." Zhu ended by asking Schurman to consider whether these activities were infringements on Chinese sovereignty.[72]

On the return leg of his journey, Schurman met with Zhang Zuolin, who referred to Schurman's speeches in support of the CER and its Land Department. Speaking with some agitation, Zhang mentioned previous colonial projects carried out by the Imperial Russian government in Manchuria and drew a direct parallel to the activities of the Land Department. His order to suppress the CER Land Department, Zhang explained, had been based on the advice of his advisors and had the full support of Manchuria's Chinese population. In February 1924, Zhang decided on a compromise. The Land Department would continue to exist and it would continue to administer and lease lands; however, the Chinese Land Bureau would register and confirm the leases. Any lands needed for administrative or municipal purposes were to be given over to the Special District's administration. Presumably, private lessors would remain under the CER's administration. The CER, in turn, admitted that it had contravened article 6 of the 1920 agreement. Zhang's apparent about-face must be placed in the context of developing talks with the Soviets, which would later result in the Sino-Soviet agreement. Zhang hoped the agreement, which would reaffirm the CER's commercial status and render any administrative pretensions on the part of the CER illegal, would finally settle the land issue. Unfortunately, the Soviets would prove to be even more interventionist than their "white" cousins – Zhang was later overheard saying that he missed Ostroumoff's rule and actively protected him from the Soviets. There was, however, no way Zhang could have anticipated Soviet imperialism in the spring of 1924. Many Chinese who worked and lived in the Special District disagreed with Zhang's decision, and saw it as a loss of face for the Chinese. Some said Zhang put his interests before those of the Special District.[73]

Schurman's tour resolved nothing. The ambassador had been charged by the US government to only gather information, not to challenge the extraterritorial status quo. Nevertheless, the tour revealed that Ostroumoff, the former colonial administrator, was proud that he had placed the CER on a sound financial footing that offered economic benefits to the Russian inhabitants of the Special District. In several disparaging remarks made about Chinese organization (that is, remarks that associated the Chinese with disorganization), the CER head revealed his feelings about his Chinese partners. He believed they were not capable of acting as true co-administrators. Meanwhile, the Special District continued to pursue a policy of Chinese control over all non-railway land. Chinese police were still arresting CER land agents, who were by then illegally collecting rent, on the grounds that the agents were acting against the interests of the Special District's Land Bureau.[74] By the spring of 1924, however, the dispute over the control and symbolic meaning of the Special District's land had moved from the level of elite discourse played out in journals and diplomatic dispatches to active resistance.

The incidents took place in and around the CER experimental farm at Station Anda. The farm had been founded in 1922 as part of the CER's efforts to diversify its activities and make the company indispensable to regional economic development. In order to create the farm, Chinese leaseholders were removed, and their leases were revoked – a development that was not mentioned in the Russian or consular sources. Chinese translators working for the CER had originally leased the Anda property from the company and then subleased it to over sixty-five Chinese families. The CER forcibly removed these families and offered them uncultivated land in return. The Chinese farmers refused. Work on the experimental farm continued, even though Chinese leaseholders of the property attempted to obstruct it.[75]

Station Anda's experimental farm consisted of a dairy-processing plant that specialized in butter and sour cream. The rationale for creating a dairy-processing farm was that it would help farmers who had difficulty finding markets for their raw milk. Dairy farming was an exclusively Russian activity, as was the consumption of milk, buttermilk, and sour cream. Thus, the benefits of the experimental farm were aimed at, and enjoyed wholly by, Anda's Russian farmers. Within six months, the farm was producing around eighty-five thousand bottles of milk, four thousand pounds of butter, and three thousand pounds of sour cream.[76] To the Russian members of the CER board, the Anda farm made economic sense. By providing a processing point for an expanding Russian market in dairy products, it diversified the economy and created jobs. From the Chinese perspective, the Anda farm was an attempt by the Russian-controlled CER to expand job opportunities for Russians by displacing established Chinese farmers – it was a Russian attempt to dominate the Manchurian landscape physically and economically.

Station Anda's experimental farm also challenged the authority of the Chinese Land Bureau by continuing to work only with the Land Department. As late as November 1923, the Anda division of the Land Department was still collecting rents, dividing land lots, and issuing leases in the CER's name.[77] Station Anda had not only refused to acknowledge the new property regime, it had also displaced Chinese farmers to come to the assistance of the Russian population. The Chinese authorities therefore extended little sympathy to the experimental farm once it became the focus of resistance by Chinese farmers. The Chinese press reported that the farm, particularly the matter of the original Chinese leases, had caused indignation among Chinese farmers.[78] In March 1924, Chinese farmers attacked the experimental farm. The farm's head agronomist reported that Chinese "armed with spades came to the field, disposed labourers of the [CER] Land Department and destroyed the work already done. Thirty men began to break and to cover with earth flowering beds, and then came Chinese with two ploughs and began to plough the field again."[79] The police, unsure about whether the CER or the Chinese authorities should deal with the matter, delayed sending men to the fields and waited for orders from Harbin. This delay was interpreted by members of the Russian and foreign press as an official endorsement of the actions of the Chinese farmers. The Russian press accused the police, who were presumably Chinese, of playing favourites and taking measures in words only. The matter was referred to Special District Head Zhu Qinglan, who ordered an investigation and gave instructions to permit no further outrageous activities on the part of the Chinese.[80] Even the arrival of the assistant manager of the Chinese Land Bureau did not restore order. The occupation continued.

On 21 March, when the experimental farm director resumed work, the head agronomist and his team were driven from the fields by Chinese farmers armed with spades. Further attempts to resume work were prevented by the Chinese, who began to build a cottage in the fields and threatened to burn the cattle barns. As the Chinese farmers attempted to destroy potentially useful buildings, buildings that were concrete symbols of the Russian dairy economy that had displaced the farmers, they were asserting what they perceived to be their legal right to the land and to an agricultural system oriented to local Chinese, not Russian settlers.[81]

During his visit to Station Anda, Schurman had met with many Chinese farmers who complained about the experimental farm's activities. They complained that Chinese were discriminated against in favour of the Russian settlers and assured Schurman that the restitution of CER land and the attempt to dismantle the Land Department were popular moves. Ostroumoff, however, informed Schurman that the troubles at Anda had been caused by the CER's efforts to modernize and improve the agricultural life of the region. He implied that it was development itself that the Chinese opposed. When Schurman asked Ostroumoff whether the CER was practising a deliberate colonization policy for the benefit of the Russian population, Ostroumoff did not respond.[82]

In the Russian émigré press, there was no attempt to see the Anda issue from the point of view of displaced Chinese farmers. The language employed by the Russian press revealed its members' fundamental prejudices and an inability to understand the Chinese position. For instance, the terms *mobs* and *marauders* were used to describe the Chinese. And phrases such as *wild Chinese actions* and *challenging manner* were used to describe their behaviour. For instance, one author reported that "passivity of the police in the matter of the destruction of the railway is really astonishing."[83] The Chinese were criticized for uncivilized and presumptuous behaviour, their administrative competence was questioned, and what was described as their essentially avaricious attitude toward the CER was highlighted. The Russian press did make an indirect connection between the CER's development project at Station Anda and the Chinese farmers' reaction to it. However, by portraying the dispute as a struggle between the forces of civilization and barbarity, between light and darkness, the press invested the case with the full weight of the Russian mission in northern Manchuria: "The debauches of the Chinese mob, the indifference of the Chinese police and its actions relating to the employees of the land department of the CER and to lease-holders are of a destructive character of a double meaning, they destroy the cultural economic work and all cultural legacy of the [CER] land department. They abolish authoritative right and make the uncultured mob believe that in certain cases one can disregard the laws with impunity and exercise violence. This strengthens the bad interests of the dark-minded mob."[84]

Station Anda was not the only agricultural station to come under attack. However, *attack* was defined broadly as any challenge, however subtle, to Russia's authority in regard to land administration and use. In the opinion of Russian and foreign observers, attacks constituted anything from direct seizures to lapses in etiquette and deference. Throughout May 1924, Chinese farmers, perhaps encouraged by events at Station Anda, invaded Russian farms and experimental stations throughout the Special District. In most cases, they were removed by Chinese authorities who upheld the Russians' property rights. In the Harbin suburb of Korpoussni Gorodok, for instance, twenty Chinese farmers took over the farm of a Mr. Yashkin, who despaired over the loss of his carefully nurtured fruit orchard. Chinese documents mentioned that there were irregularities in Yashkin's lease – perhaps this was a reference to another illegal seizure. At Station Kwanchangtze, which had another large experimental farm, the farm head was told to report to the police. According to the Russian farm head, the Chinese police, who were "rudely and affrontingly lounging on the chairs," addressed him in Russian using the familiar first person singular instead of the more formal second person plural (he did not comment on the fact that the Chinese police could address him in his native tongue). At Station Echo, experimental farm staff were told by the Chinese Land Bureau to turn over a portion of the rice fields to Chinese farmers.[85]

Russian and Chinese misunderstandings of each other's positions were clearly articulated during a dispute over farmland in the spring of 1924. From 1920 to 1924, the CER had been on a mission to develop and diversify the northern Manchurian economy. Russian CER board members saw this as politically neutral economic and cultural development. In a letter to John Stevens, head of the Inter-Allied Technical Board, Ostroumoff complained that the Chinese administration intended to restrict the CER to railway affairs rather than allowing it to play a larger economic role in the country. Although the Inter-Allied Technical Board had ceased to play a direct role in CER affairs by 1924, it remained an important sounding board for anxieties concerning the railroad and the position of Russians in Manchuria. Ostroumoff, through his comments and actions, revealed that he viewed the CER as a major player in the colonization and development of the area.[86] But it can be argued that Russian-controlled CER economic development also provided the émigré-dominated CER with a raison d'être in a changed political context. Continued Russian-led economic development would ensure Russian jobs, Russian prestige, and a continued need for Russian supervision. For those outside the Russian community, however, these émigré Russian actions inaugurated a new form of colonial authority through economic development. This is certainly how the Chinese elite, not opposed to development itself, understood CER economic development. Chinese farmers, no longer content to be the passive observers and victims of CER economic development, challenged the CER's right to administer and define the ethnic and colonial meanings of land and land use.

The dispute over land can also be situated in the context of regional control. Zhang Zuolin was in the process of discussing with the Soviet Union a possible joint Chinese-Soviet administration of the CER. The takeover of land administration established regional Chinese claims and decentred those of Russia. Zhang Zuolin's actions emphasized the CER's restriction to a commercial role. The Soviets, however, proved to be no more sympathetic to Chinese claims than were their émigré cousins. The Soviets did not support the Chinese Land Bureau, even though the USSR had renounced its predecessor's imperialist policies.[87] Soviet envoy, Yacov Davtian, interviewed in the English-language *Russian Daily News,* stated that the Soviet Union in no way supported the reorganization of the land administration and inadvertently revealed the proprietary manner in which the Soviet Union continued to view Manchuria. According to Davtian, the Soviet Union did not recognize the supplementary agreement of 1920 (signed between émigré Russian representatives, the Russo-Asiatic Bank, and the Zhang Zuolin administration): the CER was *Russia's property.* Davtian stressed that any changes to the CER's status would require the Soviet government's approval. This opinion was consistent with that of the top Soviet diplomat in China, L. Karakhan. In an interview with the Harbin paper *Zaria,* Karakhan stressed that the CER had been built with Russian labour and funds, and the land question's final solution was only possible through a Chinese-Soviet conference, conveniently forgetting that the funds had been French and the labour mostly Chinese.[88] His mention of a conference was a direct reference to the secret talks taking place in Shenyang, the reason for Karakhan's visit.

On 31 May 1924, Beijing and Moscow signed the Sino-Russian agreement. The agreement was largely symbolic, since Beijing had no jurisdiction in

Manchuria. In September a supplementary agreement was signed with Zhang Zuolin in Shenyang. Both agreements were concerned with settling outstanding issues between the two countries, particularly the question of local administration. In subsection 1 of article 9 on the CER, the CER was defined as a "purely commercial enterprise." All other matters affecting the national and local governments of the Republic of China – such as judicial matters and matters relating to civil administration, military administration, police, municipal government, taxation, and landed property (with the exception of lands required by the railway) – were to be administered by the Chinese authorities. This was how the Soviets argued for continued Soviet Russian control over land – by defining it as essential for the railway.

On the eve of the transfer of the CER to joint Russian-Chinese control, the American consul removed the consular seals that had been placed on the Land Department archives to prevent them from being seized by the Chinese Land Bureau. Although there was some consular debate as to whether the seals' removal endorsed Chinese actions, the seals were quietly removed and destroyed that September. The archives, however, were not handed over to the Chinese. With the consular corps' permission, they were turned over to the Soviet half of the co-administration and remained under Soviet control until after the 1929 conflict.[89] It was, presumably, a greater comfort to the foreign community to see the deeds to valuable lands consigned to the protection of a regime committed to eliminating private property than it was to see them under the protection of the Chinese government. In Manchuria the Soviets would not challenge extraterritoriality's basic structure. Extraterritoriality and the maintenance of the Russian colonial project in Manchuria in a new Soviet guise enabled the USSR to control a valuable economic asset and reassert its influence in a region that it viewed as a traditional Russian sphere of influence.

After the transfer of the CER to joint Chinese-Russian control, Zhu Qinglan, the Special District head, pressed the railway administration to register its title deeds and clear up the question of which lands were needed by the CER.[90] Once again, the two sides fell into disagreement over the issue. One area in dispute was the Eighth District, an industrial area between the Chinese area of Fujiadian and the mixed Russian-Chinese neighbourhood of Pristan. Falling within the boundaries of the original Russian concession, the Eighth District had its own distinct economic and racial identity. Situated where the CER tracks reached the Songhua River, the area was a warehouse district, a district of small factories and a mixed Chinese-Russian population. Chinese merchants predominated and had been paying their lease monies to the Chinese Land Bureau.

In 1924 the new Soviet general manager of the CER, A.N. Ivanov, began charging Eighth District merchants a new tax of eight dollars per railroad car for shipping goods out of the area. Merchants in other parts of the Special District adjoining the CER tracks paid no such tax. In essence, the CER was once again levying and collecting tax, a political task that under the land compromise could only be undertaken by the Land Bureau. Chinese and Russian merchants appealed to Chinese authorities, who in turn appealed to Beijing and Shenyang. In January 1925, angry Chinese and Russian merchants from the Eighth District trapped the Soviet vice-president of the CER on the Harbin station platform and claimed they had the support of the Chinese members of the CER board.[91] The vice-president escaped, and the issue was eventually solved through compromise. The CER would continue to collect a much lower tax, but it was not permitted to call it a tax – it was rechristened a transportation fee.[92]

Soviet possession and control of the district's property archive and the CER's collection of taxes reveals that joint Russian-Chinese rule did not solve the land question. The 1924 agreement had provided for the final transfer of land not needed by the CER to the Special District, but the Soviets delayed the transfer by submitting every dispute to the commission created by Zhang Zuolin to arbitrate disputes over land. In essence, the Soviets used a Chinese institution to delay property transfer. The Soviets, for instance, claimed that warehouses in the Eighth District – which were not CER property, had never been used by the railway, and were under the Special District's jurisdiction – were essential to the CER. The Soviets, by blocking the reform process, were perpetuating Russian control over land not needed by the CER.

The Soviets were also reluctant to give up the CER's hold on Harbin's lucrative residential market. Housing in Harbin was at a premium, and rent was the greatest expense for Chinese and Russian Harbiners. Said to be rising daily, rent for a three-bedroom apartment was eighty yuan a month at the beginning of 1928, more than half a white-collar worker's salary. Individual renters considered middle-class living to be three to a room, a common situation in Harbin.[93] Because housing construction could not match population growth (Harbin's population [excluding Fujiadian] almost doubled to 126,952 persons between 1913 to 1923 and rose to 160,670 by 1929), prospective renters were willing to offer landlords twice the rent to evict tenants already in residence.[94] Because of the housing crisis, the Chinese administration was kept busy with the regulation of illegal buildings. Within the Harbin Temporary Self-Governing Committee, active from March to November 1926 as a transitional body between the Russian municipal government and Chinese self-government, over one-third of the meetings contain references to illegally constructed buildings and the temporary committee's plans to demolish them. Lessees who continued to renovate or build new structures without permission had their buildings torn down.[95] The Chinese Land Bureau stressed that the regulations it imposed concerning land use were the same or better than those of the Russian land administration. In this manner, the Chinese Land Bureau, like the Special District that directed it, was continuing, expanding, and improving on the Russian project of establishing municipal codes to create a modern municipal administration. Nevertheless, many Russian landowners continued to pay lease money to the CER Land Department and did so because of the high number of Russian leaseholders in Harbin who continued to support the CER. The Chinese Land Bureau found it necessary to press these leaseholders to accept the new regime, with mixed results.

In two notices, both dated August 1926, the Chinese Land Bureau stressed that no construction could proceed without its permission and that speculation in land would not be tolerated. These notices brought attention to those who were deliberately registering their land with the CER, either to make a quick profit or to flout Chinese sovereignty by obtaining deceitful leases. The notices warned these people that they risked having their leases terminated and their land seized, and they emphasized that land not needed for the CER's technical use was controlled by the Special District.[96] The Special District was also interested in developing already-leased land to achieve maximum productivity and provide the best housing for the district's population. In two notices, one for the outlying stations and one for Harbin, the Special District pointed out that many long-term leaseholders had not developed their land; therefore, they had not increased their personal fortunes or those of the Special District. It also stressed that many still held their leases illegally – that is, not through the Special District – and that if they did not soon register these properties, it would be forfeit.[97]

Despite these warnings, the CER, especially in Harbin, continued to accept lease payments on lands that were expressly out of its control. Many of the lessees were Russian, judging from the majority of the warnings printed in Russian found in the Special District's property handbooks. (In the Chinese language handbooks, such warnings were no longer printed after 1925.) These lessees had not accepted the new regime, and in July 1926 the Special District again tried to tempt them into registering their documents by reducing the leasing fee to 50 kopecks (a kopeck is one hundredth of a ruble) per square sashin (roughly half an acre). By comparison, the CER charged 2.5 to 3 rubles per square sashin.[98]

Several conclusions can be drawn from these notices. First, the Special District saw itself as inheriting, enforcing, and improving Russian regulations concerning land use. Concerns about proper housing regulations, the exploitation of renters in an overheated housing market, and property development benefitting both the lessee and the Special District reveal that the Chinese took seriously the project of creating a modern civic administration for all residents. Their work in this manner parallels that of Harbin's city government, which took on Harbin's neglected urban infrastructure and set about to make good on the promises of the formerly Russian-dominated Municipal Council. Second, the notices also reveal that the CER continued to accept lease money, even for land legally no longer under its control, and that the Special District administration was unwilling to force the issue. The consuls wrote that the CER's Land Department continued to aggressively solicit Russian lease money and leaseholders. The Soviet Russian CER administration, through a combination of greed and a desire for administrative control, was using a combination of bureaucratic filibuster and open contempt for the Chinese administration to ensure continued Russian domination of the Special District's land. Third, the notices also reveal that a significant portion of the residents in Harbin and the Special District continued to pay lease money to the CER. The majority of these persons were Russians in Harbin, who were dealing with a joint Chinese-Russian administration. Why would they continue to support an enterprise that no longer politically supported émigrés? Perhaps some preferred a Russian administration of any political stripe over a Chinese administration. Others no doubt felt more comfortable in an exclusively Russian cultural context.

Continued Russian support of the CER's Land Department also suggests Chinese tolerance. Presumably, the Chinese could have chosen a hard line: the Special District administrators could have evicted every person not registered and paying lease monies to it. They did not, and the Chinese city government's records are filled with successful Russian (and Chinese) petitions for rent reductions.[99] In Harbin's media and administrative documents, the Chinese elite contrasted its good treatment of the Russian population with the Russian population's poor treatment of the Chinese in the pre-1919 period. A hard line, they argued, would render marginal the lives of many émigrés and severely disrupt the district's economic life. These developments would not present foreign observers with a fine example of Chinese administrative largesse toward Russian constituents.

The duties of the Land Department were officially assumed by the Special District Land Bureau in 1927.[100] However, many lessees, in particular, members of Harbin's consular community, continued to flout the Special District's authority. Immune from prosecution through extraterritoriality, angered by the 1925 suppression of their Municipal Council designated seats, the consuls continued to support the rump CER Land Department. This show of support was designed to maintain the principle of foreign privilege in China rather than to support a Soviet agenda within the CER's administration. In 1927 the Special District sent notice 50 to the consular corps to advise them that foreign leases from the CER had been suppressed and that new leases from the Special District were now necessary. Notice 51 advised the consuls that new land transfer procedures had been put in place to prevent "unscrupulous capitalist dabbling in real estate."[101] These regulations were significant because many businesses had passed out of Russian hands and into the hands of foreign nationals. This development was partly due to the difficult economic position of Russian émigré businessmen, but it was also a deliberate strategy by Russian property owners to evade Chinese taxation by placing their businesses under foreign control. In particular, the Japanese had invested 20 million yen in former Russian properties, with the French the next largest investor.[102]

In a letter dated 1926, from Zhang Huanxiang, then Special District head, to Zhang Zuolin, Zhang Huanxiang congratulated the marshal on the success of Chinese policies designed to shift control of valuable property to Chinese control: "We have acquired property to the value of over 15 million dollars in towns and villages in the Special Region of the Eastern Provinces and, what is especially important, [it is] a stupendously rich region cultivated by the Russians for 25 years which develops its economic, commercial and industrial life in a geometrical progression."[103] The Special District's policy of removing land from the CER's control was largely successful. Only in Harbin – with its concentration of Soviet citizens, émigrés, and foreign consuls – did the population resist the Chinese Land Bureau. Although Zhang Zuolin and Special District administers had been forced to slow what they considered to be a process of decolonization and to justify every sashin taken from the CER's jurisdiction, they eventually broke the CER's hold over the territorial administration of the Special District's land.

The Special District's administration demonstrated the essentially pragmatic nature of its policy to administer land and land tenure in an area with a foreign population. The policy was compatible with those pursued in the areas of law and municipal government. Former structures and institutions were left more or less intact, with the addition of Chinese supervisors and some Chinese staff. Otherwise, after gaining control, China's first priority was the Special District's ongoing prosperity. This was demonstrated through the careful attention administrators paid to land regulations, registration, and building codes and through rent reductions and the maintenance of Russian administrative practices that benefitted the Russian community. The Special District's administration made it clear that its problem lay not with the Russian population but with what it perceived to be the CER's colonial structures.

In cases where the Chinese felt that the Russians had unfairly displaced them, however, the result was popular violence. The violence that broke out at Station Anda, for example, was not aimed at the Russians themselves but was a response to the CER's use of land and the eviction of Chinese tenant farmers in favour of farmers from the Russian community. Many in the Russian community and in the CER administration did not understand the Chinese point of view. In the opinion of many Russians, the CER was fostering modernity and progress in Manchuria. The failure of both sides to understand each another would, in the long term, affect the Russians' efforts to create a new role for Russians in Manchuria.

According to the Chinese, the activities of the CER's Land Department were colonialist because the Land Department existed solely for the maintenance and growth of the Special District's Russian community. The CER's Russian board members could not easily evade this accusation because their first priority was the protection and maintenance of the area's Russian population. By choosing to put off substantive changes to the CER's organization and landholding rights in the Special District and by citing the sanctity of the original contract and the absence of a clearly defined Russian owner, Russian board members hoped to evade questions about jurisdiction to perpetuate Russian control of land. In response, the Chinese argued that the CER was not, nor had it ever been, legally part of the Russian government. According to the Chinese, the CER was a private company, and because it had operated after 1920 without Russian state protection and under the supervision of the Chinese state, it was obliged to relinquish all former political and colonial functions.

Control over land – either in the form of private property or in a nation's right to exercise political power over a bounded area – is the foundation of claims to sovereignty. By 1920, political and economic control of territory by foreign governments and their nationals in China had become a highly politicized subject. Although the concession areas and treaty ports had been based on traditional Chinese ideas about allowing lesser peoples to organize their own affairs within the Middle Kingdom, the Chinese elite in the twentieth century viewed the treaty ports and concessions as material proof of China's weakness and victimization. Chinese demands, not only for political rights but also to simply walk and be seen in areas such as streets or parks within concessions, reveals that the issue of land control went beyond contractual rights over public space. Disputes over Harbin's or Shanghai's parks or the appearance of Chinese along the formerly Chinese-free Hankou concession bund were public acts of reclamation that revealed that the Chinese, by the 1920s, were no longer willing to accede to being strangers in their own country. This point was not lost on foreign citizens in Harbin, Shanghai, or Hankou, who saw Chinese interlopers as symbols of contested rights of ownership and administration.[104] In the Special District and Harbin, the struggle over the department that administered, taxed, and supervised the land under the CER's control was not simply about controlling revenue or ensuring employment parity for the Chinese. Control of the Land Department symbolized the Chinese struggle to control the CER concession. The Special District had absorbed the Russian police, military, and courts. By claiming control over land – by taxing, regulating, and physically reshaping it – the Chinese elite hoped to make Harbin Chinese in all respects.

The land dispute was also fought in the realm of contractual language as each side challenged the meanings of words and phrases such as *administration, political role,* and *business enterprise.* Harbin's foreign consuls defended the Russian position because the superstructure of foreign privilege in China rested on similar contracts signed between China and foreign powers. The Chinese saw this defence as a betrayal because the Chinese perceived that their own intent was not to deprive foreigners of economic rights but to deprive a corporation of political rights it did not legally hold. Neither the Russians nor the foreign consuls admitted the validity of this point, for to admit the Chinese had a case was to place extraterritoriality itself into question. Thus, the uneasy, face-saving resolution of the dispute over the CER's Land Department, while temporarily solving a property conflict between the Russian and Chinese administrations, simultaneously covered up the fundamental differences in the manner in which each party legitimized its place in Manchuria.

At the heart of the Chinese-Russian conflict over the Land Department was the manner in which each side sought to define its authority in Manchuria. To the Russians, their right to control the concession's land, through the

CER, was a natural extension of their having opened up and settled the area. Russian discourse on the Land Department was dominated by two connected themes: (1) Russia, through the CER, had brought modern civilization and industry to the area, and (2) this articulation of a Russian *mission civilisatrice* was not a political act.[105]

In many ways, both the Chinese and Russians acted as colonial powers. Each power viewed the "empty" landscape of Manchuria – homeland for only the Manchus – as a canvas on which to inscribe its own image. The struggle for control of the Special District's property struck at the heart of the two nations' colonial projects on the Manchurian frontier. The Russian directors of the post-1920 CER saw control of the land as a way for the company to continue its project of developing and modernizing northern Manchuria. The Chinese elite saw control of the land as way to modernize the district in its own image, to adapt and improve on the Russian model and take into account the district's multi-ethnic population. The elite achieved this end by retaining Russian Land Department staff and permitting the use of the Russian language.

The function of the CER's Land Department was still being negotiated in 1929. The Chinese argued that the existence of two institutions caused many misunderstandings and that the remaining functions of the department would be better served under the Chinese Civil Administration. In April 1929, when the Land Department placed ten tractors for Russian tenants to use in fields on the western line, the department was again accused of carrying on agricultural work for the benefit of its Russian lessees. Tired of continued Soviet Russian delays, the Shenyang government turned the Land Department and other CER departments that were deemed not essential to the railway (for example, Veterinary Science and Education) completely over to Chinese control.[106] The Land Department was seized on 15 July 1929 during the Sino-Russian incident over the CER. Because the accord that ended the incident specified that the CER should return to its *ante bellum* status, the CER resumed control of the Land Department. The department, however, had a Chinese director and a reduced mandate. The Special District continued to have two land administrations until 1935, when the new Japanese-controlled state of Manchukuo forced the USSR to sell the CER to Japan. By this point, the issue of who controlled the Special District's property had assumed a much different character, for Japan's overt colonial project had replaced the indirect and, in hindsight, relatively easily negotiated émigré and Soviet versions of Manchurian frontier colonialism. For China, colonial control of Manchuria would have to wait until after 1949, at which point Manchuria was no longer a nuanced colonial project directed and managed from within for the benefit of all of the region's populations.

7

Whose City Is This?
Special District Municipal Governance

In China the mundane subject of municipal politics was rarely conflated with flagrant displays of sexuality or concerns about foreigners' rights. In December 1926, however, a Japanese journalist observed an incident in a park in Harbin that he felt illustrated the depths to which the Russian administration had fallen. In his opinion, loose Russian morals, coupled with an inability to provide a proper example for the Chinese, had led to the crisis in municipal governance that was sweeping through Harbin and the Special District:

> On last Sunday and in the early afternoon I, in the company of many others, saw three young fellows and a young maid engaged in what appeared to be a kissing contest. Two of the fellows would hold the girl and the third would kiss her. Such scenes cannot but reduce the prestige of whites in the eyes of the Chinese. Is it any wonder that with all these exhibitions of incompetence and lack of morality the Chinese should bit-by-bit seek to oust the Russians from their rights? The Russian Municipal servants are being gradually replaced by the Chinese, and in many other directions the latter have made their encroachments felt. Complaints are heard all around that the Chinese have not treated the Russians fairly, but it cannot be denied that the latter are equally responsible for their predicament.[1]

Despite the journalist's belief that the Russians were getting what they deserved, his newspaper, which was published in Dalian, had supported the Special District's Russian-controlled municipal councils in their conflicts with the district's Chinese administration since 1920. By 1926, the Special District's administration, tired of prolonged Russian attempts to block Chinese participation, had decided to overhaul the councils to remove their Russian majorities. By doing so, the Special District indirectly admitted the failure of its policy of accommodation, for these councils had been left intact so as not to disturb the district's Russian population. Russian council members, caught in the émigré trap of clinging to any source of institutional support, had not recognized the sprit of compromise that motivated the Special District's Chinese administrators. By refusing to co-operate, the Russian members of Harbin's Municipal Council sealed their fate.

Disputes over municipal governance were particularly intense because ethnic divisions in Harbin, northern Manchuria's largest city, were reflected in its city council. The city stands on the south side of the Songhua/Sungari River. The south bank is a broad marshy area that rests beneath a high promontory and is prone to flooding. Harbin's first Russian settlement was built on this promontory, well back from the river to avoiding flooding. As the city developed, the main administrative section moved southward, until it sat on the edge of the promontory overlooking the flood plain and river. This section, called Newtown (Nangang or "south hill" in Chinese; Novoi gorod or "new town" in Russian), is where Russian Harbin's finest buildings were constructed. If one moved east along the Bolshoi (Main) Prospect, the tree-lined boulevard that bisected Newtown, one would pass the imposing stone headquarters of the Chinese Eastern Railway (CER). Across from the CER stood the Railway Club, the residence of the CER's head, the Russian consulate, and the Law Institute. All were built in the Art Nouveau style and stood well back from the road. One would then reach a traffic circle. In its centre stood the Cathedral of St. Nicholas, a masterpiece of Vologda-style wooden church construction. From the church, one could look south down Railway Street, past large financial institutions, to the imposing railway station. Continuing to the east, one would pass several large churches and Chuirin's, Harbin's principal department store. The boulevard ended at the main Russian cemetery. The boulevard was, as Historian James Carter calls it, a ceremonial way. It was a spatial and architectural ensemble designed to impress and intimidate observers with the weight of Russian power.

Pristan and Fujiadian sat below the promontory. Pristan (Daoli or "the area within" in Chinese; Pristan or "wharves" in Russian) was the business centre of Harbin. Pristan rested on the western side of the marsh and was surrounded by the tracks of the CER, tracks that roughly mirrored the concession's physical border. Less grand and less expensive than Newtown, Pristan was where most of Harbin's shops and apartments were located. The main street – called, ironically, China Street – was lined with pastel neo-classical buildings. The street earned Harbin the nickname "the Chinese St. Petersburg."

The Eighth District was on the eastern side of Pristan and bounded on both sides by railway tracks. This area, which was within the Russian concession, served as a boundary or barrier between Russian Pristan and Chinese Fujiadian. The Eighth District contained industrial sites, such as soya bean oil plants, locomotive repair shops, and vodka distilleries.[2] It was home to the majority of Harbin's Japanese and Korean communities. It also was home to a sizeable number of Russian and Chinese workers. Contemptuous of all local governments, the Eighth District's inhabitants were a thorn in the side of both the Russian and Chinese administrations. From 1898 to 1920, Newtown and

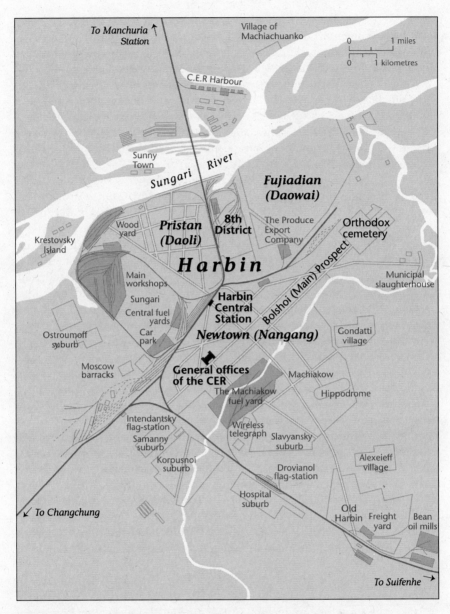

To Manchuria
Station

Village of
Machiachuanko

0   1 miles

0   1 kilometres

C.E.R Harbour

Sunny
Town

Sungari   River

Fujiadian
(Daowai)

Krestovsky
Island

Wood
yard

Pristan
(Daoli)

8th
District

The Produce
Export
Company

Orthodox
cemetery

H a r b i n

Main
workshops

Sungari
Central fuel
yards

Car
park

Harbin
Central
Station

Bolshoi (Main) Prospect

Municipal
slaughterhouse

Ostroumoff
suburb

Newtown (Nangang)

Gondatti
village

Moscow
barracks

General offices
of the CER

Machiakow

Hippodrome

The Machiakow
fuel yard

Intendantsky
flag-station

Samanny
suburb

Wireless
telegraph

Slavyansky
suburb

Korpusnoi
suburb

Drovianol
flag-station

Alexeieff
village

Hospital
suburb

To Changchung

Old
Harbin

Freight
yard

Bean
oil mills

To Suifenhe

Harbin and Environs, c. 1930 I Source: Railway Economics Bureau, I.A. Mihailoff, ed. *North Manchuria and the Chinese Eastern Railway* (Harbin: CER Printing Office, 1924), 304.

Pristan were administered by the CER and referred to as "Russian Harbin." After 1920 they became part of the Special District and were administered by Harbin's Municipal Council. Fujiadian remained under the Chinese-administered Binjiang County until 1922, when it was transferred to the Special District. It was, however, economically inseparable from the other two districts. The Chinese officials who worked in the Special District began their careers in Fujiadian, and most of Newtown's and Pristan's Chinese workers lived there.[3]

Like the city itself, Harbin's population was segregated. Newtown and Pristan were home primarily to Europeans. According to journalist Mao Hong, who lived in Harbin in the 1920s, only 20 to 30 percent of the districts' populations were Chinese.[4] Wealthy Russians lived in Newtown, while poor Russians lived in Pristan or the Eighth District. However, wealthy Chinese also took up residence in Newtown. Some, like Ma Zhongjun, the vice-head of the Special District's Municipal Administration Bureau and later mayor of Harbin, lived in large foreign homes. His children attended Russian schools, and Ma made his way about the city in a car chauffeured by a Russian. Well-off Chinese also chose to live in Pristan. Most Chinese, however, lived in Fujiadian and were migrants from Shandong and Hebei provinces who worked in Harbin's industrial plants for eleven hours a day and an average monthly wage of fifteen dollars.[5] They could not afford to live in either Pristan or Newtown, which were both divided along race and class lines.

Harbin's population grew rapidly between 1906 and 1929. In 1906 Newtown's and Pristan's combined population was 95,000 (62,000 Russians and 33,000 Chinese), and 50,000 Chinese lived in Fujiadian.[6] In 1921, according to the Chinese census, the total population of the three districts was just over 220,000 (150,000 Chinese and 70,000 Russians). Four years later, the Chinese population had increased to 212,000 and the Russians, to 92,000. By 1929, the census listed 274,000 Chinese, 28,800 Soviet Russians, and 31,400 stateless Russians.[7] The figures indicate that, demographically, Harbin had always been a Chinese city. However, a demographic majority did not translate into political or economic power for Harbin's Chinese. The sharp rise in the number of Russians in 1925 reflected the high point of the émigré flood into northern China. After that year, the number of Russians in Harbin dropped as formal Russian control over the city's institutions waned and as émigrés left for Shanghai or overseas.

Harbin's Chinese population was divided by provincial origin and occupation. According to the 1925 census, the majority – 15 and 23 percent, respectively – came from the provinces of Shandong and Hebei. Another 23 percent came from Manchuria (Jilin, Heilongjiang, and Liaoning). The Chinese population's contribution to Harbin's economy was far greater than its numbers. In highly lucrative regional industries – such as soya bean oil production, lumber and timber, and import/export – migrants from Shandong and Hebei owned 70 to 80 percent of the enterprises.[8] Their success was ascribed to their understanding of Russian labour and business practices – to knowledge acquired by working in Russia as Chinese immigrants before the revolution, when Chinese dominated the economy of the Russian Far East.[9] Following the Russian Revolution, most of the Chinese were expelled from the Russian Far East. They arrived in Manchuria with little more than their clothes and the linguistic and commercial skills they had acquired in Russia. The capacity of the Chinese community to learn Russian has been described as a triumph of Russian power, but it can equally be seen as evidence of Chinese flexibility and adaptability on the frontier. Mao Hong certainly described the predilection of Harbin's Chinese to speak Russian, follow Russian trends, and marry Russians as a contradiction of the belief that Chinese culture absorbed all others.[10]

Simon Karlinsky, a former resident of Harbin, commented on the predominance of the Russian language among the Chinese: "The only difference (between Harbin and any Russian city) was the presence of numerous Chinese shopkeepers, itinerant vendors, artisans and servants. But it was *they* who had to learn Russian, or, rather, the amusing Russo-Chinese pidgin called 'Moia-tvoia,' originated by Chinese peddlers in Siberia in the nineteenth century, which became the lingua franca for Russian-Chinese transactions in Harbin."[11] This linguistic capacity was, however, a Chinese strength that set the stage for successful joint administration. The Chinese were able to turn the "day-by-day diminishing of Russian power" to their advantage.[12]

Harbiners of Manchurian Chinese origin were not as well represented in Harbin, but they dominated the real estate industry, banking, and the fur trade. Well-educated Chinese from the provinces of Jiangsu, Jiangxi, Fujian, and Guangdong dominated government offices. Although empirically difficult to prove, it would seem that the very newness of Harbin attracted Chinese settlers who were willing to take a chance on a fluid situation and that those who succeeded were those who understood and could manipulate Harbin's Russian linguistic and cultural context. Of course, not all Chinese were business magnates. The Chinese represented the top and the bottom of the economic hierarchy, while the Russians formed an uneasy middle stratum. People from Jiangxi and Jiangsu provinces monopolized the restaurant trade, those from Hebei dominated the hair-cutting business. Industrial labour, construction work, street maintenance, and rickshaw pulling were the province of poorer people from Shandong and Hebei.[13]

Harbin's Russian community was also economically stratified and socially diverse. It is impossible to speak, in this period, of a single Russian population. Prior to the Russian Revolution, the Russian community was divided economically between administrators and workers. From the city's foundation onward, some Russians thought of themselves as the administrators, educators, directors, and employers of the Chinese and their fellow Russians. Yet, during the imperial period, these internal divisions were overlaid by an external unity. All Russians were either directly employed by the CER or lived in and benefitted from the colonial society it created. After the CER and local administration passed, partially or wholly, into Chinese hands, this externally imposed Russian unity fell to pieces. Historian Olga Bakich writes that the pre-1917 Harbin Russian population consisted largely of the petty bourgeoisie and bourgeoisie, "with urban proletariat and intelligentsia represented in much smaller numbers. The city had three main professional groups – the railway employees, the military, and the merchant-business circle; each group had its own class structure, its social club for the upper echelons, and its social life. The CER employees received higher salaries than their counterparts in Russia, and in many cases the salaries were supplemented with merit pay, living quarters, firewood, travel vouchers, treatment in the CER hospital, tuition for children in the CER schools, etc."[14]

The top of the Russian hierarchy in the CER zone was the administrative class, which worked either for the railway or pseudo-colonial offices connected to the railway. Wealthy and well educated, members of this class tended to look down on their less-well-off compatriots. There was also a sizeable working-class Russian community in Harbin prior to the revolution. The Russians brought with them class prejudices that resulted in tensions between ordinary workers and the CER's administrators. These tensions exploded into strikes in 1905 and between 1917 and 1920. Differences between Russian workers and administrators were moderated, however, by the high wages paid to all Russians working in the CER zone relative to the Chinese.

After the Russian Revolution, the goal of Russian domination in Manchuria was shattered, and Harbin's Russian community had to adapt to changing political circumstances. In addition, the community was inundated with refugees, many of whom cared little for the maintenance of the pre-revolutionary status quo. Karlinsky, who came from a pre-revolutionary family, was emphatic that Harbin was "not primarily a city of refugees" and drew a clear line between Old Harbiners and those recently arrived.[15] The older generation of CER founders and workers, called *starozhily* (veteran residents), were at odds with the new arrivals.[16] Cleavages within the Russian community over loyalty to the CER and to the project of Russian domination of the concession were deepened by the Sino-Soviet accord of 1924, which provided for joint management of the railway.

Not surprisingly, Harbin was similar to other urban outposts of Russian power in the Russian Far East and Caucasus. Like Vladivostok, Tiflis, Orenburg, and Baku, Harbin had been constructed as a centre of Russian political and economic power. These cities acted as both oases and fortresses for Russian identity in non-Russian parts of the Russian Empire. Although the CER concession was a colonial-commercial arm of the Russian government, its imprecise identity – commercial enterprise or colony? – allowed it the space to develop an identity separate from Russia. Many who immigrated to or were born in the region identified themselves as Manchurian Russians and celebrated the taming, through hard work, of a frontier of ambiguous political affiliation.[17]

The complexity of the Russian community was enhanced by the creation of a large Soviet community between 1924 and 1935. Thousands of Soviet citizens came to Harbin, and many previously stateless Russians chose Soviet citizenship as a convenient means of overcoming their ambiguous national status. The period of joint administration gave the USSR a chance to reconstitute the Russian mission in Harbin and the CER zone. The Sino-Soviet accord enabled the Soviet Union to infiltrate the CER and various departments, notably education, to carry out political work expressly forbidden by the accord. This political work, conducted in the name of transnational Socialism, had the smell of Great Russian nationalism. To their displeasure, the Chinese government found it had exchanged one form of Russian domination for another. After 1924 there were two competing versions of the Russian mission in Harbin, complete with mutually hostile populations.

Before the Special District's establishment, the CER had been responsible for administration in Newtown and Pristan and along the entire CER concession. The company's judicial, commercial, financial, land, police, education, and medical departments shared local administration. Some of these powers were delegated to the newly formed Harbin municipal government in 1909, but the CER retained veto power over all decisions made by the municipal government.[18] The relationship between the CER superintendent's office and the Harbin municipal government paralleled the supervisory-authoritarian relationship that the Russian government shared with its own municipal governments. By 1920 Chinese who had lobbied for the takeover of municipal government understood that the CER's power meant that Harbin's Municipal Council was self-governing in name only: "There is only one supervisory body, the CER. The current board of the CER is the supreme authority. Far from the stated goals of autonomy, the CER and its administration must approve the work of the Municipal Assembly. Then they can be put into practice. As for the most important cases, these are transferred by the CER to their proper bureaus or delegations of leading members. This not only despises the intention of the assembly but also gives the assembly no character of independence."[19]

Founded in 1909 as part of the Russian government's cost-cutting measures, the Municipal Council's principal tasks were tax collection and infrastructure maintenance, neither of which it accomplished fully. Harbin did not present a very pleasing face in 1911: "The streets are badly paved and drained and covered with dust, which rises in clouds during the windy weather; there are too many empty patches of ground lying waste in central and otherwise desirable places, while in others, miserable huts and shanties are crowded together in squalor and dirt."[20]

Although street paving was the raison d'être of the municipal government, by 1911, only 52 percent of the streets in Pristan and 55 percent of the streets in Newtown had been paved; of these, only 7 percent had proper paving stones.

During the rainy summer of 1910, some carriages became so mired in mud that owners had to wait until winter to chop them out of the frozen street. Harbin was described in 1916 as a city where "everything was on a large scale," but it still lacked many basic amenities such as sewers, waterworks, a central electric plant, and properly laid streets.[21] The proper construction of most streets would have to wait until the 1920s, when streets fell under the Special District's supervision.

Harbin's municipal government was never a popular institution, and voter turnout was always low. During the 1908 election, only 588 of the 1,140 Russians who were granted the franchise voted. During the 1911 election, only 344 of 852 registered voters exercised their franchise, and only forty of the sixty municipal delegates received enough votes to take their seats. The CER appointed the remaining twenty. During the 1914 election, only 566 of 1,132 eligible voters cast a ballot. Council meetings were sparsely attended, and many had to be postponed or cancelled when a quorum could not be met. Bakich reports that the city budget was "always late, while the task of regulating the length of a working day and holidays for workers took six and a half years."[22] A satirical poem published in April 1914 poked fun at the council's dismal atmosphere:

In the City Council

The accountants hum sadly.
One hears the bang of typewriters,
But there is no bustling activity.
There is not one delegate present,
And the tea stands cold.
And it is necessary not to notice
That in the corridors
No business takes place,
All is depressed and gloomy.[23]

Fiscal requirements for the municipal franchise "practically excluded all non-Russians and the Chinese from participation," even though the franchise regulations also excluded most Russians.[24] Harbin's Chinese believed that the city was not theirs politically before 1920; in reality, they were also excluded geographically and physically. Journalist Mao Hong observed that numerous Harbin Chinese did not dare to stroll along the sidewalks of Newtown and Pristan, even in Western clothing, for they risked being pushed into the street by Russians. Even if accounts such as this, like Shanghai's "no dogs and no Chinese" signs, were urban myths, they do reveal that Chinese residents felt unwelcome on the badly paved streets of pre-war Russian Harbin.[25]

The return of concessions and the municipal reform of Chinese cities became topics of national debate in 1917. The inability of Chinese to vote in concessions in which the majority of the population was Chinese was the principal issue, and most demands were limited to permitting Chinese to vote for municipal councils.[26] The First World War brought the issue of the retrogression of political privilege to the forefront of Chinese domestic politics.[27] China's involvement in the war was conditional on Allied powers' not enlarging existing concessions and returning concessions held by Entente powers to China's jurisdiction. In addition, the Chinese government asked that the entire package of foreign privileges, concessions, municipal governments, and extraterritoriality be subject to review at the war's end. In 1919, at the Paris Peace Conference, the Chinese delegation repeated this request and laid out its four-point position: (1) concessions were a form of internal colonization that impaired China's sovereignty; (2) cultural and political change within China made the separation of foreign populations unnecessary; (3) the progress made in China in municipal governance demonstrated that China was capable of assuming these duties; and (4) because China's interior was open to foreign trade, separate concessions were now unnecessary.[28]

The popularity of the Chinese movement for municipal self-government is evident in the fact that, by 1922, Beijing had over forty registered self-governing committees, and meetings on the topic regularly drew over a thousand participants.[29] In the CER concession, these two issues, concession privilege and municipal politics, entwined as the Russian Revolution undid the structure of Russian political, economic, and social control and undermined claims that that control was natural and inevitable. Seeing the opportunity presented to them, China's national and regional governments moved to assert Chinese control over the concession and to rewrite a contract that, in Chinese opinion, had been interpreted in such a way as to create an illegal Russian colony. China's pragmatic regional response, nevertheless, enforced Chinese supervision but continued to allow participation by the region's second founding population.

When Russian power in the CER concession began to unravel between 1917 and 1920, Harbin's municipal government challenged the CER's control by supporting strikes and organizing opposition to the CER's head, Dmitrii Horvath. In March 1920, members of the Municipal Assembly, perhaps because they were locked out of the town hall on Horvath's orders, called a general meeting at the Harbin Commercial High School to discuss the implications of Horvath's departure for the municipality.[30] Although the minutes of the meeting were not kept, the Municipal Council declared itself independent of the CER later that month. The Municipal Council's opposition to the CER's supervision did not continue when the new Special District revealed that it intended to take over the CER's role as supervisor. On 31 October 1920, a presidential order established the Special District. Although the order was concerned largely with establishing Chinese control over the Russian court system, its final thirteen articles dealt with the creation of Chinese-controlled municipal governments.[31]

The immediate task was to determine how much local government the new Special District would control. In its first incarnation, before the Special

District seized the Russian-controlled municipal councils in 1926, the district simply replicated the supervisory duties of the CER's Civil Department. This change was supported by the Inter-Allied Technical Board, which recommended that elected bodies "without regard to nationality" should continue to govern and that the CER should continue to cover any deficits.[32] Nevertheless, the Inter-Allied Technical Board agreed that, eventually, "the municipal administration of the Railway zone should also pass from the railroad to the Chinese government." Its members acknowledged that the transfer would be difficult because of the expense and cultural and linguistic differences between Chinese and Russians.[33]

In February 1921, the Special District's administration had the following sub-departments of the CER's Civil Department placed under its supervision: medical, veterinary, passport control, land, education, civic construction, prisons, and public sanitation. The CER's Civil Department was renamed the Department of General Affairs because its title was too close to that of a government institution for the Chinese administration's comfort. All functions and property of departments required for the railway were left in the CER's control.[34] Administration of the mental asylum, the Russian Orthodox Church, and the meteorological department were left under the CER's control but passed to the Special District within a decade.[35]

The Special District's administration also created the Municipal Administration Bureau (hereafter referred to as the Chinese Municipal Bureau). The order did not come from Shenyang: it came from Beijing, from whence the man who would become the Chinese Municipal Bureau's first director, Dong Shien, had just returned after discussing the subject of new municipal regulations with the president.[36] The bureau was authorized by presidential order 2009 in February 1921:

1 The Chinese Government authorizes the establishment of the Municipal Administration Bureau with a view to coordinating and developing the municipal administration in the Special District of the Eastern Provinces.

2 In the Municipal Administration Bureau there shall be a manager and an assistant manager to be nominated by the Ministry of the Interior, and appointed by the President, and a certain number of employees to be nominated by the manager and appointed by the Minister of the Interior.

3 The Municipal Administration Bureau shall have the power to engage advisors, who shall offer advice in regard to development and improvement of municipal affairs.

4 All important steps concerning the municipal administration in this Special District shall be taken upon the suggestion of the manager with the approval of the Minister of the Interior.

5 The various organizations and public works already existing in the Special District shall be continued.

6   Any of the existing Municipal regulations and systems, which shall be
     found to be inconsistent with the existing conditions, can be revised at the
     suggestion of the Manager of the Municipal Administration with the
     approval of the Ministry of the Interior
7   All matters, which are not covered by these regulations, shall be considered
     by the manager with the consent of the Ministry of the Interior, and the
     Head of the Special District.[37]

A number of conclusions can be drawn from these regulations. The national government was very interested in the project of municipal government in the Special District, and it considered foreign (that is, Russian) advisors important to the Special District's continued prosperity and good government. The institutions that governed the Special District, their Russian staff, and the Russian language would be retained. Finally, the Special District and its Chinese Municipal Bureau put the district's municipal councils on notice that the old system would not remain unchanged: the administration intended to reform municipal government eventually.

Following discussions between Dong Shien, the Chinese Municipal Bureau head, and the national government, the Chinese national government promulgated new national regulations for municipal self-government in July 1921. They were adopted by the Chinese Municipal Bureau that year as guidelines for the reorganization of the Special District's municipal governments. As part of the proposed changes, municipalities were given the right to make and enforce bylaws, under the supervision of the Chinese Municipal Bureau (article 5), "for all matters concerning the rights and duties of its residents." The change gave the Special District's municipalities more autonomy than they had had under the CER. The proposed new municipal franchise was restricted to Chinese nationals who had been resident in the district for more than a year and who had either paid a minimum of one dollar annually in tax, possessed three hundred dollars of immovable property, had held or were holding public office, had been engaged as schoolteachers, or had graduated from an elementary school (article 9). Election to the Municipal Council or the Municipal Assembly was restricted to Chinese citizens, twenty-five years or older, who paid two dollars annually in taxes, owned property worth five hundred dollars, or had graduated from a high school or institution of higher education (article 10). Although the franchise was restricted to Chinese citizens, the proposed regulations would have greatly expanded the number of voters.[38]

In form and duties, the planned municipal government followed the Russian model of having both an assembly and a council. The assembly would be able to pass bylaws; decide questions of reform, the abolition of abuses, and other matters of adjustment, as well as "all financial matters, taxes, fees and budgets" (article 25); and choose bills for debate in the assembly (article 33).[39] The mayor would be elected from among the assembly members and would be able to return a decision to the assembly once; if it passed again, the veto decision would pass to a provincial authority (article 38). The assembly and the council would have the right to petition against all decisions made by the mayor and his advisors, the local magistrate (who supervised ordinary municipalities), and the National Municipal Bureau (for special municipalities such as Harbin's).

The similarities between the new national regulations and the former Russian municipal system are striking. It appears that the Special District's municipal reforms influenced the national municipal reform project. Dong Shien – long interested in municipal reform – was appointed head of the Chinese Municipal Bureau immediately after his return from Beijing in January 1921, and the national municipal government regulations were tabled in July 1921, only six short months later. The Russian model of municipal government, albeit one with a greatly extended franchise, had become the national model for Chinese municipal government, and this 1921 code became the basis for all future Guomindang municipal codes.

The similarities between the Russian municipal code and new national regulations are even more striking if the Chinese municipal code of 1919 is taken into consideration. The District Self-Government Law concentrated power in non-elected, regionally appointed magistrates, and there was less opportunity for elected members to initiate and pass legislation. Powers were much more narrowly defined, and there was much less opportunity for debate. Local magistrates had the power to revoke decisions and to dissolve the assembly, a power that was removed by the 1921 code. The 1919 code was restrictive and difficult to modify. By contrast, the makers of the 1921 code envisaged a municipal code that would change as conditions changed. Finally, the 1919 code declared that residents alone "shall have rights and duties in accordance with the provision of the Law and the by-laws of the self-government body" (article 3).[40] By contrast, article 5 of the 1921 code stated that "a Municipality may make and enforce by-laws for all matters concerning the rights and the duties of its residents and matters of self-government provided that such by-laws shall not conflict with the provisions of those Regulations and other laws and ordinances." And article 8 stated that "all persons living in a municipality shall be residents of such municipality, and shall enjoy all the rights and fulfill all the duties provided for by these Regulations and the by-laws of such Municipality."[41] The language concerning rights and duties in the 1921 code was much more complex than that employed in the 1909 code, and municipal government was conceived as a dynamic process that initiated change rather than adhering to the status quo. Residents were not passive electors who were granted rights but rather individuals with municipal duties. The new code echoed the observations of the Chinese critic of Russian-controlled city government who, in Harbin's *Binjiang shibao*, reminded his readers that self-government involved the right to equal representation and the obligation of political duty for Harbin's Russian and Chinese citizens.[42]

Harbin's City Hall. | *Charoff Album of Harbin, Town and its Suburbs* (Harbin: Charoff Typesetters, 1930), 59. Author's collection.

In keeping with the Special District administration's conciliatory attitude, the new municipal regulations were not implemented until 1926, because the intransigence of the Russian members of Harbin's Municipal Council forced the Special District's administration to suppress them. Harbin's Municipal Council, still under Russian control, had one consistent position on the nature of its administrative mandate: Harbin's city government had an economic-administrative role, it was not a political administration. This argument was identical to the CER's justification for its administrative role before 1920, offering a rationale for the illegal assumption of administrative privileges in both cases. George Constantine Guins, an important figure on the Municipal Council and an active participant in city politics, argued that self-government was the council's supervision of the city's economy, not the extension of the franchise to Harbin's population. Employing a narrow definition of politics that was based on the 1909 and 1914 accords, Harbin's Municipal Council agreed that Chinese could have a supervisory role, but it argued that the number of appointees and the scope of their powers should be limited. The council members argued that the essential form and content of the city government, which left Russians in control of the franchise and decision making, should not be changed.[43]

In contrast to the Harbin Municipal Council's somewhat conciliatory position, the CER vigorously protested the removal of municipal government from its jurisdiction, even though the expense of municipal government had cost the railway in the past and despite the fact that the 1920 supplementary CER agreement had removed all political power and administrative functions from the company's mandate. In response to Dong Shien's declaration that municipal government reform would put an end to the CER's veto power and appointed positions, the company, in a letter dated 10 May 1921, stated that any changes to municipal administration had to be approved by the CER's board of directors, which still had a Russian majority. This declaration was made even though the Harbin Municipal Council had declared its independence from the CER in March 1920. The company based its position on article 6 of the 1898 contract, which stated that power to revise municipal regulations was vested in the Municipal Council and subject to the approval of the CER's board. The article, if applied, would have effectively prevented any attempts to reform municipal government to increase Chinese participation.[44] The Chinese Municipal Bureau's pragmatic decision not to immediately change the existing municipal system – it went so far as to leave CER appointees in their council seats until 1921 – was cited by the CER as proof that the system need not be changed. The Chinese Municipal Bureau pressed forward and removed the CER appointees from the municipal councils. It replaced them with a combination of elected and appointed Chinese officials.

Attempts to change the municipal government, particularly its institutionalization of foreign – that is, Russian – privilege drew immediate criticism. Dong Shien was at pains to calm the fears of the foreign community. In a speech made from Harbin's mayoral office on 12 February 1921, Dong appealed to all residents of Harbin, Russian and Chinese alike:

> The City of Harbin, with its command of railway and waterway facilities has acquired great importance as a commercial center, entering into complex relations with foreign nationals. As the city is composed of different nationals, dissimilar in customs, the habits of the administration of the city must be adapted to its peculiar circumstances. By virtue of article six of the supplementary regulations of the CER treaty, I have received the appointment to exercise the control of municipal affairs. My aims are to only further the interests of the residents of Harbin. I sincerely hope for the successful administration of the Harbin Municipal Council.[45]

In another letter to the consuls, Dong emphasized that article 6 of the accord prevented the CER from having any political role. He promised that the Chinese administration would respect the 1909 and 1914 municipal accords in the short term but that the Special District did plan future reforms.[46] The Chinese Municipal Bureau was at first under the jurisdiction of the Special District police. This arrangement reflected the bureau's early role as a supervisory institution that did not interfere with the workings of Harbin's municipal government. Although the Chinese Municipal Bureau, as the supervisor of the district's seven municipal governments, filled the position formerly held by the

CER, it was far less interventionist than its predecessor. Under its original mandate, the Chinese Municipal Bureau did not seek to change Russian institutions but instead established nominal Chinese control over municipal government and parity by appointing Chinese to important positions. Harbin's Municipal Assembly and Municipal Council, in both structure and personnel, were left intact. The number of Chinese in the Municipal Assembly was increased to nineteen, and the Municipal Council was increased to twelve members, with the addition of three more Chinese. For the next five years, Harbin had two parallel municipal powers: the Chinese Municipal Bureau and the Harbin municipal government. The Chinese Municipal Bureau would eventually be moved to the Special District's administrative branch to better reflect its role as an office committed to the reform of the district's municipal government.[47]

The Special District's administration appointed Li Xiaogen to replace the CER's appointee to the Harbin Municipal Council. The latter position was abolished by District Head Zhu Qinglan because "there was no longer any need for either direct or indirect activity of the [CER] Board in Municipal Affairs." Li had been educated in Harbin's Russian schools and had worked in the Jilin Foreign Affairs Bureau. Other CER-appointed members in town councils along the line were told to relinquish their seats to Chinese appointees.[48] The Chinese Municipal Bureau's success was due to these regional administrators, men such as Li Xiaogen; Li Lanzhou, a fluent Russian speaker and negotiator during the 1909 Municipal Council debate; Dong Shien, daoyin of Binjiang, Jilin Foreign Bureau head, and friend to Russian administrators; and Ma Zhongjun, vice-head of the newly founded Chinese Municipal Bureau and a future mayor of Harbin who was sympathetic to the Russians.[49] These men, who were native to the district or immigrants who made their careers in it, combined Chinese nationalism and knowledge of the Russian population to craft policies of municipal accommodation.

The head of the Special District himself took a keen interest in Harbin's municipal affairs and focused in particular on Harbin's potential to be a showcase for Chinese modernity and good governance. In his inaugural speech as head, Zhu Qinglan emphasized the urgent need for trained personnel in the Special District's administration to transform Harbin "into a most up-to-date city comparable with any in Europe and America."[50] Zhu emphasized that the principles and practices of municipal self-government in the Special District were not well developed and that it was necessary to study social and municipal evils and suggest suitable reforms, a reference to the Harbin Municipal Council's attempts to resist reform. It was Zhu who oversaw in 1923 the construction of two major projects that announced that Harbin was under Chinese, not Russian, control. The Paradise Temple (Jilisi) was built on Bolshoi Prospect, close to Harbin's Russian cemetery, and Number Three Middle School was the first school built in Harbin with Chinese architectural features.[51]

The Special District administration was also responsible for changing Harbin's street names from Russian to Chinese. Harbin's streets had been named after places (Amur, Mongolia, Shenyang, Manchuria), functions (School Street, Artillery Street, Police Street), or famous persons connected with either the CER (Horvath Street, Gondatti Street) or Russian culture (Tolstoy, Chekov, Nicholas). In 1925 the Special District's administration gave all the streets in Pristan and Newtown Chinese names. For instance, Nicholas Street was renamed Temple Street *(miaojie)*. The Russian-controlled Municipal Council had made the ex-CER head and its old nemesis, Horvath, an honorary citizen of Harbin in 1921. Harbin Street, an avenue north of the Cathedral of St. Nicholas, was renamed Horvath Street by the Municipal Council, a gesture that indicates that old inter-Russian rivalries were forgotten in the new context of growing Chinese control.[52] The Special District let this pass until 1925, when Horvath Street became Railway Station Street *(Chezhan jie)*.[53]

Carter argues that this act of renaming represents the highpoint of the Special District's sinification of Harbin. However, these efforts to establish a Chinese presence must be examined alongside the Special District's efforts to treat its Russian constituents fairly. Even the symbolically important act of imposing Chinese nomenclature involved compromise. Both Russian and Chinese names continued to be used on city maps well into the 1930s. Even that most controversial figure, Dmitrii Horvath, first CER General Manager, continued to have his own street. That street appears as *Railway Station St.* on Chinese maps and *Horvath St.* on Russian maps, although south of the Majiagou River, *Horvath St.* became, in Russian, *Old Harbin St.*, perhaps a compromise, or aknowledgement that Horvath was very much old Harbin. Most street signs were bilingual (as were storefront signs). Although street signs were to have been converted to Chinese by 1925, the Municipal Council's Chinese-controlled taxation committee could not find a Chinese city map in the municipal archives in 1927. The effacing of Russian street names and the removal of Russian signs was accomplished under the Japanese, not Chinese, regime.[54]

Revoking the CER's right to supervise municipal government provoked the consuls, but their criticisms reflected few concerns with the details of good governance. Rather, the criticisms of consular officials fell into two broad categories: criticism of the Special District's taxation policy and criticism of the dilution of foreign influence by the appointment of more Chinese members to the Municipal Council. In March 1921 the Chinese Municipal Bureau had requested revenues from CER taxes on wine and liquor and cargo arriving by rail. Throughout the same year, over a four-month period, the Special District police had also announced five new taxes, ranging from an automobile tax to entertainment and printing taxes, whose revenues would be used to fund the Fujiadian police, renovate Harbin's prison, and support Jilin Province's Negotiation Bureau (the successor to the Railway Bureau). All of these taxes were within the Special District's administrative scope, which now included the formerly separate city of Fujiadian, and were in the interest of fiscal and administrative rationalization. As a result of this policy, the CER in 1922 contributed 360,000 rubles out of a total yearly expenditure on the police of 1,250,000 rubles. The Chinese administration stated that this amount was in proportion to the CER's property, which constituted most of Harbin in 1923.[55]

The consuls also protested the appointment to the Municipal Council of Chinese who were "not elected in accordance with municipal procedures" – that is, they were not appointed by the CER but by the Chinese Municipal Bureau. The consuls insinuated that the Chinese authorities were using these appointments to interfere with municipal delegates.[56] Even though the consuls had their own designated consular seats, they were presumably opposed to the three new Chinese delegates on the Municipal Council speaking for Chinese interests. The consuls' actions showed little concern for the principle of equal participation, a principle they claimed to champion. Although they had expressed concerns that additional appointments would lead to voting irregularities, the consuls sent a note to the Special District on 24 November 1923 to request the addition of another consular seat on the council. The Special District ignored the request.

The consuls were not the only group that opposed new taxes. When a new grain tax was announced on 14 December 1921, there were riots in Harbin and Fujiadian, and grain stores were attacked. The new administration was more responsive to popular protest than it was to the protests of the consular corps. On 21 December the daoyin cancelled the new grain taxes, and on 28 December, because of complaints from Chinese businessmen, the Songhua River police tax was cancelled. The pragmatic solution of allowing the CER to continue to collect taxes and forward them to the Chinese Municipal Bureau had had negative consequences – the CER simply raised taxes to ensure its cut. Chinese businessmen petitioned against these taxes in 1924. They claimed that taxes had almost doubled, and appealed to the bureau to lower them. The decision was put off by the city government.[57]

In March 1924, long after municipal government had been removed from the CER's jurisdiction, and even as talks with the USSR concerning the railway's future were underway, the émigré-controlled board still claimed that article 6 gave the CER full right of administration over the Special District. In an *aide-mémoire* prepared by the board for the American consul, the CER claimed that "from the Chinese point of view and the point of view of the Chinese state constitution, such a transfer of the administrative power [to the CER] was fully lawful and natural." All levels of the Chinese administration had considered this interpretation incorrect since 1898. The CER's board claimed that because the municipal government was responsible to the company and not to the Russian government, the company could not be defined as political. The board members ignored the political and colonial precedents set by the illegal creation of Russian municipal governments. In the émigré board members' opinion, the Chinese government was, by the original 1898 contract, "deprived of the right of keeping in the zone of alienation any kind of organs of its own Government." Even the creation of the Special District was deemed illegal because "the position of a High Civil Administrator, not subordinate to the Board of Directors [of the CER] is illegal, because, in accordance with the contract [of 1898] the district where he can enjoy his power is in absolute and exclusive competence of the railway company."[58] The CER board's stubborn position must be put into context. Each Russian board member believed the CER zone and railway was Imperial Russian property and they were the only remaining representatives of the imperial mandate. Continued Russian economic domination in the zone, and their own positions, they believed, rested on continued Russian control of the railway. Ongoing negotiations with the Soviet Union (in 1924) made these men very nervous. Finally, Chinese administration and control created a negative precedent for those who defended foreign concession privilege and extraterritoriality in China.

The Harbin municipal government did all within its power to resist the Chinese Municipal Bureau. The Municipal Council protested the bureau's establishment, stating that the reforms completely changed the legal relationship between "the rights of the controlling body, the CER, and the municipality." The Harbin Municipal Assembly made the dubious argument that the CER's relationship to city government had been purely economic, not political, and resolved that the Chinese had no authority to change the existing status of the assembly. The assembly's compromise, that all proceedings be forwarded to the daoyin, sacrificed nothing, for this was required according to the assembly's original statues (1909).[59]

Official language disputes also poisoned relations between the municipal government and the Chinese Municipal Bureau. The Special District went to great lengths to accommodate the Russians, especially by continuing to use Russian as the language of business. In 1922 the administration hired Russian teachers to improve the Russian-language skills of its Chinese staff. And when rumours circulated that the Russian school curriculum would be radically changed after the Soviets took over their half of the CER, General Ma Zhongjun of the bureau moved to silence them. In October 1924, the bureau prohibited changes to the curriculum in all Russian schools in the Special District, including schools under the control of the CER. Due to the administration's efforts to accommodate the Russians within the Russian-dominated Municipal Assembly and Municipal Council, as decreed by the 1909 agreement, the language of business remained Russian, even though Chinese and Russian had become the Special District's working languages. The Chinese Municipal Bureau communicated with the Harbin municipal government in both languages, and members of the municipal government replied only in Russian. Not surprisingly, their refusal to speak Chinese provoked complaints. When the municipal government was forced to hire Chinese interpreters and translators, it complained that it cost 945 rubles a month.[60]

In a July 1924 interview in the Russian newspaper *Novosti zhizni,* Fu Guicheng of Harbin's Municipal Assembly criticized both the Russian and the Chinese members of the assembly and council. Many Chinese members, in his opinion, did not understand enough Russian to protect the interests of Harbin's Chinese citizens. The Russian members, in turn, were unsympathetic to their Chinese colleagues and refused to learn Chinese or permit the use of Chinese in government transactions. For example, given the increased number of Chinese patients attending the City Hospital (which was funded by the Municipal Council and the Special District), Fu had requested the appointment of additional Chinese and Chinese-speaking doctors. The request was defeated by the Russian majority. (Fu would later spearhead the transition to complete Chinese control.) The frustration of Chinese members such as Fu is understandable. Chinese was not an official language of business in Harbin's municipal government, although French, English, and even Japanese were sometimes used and accommodated. Letters of complaint from Chinese members to the Special District all mention the exclusive use of the Russian language and the exclusion of Chinese. One delegate complained that the Russian language was being used as a form of cultural capital to control Chinese members.[61] A compromise could have been to the benefit of the Russian members because many Chinese members already spoke Russian. But Russian would remain the working language of municipal government in Harbin until the early 1930s. Had the Russian members agreed to a policy of official bilingualism, most of the business would still have been conducted in Russian.

Instead, Russian members, in a series of interviews, stood by their position that Russian was the principal language of the majority of residents of Pristan and Newtown and would remain the only language of Harbin city government.

From *Novosti zhizni:*
The Harbin Municipal Council is neither a Chinese funded nor administered institution. It is a political and economic organization of the residents of Harbin. In as much as Russians form the majority of Harbin residents, the Russian language was made the official language of the city. The Chinese language is too complex to be used in the extensive interests of a few tens of thousands of foreign residents.

From *Russkoe slovo:*
Despite the fact that Harbin stands on Chinese territory, it is not a Chinese city, since it was constructed with Russian money and its population mostly consists of Russians. Therefore, it is quite just that there should be maintained the already existing order.[62]

Each of the articles reveals the deep chasms between the Special District's Chinese and Russian citizens. Many Russians continued to believe that they were the dominant population and that the concession's economic success was due to the Russians. That the Chinese administration was now in control did not register with the Russian population, perhaps because the Municipal Council and the CER board still perpetuated the myth of Russian control. Consuls supported the Russian position to further their agenda: to preserve concessionary privileges. According to the American consul, it was impossible for the municipality's business to be conducted in Chinese because the organization was "purely Russian" in operation and because few Russians spoke Chinese.[63] An editorial in the Japanese-owned *Manchuria Daily News* stated that Russian should be the city government's working language because 75 percent of its members were Russians. The article sidestepped the fact that the majority of the city's population was by then Chinese.[64]

Parity in the allocation of resources also divided the Russian and Chinese members of the municipal government. The Chinese position was that monies were being unfairly allocated for the benefit of émigrés and Russian institutions. In June 1923 council member Li Xiaogen complained that 800,000 rubles of the council's annual salary budget of 1.8 million rubles had been spent on Russian staff and that the Chinese Municipal Bureau's advice to the council to lay off some employees had been ignored. The Chinese members pointed out that the municipal government's expenditures for 1923, when the city was 16,500 rubles in debt, were revealing. Repairs to the Songhua River embankment cost 10,000 rubles, 18,000 rubles were spent on care of the insane, and 55,000 rubles were dispensed as cash gifts to city employees about to retire. For the fiscal year 1924, the assembly and council spent 1,670,000 rubles on schools, hospitals, public health, road repair, and charities that were, primarily, for the benefit of the Russian community and within the Russian sections of the city. According to the Chinese members' calculations, Chinese constituents received only 10 percent of the city budget, and only ten of six hundred municipal government employees were Chinese.[65]

In defence of the assembly and council, their mandate covered only Newtown and Pristan, areas that had been traditionally controlled and populated by Russians. The Chinese population in these neighbourhoods was growing, however. Chinese, according to one Russian source, paid only 21 percent of municipal taxes, whereas Russians paid 45 percent and the foreign community 34 percent. Russians and Chinese made up 51.4 percent and 41.2 percent, respectively, of Pristan's population in 1923; however, 64 percent of the Russians owned property, whereas only 25 percent of the Chinese did so. In Newtown, the figures for the Russian and Chinese populations were 71.7 percent and 25.5 percent, respectively. While 69.4 percent of Russians owned property, only 14.6 percent of the Chinese counted themselves as property owners.[66]

The Russians could not accept equal Chinese participation in city government for these reasons but also for reasons of national pride, demographic and ethnic insecurity, and prejudice against their Chinese neighbours. The disappearance of formal Russian power in Manchuria had increased the symbolic and economic importance of municipal government to Harbin's Russian community. Formerly ignored by the Russian population, municipal governments acquired a new significance as one of the few institutions still controlled by a Russian majority. They were an important source of funds, status, and employment for émigré Russians. By 1921, Harbin's Russians had been stripped of their former extraterritorial status and were subject to Chinese control. As émigrés, they felt under siege by both the USSR and China; consequently, any issues of linguistic, economic, and franchise participation in the Special District's municipal governments were highly charged.

The municipal elections of 1922-23 revealed just how much the Russians were unwilling to concede to the Chinese. These elections, fought over the issue of Chinese seats in Harbin's Municipal Council and Municipal Assembly, saw some Russian members rally the Russian population to the defence of a Russian city government. They equated a Russian-controlled city administration with European norms, and covert and overt racial slurs were used against Harbin's Chinese citizens. The electoral system itself was a complicated matter, designed initially by the CER to block true representative politics. The municipal government was not directly elected; instead, electors were divided into blocs, and each bloc submitted two lists – sixty delegates for election to the assembly and twelve for election to the council. The blocs then negotiated among themselves for a final list – or ticket, as it was referred to – of delegates' names. The decision, by custom, had to be unanimous. The election itself was not by secret ballot. Potential delegates' names were placed on jars, and the electors filed by and placed either white ball (yes) or a black ball (no) in the jar. Those who received the designated minimum number of white balls were elected. In the event that some of the seventy-two seats went unfilled, the CER had the right to fill the seats by appointment. During the 1922 elections, the blocs represented the spectrum of political views. There was a CER bloc, a Japanese bloc, a Russian professionals' bloc, a Chinese bloc, a Russian liberal bloc, and a workers' bloc. In the Municipal Assembly, nineteen seats were set aside for Chinese members; in the Municipal Council, two of the eight seats were reserved for Chinese.[67]

On 15 September 1922, the bloc representatives met at the Russian Chamber of Commerce to discuss the ticket of council and assembly delegates. The Chinese electors wanted to increase the number of Chinese delegates by sixteen to bring the total number of Chinese seats to thirty-five – a majority in the lower house (Municipal Assembly). A Chinese majority of thirty-five in the assembly would not necessarily have given the Chinese a true majority. The remaining thirty-seven seats were divided between Russian and consular delegates, and the latter often voted with the Russians.[68] In the upper house, or Municipal Council, Chinese electors wanted to add three council seats to the two reserved for Chinese (the Russians had four council seats, and two were reserved for foreigners). The Russian electors offered the Chinese eighteen seats in the assembly, one fewer than in the previous sitting, and no additional seats in the council. The two sides refused to compromise, and the stormy meeting ended. Because of the blocs' inability to agree on a common list, all of the blocs submitted a full ticket of names for election – 243 names for eighty seats. The Chinese electors threatened to boycott the election and refuse to make their tax payments. Meeting with the Russian and Chinese blocs' representatives, Ma Zhongjun, the vice-head of the Chinese Municipal Bureau, urged the two sides to co-operate in the interests of the city. The Russians pointed out that although the Chinese were demographically superior, Russians paid more taxes. The Chinese did not deny this – Russians in both Newtown and Pristan paid a total of 880,651 rubles in tax, while the Chinese only paid 264,099 rubles. The Chinese argued, however, that population, not taxation, should determine representation.[69]

The conflict revealed a fundamental gap in the two sides' understanding of the municipal government's purpose. If the government was, as the Russians argued, purely an economic body, then participation should be based on economic contribution, for an economic body had no political role. If municipal government was political, as the Chinese argued, then representation should be based on the principle of one person, one vote.[70] The election provoked an interesting semantic discussion about the true nature of Harbin's municipal government and revealed just how far the émigrés would go to deny that they were under Chinese control. The Russian characterization of the municipal government's role also offers insight into the dynamics of émigré politics. Before 1920, municipal government in Harbin had been Russian in ethnicity, language, and composition. Consular efforts to restrict the powers of the Municipal Council (or efforts to increase non-Russian foreign participation) had been soundly resisted in the name of preserving Russia's mandate in Manchuria. After 1920, faced with Chinese pressure and the disappearance of the Imperial Russian state, the Russian-controlled Municipal Council chose to transform its Russian identity into an international identity. Significantly, it did not choose to become a Russo-Chinese institution. The CER and the Municipal Council encouraged consular participation and increased consular representation to counter Chinese participation. In some cases, the Chinese were described as being culturally unable to administer foreigners, a charge echoed in other Chinese concessions. In one case, *Russkii golos,* a right-wing émigré paper, urged the municipal government to allow more foreigners to participate. Along with an increased tax base, the foreign presence would "play an important role toward making Harbin a cultured town."[71]

The aforementioned foreigners were Americans. Americans in Harbin boycotted municipal politics because they refused to acknowledge a government that could tax Americans but would not allow them to vote. Harbin's mayor, Peter Tishenko, in a not so subtle jab at the Chinese, pointed out that "the submission of American citizens to the regulations of the municipality and their sincere participation in Municipal affairs will do much for all concerned voters in developing the activities of the Municipality and town economy on principles of European culture."[72] N.N. Bektjaschinsky, in his 1925 article on Harbin's municipal government, characterized the government as international and claimed that it had a "purely economical nature."[73] His meaning was clear. Harbin's municipal government could have multiple identities: it could be Russian or European, non-political or international. It could not be Chinese or Sino-Russian. The Russian majority not only denied Chinese participation in Harbin's government, it also denied the government even a modicum of Chinese identity.

As the elections approached, Russians were urged to support Russian candidates. In one newspaper article, Russians were called on to vote for a united Russian bloc to "oblige the Chinese to be more moderate in their seeking for places." Chinese delegates, the article explained, "do not possess enough steadiness ... and the lack of experienced city workers among the Chinese will decrease the quality of work of the Harbin City Administration."[74] Another paper called the election the "most important test of Russian civil rights in Manchuria" and urged its readers not to let the Russian majority slip out of their hands.[75] The election had come to centre on the issues of the suitability of the Chinese for participation in municipal politics and the preservation of Russian rights in Manchuria.

The election revealed the weaknesses of the electoral system. The voting itself was tense: "Suddenly the crowd heard that the Chinese voters were placing black balls without exception into all urns of Russian candidates. There was a strong propaganda against permitting foreigners [the Chinese] to enter into the administration. Voters grew more and more excited. Somebody shouted, 'Do not make a *Hoocha* [a common Harbin nickname for a Chinese coolie] city out of Harbin!'"[76] There are several interesting points to be made about this spontaneous expression of civic and ethnic nationalism. First, some Russians characterized Chinese, in whose country they resided and under whose governments they lived, as foreigners. This reflected the Russians' belief that Harbin, Manchuria, and the Special District were their home, and it denied that same sense of belonging to their Chinese neighbours. The profound anxiety that Russians experienced at the thought that Harbin would become a Chinese city was reflected in their use of the pejorative term *hoocha*. As for the Chinese electors, they responded by using their greater numbers to place black balls – that is, no votes – in the jars of Russian candidates. Five hundred of the 1,357 electors were Chinese, and they capitalized on a politically divided Russian electorate. The Chinese voters responded to racist taunts by voting as a group against the Russian candidates. The Russians, in turn, voted as a group against the Chinese. Only four of the 253 candidates – three Chinese and one Japanese – received a sufficient number of white balls. That one of the Chinese was Li Xiaogen was a testament to his popularity among both the Chinese and the Russians.

A second election was called for 21 January 1923, and a new Russian bloc, the Democrats, attempted to form a coalition with Chinese electors. The

Democrats drew the criticism of Russian traditionalists who said they were traitors: "Thus does one of the Harbin groups, proudly calling itself democratic, understand its civic duty toward the Russian population, the defence of the Russian cause in the Railway Zone." Russians eligible for the franchise were urged to pay their tax debt and vote for the General City Bloc, which had traditionally controlled the municipal government.[77] Because of Russian agitation, 1,738 Russian electors (an increase of 481) voted in the second election, while the number of Chinese electors remained at 500. Only twelve candidates – all Russian – were successful. That even prominent Chinese candidates such as Li Xiaogen received only three hundred votes was a testament to Russian determination not to allow a Chinese majority. Chinese may also have been angry with their own candidates. As a result of the election, the Chinese Municipal Bureau was permitted to appoint the remaining forty-eight seats. In a spirit of compromise, the bureau chose those candidates who had received the most white balls – they were all Russian. The Chinese retained the same nineteen assembly seats. Mayor Tishenko was re-elected, but two other men (like Tishenko, graduates of the Far Eastern Institute in Vladivostok who spoke Chinese and were described as Harbin liberals) were not and had to be appointed.[78] Why had these men not reached out to Chinese delegates and formed a coalition? The answer lies less in their liberalism and more in their primary Russian identity.

In the subsequent Municipal Council elections, four Russians, one Chinese, and two foreigners were elected, and the bureau appointed one additional Chinese member, Liu Minshen. The Chinese assembly members were unhappy with the same number of seats, and at an assembly meeting on 20 January 1923, they asked for three additional seats. After a two-hour debate in which Liu spoke for the Chinese side in excellent Russian, the council agreed that the assembly could elect one more Chinese. But when the assembly rejected this motion, the Chinese members walked out in protest.[79] Russian members justified their decision by citing the Chinese population's lack of experience with municipal government. They clearly saw the Chinese as bad losers: they stated that in Europe and America "one knows how to submit to the decision of the majority."[80]

Ma Zhongjun, the vice-head of the Chinese Municipal Bureau, once again tried to act as a mediator during a meeting of Municipal Assembly members at his home. Arguments for more Chinese seats were countered by arguments about Russian tax dollars and Russian experience with municipal government. The final proposal, for one additional Chinese seat and one seat for a member without nationality (providing he was ethnically Russian), was passed, and, in March 1925, one new Chinese delegate took his seat on the Municipal Council.[81] The Chinese Municipal Bureau was convinced by the election debacle that more needed to be done to effect Chinese control over the Special District's municipal government. In a secret letter to the Special District concerning the Russian-dominated municipal government, the bureau's head argued that because Russian municipal councils were more powerful than the Special District's bureau, they damaged China's sovereignty and limited local Chinese power. He stressed that the CER's new commercial identity negated its former influence over municipal government and that China could take control of the assembly and council before the next election, which was scheduled for 1926. The 1920 CER accord, he explained, cancelled the older 1909 and 1914 treaties, which were "garbage." The head suggested that the new municipal government should be constituted with a number of foreign advisors, "so as to make the foreigners feel as if they had input, but not giving them legislative power." An administrative body elected by all nationalities and similar to the assembly should be created. The new administrative body would, in turn, elect a supervisory body, similar to the council, whose head and vice-head would both be Chinese and to which a few token foreigners could be appointed. He admitted that his solution was only "half-and-half": foreigners would still have a role, but the Chinese would be in the majority and control administrative power.[82]

The Chinese Municipal Bureau, commenting on the "usurpation principles" that characterized the original municipal agreements, proposed new regulations based on the 1921 national municipal regulations. These regulations, it believed, would not offend "Chinese sovereignty in the settlements with municipal government" and would extend municipal government to settlements that presently had none.[83] Despite the bureau's concern about the original colonial nature of municipal government, its members continued to value Russian participation. The sole difference from the 1921 regulations was that Chinese citizenship would now be required for the franchise, a nod to the fact that stateless Russians still dominated the municipal governments.[84] Both the Chinese and the Russian languages were to be used for municipal business, but Chinese would have priority. All "measures of a social character started by the CER" would be absorbed by the new councils, as would the leasing or purchase of property. The emphasis placed on control over land in the 1923 regulations reflected the Special District administration's efforts to take over the CER Land Department (see Chapter 6). CER workers who resided in CER-owned homes would not be eligible for the franchise, presumably because they paid no taxes and did not own property. Because most of the outlying stations' populations consisted of CER workers, many Russians would be disenfranchised, as would Chinese workers. However, no mention is made of a franchise restriction for CER employees in the 1924 provisional statute. Finally, the new councils would be supervised by the Chinese Municipal Bureau.[85]

When this information became public, the response of the Russians and the consuls was uniformly negative. Some argued that the proposed regulations would "chinafy" the entire municipal system and put an end to the "settlement self-administration of the Russians and, consequently, of the general European type."[86] Despite this opposition, Chinese authorities went ahead and published the new electoral rules in October 1923. But further reform was put aside during Sino-Soviet talks about the CER's future. Some Chinese, unconnected to the Special District, saw the Shenyang agreement as an opportunity to seize municipal power for China. At a meeting of the nationalist group Young China, it was suggested that any future municipal settlement should permit only Chinese on the council. A majority of the club's members, however, voted down the suggestion because Russians retained too many interests in the city to be eliminated. If the Chinese attempted to dislodge the Russians, they argued, the Russians would cease to pay taxes. The club's compromise was the appointment of a Chinese vice-director and the inclusion of Chinese as an official council language.[87]

During celebrations to bring in the new year, all talk of municipal reform was temporarily forgotten. The Moderne Hotel, the Railroad Club, and cabarets were packed, and celebrations continued until late the next morning. At their customary levees – given by the CER, the Special District's administration, and Harbin's municipal government at their respective headquarters – there was much talk about the upcoming Sino-Soviet conference. At the Railroad Club, after the Russian Orthodox service, a telegram of congratulations from Dmitrii Horvath, now retired in Beijing, was read aloud and toasts were made to his health. Special District Head Zhu Qinglan and Municipal Bureau Vice-Head Ma Zhongjun made the rounds of the festivities, and Zhu was congratulated for opening a senior's home for over five hundred Russians as part of his work as chairman of the International Committee for Indigent Russians. Feeling generous, Zhu gave the CER club permission to play cards until the early hours, so long as no gambling took place.[88]

The transfer from émigré to Soviet Russian co-administration of the CER did not greatly affect Russian control over the Special District's municipal governments. Most assemblymen read Soviet papers and kept their seats. The new Soviet administration proved reluctant to give up the Russian-controlled councils, although the transfer had been mandated in the Shenyang and Beijing agreements. As a consequence, conflicts over municipal government continued throughout 1925. In December 1925 the Chinese Municipal Bureau asked that Harbin's municipal government be placed completely under its jurisdiction. When the assembly's Chinese and pro-Chinese members attempted to pass these changes, a bloc of delegates that favoured the new Soviet co-administrators killed the measure. This confirmed the Special District administrators' concern that Soviet administrators of the CER were unduly influencing Russian delegates. A strong CER bloc of voters and municipal delegates who were openly pro-Bolshevik and held Soviet passports had consistently opposed all Chinese attempts to revise either the membership or the content of municipal government. After Russian municipal government was suppressed, the Soviet members of the CER's board would refuse to pay taxes to the municipality for three years.[89]

In 1925 the head of the Special District, Zhang Huanxiang, secretly agreed to the Chinese Municipal Bureau's request for a new provisional municipal government.[90] This request, not published until 1931, explained how the assemblies and councils could be suppressed and how the Special District's administration could finesse the legal conflict. Written by Zhang Huanxiang himself before the Shenyang accord was signed, the report represents Zhang's personal views on the subject. Zhang explained that the CER had controlled the concession before 1920 and that municipal governments had been independent in name only. The Special District's administrators had hoped that the publication of new municipal regulations in 1921 and 1923 would prompt the institution to reform itself, but this failure, and the failure to pass language and proportional representation motions, left Zhang to conclude that the Chinese would never control the assemblies and councils as they were presently constituted. Therefore, as long as municipal government remained under Russian control, no change was possible.

Zhang specified three problems with the municipal government. The first was the unequal allocation of resources to the Russian community. The second was municipal regulations that specified that the council head must be a Russian national and that the language of business must be Russian. Finally, Zhang worried that a Soviet Russian majority might dominate the council; if it did so, control of the city would slip completely from Chinese hands. Zhang defended the original 1921 regulation that only Chinese nationals could vote by arguing that émigrés would be retained in municipal governments in a consultative capacity by a Chinese-controlled administration. However, foreign taxpayers, the report stated, would probably refuse to pay taxes. Zhang Zuolin, according to the report, was against Zhang Huanxiang's reorganization and specified that it could not be accomplished before a settlement with the USSR.[91]

Perhaps emboldened by the prospect of reform, in January 1926, Chinese delegates pressed for the addition of more Chinese members to the council and the assembly and for the inclusion of Chinese as an official language in municipal government. The majority of Russian assemblymen rejected this proposition, and the Chinese delegates walked out. In February the Chinese Municipal Bureau asked the Municipal Council and Municipal Assembly to enact the 1923 regulations. In order 1202, issued by the Special District, the bureau sent the council a copy of the regulations and "awaited the completion of their examination."[92] The city government did nothing until March, when its members agreed to divide the city into electoral districts and introduce a proportional system of elections based on the Chinese model.[93] By then, however, it was too late. On 23 March 1926, Harbin's Municipal Council passed a motion to formally replace the CER's authority with that of the Chinese Municipal Bureau. The motion to have both Mandarin and Russian as official municipal languages, however, did not pass, and the Chinese delegates stormed out. George Constantine Guins, head of the Municipal Council, unsuccessfully tried to tone down the Chinese delegates' rhetoric by refusing to allow the term *sovereign rights* to enter into debates about a "non-political Municipal Council."[94] Three days later, on 26 March, at 12:30 p.m., the head of the Chinese

Municipal Bureau, Li Xiaogen, arrived at City Hall and asked the delegates to come to the chairman's room. There, Li announced to the mayor and his assistants that the assembly and council were dissolved by order of the Special District's head and that a provisional committee had already been formed. Fu Guicheng, advocate of the language issue, replied in Chinese and Russian that he understood the order and took up the role of temporary chairman. The Russian delegates were told to hand over all documents before they left. There was some unpleasantness: Russian delegates found their way barred by Chinese guards, who refused to let them pass and who understood no Russian other than "Interpreter, please!" Following Fu's intervention, the Russians were allowed to leave.[95]

In a meeting held at the end of March between the consuls and District Head Zhang Huanxiang, Zhang acknowledged that he had given the order for the municipal government to be suppressed after the quarrel over the language issue. He also disclosed that the plan to radically change the municipal government's form had been in place since the signing of the 1924 Sino-Soviet accord. Zhang complained that it was impossible for the present municipal government to satisfy Chinese demands because the Russians had, according to the electoral rules, a majority. He stated frankly that the goal of the municipal reform was to create a Chinese-controlled government. Even though he would take into consideration Harbin's particular circumstances, he was not willing, at that time, to discuss arrangements with the Russians. The patience of the Special District's administrators had run out.

A temporary committee of twelve Chinese, headed by Fu Guicheng – a Harbin businessman and graduate of the Harbin Russian Commercial School who had boarded with a Russian family and spoke fluent Russian – took over the Municipal Council's duties.[96] During a meeting with the consular corps, General Zhang said it was chiefly at the urging of the Chinese business class that the old municipal system had been taken over. Of the twelve committee members, nine were businessmen who managed businesses that ranged from oil factories, hotels, and teahouses to steamships and newspapers. Eight had been members of the former Municipal Assembly. The temporary committee met from March to November, and its minutes are revealing. Conscious that they were crafting a new form of municipal government, the committee members wanted the new regulations to be comprehensive. The regulations were reviewed several times, rejected, and returned for rewriting. Chinese were appointed to important positions, and, throughout June and July, the reorganization of municipal departments included the firing of Russian staff. Russian staff members were retained if they were deemed useful, and the committee attempted to fairly allot funding to the two communities. Two new committees were struck to take over the revenue and revision departments. Chinese institutions, such as the Confucian Temple (in the process of construction), were given money, but Russian Orthodox churches were also provided funding in the form of municipally subsidized repairs. Many of the committee's meetings

Cartoon from the Japanese-published *Manchuria Daily News* criticizing the forced closure of the Harbin Municipal Council. This depicts General Zhang Huanxiang closing the Harbin Municipal Council in March 1926. | *Manchuria Daily News,* 1 June 1926. Author's collection.

concerned the reconstruction of Harbin's sidewalks. Pensions for former municipal workers were cancelled, but individual cash settlements were paid to prominent former members such as Dr. Guins. Much attention was paid to equipping Chinese and Russian schools (see Chapter 8), and committee members noted at several meetings that Chinese was still not the working language of municipal business. Despite the efforts of the Chinese administration to impose the use of Chinese, Russian remained the working language of municipal business. Several taxpayers, both Russian and Chinese, approached the committee to have taxes lowered or commuted. These petitions were judged on a case-by-case basis; in cases where the committee saw genuine need, taxes were lowered and fines were waived.[97] When contracts were tendered, the work most often went to Russians, who tended to submit the lowest bids.

On June 1926, "with the opinions of Marshall Zhang Hwan Hsien [sic] as well as the public opinion of the people of the city, who gathered together and discussed harmoniously in accordance with local conditions and in reference to the systems of Eastern and Western nations with the spirit of self-government," new municipal government regulations were promulgated.[98] Under the new regulations, Harbin's new Municipal Assembly would consist of forty Chinese delegates. Seven seats would be reserved for foreign members and three for Russian members without Chinese passports. The new Municipal Council would have twelve members, six elected by the assembly and four appointed by the Special District. One foreigner and one Russian would be appointed by the Special District, and the Special District's head would appoint the mayor and would be able to veto any municipal decisions. His two deputy mayors would be appointed by the Special District and the Municipal Council, respectively. Only those Chinese nationals who were twenty years old or older and paid at least two dollars in tax annually would be enfranchised. Russians with Chinese citizenship could have been a potential fifth column, but Zhang Huanxing, in an uncompromising fashion, stated that if every Harbin Russian took out Chinese citizenship, franchise regulations would be changed again.[99]

The consular powers protested, especially what they considered to be Zhang Huanxiang's undue influence and the power of the Special District to appoint members (they conveniently forgot the extensive powers once exercised by the CER). The Special District's head avoided the issue by explaining that the self-governing capacities of the Chinese were different from those of foreigners – the "municipal council of their hearts' desires" might be formulated in a few years.[100] The consuls decided to reject the draft regulations. The foreign-owned *Manchuria Daily News* wrote that the Chinese should be allowed to formulate a political system with Chinese at the centre, for it would teach them to respect regulations and teach them good governance.[101]

Like Harbin's Russian population, the Chinese did not respond quickly to changes in municipal affairs. According to the 1926 census, 5,197 Chinese in Pristan and Newtown qualified for the right to vote under the new electoral qualifications, and 1,448 could stand for either the assembly or the council. Voting was now by secret ballot rather than the notorious ball system. In the elections held on 16 October 1926 to fill forty assembly seats, only one candidate received sufficient support. Supplementary elections were later held for the other thirty-nine seats. Zhang opened the new council in October, and Harbin's self-government – which included Newtown, Pristan and Majiagou – was proclaimed an established fact on 1 November. There were no Russians or other foreigners present at the opening, although Russian members had been elected. The new mayor was Zhu Chen, the former head of the Chinese Municipal Bureau.[102]

In March 1928, during celebrations of the Special District's fifth anniversary, the Chinese paper *International* praised the appearance of Harbin's streets and sidewalks since the assumption of full municipal control by the Chinese. J.B. Powell, a European observer, likewise wrote that the Chinese administration had paved many of Pristan's worst streets and was beginning to install a sewage system. China Street, formerly "impassable in muddy weather ... has been paved and double tracked for the street car system in modern American fashion with a row of ornamental lampposts down the middle."[105] In other articles, local municipal authorities were praised for having a Russian education that familiarized them with European ways. These same Chinese authorities were complimented for having the good sense to employ Russians and for continuing plans for the city's development that had been made long ago by Russian employees.[104] These same Russians, however, were slowly losing their dominant economic position to the Chinese. Even Pristan's China Street, a main street known for its Russian shops, was being taken over by Chinese owners, and "all over town more tracts of land and houses are being transferred to Chinese ownership, and the rents are being raised by avaricious landlords at every chance."[105]

In December 1929, the Three Northeastern Provinces officially rejoined the central Chinese government, although the Guomindang (GMD) flag had flown over Harbin since December 1928. According to the American consul, however, the populace showed little interest in the change.[106] Following formal acknowledgment of the GMD's control over the Special District, the region implemented the GMD's 1930 municipal law, which stipulated that citizens had to have been naturalized for ten years before they could participate in municipal politics. The law sought to curtail the participation of Russians who held Chinese citizenship. Despite these losses, within the context of the new municipal politics, the Russian population could make its presence felt. For instance, when Chinese drivers in early December 1928 intimidated Russian patrons of the Chinese-operated tram service, the Russian population boycotted the municipally owned trams. An official apology from the Chinese administrators of the Special District ended the boycott.[107]

The Chinese authorities did attempt to tame Harbin's wild nightlife when the Municipal Council promulgated new regulations that obliged restaurants and cabarets to close by 2 a.m. and 5 a.m., respectively. Article 11 of the dance hall regulations prohibited any female dancer from appearing nude and from waiting on any member of the audience.[108] The first offence was punished with a fine, while a second offence meant the establishment would be closed. Dance clubs and schools were placed under strict supervision, and shows were to wind down by midnight. The Municipal Council slowly changed "wild and wicked and wet" Harbin into a respectable town. The change reflected the aspirations of the middle-class Chinese elite who controlled municipal politics.[109]

Certainly, the days when Chinese felt unsafe walking the streets of Pristan and Newtown were gone. Fujiadian Chinese, Mao Hong reported, no longer scattered when a Russian car and chauffeur entered their neighbourhood. Instead, the car now moved to avoid them, and if the Russian chauffeur dared to strike anyone, the result was a damaged car and a driver chased back to Pristan. Chinese now felt free to stroll in the municipal park, which had formerly restricted their admission. The Pristan park, under the former Russian municipal administration, had only admitted prosperous-looking Chinese who wore Western clothing. After the administrative transfer, the park became very popular with Chinese, and they gradually replaced the Russian park workers. Nevertheless, dominant values about what was considered appropriate dress and behaviour did not change under the middle-class Chinese administration. For example, in August 1926, a Chinese woman was beaten by a Chinese worker because she was judged not well dressed enough to enter a park.[110]

While Russians claimed that the Special District's municipal governments were not political bodies, the Chinese elite claimed that the municipal government was a political tool of the Russian government, under the control of the colonialist CER. The Chinese sought to correct this imbalance by removing the CER's authority and replacing it with that of the Chinese Municipal Bureau. By not altering the Special District's municipal governments, by allowing the Russians to continue to exercise their franchise, and by extending civic government through new regulations, the Chinese authorities demonstrated a remarkable sensitivity toward the Russian community under their control. They were willing to ignore the colonialist origins of city government to construct an institution that would reflect the needs of all residents in the district. Despite conflicts with the Russians, the Chinese profited from the experience. The administrative structure the Chinese elite created in the Special District was the most sophisticated municipal government in China and continued to be so until the Japanese invasion of 1932.

Colonialist and racist attitudes held by Russian Harbiners did not allow them to compromise with Chinese citizens. Abandoned by their home country and believing that they had to preserve the last piece of czarist Russia, Harbin Russians were unwilling to give up control of the one institution left to them. Instead, the Russian community retreated into a fortress of legal nitpicking and discourses about Russian racial and administrative superiority. They resisted the opportunity to create a new identity for the city based on its bicultural origins. In their racist insults, the Russians showed a great deal of contempt for their Chinese citizens. In the end, the Harbin Russians were, in the words of a Chinese columnist, "unsure if they were guests or hosts in North Manchuria."[111]

The end of Chinese rule in Harbin came with the Japanese conquest of the northeast and the creation of the state of Manchukuo in 1932. In a pro-Japanese Russian paper, an unknown author lamented the demise of Harbin's international city government and its replacement with a government that was based on "narrow chauvinism," that is, Chinese control.[112] Some Russians briefly held out the hope that the Japanese would restore the old form of municipal governance in the name of Harbin's international identity. After the Japanese entered Harbin, Special District administrators were among the provincial leaders from Jilin and Heilongjiang who were called on to create the new state of Manchukuo.[113] Despite slogans on leaflets dropped by airplane over Harbin that proclaimed "Everything is new!" very little changed in Harbin's administrative landscape. Many of the Chinese elite stayed on to rule Japanese-dominated Harbin. Zhang Qinghui remained the Special District's head, and Li Xiaogen became the CER's president.[114] Despite assurances that Harbin's population had welcomed the new rulers, photos of an inaugural parade for Manchukuo show a few unhappy Chinese and almost no Russians. By 1934, with the exception of Director Li at the CER, no familiar names remained in Harbin's administration. The Municipal Council had all new Chinese members and several Japanese in key positions.[115] It had no Russian members.

8

Making Russians Chinese:
Secondary and Post-Secondary Education

The first book ever published on the Chinese Eastern Railway (CER) concession was an ABC primer, written in 1898 by Harbin's first Russian primary
schoolteacher for Harbin's first school.[1] This school also set an example for the
Chinese on how to get ahead in the new concession by offering evening courses
in the Russian language. That a school was built even as the first railway ties
were being laid indicated that the CER was more than a railway company. The
education of the concession's growing Russian population was one of the reasons given by the Russians for their extension of the CER's commercial mandate. In time, the CER would establish a comprehensive education system that
extended from the primary to the post-secondary level and had many specialized training courses. The attention paid to the education system – the money
lavished on schools, libraries, technical institutes, and research societies – was
an indication of the pride that the CER and its Russian community took in their
pedagogical institutions. A cynical view of these institutions would be that they
were an extension of informal Russian power throughout the concession. In a
fashion, this view is correct: education and research was a component of Russian power. The education system established the Russian language as the
concession's language of commerce and administration. Russian research into
the history, regulation, and development of northern Manchuria established
Russian education and culture as the baseline from which modernity and
progress were measured. After the Russian Revolution, Russian education
became a means of preserving pre-revolutionary Russian culture and identity,
and it became a means of ensuring employment for Russians and of preserving
Russian influence in a changed political context.

Nevertheless, education in the CER concession, later the Special District,
was not simply about Russian hegemony. In education, more than any other
facet of the Special District's history, we can see how the region became not
only a site of Russian cultural penetration but also a site of Chinese-Russian
cultural exchange. By building the region's first schools, the CER ensured that
all Chinese who hoped to advance could have access to a Russian education.
Chinese merchants had to speak some Russian to deal with their Russian

customers. Nevertheless, the CER itself needed a corps of trained specialists in Chinese language and culture. By drawing on specialists from St. Petersburg and the Institute of Far Eastern Studies in Vladivostok, the CER would lay the foundation for a brilliant period of regional studies and cross-cultural exchange.

In northern Manchuria, it would be easier for the two cultures to mix precisely because neither side really had a comprehensive cultural claim to the region. Culturally and linguistically, it was Manchuria's indigenous peoples – the Daur or Manchus – who had the best claim. But like the indigenous peoples of other colonized regions, the Manchus claim was lost through Chinese and Russian colonization. The Chinese and Russians entered North Manchuria at the same time as pioneers and settlers. While both would construct their own Manchuria, neither had to defend prior claims because they viewed northern Manchuria as a blank slate on which they could fashion their own versions of state and nation. The Russian elite viewed indigenous tribes as objects of ethnographic interest, while the Chinese elite, in the 1920s, dismissed them as undeveloped and pre-modern.

Nationalist histories, especially of China, have emphasized the building of a purely Chinese nation and state. However, the Special District serves as an example of a more complex history. Members of the Chinese elite who moved to or were raised in the concession were often bilingual and, more often than not, bicultural. According to journalist Mao Hong, those Chinese who crossed the cultural divide often crossed it forever. Harbin's Chinese elite, especially those members associated with the Special District's administration and the CER, dressed like their Russian colleagues and spoke Russian. If they married Russian women, their homes were more Russian than Chinese. Indeed, even as late as 1929, when the project of creating a Chinese Harbin was well underway, Mao reported that many of these Chinese, especially their children, spoke better Russian than Chinese.[2]

Ma Zhongjun – vice-head of the Chinese Municipal Bureau and prominent member of the district's administration, who would later be mayor of Harbin – is a good example of the region's creole elite. Although Ma is identified in Chinese nationalist histories as an example of a patriotic Chinese dedicated to regaining sovereignty from the Russian colonizer, the details of his personal life suggest he was more than simply a patriotic Chinese. His home, located in Harbin's finest Russian neighbourhood, was furnished in the Russian style. Although Ma was married to a Chinese woman, he taught himself Russian and sent his daughters to the best private Russian girls' school. His daughters' piano recitals of the Russian classics were the highlight of social evenings spent with Chinese friends and family. The Ma family, like many other upper-class Chinese, were fans of opera and attended performances at the lavishly funded and maintained theatre in the CER Railway Club, which also housed a stage for Chinese opera.[3] There was more going on here than simple cross-cultural interaction. Issues of class, conflicting definitions of modernity, and competing cultural claims were all in attendance, but what was unmistakable was that the Chinese elite in the Special District measured education, modernity, culture, and power by Russian norms.

The challenges faced by the Special District's administrators after 1920 were how to lay claim to a Russian education system built and funded by the CER and how to best ensure that the concession's Russian population continued to be satisfied as the Chinese education system expanded and modernized. As in other areas of administration, the Special District's Chinese administrators forged a middle way between demands for the sinification of the Russian system and the need to maintain good relations with Russian clients and fellow citizens who saw education as crucial to maintaining Russian identity. The process was not always smooth. In the realm of secondary and post-secondary education and specialized research institutes – where not only the issues of language, prestige, and access to funds were at stake but also the manner in which Manchurian development and modernity would be defined – there was significant Russian resistance. The power of knowledge dissemination to define and maintain Russian identity when the source of that identity was gone became a crucial concern and source of conflict. Within the Special District's publicly funded research societies, the use and application of seemingly neutral facts concerning anthropological classification, industrial development, and the politicization of knowledge exposed the deep cleavages between the district's two populations.

Between 1898 and 1917, the CER built and funded twenty-two elementary schools and the Harbin Commercial High School, with separate buildings for boys and girls. By 1921, this system had expanded to fifty-seven elementary schools and four secondary schools that serviced 8,849 secondary students, evenly divided between the genders. The CER also ran one Chinese elementary school. The system was founded on the principles of Russian education, and few concessions were made to the Chinese milieu in which instruction took place. Harbin's commercial school for boys had some Chinese-language instruction – four to five hours of practical spoken Chinese and three hours of literary Chinese per week. The CER not only had control over its own schools but also complete control over all schools in the concession. This control was challenged in January 1910, when the newly founded Harbin Municipal Council and some private schools launched a protest against the CER's supervision. The railway informed a girls' high school in Harbin, funded directly by the Russian Ministry of Education and under the supervision of the governor of Amur, that if it resisted CER control, it would be closed.[4]

The railway's bid for complete control was not successful, and a number of schools, private and municipal, remained outside its control. By 1921, twenty-one schools were being maintained by municipal or national organizations, including six Polish, Ukrainian, or Islamic schools.[5] In 1920, with the former Russian government gone, the CER had also attempted to extend its mandate over all Russian schools within the concession. The head of both the CER's Education Department and the Commercial High School, N.V. Borzov, tried to purge the schools of teachers he believed were sympathetic to the left. In its complaint, Harbin's Municipal Council showed uncharacteristic flexibility. It reported that N.V. Borzov "wanted to make distinctions of nationality between teachers, perhaps tomorrow he will make distinctions of nationality or religion among the children. We must not forget we are living in Manchuria and therefore make allowance in our local legislation for local conditions." The Municipal Council also criticized Borzov, and by extension the CER, for using an ideological excuse to extend the railway's jurisdiction over areas the council believed were not in its province. In December 1920, the council wrote, "Who would have thought that the railroad [would] have insisted on undertaking the supervision of the education of the children and imprinting all educational matters with its official stamp. The company wanted to consider itself as a little government in a special Manchurian state."[6]

From 1920 to 1924, from the creation of the Special District to the Sino-Soviet Shenyang accord, Chinese control over the Russian school system was nominal. As with the courts, the police, municipal politics, and the CER itself, the Chinese administration was content to exchange institutional continuity for acknowledgment of Chinese control. The Russian curriculum was not changed, municipal schools continued as before, and schools remained under the purview of the CER's Education Department, but with the addition of Chinese school inspectors.[7] The Special District's administration could have radically changed these schools, but it chose not to. This was partly due to other pressing concerns and partly due to the influence of the first generation of Chinese officials to hold positions within the Special District. These officials were local men, men who had experience in a bicultural city and whose Chinese nationalism had been shaped by the objective conditions in which they lived and did business. They were not threatened by the continuance of Russian schooling.

The decision to maintain the Russian school system virtually unaltered was also made during a period of regional autonomy and consolidation. In 1922, after his failure to establish a national regime based in Beijing, Zhang Zhuolin declared the Three Northeastern Provinces autonomous and embarked on a period of regional consolidation. This policy of regionalization was based on Zhang's need to extract as much capital as possible through the rational administration of Manchuria. However venial Zhang's intention, it did have the effect of bringing into his administration men for whom military concerns were not the bottom line. These men were also practical administrators who knew that radically changing the Russian school system would not only upset the Russian population, it would also be very expensive. These years were also marked by the increased attention that Zhang's government paid to education. In 1923 Zhang pointed out that control over education, particularly Japanese control, was an area of special concern, and, in that year, the Northeast University was founded in Shenyang. In 1924 there was general agitation in the region to recover the education system from foreign control. Resistance began in the Kwangtung leased area and moved to Jilin Province, and it focused on Japanese schools.[8]

It was during this period of heightened awareness of increased Chinese control that the Special District's Education Department was founded. The department's mandate was to extend Chinese control over the Special District's schools and then extend Chinese education within the district. Although Russian education was left untouched, there was considerable expansion of Chinese education: more Chinese primary schools and up-to-date secondary schools were founded. The biggest school was the new Chinese Third Middle School, which was built in the Chinese architectural style near the Jilesi Temple. On 3 January 1924, Wang Jingchun, president of the CER, opened five more CER Chinese schools, three in Harbin and two in other stations. The schools increased the number of Chinese students by five hundred. An additional school that was funded by the Chinese government was also built. Recognizing the importance of Russian-language instruction, the Sixth Jilin Gymnasium hired three Russian teachers, and special preparatory courses for Chinese students entering Special District Russian schools were created.[9]

In the early 1920s, the Special District's administrators encountered the problem of where to educate the children of recently arrived refugees. Under the former system, only children of CER workers, the majority of the Russian population, could attend the CER's schools. Under the new administration, the CER wanted to contract rather than expand the company's commitment to funding education. The Special District's administration decided to allow Russian children of parents not connected to the CER to attend CER schools. The decision accommodated the needs of thousands of refugees flooding into the Special District and, at the same time, passed the fiscal responsibility to the CER. The CER added more schools, bringing the number of schools under its control to seventy-six and the total number of students to 11,114. The students were served by 991 staff members. The CER also established two specialized language courses, one for Russians learning Chinese and the other for Chinese learning Russian.[10]

When the Special District was founded, the number of Chinese schools and students lagged behind their Russian counterparts. There were twenty-seven Chinese schools in Harbin and Fujiadian in 1921 – four primary (three for boys and one for girls) and twenty-three secondary (twenty-one for boys and two for girls). Nine were private, one was funded by the CER, and nineteen were funded by the Chinese government. Together, they offered instruction to 2,188 students, 349 of them female. Before the Special District was established, Chinese education was neither as well funded nor as systematically controlled as Russian schooling. Much of the funding and the initiative for Chinese schools relied on individuals or native-place groups. For instance, the first Chinese secondary school had been founded in 1912 for the children of Shandong immigrants. Chinese education in the Special District was caught between the demands of establishing a Chinese school system and the practical needs of educating children to live and work in a region with a large non-Chinese population. James Carter's study of the Donghua Private Middle School reveals that the Chinese mercantile and educational elite who founded the school wanted to instill in their students national pride and a modern education. Yet, Carter's study also shows that these same Chinese elites had been marked by the cosmopolitan milieu in which they lived. The founder of the private school, Deng Jiemin, had worked in the Binjiang Negotiation Bureau; spoke Russian, English, and Japanese; and had been educated in Japan. Like Deng, any Chinese who hoped to advance in the Special District, especially Harbin, needed to speak Russian. In addition to the CER's Chinese primary school, where Russian was taught, Chinese students were also admitted to the CER's commercial school after 1911 at the special request of Li Lanzhou, who was then intendant of Binjiang. Li, a fluent Russian speaker who was married to a Russian and would later become the first head of the Special District Court, understood the importance of Russian-language education. Many of the first class of thirty-two Chinese students admitted to the commercial high school (twenty-two boys and ten girls) would later be employed by the CER and the Special District.[11]

Following the takeover of the municipal councils in 1926, the Special District's Education Department was directly responsible for schools that had previously been under municipal control.[12] In Harbin there were six Russian schools funded by the Municipal Council that were allowed to function virtually without change. The curricula for municipal Russian high schools bore no sign, other than an index in Chinese, that the schools were under Chinese control. Students were responsible for studies in Russian language, arithmetic, geography, modern and ancient history, physics, algebra, natural sciences, English, commercial accounting, art, music, physical education, and religion. Several of these subjects – history, art, music, and religion – were aimed at instilling Russian identity in students. Remarkably, although Chinese-language instruction was offered, it was still not a compulsory subject in 1926.[13]

From 1926 onward, Harbin's new Chinese Municipal Assembly and Municipal Council set about improving schools under their control. Money was transferred to Chinese education from a fund earmarked for building more Russian schools, plans were made to build new schools, and eight more higher-education teachers were hired for both Chinese and Russian schools. The council allotted more funding for art supplies and teachers in Russian schools and approved the expansion of the music program in Russian primary and secondary schools. These changes resulted in a budget increase of 675 yuan and the employment of two more teachers. When the extension to the music program went over budget, the council allotted additional funds to cover the difference. Funds were also offered to the Chinese schools to create a music program. The new council, however, did not honour all of the previous council's commitments: it refused to pay 300 yuan to an émigré swimming coach for a book on swimming techniques commissioned by the former council.[14]

The Chinese council increased the number of tuition-free Russian children in the Special District's municipal schools. According to the regulations of the former Russian-controlled council, only 233 students were to be admitted to municipal schools without tuition. When constituents informed the council that an additional 239 students could not pay tuition because of extreme poverty, the council passed a motion to grant an additional 5,020 yuan in the form of tuition waivers. Chinese and Russian schools were encouraged to interact by sharing buildings and even graduations. After the first joint graduation celebrations, the Municipal Council covered the 400 yuan that each of the Chinese schools had overspent and the 170 yuan that each of the Russian schools had overspent. The council also approved the purchase of new property for the creation of two new schools, one Chinese, the other Russian. In total, 60,000 yuan was used to build new school buildings.[15]

Of the two versions of the Sino-Soviet CER accord signed in 1924 (one signed in Beijing in May, the second signed in Shenyang in September), only the Shenyang accord mentioned education. Its inclusion in the Shenyang accord reflected Zhang Zuolin's and his government's interest in the topic. The Shenyang agreement specified that the CER would retain departments essential to the administration of the railroad. The CER's Educational Department, nominally under the Special District's control, should have been transferred completely to the Chinese administration. This possible change worried émigré parents, for whom the prospect of transferring the CER to joint Chinese-Soviet administration raised the possibility that their children might be educated in a radical system that the parents despised. The Soviets wanted to retain control of the CER's Education Department for the same reason – they did not want the children of Soviet workers, soon to arrive in the Special District, educated in émigré-controlled schools. The Special District compromised by assuring émigré parents that nothing would change in the Special District's schools and supporting this promise with articles in the Shenyang accord that forbade the Communists from propagandizing or changing school curricula.[16] Unfortunately, the Special District initially had no control measures in place to ensure that the Soviets kept their promise; as a result, Soviet influence in CER schools would become a serious problem from 1925 onward.

Perhaps to calm concerned Russian parents, in December 1924 Ma Zhongjun, the director of the Chinese Municipal Bureau, brought out new regulations for Harbin's six Russian municipal schools that likewise specified that no alterations would be made to the curriculum. In the same month, the newly appointed head of the Education Department, Chan Yuwen, in an interview with the *Harbin Daily News,* specified that Chinese and Russian children would be treated the same and their schools would keep strictly to the business of teaching. No changes would be allowed. To support this promise, a soon-to-be-very-busy special inspector was posted to the CER's Education Department to ensure that no curriculum changes occurred in CER schools.[17]

The directive against propaganda, however, also meant the end of religious instruction in CER schools. In November 1924 the CER's Church Department was closed, and religious instruction was forbidden in CER schools. Religious instruction continued in municipal and private schools with the Special District's support.[18] By 1925 the CER's Russian schools were also beginning to modify the curriculum to introduce new Soviet pedagogic theories. This development was in direct contravention of the Shenyang accord. In March, Dr. Nikiforov, head of the CER's Education Department and an opponent of the ongoing reorganization of CER schools on the Soviet model, was fired and replaced by a Dr. Nikolai Vasil'evich Ustrialov, a Soviet citizen.[19] Dr. Borzov, head of Harbin's commercial school since 1906 and well-known anti-leftist, was fired "owing to the inability to meet with service requirements," that is, because of his opposition to Soviet pedagogy.[20] With the two strongest opponents of the Soviet curriculum gone, the CER's Education Department, under Soviet direction, continued to illegally change the curriculum of Russian schools under its control. The CER's special inspectors, who were Chinese and without any specific training, did not have the linguistic or pedagogical capacity to judge the changes initiated by the new Soviet administrators. According to one observer, they were "policeman, nothing more."[21] New pedagogy courses based on Soviet principles were taught to the teachers, and in the words of two supporters of curriculum change, "the best modern teachers were invited to the schools and the schools were gradually cleaned of the mould of monarchist education. The schools became a living organism more connected with realistic life and the surrounding labour classes."[22] Classes were based on the "labour school and those new principles which are now applied in advanced schools of Western Europe and Russia particularly."[23]

One can imagine the effect these changes had on émigré parents. The previous Russian curriculum had embraced the values and symbols of the old Russian regime. Religion had been taught in most schools, and the czar's portrait had hung in some CER classrooms. Because only Soviet and Chinese citizens were allowed to work on the CER after 1924, the new curriculum, in the opinion of the Soviet administrators, had to be tailored to Soviet children to instill Soviet values in a foreign land. There was no place for the children of émigrés who also wanted to pass on their national values. The Soviet head of the CER's Education Department countered a charge by the company's Chinese president that it was "sovietizing" the schools by presenting the changes as part of a national – not a political – pedagogy. He claimed that the subjects of this experiment would mature into allies, rather than foes, of the Chinese government:

It is quite plain that this money can be expended only for the education of such children who would be connected with their mother land and would know how to defend and protect her interests, being full of the friendly spirit which was the foundation of the Soviet/Chinese intercommunications. It is not a question of creating centers for communistic propaganda or agitation or a question of sovietization of railway schools, as the new manager declared, but that Russian schools must have such an organization as would prepare proper and actual citizens of the USSR who would know how to act in the interest of the USSR and China.[24]

Russian education was now split between the better-funded and equipped Soviet-controlled schools of the CER and municipal and the private schools under Chinese control. Despite the advantages enjoyed by Soviet schools, the Russian schools in the Chinese system continued to be more popular among the émigrés because they used the former curriculum. Soviet-controlled schools, which used experimental teaching methods, were derided for their poor discipline.[25] Although the Russian schools under Chinese control were not as well funded, the Special District did what it could to protect its Russian employees. In 1926 the Soviet head of the CER's Education Department, Nikolai Vasil'evich Ustrialov, fired eleven émigré teachers who had become Chinese nationals, even though they were legally allowed to work for the CER. In response, the Special District's administration fired eleven Soviet teachers who were working in the district's schools and replaced them with the Chinese nationals who had been fired.[26] That the Special District had allowed, up to that point, Soviet citizens, more than likely émigrés whose citizenship did not reflect an attachment to the USSR, to teach highlights the tolerance that was typical of the Special District administration.

The Special District hired several more school inspectors, Russian émigrés who knew what to look for, to check on student progress, school holidays, final exams, and for the presence of propaganda. According to the French consul, these émigrés found pro-Soviet and anti-Zhang Zuolin propaganda in the curricula of the Soviet-controlled CER Russian and Chinese schools. They discovered that the CER's Education Department favoured schools for Soviet nationals by increasing their funding, even though money allocated to the department was to be split equally between Soviet and Chinese schools. Of the Education Department's budget of 2 million gold rubles, only 300,000 gold rubles was spent on Chinese schools. The Soviets argued that because only five of the seventy-six schools were Chinese and because Russian employees outnumbered Chinese, the discrepancy was justified. In the first two years of joint administration, however, the railway had opened no new Chinese schools, even though the number of Chinese employees had increased. The Chinese argued that complete parity in every aspect of the railway's operation was necessary.[27]

The crisis came to a head in May 1926, when a conference between the co-administrators to resolve these problems broke down. Soviet delegates showed no inclination to consider Chinese requests. Soviet officials refused to provide estimates of their educational expenses, opening the possibility that money was being spent on purposes other than education, and refused to yield control over the budget to the Chinese. The Soviet schools were threatened with closure, and the staff went unpaid. The incident was serious enough that the new Chinese head of the Special District's Education Department, Li Xiaogen, made an emergency trip to Shenyang. On 27 August 1926, the CER's Education Department was closed on Shenyang's orders.[28]

The Special District's administration chose to solve this debacle by creating another level of bureaucracy. On 4 September 1926, the district head, Zhang Huanxiang, created the Special Administration Department of Public Education, and all schools – CER, municipal, private, foreign, and Chinese – came under the department's inspection and management. The head, Li Xiaogen, requested that all schools send lists of their faculty and curricula to the new department. Teachers in CER schools were told by the company not to comply – a directive that was rightly interpreted by the Special District as resistance to its new department. On 7 September, Li arrived at the CER's Education Department with a police escort. He found the department head directing his typist to copy a course curriculum titled "The New Program of the United Labour School." Interpreting this as an intention to spread propaganda, Li ordered the department closed, and the police instructed the employees to leave.[29]

The Soviets argued that since the schools were for the benefit of children of the company's Soviet and Chinese employees, the CER had the right to continue to administer them. In an interview with the pro-Soviet newspaper *Zaria*, the CER's vice-president, Savrassov, stated that Soviet citizens feared that their children would have to attend municipal Russian schools if the CER's schools were closed. He mentioned that eleven Soviet teachers in the municipal schools had been fired and replaced with émigré teachers, but he neglected to mention that the émigrés had originally been fired by the Soviets. Savrassov argued, in essence, for a form of Soviet extraterritoriality – the right to be above Chinese administration and law. According to Savrassov, the CER's schools did not violate the Shenyang agreement because private schools were allowed in China. He confirmed China's right to inspect schools, but because the CER provided the majority of funding, Savrassov objected to the CER's limited control over their schools. In his opinion, either the Special District should assume full power over the schools, along with their funding, or the CER should have the same rights as any other private school in China.[30] Savrassov's other argument in favour of the CER rested on the necessity of having children schooled in a Soviet atmosphere. "Naturally Soviet citizens working in the CER and residing in Manchuria cannot have all of their children educated in the USSR. Of course they should have here their own schools which should naturally be under the control of the Chinese government and enjoy the same rights as Chinese schools in the USSR."[31]

Savrassov's arguments had several weak points. The Shenyang agreement had forbidden the dissemination of propaganda and gave full control over all civil affairs to China and its representatives in the Special District. The argument that the new Soviet curriculum was not propaganda was disingenuous because the Special District had forbidden the symbols and ceremony of czarist Russia in the schools and expected the Soviets to do the same. Although the CER had a legal right to educate all of its employees' children, Savrassov did not mention the Chinese argument that both Chinese and Soviet CER schools should be equally funded. Finally, Savrassov's suggestion that the CER was only a private corporation ignored the important role that the railway played in the Special District. Everything the CER did have political meaning.

On 1 December 1927, an agreement was signed to end the conflict. The CER's Education Department remained intact, but it was renamed the CER Fourth Division and was under the nominal direction of the Special District's Education Department. In cases in which the Special District and the USSR differed over educational matters, compromises were made. Funds were divided into two funding streams: those transmitted to the Special District for Chinese schools and those sent to the Fourth Division for Russian schools. The system's budget was increased to 3.4 million rubles. The Special District appointed all Fourth Division employees from lists provided by the CER, and Soviet citizens were appointed as inspectors for the Soviet schools. The Chinese considered the agreement a great success. The Special District got the best of the agreement – no direct financial responsibility for the schools but control over their curriculum and staffing. In addition, Harbin would be transformed into Manchuria's educational centre. However, the agreement was also a compromise, one of many made between the Special District and its Russian partners. The CER's school system became two systems – one for Chinese and the other for Soviets (although, if they wished, Chinese workers or Russian workers with Chinese citizenship could send their children to the Soviet schools). Each system would develop with different curricula and political goals. The Soviet system was largely autonomous. Although its funding had been halved, it retained control over course content, and the annoying émigré school inspectors had been removed.[32]

For his success in mediating the crisis, Li Xiaogen was admitted into the CER's directorate. His position as head of the Special District's Education Department was taken over by Zhang Guochen, Zhang Xueliang's former secretary. Also known as Zhang Guo, Zhang Guochen was a native of Liaoning who had graduated from the Commercial High School. He had been appointed an expert on Russian law to the Foreign Ministry and was a professor of Russian language at Beijing's Sino-Russian University. He had been chief of the Office of Foreign Affairs for the Three Northeastern Provinces and was also the author of a Chinese survey of Russian literature and a translator of documents seized during the 1929 Soviet consulate raid.[33] Zhang Guochen would lead the next assault on the Fourth Division Soviet schools.[34] With his language skills and familiarity with the Russian community, Li's entrance into the CER's highest rank marked the beginning of his policy to staff the CER with Chinese with Russian experience. During the 1929 crisis, many more Russian-educated Chinese, along with naturalized Chinese Russians, would be appointed to the railway administration. In July, for instance, the Chinese board elected a Mr. Fan, who had been educated in Russian schools, as the CER's general manager. His first act was to replace the Soviet department heads with Chinese personnel or with Russians who had taken Chinese nationality. The promotion of men like Li and Zhang, men who were instrumental in the recovery of educational administration and municipal administration, respectively, sent a strong signal that the Chinese were in control. Appointing men who were familiar with Russian affairs and well liked by the émigré Russian community also signalled that the interests of émigrés, not Soviets, would be paramount.[35]

The Fourth Division compromise sowed the seeds of future conflict. The CER's Soviet schools continued to teach the Soviet curriculum, while its Chinese schools taught the same curriculum as the Special District's public schools. The Soviet-controlled Association of Russian Teachers came under the particular scrutiny of officials. According to Chinese sources, the teachers spread anti-Zhang Xueliang and anti-Guomindang propaganda and tended to communicate secretly in Russian. (By this time, Zhang Xueliang had succeeded his father, Zhang Zoulin, and was bringing Manchuria into the Guomindang orbit.) This issue became part of the greater breakdown in Chinese-Soviet relations in the months before the 1929 crisis. In April 1928, nineteen Russian schoolteachers were arrested and released on bail for attending an illegal conference.[36] In December the police raided the offices of *The Educator,* a journal for Soviet teachers, and Zhang Guochen accused the Fourth Division of exhibiting "exceptional independence" and teaching propaganda. He specified that all future Fourth Division correspondence would require his signature and all documents would be translated into Chinese.[37] Filipovich, the Soviet head of the Fourth Division who had been charged by Li Xiaogen for illegally disseminating "The New Program of the United Labour School," was to inform Zhang of any changes to the Soviet school curriculum.

Relations continued to deteriorate. In January 1929, Zhang dismissed twelve Soviet Russian teachers and replaced them with émigrés, and, in February, Filipovich himself was dismissed and deported to the USSR by the Chinese CER head for his "strong communistic activities" and for spreading Communist propaganda in schools.[38] On 19 February, Zhang accused the Fourth Division of educating "the growing generation in a manner entirely contrary to political and educational methods in China," and, on 22 February, all Chinese students were pulled out of Soviet schools. Those who were naturalized

Chinese of Russian parents were allowed to attend the Special District's Russian public schools.[39] Although the propaganda ceased, Chinese officials decided the overall atmosphere of the CER's Soviet schools had been "contaminated with undesirable influences." In an effort to control information from the Fourth Division, the Special District's administration announced once more that all division correspondence would be in Chinese and Russian and that all Fourth Division Russian students and teachers would be required to learn Chinese.[40] In August 1929 Zhang discharged five hundred Soviet teachers and replaced them with émigrés whom the Chinese administration saw as a significant source of support.[41] In October 1929, during a speech to a Russian relief committee headed by Zhang Guochen, Zhang asked all of Harbin's Russian and Chinese high school principals to support the Chinese cause, a request to which they "pledged their support."[42] That same month the Special District seized the CER's libraries.[43]

Although these actions were cited in the Japanese press as an attack on the entire Russian-language school system, only Soviet-controlled schools were affected. From the Chinese point of view, the dispute was legitimate. Soviet officials had refused to conduct correspondence in the two official languages of the CER and had continued to disseminate propaganda that was forbidden by the Shenyang agreement. During a search of the Soviet consulate in May, a plan for the dissemination of political propaganda among the CER's professional unions and teachers had been seized.[44]

The settlement of the 1929 conflict specified that the CER was to return to its antebellum status. Although the settlement was interpreted as a great blow to the Chinese administration because it failed to provide China with complete control over the railway, the Chinese did obtain significant advantages. Soviet propaganda activities on the line diminished considerably, and there was more parity in the hiring of Chinese and Soviet employees and more day-to-day control by Chinese or naturalized Chinese administrators. Most of the émigrés hired during the crisis were retained or, if let go, either employed by the Special District or given a cash settlement. There is no evidence that the émigré teachers who were hired during the crisis were subsequently released. All CER schools after 1929 were designated public schools under the control of the Special District, and as of 1930 the new curriculum for Soviet schools was based on that of Harbin's Russian Commercial High School – the same curriculum the Soviet school administration had attempted to subvert.[45] The Fourth Division ceased to exist as a locus of Soviet power in the Special District as the division's curriculum was harmonized with that of Russian public schools. All other educational institutions and research groups seized during the crisis remained under Chinese control, with the exception of the CER's libraries, which were returned to joint Chinese-Soviet control. Although the libraries remained in the railway's hands, increased Chinese influence can be discerned. After 1929 the Asiatica section and the Chinese collection both underwent significant expansion.[46]

The question remains, how did the Russians and Chinese influence each other through education? Two articles published in the *Binjiang shibao* newspaper in 1922 speculated on the influence of Russian education in Harbin. In one, the author, who, according to a Chinese scholar, was not an educated man, condemns the Pristan Chinese-Russian Business Association for being an association in name only and accuses the association of using money, meant to be divided evenly between Chinese and Russians, to support Russian charities and schools. Four months later, another article appeared on the opening of a Russian school for Chinese, taught by two Russian women skilled in written and spoken Russian. In it, the author praises the school and recommends that Chinese take advantage of the opportunity to improve their knowledge of Russian.[47]

These two articles capture the spectrum of Chinese feeling concerning Russian education in Harbin and the Special District. Russian education was resented as an expression of Russian colonialism, which had once been political but was cultural by the 1920s. Russian education was also admired for its connection to modernity, especially by those Chinese who had some experience with the language. Russian culture and education played a great part in the worldview of the Special District's Chinese elite. Numerous members had a Russian education and spoke Russian. The experience of this group and the manner in which they went about trying to administer the Russian community reveals that the region had a cross-cultural dimension that has been overlooked.

A large number of Chinese spoke Russian because Russian was the language of commerce and administration in the Special District, but there was little impetus for Russians to learn Chinese. After the publication of the first Chinese textbook for Russians in 1905, the Chinese language was offered at the Harbin Russian Commercial High School for four to five hours each week. But Chinese-language instruction was not a priority in Russian schools.[48] Most Russian high schools included Chinese geography and some history but no Chinese-language instruction. The schools offered three hours each week of English-language instruction but nothing in the language spoken by the majority of the Special District's inhabitants.[49]

After 1920 Chinese-language instruction was expanded to most schools in the Special District. The authorities, however, complained that the quality of instruction in the first years was poor and that students graduated without sufficient knowledge of Chinese. After the municipal councils were absorbed into the district, funds that had been earmarked for building Russian schools were transferred to Chinese education. In 1928 a committee of both Chinese and Russian teachers was struck to encourage Chinese as a second language and to make the Chinese language compulsory. As a result, primary school students received four hours per week of instruction in the Chinese language. In the first year, they memorized tones and 700 characters; in the second year, they advanced to simple stories and learned another 750 characters; in the third year, they were expected to know 800 characters and began to learn colloquial Chinese; by the end of the fourth year, they were expected to know another 850 characters; and in the fifth year, students were introduced to specialized knowledge about the CER, telegraphs, and post offices.[50] Middle school students received eight hours of Chinese study each week, while high school students received twenty hours. By the end of high school, students were expected to know from two thousand to three thousand characters. I.G. Baronov, writing that the teaching of Chinese to Russian children was of the utmost importance, admitted it was an ambitious program and that the main obstacle was a lack of trained teachers.[51] To prepare its students for work with the CER and in acknowledgment that Russian alone would no longer be sufficient, the V.L. Anders Private High School began to require not only Chinese and English of all its graduates in 1927 but also completion of courses on the CER, Chinese history, and the economic geography and history of Manchuria. Taught at the Moscow Bazaar, in the heart of Newtown and facing the Cathedral of St. Nicholas, the courses injected Chinese content into the most Russian part of Harbin. Chinese faculty expected students to master Chinese history, geography, everyday spoken Chinese, literary Chinese, and the history of Chinese literature. The students were predominantly children of CER employees who hoped to obtain positions in the company. Vladimir Shkurkin, one of the teachers in the CER's schools, was a prominent Orientalist who wrote extensively on Chinese history, fables, and children's stories.[52]

One of the hallmarks of Chinese educational reform in Harbin was the addition of classes in physical education. James Carter, in his study of the Donghua school, points out that its Chinese founders paid particular attention to physical fitness.[53] Strong, healthy, and competitive bodies were seen by Chinese reformers in this era as proof of national and intellectual vigour. The Russian influence on attitudes toward physical fitness among Harbin's Chinese elite was striking. As early as 1922, it was noted that Russians allocated more class time to physical fitness. One newspaper article in a Chinese paper exhorted the Chinese to learn from the Russians' example – to exercise, even in hot weather. According to Wang Lijiang's memoir, there were sports facilities in all three sections of Harbin; the best, however, were in Newtown, and the worst were in Fujiadian. Wang described the facilities in Fujiadian, which were for the Chinese, as a sea of mud. Wang noted that the Russian habit of exercise was unknown to the Chinese. Only the Russian schools formerly administered by the CER had physical education classes. Chinese were not allowed into the Russian facilities until 1926, the year that municipal facilities came under Chinese control. Although Wang records only acrimonious relations between the two peoples, accounts from the early 1920s reveal that Chinese and Russians competed against each other and shared facilities.[54]

Athletics were a source of competition and co-operation. In 1926, during a game between the Donghua School and the Russian YMCA, the Russian team won 29-17, and a riot between the Chinese and Russian students followed. The

Russian coach later claimed that a group of two hundred screaming Chinese students had pursued him, then left the building and proceeded to break windows. Students of both nationalities were injured in the fighting.[55] According to Chinese sources, it was Russian students, aided by a Russian policeman, who had provoked the fighting. The event was commented on extensively in the Chinese and foreign presses. The Chinese press linked the riot to the changing power structure in the city:

> The white Russians who live now in Harbin are ... without nationality, like
> the Poles and Indians. When we look back, we find that in the past Russia
> was a powerful monarchy, but now the Russians live in China as guests. In
> the past the Russians treated we Chinese very arrogantly, yet the Chinese
> have forgiven these past abuses and have not sought revenge, but instead
> treat the Russians very well. Because of these circumstances, the Russians
> must accept Chinese hospitality graciously and live without creating
> disturbances. China today is not the China of twenty years ago where
> Chinese could be abused.[56]

The author of this piece made it clear that conditions in China had changed and that the Russians were permitted to stay only because of the good graces of the Chinese.

The introduction and spread of physical education in the Special District's schools was a direct result of the subject's having been taught in the Russian system. Its presence was noted and approved of by reform-minded Chinese. Wang credits the fact that Harbin had the most comprehensive physical education program in China to the influence of the Russian system. Following the Russians' example, the Special District's Education Department made physical education mandatory in all of its schools in 1928 – so that "all schools would have the same opportunities."[57]

After the Russian Revolution and the loss of the Russian motherland, the CER's administration and the Russian elite were forced to debate the purpose of the railway and its educational institutions. Was the CER and its concession merely a business enterprise to be administered on an economic basis, or was it the means of preserving a society and culture that no longer existed in the mother country? Because of the importance of education to the émigrés, higher education in the Special District was politicized. Harbin, as a world centre of Russian immigration, was now a centre for Russian education. The émigrés' determination to maintain pre-revolutionary education and culture took their community in two directions. One was inward-looking. In their desire to perpetuate pre-revolutionary Russian culture, many émigrés actively opposed redefining their culture and education, a process that could have acted as a bridge and an anchor in Manchuria.

For others, the establishment of institutions of higher education such as the Russian Law Faculty and the Russo-Chinese Technical Institute was a proactive means for the Russian elite to find a new purpose in Manchuria. The Bolshevik government was not going to fall, and Harbin, the only intact pre-revolutionary Russian community outside of Russia, was being overrun with refugees. The Chinese government was taking advantage of this power vacuum to reassert its rights in the railway zone. The CER and the Russian elite had to find a new purpose and accommodate themselves to a new political reality. As the railway's ownership was debated between Chinese, émigré Russian, and Soviet Russian interests, the CER and its Russian elite sought a role that was not overtly political. Under the temporary émigré-Russian–Chinese joint administration (1920-24), the Russian elite promoted the economic and cultural development of Manchuria through the CER's Economic Department and the creation of institutions of higher education. Russian émigré professionals served as brokers between the Chinese and international capital. They hoped the latter would both invest in the region and buy its raw materials. In this manner, Russians hoped to assist in the development of the region that had become their home. Some Chinese, however, believed that this project would ensure the continued Russian domination of Manchuria's economy and culture.

In 1916, even as czarist Harbin began to unravel, a Committee for Higher Education was formed to found and open a university in Harbin. Even though revolution and the devaluation of the Russian ruble forced the committee to abandon its goal, Harbin, as a centre of immigration, attracted the cream of Russian academe.[58] In 1920 two new institutions – the Law Faculty and the Russo-Chinese Technical Institute – were created, and they were followed by the Harbin Polytechnic, an ancestor of the present-day Harbin Institute of Technology. During this period, Russian institutions such as the CER were being forced to adapt to changed circumstances, for formal Russian power in the Special District had been severely curtailed. The only recourse was for Russians to retain strategic posts in industry and education and to make themselves indispensable to the new regime.

Harbin's premier institute of higher education, the Russo-Chinese Technical Institute, was, like the Law Faculty, subsidized by the CER and the Municipal Council. Because the institute's purpose was to train CER personnel, the courses were only in Russian, although there was a preparatory course in Russian for non-Russian speakers (there were 7, all Chinese, in the first class of 103 students). Between 1922 and 1928, the college expanded considerably and came to be known as China's best technical university. The number of Chinese graduates was small, but very few students completed the rigorous four-year program. For instance, in the first class of 103 students, only 22 graduated.[59] Despite its primarily Russian identity, Chinese students continued to be attracted to the institute because it was associated with modernity and development. In 1926, however, the Special District, insisting on greater Chinese participation and content, appointed a Chinese vice-principal.[60] Until

1928, although it was nominally an independent institution, the institute was still under the control of the CER. It then came under the Special District's administration and funding. Renamed the Harbin Technical University, it was run jointly by the Chinese and the Soviets, and Zhang Huanxiang was appointed dean.[61]

The Law Faculty was founded in 1920 by Russian émigré scholars who wanted to preserve the best of Russian academic thought, to teach a new generation of scholars who would have no access to Russia, and to provide employment for unemployed academics. Unlike the Russo-Chinese Technical Institute, which was viewed by the Chinese as a practical and essential tool for the region's development, the Chinese associated the Law Faculty with the Russian elite and a less practical education. It was, consequently, subjected to more scrutiny by the Special District's administrators. Like the college, the Law Faculty was funded by the CER and the Russian-controlled Municipal Council. Although the curriculum was based on the Russian model, there were some courses in regional studies and Chinese state and civil law, and eleven professors taught in the Chinese language. After the Chinese took over the municipal councils in 1926, the Law Faculty, autonomous in theory but in practice beholden to the CER, continued to be funded by the CER but under a joint Soviet-Chinese administration. A preparatory course was introduced to prepare Chinese students for the Russian and European content and for studies in Russian. Despite attempts to make the Law Faculty more relevant to the Chinese community, the institution was still oriented to the Russian community. During the 1929 crisis, the Law Faculty was put under full Chinese control, and it lost its CER subsidy because, according to Olga Bakich, "China opposed the existence of this private Russian institution subsidized by the Soviet Union." The new administration aggressively attempted to sinify the Law Faculty: Chinese replaced Russian as the language of instruction, strict control over the activities of Russian staff was introduced and, after 1929, no additional Russian students were admitted. These harsh terms were rescinded following the 1929 Sino-Soviet incident. As a compromise, two streams, one Chinese and one Russian, would be permitted in the school. The one concession to the linguistic majority was that Chinese students would now take special one-year preparatory classes in Russian.[62]

Members of the Law Faculty published extensively on diverse subjects of regional interest: Chinese law; Chinese, Mongolian, and Manchu ethnography; and local industry and commerce. The Law Faculty was a good example of how the Russian émigré community maintained a hold on higher education and on its status in Harbin. The Chinese allowed the institution to remain outside of effective Chinese control for most of the 1920s because of the useful purpose the faculty claimed to serve. When the Law Faculty was placed under Chinese control, a compromise was worked out that retained Russian professors and students. Relatively few Chinese were admitted to the Russian system of higher education because the Faculty of Law's system did not allow Chinese students to be easily incorporated into the curriculum. Only 19 of the 297 students who graduated from the Law Faculty before 1933 were Chinese.[63]

Unlike the Russian Orthodox Church, which used religion to build a sense of Russian identity in Manchuria and rarely interacted with the Chinese community, institutions of higher learning attempted to adapt by introducing some Chinese content to their curricula. The Russian elite used what the émigré Russian intelligentsia considered to be the best legacy of pre-revolutionary Russia – its culture, education, and training – to bridge the gulf between peoples and cultures. However, neither the Russian Orthodox Church nor the Russian elite questioned the primacy of Russian and European cultural values. Both assumed that the Russians would continue, and would be allowed to continue, to dominate agencies of economic and cultural production in Harbin. The Special District's Russian-controlled institutions were, in fact, a continuation of Russia's pre-1917 colonialist project, albeit without the military threat posed by the mother country. Instead, Manchuria would be colonized through the values of trade and culture, which assumed continued Russian leadership. This assumption was particularly pronounced in the debate over the Special District's Russian-controlled research institutes.

In émigré historiography, Harbin's institutions of higher education and its research societies are represented as examples of the superiority of Russian émigré culture in China. Within Chinese historiography, these institutions are ignored and forgotten. Those institutions that have survived, such as the Harbin Institute of Technology, barely mention their Russian origins.[64] This oversight has traditionally been explained as a product of Chinese nationalism, the Sino-Soviet split, and Maoist emphasis on Chinese self-reliance. Although all of these explanations are valid, the absence of details regarding the Russian influence on higher education points to fundamental differences in how the Chinese and Russian elites saw the production and use of knowledge.

The history of Manchurian research institutes – in particular the Manchurian Research Society (Obshchestva izucheniia Manchzurskogo kraia, hereafter referred to by its Russian abbreviation, OIMK) – offers a glimpse into competing visions of culture and modernity among the three principal actors: the Russian émigré community, the Chinese elite, and Soviet representatives. The society's strategy of knowledge formation and dissemination to establish Russian cultural hegemony over Manchuria's supposedly empty land resulted in the alienation of the institute's Chinese partners, who perceived OIMK as a Russian institution that had a questionable political vision. The research society was devoted to the ethnographic, economic, anthropological, botanical, and historical study of Manchuria, and it functioned as the research and development arm of the CER, which was OIMK's chief source of income (in 1928 the CER provided 73.5 percent of the society's funding), and acted as an information clearing house for potential investors who wanted information on Manchuria. During its seven-years' existence [1923-30], the society published numerous proceedings, and it grew to eight hundred members by 1929. The society operated a museum with over sixty-two thousand artifacts, a publishing house, a botanical garden, and a library and archive. It had many successful exhibitions in Harbin and abroad and sponsored numerous research expeditions across Manchuria. The research society was also an important institution within Harbin. Its members were acknowledged as the intellectual leaders of the community, and the society was supported by the CER, during both the émigré and Soviet administrations.[65]

The CER's twenty-fifth anniversary jubilee in 1923 had reflected the new vision of Russian leadership in Manchuria that dominated OIMK and other institutions of Russian higher education. And OIMK had been founded in the wake of a highly successful jubilee exhibition to advance the modernization and economic progress of the northeastern frontier. The exhibit, which eventually grew into OIMK's Museum of Northern Manchuria, had one hundred thousand artifacts divided into four sections: industry, ethnography, archaeology, and natural science. Natural science, the biggest section, stressed cross-border regional flora and fauna; ethnography, the second largest, which sought to delineate "the level of existence and culture attained by the indigenous races inhabiting the territory," displayed the traditional costume and homes of the Manchus, Mongolians, Daur, and Han Chinese.[66] There was also a large section on Mongolian and Chinese Buddhism. In the archaeology section, the Han Chinese came last in the periodization of the region's peoples because OIMK divided Manchurian history into two stages: ancient and modern. According to the society, ancient Manchurian history had begun 2,200 years before 1889. The modern period began with the CER's construction. From the Chinese perspective, this version of history was problematic for several reasons. First, modernity was associated with the arrival of the Russians. Second, OIMK's depictions of Manchuria made insufficient reference to modern China's ethnic or political claims.[67]

In OIMK's publications, the most common geopolitical term for Manchuria is *region (krai)*. According to the OIMK, Manchuria shared political, economic, and ethnic characteristics and development potential with the Russian Far East and Korea. In these publications, OIMK extols the virtues of Manchuria's untapped natural resources, and it presents the OIMK and its Russian researchers as the best tool for tapping them. The use of the geographical term *krai* in OIMK's name and its publications is significant. *Krai* means territory, in the sense of an administrative unit. The term was used in the title of various territories of the Russian Far East such as Amurskii krai (Amur territory or region) and Primorskii krai (Maritime territory). The use of *krai* instead of the Chinese word *dong sheng* (eastern provinces) and the use of the even more vague term *Manchuria* in the English translation implicitly highlighted the territory's ambiguous relationship with China. The use of the transnational regional designation of *krai* [region] did acknowledge that Manchuria was a land of competing geopolitical visions, but by portraying Manchuria as a land

Harbin's Manchurian Research Society Museum (OIMK), located at the heart of Newtown across the traffic circle from the Cathedral of St. Nicholas. Russian researchers and Chinese politicians struggled for control of the society and its museum in 1929. | Courtesy of the collection of Olga Bakich.

of ambiguous political affiliation that could be conquered by technology and research, the Russians offended their Chinese patrons.

From the perspective of the Chinese, OIMK's production and dissemination of knowledge was not value-free; rather, its choice of research categories had political, cultural, and racial meaning for both the researcher and the object of research. The creation of specific subject areas such as ethnology, anthropology, archaeology, and oriental studies placed the known world in a hierarchy of peoples and histories. Long the handmaiden of the colonial and imperial enterprise, OIMK's research became an effective means of marking territory and claiming it for a new Russian development project. The subjugation of India by the British and southern Manchuria by the Japanese was accompanied by research into the history, religion, language, and culture of local societies in order to better administer the newly conquered territories. From the Chinese perspective, OIMK's goals were, like those of the Japanese South Manchurian Railway Company Research Institute, colonialist. Because OIMK envisaged Manchuria as a zone of Russian research and development, its goals were compatible with those of the Soviet administration that took over the CER in 1924, and the Soviets continued to fund the institute even though most of its members were émigrés.

The administrators of the Japanese-owned South Manchurian Railway Research Institute were quite forthright about their purpose, which was dubbed "military preparedness in civil garb" by the first director of the SMR's research institute. "We have to implement a cultural invasion with a central laboratory, popular education for the resident population[,] and forge other academic and economic links."[68] Although the research institute attracted a substantial number of liberal and dissident Japanese scholars who produced seemingly non-political regional studies, its members never forgot the primary goal of Japanese domination and the eventual detachment of Manchuria from China. Although it was not as openly political, on a smaller scale, OIMK served a Russian constituency for which a Chinese Manchuria was not a priority.

OIMK filled the needs of two constituencies: it functioned as the CER's research and development body, and it provided employment and social prestige to Russian specialists. The population of the CER concession was the most highly educated in the former Russian Empire. At seventy percent, Harbin's literacy rate far exceeded that of the Russian Far East. This was in part because, before 1920, the CER hired skilled Russian labour and administrators, and hired Chinese workers as the unskilled labour, which resulted in the higher Russian literacy rates than in Russia proper. The Russian researchers formed a large pool of highly trained specialists whose worldview had been formed by the pre-revolutionary Russian Empire. They saw Manchuria as a region rather than as a Chinese administrative unit, as a place where no one particular culture or nationality had predominated historically. For example, OIMK followed the established Russian scientific practice of placing ethnic groups in a timeline according to criteria that related to the concept of development. Since the Chinese settlement of northern Manchuria had occurred primarily in the 1890s, at the same time as Russian settlement, OIMK's history of Manchuria stressed indigenous groups such as the Manchus and the Mongolians, particularly their dress, customs, language, and economic life. Studies of the Chinese were confined to either ancient China or contemporary studies of labour, marriage, and economic life. OIMK's studies created a hierarchy of contributions by the different ethnic groups to the economic and political development of the region. Ultimately, this hierarchal scheme placed a greater value on the Russian rather than the Chinese contribution to the region. Therefore, in the opinion of the Chinese, these studies and the institute served only to perpetuate a perceived hegemonic Russian influence in Manchuria.

The Chinese community's belief in OIMK's hidden agenda was based on several aspects of the society's work, including the prominence of economic studies that underscored the society's role as a promoter and disseminator of information on Manchurian economic life. In 1926, 177 of the society's 460 members were involved in economic studies. The subjects of these studies ranged from forestry to the soya bean, the main agricultural export of the area, and highlighted the unique characteristics of the area's flora and fauna. It contrasted traditional Asian methods of cultivation with the modern Russian methods promoted by OIMK. The society's publications repeatedly gave the impression, not only to the Chinese, that modernity was Russian.[69]

Members of the Russian elite did not question their model of Manchurian science and research, for it was through this activity that they created and perpetuated themselves, both economically and socially. OIMK was, like the Law Faculty, an elite that dominated Harbin society. Through the act of naming, studying, curating, and cataloguing, this Russian elite created a new role for itself and the culture it represented. Using the tools that these researchers knew best, the members of OIMK, in a less overt manner than the Japanese, dominated their physical and social landscape. Only once were the society's proceedings published in both Russian and Chinese, and the sole concession to OIMK's home was the translation of the titles of publications into both Chinese and English.[70] This linguistic prejudice did not go unnoticed by the Chinese press – it was noted that OIMK's objectives were "not for China and Russia to research together."[71] The research practices of OIMK were in sharp contrast to those of Japanese research groups, who published in Chinese and actively tried to recruit Chinese members. OIMK missed the opportunity to build a bridge between the Chinese and Russian elites, and when it needed them, the society found few Chinese defenders.

Unlike other spheres in which émigrés and Soviets clashed, the CER's transfer from émigré to Soviet co-administration in 1924 had little effect on OIMK. Although the Soviets tried to eliminate émigrés from other branches of the CER, they retained OIMK's émigré staff, and the society continued to disseminate information about Manchuria. The society functioned as a key vehicle for promoting Sino-Soviet trade, modernization, and development – values the Soviet regime, much like the former CER émigré board, promoted in order to build regional legitimacy. With this goal in mind, the society produced several exhibitions that extolled the virtues of cross-border trade, inter-regional dependency, and Sino-Soviet friendship in the Special District and abroad. The subsidy to the society and the number of honorary Chinese members were was increased. Chinese members, who were local dignitaries and representatives of the provincial and civic elite, were honorary members only.[72]

In 1927 OIMK attempted to have its taxes waived, a privilege granted to other Russian societies registered as charities. The denial of OIMK's request indicated that Chinese administrators did not view the society as a neutral educational organization.[73] By 1929, the Chinese municipal and provincial elites were actively campaigning to incorporate OIMK into Manchuria's education system. Their campaign was sparked by worsening relations between the CER's Chinese and Russian co-administrators during the CER 1929 crisis, as well as the controversy around the ethnographic and archaeological exhibits on the region's "traditional" peoples in OIMK's Harbin museum. Exhibits on the Chinese peasantry and merchants were removed by OIMK's new Chinese director, and "carefully researched exhibitions of regional dress and daily life" were replaced by an exhibition on Soviet industrialization. According to the new Chinese administration, the original exhibits were "uninteresting."[74] The Chinese elite was not interested in seeing another ethnological exhibit that placed China and the Chinese only slightly ahead of tribal peoples the Chinese considered pre-modern. Nor did it want the Chinese to be placed second in a Russian-constructed narrative of Manchurian development and modernity. The Chinese wanted to see exhibits that highlighted the cutting edge of modernity, a subject of interest to them, and exhibits that did not challenge Manchuria's Chinese identity.

OIMK's Russian émigré members expressed disappointment and anger at the removal of these exhibits. That they could not understand their Chinese partner's point of view indicates that they had internalized OIMK's message of neutral development and did not see OIMK as a bastion of Russian colonial values.[75] OIMK's emphasis on the region and the hierarchy of cultures within it did not endear the society's work to Chinese nationalists. What was for the Russian researcher a scientific analysis of local culture was for his Chinese supervisor an Orientalist exercise, at best, or a covert refusal to acknowledge Chinese rule in the Special District, at worst. The Chinese elite's distaste for OIMK's research must also be considered in the Russian context in which the research was presented. Although OIMK was never explicitly promoted as a Russian cultural institution, it was in language, socialization, and intent purely Russian. Aside from a few exceptions, there were no active Chinese members and no effort to organize a Chinese-language section. OIMK remained a source of employment for Russian academics centred on the railroad, which was itself a reminder of Russian imperialism. Like the other Russian cultural institutions in the Special District (the Law Faculty and the Chinese-Russian Technical Institute), OIMK held itself above the linguistic, national, and geographic context in which it resided. During the 1929 crisis, the society was placed under the authority of the Special District's administration, which announced that OIMK was placed under the district's Department of Education and would lose its status as an independent body.[76] The Russian staff, however, was retained, and OIMK's researchers continued their work until the Japanese occupation.[77]

The experience of Russian primary and secondary schools under Chinese control demonstrates that the Special District ruled with the interests of both its Russian and Chinese populations in mind. The Special District's administration left Russian education relatively untouched and insisted only that Chinese-language studies be included in the curriculum. When émigré schools were threatened by Soviet incursions, the Special District protected them. The Special District also expanded Chinese education under its tenure and introduced the elements of the Russian school system that it admired, such as music and physical education.

OIMK's ethnographic and historical expositions concerning Chinese bronzes, Mongolian Buddhism, or Manchu costumes and its expositions on contemporary themes such as art, photography, or industry reflected the dominance of the Russian or European vision of culture. The society's members presented themselves not only as Russians but also as Russians educated according to the superior standards of Russian liberal and post-Enlightenment thought. Although OIMK's work and the work of Russian higher education in Harbin represented an attempt by researchers to create a new space and vision for Russian learning and culture in Manchuria, the Russian elite could not overcome barriers between Russians and Chinese, nor could they demonstrate that their project was different from those of Imperial Russia, the USSR, or Japan. Whereas Russians in European or American émigré centres tried to build lives based on shared European culture, those in China could not reach out beyond self-imposed linguistic and cultural barriers to their Chinese neighbours. Harbin's physical monuments to Russian culture and creativity – the CER, the churches, its architecture – all worked to reassure some émigrés that they need not compromise. Unlike members of the Chinese elite, who were busy with the project of remaking Chinese language and culture, and had accustomed themselves to borrowing and adapting, émigrés used education and culture to build a barrier between themselves and the Chinese. The fragile structure of émigré identity, the need to preserve this identity in the face of an overwhelming political and economic instability, and the undeniable fact of Chinese numerical superiority in the Special District account for the fact that relatively few Russians learned the language and culture of the country they called home. Russian higher education did not offer a new vision to the Chinese, nor did the Russian elite get past its own preconceptions about Manchuria and China in general. Because the Russian elite failed to speak to the Chinese elite, their work did not escape identification with the private interests of the Russian community. Nor did the elite want it to, for these men saw their research as the best that their community had to offer its old home, which was now situated in a changed political and ethnic context.

Unfortunately, their new home ultimately rejected them and their work. Unlike Russian primary, secondary, and post-secondary schools, which the Special District's administrators considered to be essential not only for the education of the Russian minority but also for the continued development and modernization of the district, the OIMK did not maintain its relevance in the district's changing political environment. The Special District's administration protected and enhanced Russian education when the goals of the Russian community and the administration coincided and when the Russians did not challenge the principle of Chinese supervision. OIMK, like other institutions that challenged Chinese authority, was altered so that it could no longer pose a threat to the Special District's dual mandate to ensure Chinese supervision over its institutions, while fairly administering the Russian minority. OIMK, like Russian education in general, survived until the 1930s, when the new Japanese-controlled regime put an end to the Chinese policy of ethnic accommodation. The creation of Manchukuo and the "Japanization" of Harbin would "deal a death blow to the integrity and continued existence of Harbin as a center of dynamic Russian culture."[78]

9

Conclusion:
Playing Guest and Host on the Manchurian Stage

On the evening of 12 January 1924, the curtain rose for two keenly awaited performances in the lavishly appointed club theatre of the Chinese Eastern Railway (CER). The event was the culmination of a series of charity events for impoverished students of the Russo-Chinese Technical Institute. On the play-bill were two pieces, *The Mandarin's Son* by César Cui and *The Geisha* by Sidney Jones. The former was a play on a Chinese subject by a Russian; the latter was a light operetta on an Asian subject by an Englishman. It was hoped that the performances would reflect the varied interests of the audience and acknowledge the growing importance of the Special District's Japanese population. The audience represented the cream of the Special District's society: a full complement of the district's directors, Chinese and Russian, and their families; all of the Special District's administration; the Harbin Municipal Council; members and faculty of the district's varied schools and research institutes; representatives from Zhang Zuolin's government; foreign consuls; and the business class of all nationalities. The curtain rose to reveal a trad-itional Chinese inn and a Chinese servant bowing and scraping to his employer. The servant, in turn, would attempt to bribe a visiting Chinese offi-cial. Whispers in Chinese rose from the audience as the spectacle of slavish and corrupt Chinese was presented for an international audience. When the curtain fell, there was a particular chill among the Chinese members of the audience, and a number of Russians gossiped about the wisdom of choosing such a play. The head of the CER, Boris Ostroumoff, fresh from his dispute with the Special District and surrounded by Russian CER board members, dismissed the criticism.

The audience returned for the second performance. *The Geisha* is set in a Japanese brothel managed by an obsequious Chinese man who speaks in ter-rible pidgin. For most of the first act, the manager is humiliated and bullied by Japanese and foreigners; in one scene, he is slapped repeatedly by the Japanese owner.[1] The cries in the audience, in both Russian and Chinese, were loud and prolonged. Ma Zhongjun – head of the Special District's Municipal Bureau and a devotee of European, particularly Russian music – rose with his

The Chinese Eastern Railway Club, scene of the 1924 opera scandal. | Courtesy of the collection of Olga Bakich.

family and marched out of the theatre. He was followed by all of the Chinese audience members and some of the Russian. The remaining audience members did not understand the reaction – surely these were only light and harmless theatrical pieces?[2] Within a few days, the Chinese press was calling for Ostroumoff's head, and the streets of Harbin's Russian neighbourhoods were filled with Chinese students, protesting what they believed had been an insult to China's honour.

This episode illuminates fundamental problems and misunderstandings at the heart of the Chinese-Russian relationship in the Special District. Although these problems were not fatal to the administrative, cultural, and economic experiment being carried out in the Special District, they did limit the extent to which either side was willing to compromise. The Special District, as an administrative and geographical entity, was based on compromises between Russian pride and Chinese nationalism and both peoples' colonial aspirations. The Special District owed its very existence to the Russians' recognition that they could no longer lord it over the Chinese, who were now their protectors. For the Chinese, the Special District's administrative arrangement recognized that both peoples had claims to the region and that displacing the Russians would be impractical, given their importance to the district's continued functioning. Nevertheless, there were limits to the compromise, moments when the hard borders of national identity trumped the soft borders of shared history and geography.

Ostroumoff's perceived insult to the Chinese people was that much worse because it took place in a venue in which the Russians excelled and to which the Chinese aspired. Opera in Harbin was serious business. At a time when many North American cities could not support a permanent company, opera was performed in Harbin twice a week at the Railway Club, and there were opera and other musical performances scheduled around the city in different venues. No expense had been spared in the construction of the CER's theatre. The venue was considered the best in China; indeed, it was said that one would have to travel to Moscow to experience its equivalent.[3] Performances were subsidized by the CER, which was committed to promoting the best of European civilization. According to one American resident in Harbin, everybody went to the opera, including Chinese.[4] The incident in question involved benefit productions by the avant-garde Soviet art troupe RABIS for disadvantaged students of the Chinese-Russian Technical Institute.[5]

Both *The Mandarin's Son* and *The Geisha* depicted the Chinese and Chinese life in a manner that Chinese members of the audience found insulting. To some non-Asian members of the audience, however, the performances were entirely consistent with their views of the Chinese; consequently, they found nothing provocative in them. *The Mandarin's Son,* composed in 1858, is an Orientalist fantasy that depicts the romantic difficulties of a young Chinese servant who is in love with his patron's daughter. The inn where he works is visited by a high official. When it is revealed that the official is the boy's father, all the romantic difficulties are resolved. The Chinese objected to the opera's portrayal of slavish relations between the classes and its depiction of a hopelessly corrupt Chinese ruling class.[6] One Russian source said the piece portrayed the Chinese as total idiots.[7]

The Geisha was a popular, widely translated English music hall piece that depicted a day in a Japanese brothel. The brothel is run by a Chinese named Wun-Hi, who is described in the libretto as devious. The plot centres on the efforts of a geisha to marry her Japanese lover and an Englishwoman's attempt to disguise herself as Japanese to woo back her fiancée. During the performance, both the Japanese and the English characters speak in correct English. Only the Chinese character, Wun-Hi, speaks in broken pidgin English – presumably translated into the pidgin Russian used in Harbin.

Wun-Hi.   Oh dearee me! Oh dearee me! This is very awkward – and most obstrepulous! He wantee O Mimosa San, and O Mimosa San makee sing-song for English officer, who givee me plenty much money. What will Wun-Hi tell Marquis?

JULIETTE.   A Chinaman is never at a loss for a lie.

Wun-Hi.   Me very like a woman! Oh, here he comes! This very awkward, most unrelishable. What me do? You, Frenchee girl, be very nice to Marquis. Perhaps Marquis like French girlee – leave Mimosa San – makee much money for me![8]

In Act 2, Wun-Hi bows repeatedly to a Japanese official, and he was slapped repeatedly in the Harbin production.[9]

When Ma Zhongjun and the others walked out of the theatre, they triggered a furor in the Chinese press and demonstrations against Ostroumoff and the CER's Russian émigré administration. The Chinese press condemned the two performances as degrading and insulting to China and took particular offence to the pleasure-quarters setting of the Jones piece and its depiction of Chinese life as corrupt and backward. Wun-Hi's obsequious behaviour toward a Japanese official garnered much anger. On 20 January, at a joint meeting of three Binjiang self-governing societies that had ostensibly been called to discuss Fujiadian's roads, the participants called the operas an insult "to the dignity of the state and all Chinese" and formed a committee to collaborate with CER employees to launch a protest.[10] The largest protest took place on 19 February, when a crowd of several hundred men, described as "mostly coolies and boys," marched from Fujiadian into Pristan, the heart of Russian Harbin. Carrying banners and shouting "down with Ostroumoff," the crowd stopped at the office of the CER's Chinese president and then moved on to the CER's main administration building. Chinese police, who had been warned in advance of the protest, kept order, and the demonstration was described as peaceful.[11] Several schools participated, including many students from the Russo-Chinese Technical Institute (for whom the benefit performances took place): "On February 19th, there was a public meeting in which 4,000 participated, afterwards there was a march. My school had their own bicycle team at the beginning and the end. There were several tens of thousands at the end of the march. Under pressure, Ostroumoff was asked to leave."[12]

The non-Chinese papers were not at all sympathetic. The protesters, identified by the press as "rabble from Fujiadian," were said to be overly chauvinistic and were blamed for creating animosity against Russians and the CER.[13] Casting doubt on the protesters' nationalist feelings, members of the foreign press explained that they had been bribed with food and drink and made light of the protesters' anger: "It [the demonstration] is not an indication of popular feeling. It is not an expression of popular wrath, but merely a rude imitation of it. The people of Harbin know full well by what means Chinese popular wrath is staged."[14] According to the press, the demonstrations were illegitimate because they represented sentiments manufactured by the Chinese elite for their own selfish purposes.

This expression of Chinese nationalism may, to a certain degree, have been encouraged by the Special District's elite. This elite was frustrated by the Russian board members' opposition to increased Chinese control of the district, notably the CER's resistance to giving up control of non-railway land it owned (and taxed). Even proposals to have Chinese, along with Russian, made an official language on the CER had been blocked. What is striking is the absence of any Russian or foreign attempt to see the issue from the Chinese point of view. The Russian and foreign press never conceded that the Chinese may have had a point, and the foreign consuls described the Chinese, elite and otherwise, as children having a tantrum. The possibility that the two performances had either been chosen as a deliberate insult or represented a severe lack of judgment and an exercise in bad taste was not entertained. Certainly, Russians and other foreigners were aware of growing Sino-Japanese tensions, and it was obvious that many foreigners found nothing offensive in the performance's portrayal of the Chinese. The few Russians who did sympathize with the Chinese demonstrated the distance between the two communities and revealed that the foreign community felt it could give no support to the Chinese in a district where foreign privilege was already under siege.

Over one thousand CER employees, all Russians, gathered in a counter-demonstration. The Russian press reported that "the Chinese employees, who once more showed their solidarity with the Chinese crowd of ruffians," were not present.[15] This Russian demonstration, too, is telling. Despite generally good relations between the CER's Chinese and Russian administrations, Ostroumoff was able to gather a large all-Russian crowd by appealing to national prejudices. It appears, however, that Ostroumoff organized the counter-demonstration to rally support for the besieged Russian members of the CER's board. For his part, Zhang Zuolin demonstrated that he was not going to put national pride before the smooth functioning of the Special District when he instructed Zhu Qinglan to prevent the Russian press from spreading rumours that the Chinese planned to expel all Russians. Zhu announced that every effort would be made to stop these rumours and that the Chinese and Russian populations would be treated with complete equality.[16] Zhang prohibited all further demonstrations and ended the incident.

The opera demonstrations were relatively tame. By consular standards, even the Fujiadian nationalists behaved well. There had been much shouting but no violence during the demonstrations. What the Russian and foreign press objected to was that the Chinese had publicly protested in order to claim public space in Harbin's European neighbourhoods (Pristan and Newtown).[17] The detail of the incident that attracted the most attention in the Russian press was the claim that the Chinese protestors had chanted "We will throw the Russians into the Sungari River!" as they marched toward the Russian cathedral. Chinese sources, however, denied the allegation.[18] Even if these chants were not voiced, the fact that this detail was taken up by the Russian press shows their underlying sense of frustration and powerlessness with the changed power dynamic. The report implicitly acknowledged that the Chinese were in control and, if they desired, could indeed throw the Russians into the Sungari.

The Chinese authorities kept the incident under control. Chinese police prevented the demonstrators from approaching both the CER's headquarters and Ostroumoff's home. They acted to shut down a potentially explosive national and racial issue in the interest of preserving peace in the Special District. Given that many of the Chinese authorities had been at the performance, their willingness to defuse rather than exploit the issue demonstrated that peaceful government came before chauvinistic nationalism. Surprisingly, the demonstrations merit little to no mention in contemporary Chinese histories, even though they have all the ingredients of a successful nationalist *cause célèbre*. The incident has only one brief mention in Chinese histories of Harbin published after 1949. By contrast, anti-Japanese or save-the-nation rallies receive extensive treatment. Perhaps the Harbin demonstrations are less interesting because they highlight the city's dual cultural origins and, in their resolution, demonstrate that the Chinese administration was more interested in securing a peaceful community than defending nationalist concerns. The incident was, in other words, another example of what Rana Mitter describes as the mutability of Manchurian nationalism and identity.[19]

The Harbin demonstrations and the accompanying compromise reflected a particular juncture in the decade-long history of the Special District. From 1920 to 1924, Chinese administrators had left most of the district's political, economic, and social institutions intact and under Russian control. The results had been mixed. On the one hand, Chinese supervision had been achieved, and the Special District's administrative staff had gained invaluable experience. On the other hand, some of the district's Russian population continued to act as if Russians were the real power in the Special District. The theatre incident revealed that some Russians were profoundly ignorant about their Chinese neighbours' feelings and did not take Chinese attempts to rule the district seriously. The Russians belittled the Chinese by suggesting that they were incapable of ruling the district, insulted the Chinese by continuing to refer to Russian talent and genius, and threatened the Chinese by using the supposedly co-administered and politically neutral CER to develop projects and policies for the exclusive benefit of the Russian community (policies that the Chinese saw as dangerously similar to the overt colonial project their czarist predecessors had followed a few years before). The Russians dismissed China's claim that it was ruling in the name, and for the benefit, of the district's two populations as crude nationalism, and they interpreted any punitive measures as rapacious Chinese hatred for the Russians. In many ways, because the Russians in this period were prisoners of their own émigré identity, they found it necessary to strike out at anything that threatened their precarious position.

The 1929 crisis, which came at the end of the period of Chinese control of the Special District, revealed that the changes begun by the Special District's administration had taken root: the Russian population had, more or less, accommodated itself to Chinese rule. Five years of a substantial Soviet presence in the Special District had proved to the Russian minority that the Special District's administration supported émigré interests. The attempt in 1929 to dislodge the Soviets from the railway revealed that the Special District had the full support of its non-Soviet Russian population. The 1929 Sino-Soviet incident, an undeclared war on the Sino-Russian border, was the culmination of a five-year struggle between the CER's administrative partners. Each side had tried to increase its control over the railroad. The Soviets had attempted to gain more political and economic control of the CER, and, in turn, the Chinese had attempted to extend and consolidate their own control by employing stateless

Russians and those with Chinese citizenship in key CER positions. The struggle had not simply pitted Chinese against Russians: it had pitted Chinese and Russians long established in the Special District against Soviet carpet-baggers.[20] Beijing and Shenyang once again had different agendas. When the national government persisted in pushing the Soviet Union to the brink of war, Zhang Xueliang's regional government indicated that it was willing to settle the issue.

Frustrations, which provoked the 1929 CER incident, had been building since the 1924 Shenyang agreement. Throughout 1926 and 1927, the Chinese and Soviet members of the CER had fought over the principle of increased Chinese control. These struggles occurred principally in the CER's education and land departments and over the employment of émigrés and naturalized Chinese. The Soviets had complained about the transportation of Chinese troops, local Chinese courts, the CER guards and the railway police, the schools for CER employees, and undefined "institutions under the control of the Chinese authorities," even though the 1924 accord had, on paper, settled these issues.[21] In response, the Chinese had charged the Soviets with non-compliance in the hiring of Chinese workers and the dissemination of Soviet propaganda.[22] By June 1928, relations between the Chinese and the Soviets had declined to such a degree that it was decided that there would be no celebration to mark the CER's twenty-fifth anniversary. Many Russians did, however, celebrate the Chinese national holiday on 10 October.[23]

In July 1928, a Soviet board member, Lashevitch, died of blood poisoning after being accidentally shot during a search of his home by Chinese policemen looking for propaganda. That Chinese police would search the home of a CER board member indicated just how poor relations between the Chinese and Soviets had become. Lashevitch was treated to a Soviet martyr's funeral with the full panoply of Bolshevik ceremony and the body was sent back in state to Moscow. None of this endeared the Soviets to the Chinese or vice versa. Nine months later, on 27 May 1929, Zhang Xueliang ordered a search of Harbin's Soviet consulate. More than eighty persons were arrested, including thirty-eight CER officials and representatives of Soviet labour unions. Various Soviet companies were charged with conspiring to overthrow the Chinese government, assassinate Chinese officials, and spread Soviet propaganda. On 5 July 1929, another Soviet board member was found dead in his home. Rumours suggested that he had been killed by the Soviets because his connections to the Chinese police had resulted in the raid on the Soviet consulate. On 10 July, the Chinese authorities, to put an end to illegal Communist propaganda, dissolved the CER's Soviet labour union, the Young Men's Communist Group, and the boys' and women's Communist groups. The Special District's authorities also sought to overcome Soviet domination of the district's economy by seizing the CER's telegraph office and by closing the Soviet Trade Mission, the Soviet Merchant Marine, and the Soviet-controlled Far Eastern Trading Corporation.[24]

As Manchuria and the USSR moved toward war, émigrés, motivated by a combination of politics and pragmatism, lined up to obtain Chinese passports:

> White Russians have been going to the Binjiang county headquarters to apply for Chinese passports. Since July 1st 1929 until now, more than 1,000 Russians have applied for Chinese citizenship. To apply for a passport, besides submitting documents and a photo, they only need to pay fourteen Harbin dollars. Within ten to fifteen days, they receive their passport. After receiving their documents they can say to everyone, "I am a Chinese national, I am not of the poor party (a Bolshevik)" and can apply to the railway for a job. Although they have had many hardships and have become refugees, they do not want to change their beliefs and submit to the enemy, the Red Party. They believe in China.[25]

All Soviet departmental heads of the CER and Soviet passport holders were fired and replaced with Chinese citizens, largely Russians with Chinese nationality. In an exchange of notes issued between 10 and 17 July, the Soviet government warned that it had the means to protect its lawful rights on the CER and demanded the release of Soviet citizens who had been arrested. The Chinese refused, and the nationalist leader Chiang Kai-shek – speaking from the new Guomindang national capital, Nanjing – was quoted as saying, "Our steps are designed to take possession of the CER. Our hands contain nothing unusual – we want to first take hold of the Chinese Eastern Railway, then take up the discussion of all the questions." In response, Soviet troops gathered near the main border crossings. A conference was hastily arranged for mid-July, at which the Shenyang government would be prepared to settle the conflict. The conference, however, exposed the differences between Shenyang and Nanjing: when Nanjing forbid Zhang Xueliang to settle the issue, the conference was cancelled.[26]

In mid-August the Soviet army attacked the CER line at the two stations on the eastern and western borders. Soviet troops advanced into Chinese territory and caused considerable damage to civilian targets, villages, and towns. After the retreat, the Soviets rationalized the damage by claiming that it had been part of defensive manoeuvres. However, there had been no instances of Chinese aggression against the USSR. That same month, Chinese was designated an official language on the CER.[27] During September and October, the Soviets continued to advance, attacking Chinese shipping on the Amur River and bombing several border communities. The Chinese armies, evidently not well prepared, put up a poor defence. When thousands of Russians and Chinese fled the border communities, they put a great strain on the Special District's resources. The Nikolsk-Ussuriisk Protocol ended the conflict on 3 December, and a new joint Chinese-Soviet administration was appointed for the CER. Ten thousand Soviet Russians, waving red flags, turned up at the railway station on 27 December to welcome the new Soviet head of the CER, Yuly V. Rudy, and the

TABLE 1

CER Employees Pre- and Post-1929

		Russians	Chinese
Pre-1929	Officials	7,735	3,477
	Temporary	1,589	1,414
	Day labourers	1,735	6,627
	Total	11,059	11,518
Post-1929	Officials	5,270	4,817
	Temporary	1,100	2,642
	Day labourers	1,874	9,612
	Total	8,244	17,071

Source: "CER servants of White Russian Origin," *Manchuria Daily News*, 20 January 1930.

new Soviet consul-general. As the band struck up the "Internationale," the Chinese envoy and his party, waiting unhappily on the platform, were pointedly ignored by the Soviet appointees. Although Harbin was still under a midnight curfew, its Soviet citizens celebrated until 1:30 a.m.[28]

Although some Chinese viewed the protocol as a complete capitulation, the Soviets did not recover subsidiary CER institutions and departments that had been seized by the Chinese during the crisis. Nor did the Soviets act in a high-handed manner after 1929. Although it could be argued that the Soviets wisely did not exploit the victory, their post-1929 reticence in regard to both prescribed duties and prohibited actions (such as spreading propaganda) was remarkable. This reluctance should, I believe, be read as an unwillingness to advance a Soviet agenda in the face of Chinese opposition. For instance, after 1929 Soviet employees no longer dominated the CER's payroll (see table 1). There was even a change in how employee numbers were calculated. Before 1929 Russian CER workers holding Chinese passports were counted as Russian workers. After 1929 they were counted as Chinese workers. Before the 1929 incident there were 11,518 ethnic Chinese working for the CER. Russian employees numbered 11,059, giving the ethnic Chinese workers a slight majority. These Russian workers were Soviet passport holders (7,344) and Russians holding Chinese passports (3,715). After the 1929 incident, the number of Russian workers dwindled to 8,244, all Soviet nationals. Chinese workers, both ethnically Chinese and Russians holding Chinese passports, now numbered 17,071. An additional 2,100 Russians, who took out Chinese passports during the crisis, had joined the existing 3,715 so-called Chinese workers of Russian origin. Presumably Soviet actions had convinced these Russians that their Chinese bosses would best protect their interests. Although CER Head Yuly V. Rudy attempted to have these 2,100 new Chinese citizens fired, along with an additional six hundred ethnic Chinese employees, he failed. Chinese CER board members successfully defended their naturalized Russian workers, now fellow Chinese citizens. Only four hundred Russian Chinese passport holders were fired; however, these laid-off workers received generous severance pay from the company on the insistance of the Chinese board. For the first time, Chinese citizens (ethnic and naturalized) constituted a clear majority of CER workers.

Nor would the Soviets exploit the remnant of the school system under their control. They acquiesced to a new curriculum, which was based largely on the old émigré curriculum they had tried to eliminate. Propaganda ceased, and the unions were quiet. The CER was also forced to pay three years' worth of back taxes, which Soviet board members had blocked after the Chinese seized the municipal governments. Yet, relations between the two sides were still not harmonious. In December 1929 all of Harbin's Chinese administrative personnel were instructed not to appear at a CER reception at the Railway Club on 1 January. Although prominent Chinese officials had always gone to the reception, which was held as a gesture of "general congratulations," "not a single one turned up" that year. In return, the Soviet consul left his card at the official reception given by the Special District's head but did not attend himself.[29]

The Special District's Russian population had grown accustomed to Chinese rule by 1929 and preferred it to the Soviet alternative. Was the relative ease by which Manchurian Russians adapted to Chinese rule due to, as some have argued, a qualitative difference between Russian imperialism in China and that of the other powers? Rosemary Quested, in her pioneering work on the CER concession before 1917, argues that the Russian-Chinese relationship was less coercive and based on a greater degree of co-operation than the relationships between the Chinese and other foreign powers.[30] The degree of mateyness (Quested's term for the unusual degree of good relations between Russians and Chinese) during the period before 1918, when Russia was the dominant power in the CER zone, is difficult to measure. Many Russian and foreign observers noted that the Russians interacted with the Chinese better than other imperial powers.[31] Maurice Hindus – who wrote in his 1928 travel article about Russians and Chinese working and living together and even marrying – put this co-operation down to "a lack of race and color feeling" among the Russians who, unlike their European neighbours, were not obsessed with Nordic roots.[32] Although it is impossible to measure the presence or absence of colour feeling, many Chinese sources include references to good relations with their Russian neighbours.[33] Russian memoirs, in turn, often show respect for the Chinese.[34]

The main thrust of studies about imperialism, from the perspective of both the colonizer and the colonized, has been to accentuate the aggressive and coercive nature of the imperial relationship. Aside from studies by émigrés, most studies on Harbin written after 1949 have supported the Chinese nationalist argument that the establishment of a semi-colony, outside of normal treaty port categories, was an aggressive, premeditated act on the part of Russia, which was bent on removing northern Manchuria from Chinese control. Little consideration is given to accounts – Russian, Chinese, or foreign – that reveal that the Chinese-Russian relationship in Manchuria before 1917, both on a personal and an official level, did not have the element of mutual distrust and racial antagonism that characterized relations between the Chinese and other Europeans or, for that matter, the Chinese and the Japanese. Co-operation between China and Manchurian Russians prior to 1917 contributed to China's successful administration of the Special Districts. Of course, there are no statistics through which one cultural or ethnic group's empathy for another can be measured. What we do have are narratives and anecdotes that describe the relationship as friendly.

Are there other factors that encouraged the Manchurian Chinese to be more open to interacting with Russians? The hostility exhibited toward foreigners in the interior of China was generally not seen in Manchuria. Geography may have played a role. Unlike the concessions and treaty ports of central and coastal China, the CER concession was not established in an area that had been occupied by the Chinese for a long time. Because Manchuria was relatively unpopulated, it was a land where different types of national, administrative, economic, and even racial identities could be created. As time passed, these identities tended to be subsumed under the dominant Chinese and Russian national narratives. Yet, the possibility of openness and co-operation, present at the start, never quite disappeared.

The northern Manchurian Chinese, much like Chinese immigrants around the globe, were willing to sacrifice and to adapt to a new linguistic and cultural context to maximize the possibility of success. As immigrants to the Russian Far East, many of them had had long experience with Russians.[35] In Harbin these Chinese sent their children to Russian schools and considered the Russian language to be a necessary tool for success. Most of the Chinese officials whose names appear in this study spoke Russian, and some had Russian wives. Harbin today remains a centre of Russian-language study in China.

What of the Russians? Evidence of a less coercive type of imperialism can be found in Russia's long history as a multi-ethnic empire, one in which subjects of other races and religions were not marginalized. The subject peoples of the Russian Empire coexisted with Russian settlers, and the original ruling stratum of the subject peoples was often absorbed into the Russian ruling class. Sometimes they converted to the Russian Orthodox Church, sometimes they did not.[36] Administratively, Russian imperialists were content to impose a superstructure of Russian control over an area and allow local customs to continue as before.[37]

Of all the foreigners in China, the Russians were singled out for their famous "lack of racial feeling."[38] It is difficult to measure whether this is true. There are numerous accounts of Chinese, or persons of mixed parentage, who were raised Russian Orthodox in Harbin and were considered to be part of the Russian community. They were not excluded from the Chinese community, and often acted as intermediaries between the two groups. In comparison to other Christian denominations, the Russian Orthodox Church is notable for having no sense of mission. Unlike other denominations, it did not actively seek out converts, and it did not distinguish between converts and ethnic Russians.[39]

The task of determining whether Russian imperialism was more inclusive than that of the other concession powers in China, a phenomenon that might explain the relatively peaceful relations between Manchuria's Russians and Chinese, is beyond the scope of this study. Both peoples settled in North Manchuria at the same time, and Russians living there after 1917 had few options outside of co-operation with their new Chinese supervisors. We could point to a long-standing Russian debate about whether Russia was an Asian state, a debate that might have opened the Russians to considering themselves equal to the Chinese, especially in a context where the Russians no longer had the imperial muscle to back their colonial project in China. The other concession powers in China viewed the Russians as Asiatics, perhaps as a means of coping with the spectacle of Russian weakness in China and how far the "whites," as a race, had fallen in China. What must be acknowledged is that Russians, other foreigners in China, and Chinese often described the Sino-Russian relationship, at the level of everyday life, as relatively peaceful.

The Special District's administrators faced a unique challenge during the 1920s: they had the dual task of coping with a declining Russian power as they constructed a Chinese administrative presence where there had been none before. In their opinion, the district presented the perfect opportunity to seize a piece of the Chinese nation that had been stolen to build an illegal Russian colony. However, were they regaining something that China had once possessed? The CER concession had been built on undeveloped territory that China and Russia had settled at roughly the same time. What, then, was being taken back? The task of building Chinese nationalism in northern Manchuria was affected by the particular circumstances of the region. The area had only recently been incorporated politically into China, and it contained large non-Chinese populations. The largest, the CER concession's Russian population, had already erected a sophisticated economic, cultural, and administrative apparatus around the CER.

The CER and its concession had a defined civil administration for those Chinese living in its domain. Even the Chinese administration that adjoined the concession, Binjiang County, existed because the Chinese government required a foothold to counter Russia's presence. Does this mean that the Russian presence was an active force and that the Chinese were merely passive observers of the administrative landscape? Peoples and governments are not like chemical formulas: the human interactions they engender are complex and multifaceted. Dmitrii Horvath did not have developing China's most modern, independent, and inclusive local administration in mind when he took over the CER. Horvath's goals were those of the Russian state – to extend Russia's informal influence over the empty Manchurian landscape. However, the Chinese and Russians who peopled the landscape were changed by the Russian imperial project. Living in a region not completely Chinese and not completely Russian, their identities were formed against and alongside those of their neighbours. When the CER's control apparatus fell apart between 1918 and 1920, Chinese administrators found themselves in control of one of China's most modern, and certainly its most multi-ethnic, city.

The administrative decisions that this Chinese elite made between 1920 and 1929 were informed by the experience of working and living in a Chinese-Russian city. The option of ridding the Special District of its non-Chinese population – or, at least, of creating a completely Chinese administration – was not chosen. This policy was partly pragmatic: the Special District could not function without the Russian employees who served its various institutions. However, the Chinese elite would not have eliminated the Russian population even if their elimination had been an option. Having lived next to and among the Russians – in an area that was not historically Chinese and was, thus, free from many of the ethnic, geographical, and racial associations that informed foreign-Chinese disputes in the southern treaty ports – the Chinese elite was now faced with the hapless colonial remnant of a former great power.

The Chinese administration of the Special District attempted to create a better administration, one that took the interests and aspirations of the two dominant populations into account. Certainly, this project was not completely successful. In the CER, the municipal government, and Harbin's schools and courts, some Russians resisted the Chinese administrative project because they believed it put cherished Russian institutions, rendered more important by the absence of a mother country, into peril. Their discourse of Russian modernity and progress, of experience and culture, hid another racist discourse, one that the insult at the theatre in 1924 made visible, a discourse that held as its first principle China's inability to administer a European community according to European norms. In this case, the consuls joined the Russians. The consuls saw the experiment unfolding in Harbin as a real threat to foreign privilege in China. If the Chinese could prove themselves capable of administering a European community, the entire ideological apparatus of extraterritoriality would be rendered illegitimate.

When the Russians resisted too actively, they were pushed aside. In the early period (1920-24), the Chinese were willing to accept limited Chinese supervision over Russian institutions in the Special District. As the USSR began to reassert an imperial presence in the region, however, the Chinese elite moved to entrench Chinese control, but never with the intention of excluding the Russian population. From 1924 to 1929, the Chinese administration aggressively pursued Chinese control at the expense of the Soviets. This has been misunderstood by many of the sources that assume an unbroken Chinese assumption of power in the Special District. The takeover of the municipal councils, the extension of Chinese control over the education system, and the dispute over the CER, all occurred after 1924 and were all aimed at eliminating real and potential Soviet power bases in the Special District, not at reducing a generic Russian presence for the sake of the Chinese nation. The extension of Chinese control in the second period (1924-29) should therefore be understood as a localized regional response to renewed Soviet imperialism. Chinese administrators often had the support and active assistance of the émigré population, who saw the Special District as their best defence against the Soviets. In return, the Chinese extended protection and support during the 1929 incident to "our Russians," as Zhang Huanxiang called the émigrés.

The figures of Zhang Zuolin and his son and successor, Zhang Xueliang, were crucial to the administrative project. Zhang Zuolin, motivated to protect and enhance the CER concession, created the Special District to preserve and enhance the area. His sponsorship of the émigré population, "that most desirable of European populations," was a strategy aimed at creating an alliance with an important constituency that could be used against the USSR and Japan. As an administrative project, the Special District should be understood in the context of all forces – local, provincial, national, and international. All of these forces are important, but the regional and the provincial have to be given equal billing with the national and the international. For too long, Manchurian history has been written from the shared ideological and political perspective of Beijing and Moscow. This perspective has obscured the unique intercultural and regional administrative experiment that played out on the countries' common frontier.

If the Special District was a unique case, why study it? For one, the history of the Special District reveals a crack in the monolithic story of national resistance to the foreign presence in China. Treaty ports histories have assumed a rather uncomplicated Chinese nationalist resistance to foreign incursion, along with relatively simple Chinese imitation of foreign administrative models. The case of the Special District reveals that, given the opportunity, the Chinese could not only take over a European administration but also improve it. The experience of the Special Distract also reveals that there was not one Chinese nationalism but many regional nationalisms, and southern China was not the only site of urban and local administrative reform.

The experience of Harbin and the Special District challenges categories such as "China," "the Chinese state," and "greater Chinese civilization," which must be expanded to encompass administrative experiments that combined Russian and Chinese institutions and culture and acknowledged difference and plurality and yet were still Chinese.[40] The Special District's administration demonstrated that civilization could be both modern and Chinese. Inhabiting a fully equipped modern city and region that had been built around one of the most up-to-date railway systems in China, the Special District was noted for an absence of national despair for a lost Chinese tradition because the Special District had no Chinese past. It only had a Chinese future, one that included a substantial Russian population. By allowing full interaction between a foreign population without extraterritoriality and the Chinese, China showed that it could accept the presence of a non-Chinese population. The administration of the Special District was, in fact, what the foreigners feared: it undermined the entire racist ideological superstructure on which extraterritoriality was based. The history of the district also proved many of the émigré accounts wrong – the Chinese administration did treat them well. As the author of one newspaper article in 1924 wryly observed: "It was a bitter derision of Russian national conscience that a strange government, different in culture, proved to be more attentive, considerate, and acceptable than the Soviet government, which claimed to be Russian and pretended to be a government."[41]

Chinese nationalism was not the only type of patriotism at play in the Special District. Many of the Special District's Russian citizens were strong Russian patriots who were proud of their country's imperial achievements in Manchuria. Their pride caused them to relegate China and the Chinese to second place, which the Chinese read as an attempt to efface China's contributions to the region. This is illustrated by the account of teacher N.V. Borzov, sadly witnessing the raising of the new Chinese/Soviet jointly administered CER's flag in 1924, where he muses on Russia's contributions to North Manchuria, and China's place as the benefactor of these efforts. "This accomplishment of great Russian creativity was beautifully characterized by the Chinese and foreigners on the occasion of the 25th anniversary ceremonies [of the CER]. But this activity for the benefit of Russia and China does not need words. One should just sit on the train car from Station Manchuria and go along the entire CER in order to see what has been done by the great Russian nation and its real representatives for the benefit of China, Russia and the entire world."[42] Many – such as the head of the CER, Boris Ostroumoff; municipal councillor and Harbin mayor, George Constantine Guins; and the researchers of the Obshchestva izucheniia Manchzurskogo krai [OIMK]– believed that continued Russian supervision and control was essential to retaining the concession for a future non-Bolshevik government. They saw the concession as the last remaining vestige of an Imperial Russia that they had to preserve. Racism in the form of the idea that the Chinese were incapable of ruling the Russian community (the same patronizing attitude that allowed many Russians to justify the illegal construction of a Russian sphere of influence in Manchuria) remained a factor in Sino-Russian relations and sometimes poisoned the relationship. Finally, because the Chinese project threatened the established Russian elite's livelihood, they resisted to save their jobs and not become destitute, stateless refugees.

During the 1920s, the Special District's Chinese elite freely admitted that Harbin owed its prosperity to its Russian co-founders. These strong Chinese patriots equated modernity and development with a strong country. Many were immigrants from other parts of China; as recent settlers, they freely admitted that the Special District was different. Members of the Chinese elite had to co-operate with their Russian neighbours, and because many of them were already linguistically and culturally familiar with Russians, it was no great sacrifice to reach out to the Russian community. These compromises, however, are not the stuff of which an uncomplicated national identity is made. The Special District's administrative experiment, brought to an end by the Japanese takeover of Manchuria in 1931, stands out for its spirit of practical and pragmatic compromise. It has little to say, however, about present-day Chinese patriotism. The imagined community of post-1949 Chinese national-ism has no place for contributions by non-Chinese communities, especially those that cannot be easily absorbed by Maoist national policy. Manchuria had been the colonial frontier of Russia, China, Korean, and Japan, and the People's Republic of China has done its best to wipe away Manchuria's alternative pasts. Following the establishment of the People's Republic of China, citizen-ship laws were changed to render Russian Chinese stateless once more. Rus-sian schools, hospitals, and churches were closed, and employment for Russians disappeared. Some Russians returned to the Soviet Union. Once news of Stalin's camps and the fate of returning Russians began to circulate, many Russian Manchurians opted to leave in the 1950s and 1960s for the United States, Canada, or Australia.

Just as Harbin's many Russian buildings are now hidden behind shiny new towers, so also has the history of the Special District's administrative experiment been effectively buried. To acknowledge this buried past is to acknowledge another version of Chinese nationalism, one that does not mesh with the accepted story of a Russian aggressor and the Chinese victim. As Bei-jing's control weakens over the regions, the northeast, as it is now known, is able to explore its multi-ethnic past. This freedom is evident in the restoration of Russian and Japanese buildings for the tourist trade, but it has also taken the form of memoirs and articles that acknowledge the region's foreign influ-ences. These influences, and cross-cultural exchanges in general, were taken for granted during the 1920s:

> Despite the repeated frictions between the Chinese and the Soviet govern-ments, Chinese and Russian, regardless of political differences, are living most congenially together. When the Chinese authorities took over control of the CER and the relations with Soviet Russia were disrupted, there was not even a single instance of private animosity between the two nationals. Here, in Harbin, Russians have learned Chinese ways to a marked extent, and Chinese in turn have also acquired certain Russian customs and characteristics. Cases of intermarriage are not rare, and the happy results attained seem to disprove Kipling's dictum that "East is east and West is west and never the twain shall meet."[43]

In the Special District, everyday lived experience was not necessarily motivated by national tensions. Chinese and Russians lived next to one another and with one another. Although tensions existed, they were not the dominant mode of interaction. The Special District was unique because the two peoples managed to live together peacefully, and perhaps their greatest accomplishment was their ability to distinguish between the national struggles that could have driven them apart and the common humanity they shared as neighbours and citizens of a shared administration.

Appendix
CER, Special District, and Harbin people

Bao Guiqing, General 鮑贵卿	Military governor of Jilin province, 1919-21
Borzov, N.V., Dr.	principal of Harbin Russian Commercial School; head of the CER's Education Department, 1920-25
Davtian, Yacov	Soviet envoy during the 1924 CER negotiations
Dong Shien 筻士恩	Binjiang County daoyin (circuit intendant) until 1921; head of the Special District municipal bureau, 1920-22
Emshanov, Boris	CER general manager, 1926-29
Filipovich	head of the CER's Education Department, 1924-29
Fu Guicheng (*aka* Fu Xinnian) 傅闰成	graduate of Harbin Russian Commercial School; businessman; Harbin Municipal Council member 1923-29
Gondatti, Nicholas L.	Russian colonial official; head of the CER Land Department, 1920-24
Guins, George Constantine	head of the Harbin Municipal Council, 1923-26
Hanson, George	American consul in Harbin, 1922-30
Horvath, Dmitrii	CER general manager, 1898-1920
Ivanov, A.N.	CER general manager, 1924-26
Gerts, G.I.	Russian lawyer who worked for the Special District, 1923-35

Lashevitch	CER Soviet General manager, 1926-28; shot by the Chinese police and died July 1928
Li Hongzhang 李鸿章	Qing official, 1823-1901; CER negotiator
Li Jiaao (*aka* Li Lanzhou) 李家鳌	Chinese consul to Vladivostok, 1918-21; Binjiang county daoyin, 1911-18; first chief justice of the Special District, 1921; CER board member
Li Xiaogen 李咢苣	Harbin Russian Commercial School graduate; Jilin Foreign Bureau, Harbin Municipal Council member, 1926; head of the Special District Municipal Bureau; head of the Special District Department of Public Education, 1926-29; appointed in 1927 to CER board; acting president of CER board, 1929
Ma Zhongjun 马忠骏	member of the Jilin Province Railway Negotiation Bureau; vice-head of the Special District's Municipal Administration Bureau, 1922-25; mayor of Harbin, 1926-28
Nikiforov, N.V.	head of the CER's Education Department, 1920-25
Ostroumoff, Boris	CER general manager, 1920-24; consultant to the Special District, 1924-30
Riutin, Martem'ian Nikitich (*aka* Liuqin, in Chinese)	Bolshevik head of the Harbin Council of Workers and Soldiers, 1917-19
Rudy, Yuly V.	CER General Manager, 1929-35
Schurman, Jacob	American minister to China
Song Xiaolu 宋小濂	CER president and head of the Special District, 1920-22
Stevens, John	head of the Inter-Allied Technical Board, 1919-22
Sun Lieshan 孙烈山	Heilongjiang daoyin, 1920-22; Jilin province's top military officer, 1921-24
Tishenko, Peter	Vladivostok Far Eastern Institute graduate; mayor of Harbin, 1923-26

Ustrialov, Nikolai Vasil'evich	Soviet head of the CER's Education Department, 1925-29
Wang Jingchun 王景春	CER president, 1922-25
Wen Yingxing 溫应星	West Point graduate; chief Harbin police; CER police director; head of Special District police
Witte, Sergei Yulyevich, Count	Imperial Russian Finance Minister, 1898-1903; Russian Premier 1905-06; founder of the Chinese Eastern Railway concession
Yang Zhuo (*aka* Yang Cho) 杨卓	graduate of Harbin Russian Commercial School; CER board member and head of the Audit Committee; murdered on Zhang Zuolin's orders in 1927
Zhang Huanxiang 张焕相	Special District police chief, 1922-26; head of the Special District, 1924-29; dean of Harbin Technical University, 1928-34
Zhang Nanzhao 张南钊	Binjiang police chief 1917-19; Harbin police chief 1919-22
Zhang Qinghui 张景惠	head of the Special District police 1926-29; head of the Special District, 1929-33
Zhang Xueliang 张學	Manchurian ruler following his father, Zhang Zuolin's, assassination in 1928
Zhang Zuolin 张作霖	Manchurian ruler, founder of the Special District of the Three Eastern Provinces, 1920-28
Zhu Qinglan 朱慶瀾	military and civil governor of Heilongjiang, 1913-16; civil governor of Guangdong, 1916-17; head of the Special District, 1922-24; founder of the International Society for the Protection of Russian Refugees

Notes

CHAPTER 1: INTRODUCTION

1 Olive Gilbreath, "Where Yellow Rules White," *Harper's Magazine*, February 1929, 367.

2 Ibid.

3 Ibid., 368. Manchuria has had many names that indicate its long-contested political identity and the many peoples that have called it home. In contemporary China, the region once known as Manchuria is now known as *Dongbei*, a rather neutral and generic term that indicates that the region is in the northeast of the country. In the latter part of the nineteenth century and the early twentieth century, under the Manchu (Qing) Empire, the region was administered separately from China proper as the homeland of the Manchus. In the final years of the dynasty, the region was known as Dong-sansheng – the Three Eastern Provinces (Heilongjiang, Jilin, and Liaoning). Manchuria was also considered not quite Chinese – in the political, cultural, and ethnic sense – because it was outside of the Great Wall *(guanwei)* rather than within *(guannei)* that traditional boundary of the Chinese state. The Russians also distinguished the region from China proper, referring to it as *Man'chzhuriia*. Although the term now carries the taint of Japanese colonialism because of its association with the term *Manzhouguo*, the name of the Japanese puppet state created after 1931, I will risk drawing the ire of Chinese nationalists and use the contemporary terms *Dongsansheng*, *Man'chzhuriia*, and *Manchuria*. Thanks to Norman Smith, Ronald Suleski, and Olga Bakich for clarifying these issues.

4 The CER concession was, legally, not a concession at all. Unlike legal foreign concessions such as Hankou, where the Chinese government had formally given over local administration to a foreign power, the CER zone (as it is often referred to in order to highlight its ambiguous legal status), was a zone of alienation, *polosa otchuzhdeniia* in Russian. A zone of alienation was a Russian railway term for land on either side of railway tracks given over for the normal functioning of a railroad. As will be made clear the CER's Russian founders used misunderstandings and mistranslations of this term to create a full Russian administration in North Manchuria. Nevertheless, since most Russians, Chinese, and foreigners used the terms *zone, zone of alienation,* and *concession* interchangeably, I will use *concession* for consistency, while arguing that the Russian-controlled CER's claims to administer North Manchura were fundementally illegal.

5 *Jehu* is a nickname for an elderly Russian man. *Yamen* is a traditional Chinese term for a magistrate's bureau. Gilbreath, "Where Yellow Rules White," 368.

6 Lilian Grosvenor Coville, "Here in Manchuria," *National Geographic Magazine* 63, 2 (February 1933): 238.

7 Frederick Simpich, "Manchuria: Promised Land of Asia," *National Geographic Magazine* 56, 4 (October 1929): 400. Not all journalists disliked what they saw in the Special District. Those who tended to socialize outside diplomatic circles and expatriate clubs, spoke some Russian or Chinese,

and were familiar with the two cultures often praised both the absence of official racial prejudice and the efforts of Chinese and Russians to adapt to the changed circumstances. Most often, inter-marriage and bilingualism in the Special District were for comment. For instance the Russian-speaking author Maurice Hindus was puzzled, and then delighted, at Chinese policemen who came to his aid at the Manchurian Customs and spoke Russian. Maurice Hindus, "Manchuria, Boom Land of the Orient," *Asia* 28, 8 (1928): 626.

8 "The Foreigner Who Works with His Hands!" *China Weekly Review* (Shanghai), 18 December 1926.

9 "Notes from Harbin," *Manchuria Daily News* (Dalian), 13 May 1926.

10 Rodney Gilbert, *What's Wrong with China* (London: John Murray, 1927), 269.

11 Ibid., 272.

12 Maurice Hindus, "Manchuria: Boom Land of the Orient," *Asia* 28, 8 (1928): 629.

13 Olga Bakich, "Émigré Identity: The Case of Harbin," *South Atlantic Quarterly* 99, 1 (2000) 57.

14 Gilbreath, "Where Yellow Rules White," 371.

15 Yelena Medvedeva, "Good Neighbourliness (Sketches of Daily Life)," *Far Eastern Affairs* 1 (1994): 73.

16 Viktor Petrov, "A Town on the Sungari," in *The Other Russia: The Experience of Exile*, eds. Michael Glenny and Norman Stone (London: Faber and Faber, 1990), 208.

17 Bakich, "Émigré Identity," 71. What English term should be used for Harbin's citizens? In Chinese and Russian, the terms *haerpin ren* and *harbintsy* are both inclusive and succinct. In English I will use the term *Harbiners* to designate all citizens of Harbin: Chinese, Russian, Jewish, Japanese and Korean.

18 Yaacov Liberman, *My China: Jewish Life in the Orient, 1900-1950* (Jerusalem: Gefen, 1998), 12, 39.

19 B.A. Romanov, *Russia in Manchuria* (Ann Arbor, MI: American Council of Learned Societies, 1952); G.V. Melikhov, *Man'chzhuriia: Dalekaia i blizkaia* [Manchuria: Far and Near] (Moscow: Nauka, 1991). Translation by author. Unless otherwise stated, all translations are the author's own.

20 "Proceedings of the 100th Anniversary of the CER," Khabarovsk, August 2000, and "Gody, liudi, sud'by: Istoriia rossiiskoi emigratsii v Kitae" [City, citizens, and their fate: The history of Russian emigration in China], Moscow, 19-21 May 1998. In the case of the Khabarovsk conference, Chinese officials in Harbin must share the blame for the exclusion of a Chinese perspective in the proceedings. By judging the conference to be too sensitive to be held in China, which was the original plan, they ensured that only half of the story was told.

21 Doc. 28, General Chang-Huan-Hsiang [sic] to General Chang-Tso-lin [sic], 11 September 1920, United Kingdom, Foreign Office, *British Documents on Foreign Affairs: Reports and Papers from the Foreign Office Confidential Print*, Series E, Part 2: Asia, 1914-1939 (hereafter *BDFA* E.2), *China Annual Reports: January 1921 to May 1921*, vol. 24 (Bethesda, MD: University Publications of America, 1994), 21.

22 "Chinese and Russian Police to Learn Each Other's Language," *Binjiang shibao* [Binjiang News] (Harbin), 8 August 1922.

23 "Russians Are Easy to Marry, but It Is Hard to Change Their Customs," *Binjiang shibao* [Binjiang News](Harbin), 2 February 1922.

24 Sun Zhengjia, "Looking at the Glorious Historical Culture of Harbin through Its Cultural Relics," in *The Making of a Chinese City: History and Historiography in Harbin*, ed. S. Clausen and Stig Thogersen (Armonk, NY: M.E. Sharpe, 1995), 15.

25 The end of the Second World War saw the region occupied by the Red Army and many of the original Russian population deported. The region's Japanese population was killed or expelled. For three years the Chinese Communist Part (CCP) and the GMD struggled over the northeast. By 1949 Harbin had been depopulated. The CCP – with an eye to rebuilding the northeast's industrial plant but also, I believe, deliberately colonizing the region – increased the population by one million. For many contemporary Harbiners, history does begin in 1949; there are no references to events before

that year or the pressures put on the Russian population after it. The standard response (in 1989) from many Chinese Harbiners, not knowing their city's multiethnic past, when asked what happened to the Russians was the simplistic answer "They all ran off!" (*Tamen dou pao le!*).

26 Kong Jingwei, *Di e dui haerbin yidai de jingji lueduo* [The economic plunder of Harbin by imperial Russia] (Harbin: Heilongjiang Peoples Publishing, 1986); Zhang Chunlin. "The Foundation of the Harbin City Government," *Harbin Shijiu* [Harbin Historical Research] 9 (January 1989): 8-15; Zhang Chunlin "Haerbin tiebie shijian zhiyange" [The foundation and development of Harbin Special City], *Harbin shizhi* [Harbin Historical Records] 3, 9 (1986): 20-25; Zhang Yuanrong. *Heilongjiang shengzhi jiaoyuzhi* [Heilongjiang provincial records: Administration] (Harbin: Heilongjiang Peoples Publishing House, 1996).

27 Zhang Dongmin, "Recollections on the Foundation of the Northern Section of the Party," *Beifang Luncong* [Northern Research] 4 (1981): 11.

28 Zhang Chunlin, "The Foundation of the Harbin City Government," *Harbin Shijiu* [Harbin Historical Research] 9 (January 1989): 8-15.

29 Ding Lianglun, "A Survey of Harbin's Russian Community, 1917-1931," *Beifang wenwu* [Culture of the North] 61 (January 2000): 81-86.

30 See Li Xinggeng, *Feng yu fu ping: Eguo qiaomin zai zhongguo, 1917-1945* [Leaves in the storm: Russian refugees in China, 1917-1945] (Beijing: Central Publishing, 1997); Ding, "A Survey"; and Wang Zhicheng, *Shanghai eqiao shi* [A history of the Russian emigré community in Shanghai] (Shanghai: Shanghai Branch of the Third Publishing House, 1993).

31 Thomas Lahusen, "A Place Called Harbin: Reflections on a Centennial," *China Quarterly* 154 (June 1998), 185.

32 Lahusen, "Place," 185.

33 John King Fairbank, *Trade and Diplomacy on the China Coast: The Opening of the Treaty Ports, 1842-1854* (Stanford, CA: Stanford University Press, 1953).

34 Rhoads Murphey, "The Treaty Ports and China's Modernization," in *The Chinese City between Two Worlds,* ed. M. Elvin and G.W. Skinner (Stanford, CA: Stanford University Press, 1974), 18.

35 Ibid., 18.

36 See Joseph Esherick, "Harvard on China: The Apologetics of Imperialism," *Bulletin of Concerned Asian Scholars* 4 (December 1972): 9-16.

37 Ramon Myers and J. Metzger, "Sinological Shadows," *Washington Quarterly* 3, 2 (1998): 87-114.

38 David Strand, *Rickshaw Beijing: City, People and Politics in the 1920s* (Berkeley: University of California Press, 1993).

39 Maryruth Coleman, "Municipal Politics in Nationalist China: Nanjing, 1927-1937" (PhD diss., Harvard University, 1984); David Buck, *Urban Change in China: Politics and Development in Tsinan, Shantung, 1800-1949* (Madison: University of Wisconsin Press, 1978).

40 This also speaks to a continuing central Chinese perception that Manchuria was not quite Chinese.

41 Christian Henriot, *Shanghai, 1927-1937: Municipal Power, Locality and Modernization* (Berkeley: University of California Press, 1993).

42 Robert Bickers, "Shanghailanders: The Formation and Identity of the British Settler Community in Shanghai, 1843-1937," *Past and Present* 159 (May 1998): 162.

43 There are also a number of errors in Wang's monograph, which detract from its usefulness. Wang, *Shanghai eqiao shi.*

44 Jung-Fang Tsai, *Hong Kong in Chinese History: Community and Social Unrest in the British Colony, 1842-1913* (New York: Columbia University Press, 1993).

45 David Wolff, *To the Harbin Station: The Liberal Alternative in Russian Manchuria, 1998-1914* (Stanford, CA: Stanford University Press, 1999). Enfranchisement regulations would ensure the CER's domination of city government until the 1920s.

46 James Hugh Carter, *Creating a Chinese Harbin: Nationalism in an International City, 1916-1932* (Ithaca, NY: Cornell University Press, 2002).

47 Rana Mitter, *The Manchurian Myth: Nationalism, Resistance, and Collaboration in Modern China* (Berkeley: University of California Press, 2000).

48 Prasenjit Duara, "Transnationalism and the Predicament of Sovereignty: China 1900-1945," *American Historical Review* 102, 4 (1997): 1030-51.

CHAPTER 2: RAILWAY FRONTIER

1 David Wolff, *To the Harbin Station: The Liberal Alternative in Russian Manchuria, 1989-1914* (Stanford, CA: Stanford University Press, 1999), Chapter 1.

2 Mao Hong, "Haerbin zhong e renmin shenghuo zhuangkuang" [Harbin's Russian and Chinese citizen's lifestyles compared] *Shishi yuebao* [China Monthly] 1, 2 (1929): 115; *Haerbin tebie shizheng baoshi* [Report on the Harbin Special City: City Government] (Harbin, 1931), Introduction.

3 A railway crossing international borders to save travel time and avoid geographical obstacles is not unusual in itself. In the 1850s the Canadian National Railway struck a deal whereby the eastern portion of the railway would cut through Maine to save hours on the Halifax-Montreal run.

4 China: The Maritime Customs. Statistical Series No. 6 Decennial Reports, "Harbin Report, 1907-1911," in *Volume 1: Northern and Yangtze Ports* (Shanghai: Statistical Department of the Inspectorate General of Customs, Shanghai, 1913), 9.

5 David Schimmelpenninck van der Oye, *Toward the Rising Sun: Russian Ideologies of Empire and the Path to War with Japan* (DeKalb: Northern Illinois University Press, 2001), 75.

6 For more on the "Asian" bent in late nineteenth-century Russian foreign policy, see ibid.

7 Foreign Policy Association, "The Chinese Eastern Railway," *Foreign Policy Association Information Service, Volume 1, 1925-1926* (New York: Kraus Reprint, 1967), 1.

8 Economic Bureau of the Chinese Eastern Railway, *North Manchuria and the Chinese Eastern Railway* (Harbin: Chinese Eastern Railway Printing Office, 1924), 99.

9 Sarah C.M. Paine, *Imperial Rivals: China, Russia, and Their Disputed Frontier* (Armonk, NY: M.E. Sharpe, 1996), 186.

10 Ibid.

11 "Liu K'un-I's Secret Proposal, July 1895," in *China's Response to the West: A Documentary Survey, 1839-1923*, ed. Ssu-yu Teng and John Fairbank (Cambridge, MA: Harvard University Press, 1982), 127.

12 "Chang Chih-Tung's Memorial of August 1895," in *China's Response to the West: A Documentary Survey, 1839-1923*, ed. Ssu-yu Teng and John Fairbank (Cambridge, MA: Harvard University Press, 1982), 129.

13 "Treaty of Alliance between China and Russia, May, 1896" (Old Calendar), in *Treaties and Agreements with and Concerning China, 1894-1919*, vol. 1, ed. John MacMurray (New York: Oxford University Press, 1921), 81.

14 Although the Russo-Chinese Bank was a Russian joint-stock company, it was financed by four of Paris's most important banks. In 1910 the Russo-Chinese Bank merged with the Banque du Nord and became the Russo-Asiatic Bank. Following the Russian Revolution, the claims of the Russo-Asiatic Bank, along with those of China and the USSR, would only add to the confusion of who actually owned the line. Foreign Policy Association, "The Chinese Eastern Railway," 2.

15 "Treaty of Alliance," in MacMurray, *Treaties and Agreements*, 75.

16 "The Chinese Eastern Railway Contract," in *Zhongdong tielu* [The Chinese Eastern Railway] (Harbin: Heilongjiang Provincial Archive, 1986), 18.

17 Olga Bakich, "History of Harbin: The Establishment of the City Council," unpublished manuscript, Bakich collection, Chapter 5, "Major Events in the Life of Harbin," 259.

18 Fred Fisher, American Consul General, Harbin, to Henry P. Fletcher, US Ambassador, China, 11 January 1908, included in National Archives and Records Administration (hereafter NARA), RG 59, M862, Roll File 366/4002, 2.

19 Thanks to Olga Bakich for pointing this out.

20 "The Chinese Eastern Railway Contract," article 6.

21 Ibid., article 3.

22 Paine, *Imperial Rivals*, 188.

23 "Contract for the Construction and Operation of the Chinese Eastern Railway, September 8th, 1896," (Gregorian calendar), in MacMurray, *Treaties and Agreements*, 75.

24 The first Chinese president was killed, it is not known by whom, during the Boxer Rebellion and was never replaced.

25 "Statutes of the Chinese Eastern Railway, 4 December 1896" (Old Calendar), in MacMurray, *Treaties and Agreements*, 88.

26 Ibid., article 7.

27 Ibid., article 8, my emphasis.

28 Ibid., article 16.

29 "Convention for the Lease of the Liaotung Peninsula," in MacMurray, *Treaties and Agreements*, 119, article 4.

30 Ibid., article 5.

31 "Additional Agreement Defining the Boundaries of the Leased and Neutralized Territory in the Liaotung Peninsula," in MacMurray, *Treaties and Agreements*, 127, article 4.

32 The siege of Harbin was a relatively unimportant event – at no point was the Russian community seriously threatened. Russian soldiers in the concession numbered close to five thousand. Isolated Chinese attacks did result, however, in the cutting of the Chinese Eastern Railway and the delay of the line's completion. See R. Polchaninov, "A Short History of Harbin," unpublished manuscript, n.d., A.S. Loukashkin Papers, Hoover Institution on War, Revolution and Peace, reel 12, folder 2.

33 Howard Spendelow, "Conflict of Authority in South Manchuria: The Early Years of the Russian Leasehold, 1898-1900" (PhD diss., Harvard University, 1982), 210-17.

34 Paine, *Imperial Rivals*, 217.

35 "Russian Imperial Ukaz Regarding Jurisdiction in the Chinese Eastern Railway Zone, 2 August 1901," in MacMurray, *Treaties and Agreements*, 88.

36 Ibid., 89, article 2.

37 "Additional Agreement," in MacMurray, article 7.

38 Ibid., articles 2, 9, and 10.

39 "Agreement Regarding the Jurisdiction over Chinese Subjects in the Railway Zone," in MacMurray, *Treaties and Agreements*, 321, article 2.

40 Ibid.

41 In 1903 the entire budget for the Russian government was 1.3 billion rubles. S.C.M. Paine, *Imperial Rivals: China, Russia and Their Disputed Frontier* (Armonk, NY: M.E. Sharpe, 1996), 256.

42 Czar Nicholas II, "Russian Imperial Order Regarding the Imperial Lieutenancy of the Far East," in MacMurray, *Treaties and Agreements*, 122, article 1.

43 Russian State Historical Archive, 323:1, 1357, 13-14, 27, translated in Wolff, *To the Harbin Station*, 76.

44 Czar Nicholas II, "Russian Imperial Order," 122.

45 E.I. Martynov, quoted in David K. McQuilken, "Soviet Attitudes towards China, 1919-1927" (PhD diss., Kent State University, 1973), 19.

46 Russian Council of Ministers, quoted in ibid., 20.

47 Ibid., 21.

48 Russian Council of Ministers, quoted in ibid., 22.

49 Sir Claude MacDonald quoted from George Alexander Lensen, *Balance of Intrigue: International Rivalry in Korea and Manchuria, 1884-1899*, vol. 2 (Tallahassee: University of Florida Press, 1982), 796.

50 Paine, *Imperial Rivals*, 244. The Chinese city of Fujiadian was located immediately across the eastern side of Harbin's CER concession border. In Chinese it is sometimes known as Daowai (the area outside the tracks). *Fujiadian* (in English, the domain of the Fu family) was the name used in official Chinese documents and by the foreign population of Harbin. Chinese Harbiners referred and still refer to the area as either Fujiadian or Daowai, although today it is part of Harbin. During the 1920s, it was administratively separate from Harbin and lay within Binjiang County. Fujiadian was the seat of the intendant, the *daoyin*, the county's chief military and administrative officer, who helped co-ordinate administrative policy for the Special District. There is some confusion about the term *daoyin*. James Carter translates *daoyin* as "circuit intendant," a position that was distinct from the Binjiang magistrate or *zhishi*. The daoyin, as a military officer, was superior to the magistrate. James Hugh Carter, *Creating a Chinese Harbin: Nationalism in an International City, 1916-1932* (Ithaca, NY: Cornell University Press, 2002), 27. Fujiadian was also the area where the Special District's future Chinese administrators learned Russian and the challenges of interacting with the Russian population, lessons they brought to the district after 1920.

51 Paine, *Imperial Rivals*, 245, 256.

52 Economic Bureau of the Chinese Eastern Railway, *North Manchuria and the CER* (Harbin: Chinese Eastern Railway Printing Office, 1924), 401.

53 American Consul Fred Fisher to the Secretary of State, Harbin, 25 November 1906, NARA, RG 59, M867, File 3562, 4002/Nov. 25/190, 2.

54 Notes reg the Civil Departmentof the CER Administration, NARA, RG 59, Roll 151, File 861.77/2053, 18 March 1916, 16.

55 Ibid.

56 Ibid.

57 Overview of the Dmitrii Leonidovich Khorvat memoirs (hereafter Khorvat memoirs), Chapter 7, p. 11, Hoover Institution on War, Revolution and Peace.

58 Bakich, "History of Harbin," 257.

59 China: The Maritime Customs. Statistical Series No. 6 Decennial Reports, "Harbin Report, 1907-1911," in *Volume 1: Northern and Yangtze Ports* (Shanghai: Statistical Department of the Inspectorate General of Customs, Shanghai, 1913), 8.

60 For a detailed examination of interministerial rivalry in Manchuria, see Wolff, *To Harbin Station*, Chapter 2.

61 After Witte's fall, the Finance Ministry, which had under Witte assumed the duties of other government departments, was scaled back, and its many obligations returned to their former ministries.

62 "Plans Peace for Harbin," *New York Times* (New York), 6 March 1909.

63 United States, Department of State, *Proposed Establishment by the Chinese Eastern Railway Company of a Municipal Administration at Harbin* (Washington, DC, 1910), 1.

64 Ibid., 38.

65 Dong was also deeply interested in administrative and municipal reform and, after playing an active role in the takeover of the concession's police force, would be appointed head of the new Special District in 1921. Zhang Nanzhao, "Memoirs," in Dongchui shangbao [Northern Frontier Business Association], *Haerbin zhinan* [Guide to Harbin] vol. 1 (Harbin, 1922), 7.

66 United States, Department of State, *Proposed Establishment*, 8.

67 Ibid., 17.

68 Governments of China and Russia, "Preliminary Arrangement for the Municipal Organizations in the Zone of the Chinese Eastern Railway," *American Journal of International Law* 3, 4 (October, 1909): 290.

69 Ibid., 292.

70 China and Russia, "Preliminary Arrangement," 291.

71 Only Chinese copies of these regulations have been found.

72 *Haerbin tebie shizheng baoshi*, 2.

73 Article 3 of the 1909 agreement gave control of all property determined to be public over to the municipal governments. Individual leases were still paid to the CER Land Department. China and Russia, "Preliminary Agreement," 289.

74 *Haerbin tebie shizheng baoshi*, 3.

75 Ibid., 1.

76 Rosemary K.I. Quested. *"Matey" Imperialists? The Tsarist Russians in Manchuria, 1895-1917* (Hong Kong: University of Hong Kong, 1982), 199.

77 Fred Fisher, to American Secretary of State, 21 July 1909, NARA, RG 59, M862, Roll 367, File 1198.

78 United States, Department of State, *Proposed Establishment*, 58.

79 Robert Thurston, *Liberal City, Conservative State: Moscow and Russia's Urban Crisis, 1906-1914* (Oxford, 1987): 37-41

80 United States, Department of State, *Proposed Establishment*, 34.

81 Fred Fisher to American Secretary of State, 21 July 1909, NARA, RG 59, M862, Roll 367, File 1198.

82 "Russia Would Rule by Chinese Treaty," *New York Times* (New York), 8 July 1909.

83 In 1914 the appointment of the CER's delegate was delayed when St. Petersburg could not make a decision about whether the appointed candidate was suitable. "The Appointment of Delegates," Kharbinskii den' [Harbin Day](Harbin), 16 April 1914.

84 Letter from Harbin Counsul, "Chinese Members, Municipal Council," NARA, RG 59,M329, Roll 99, File 893.102 H/303, 6 October 1911.

85 Consul Fisher to Secretary of State, NARA, RG 59, M862, Roll 367, File 1906-1910, , 21 July 1909.

86 Bakich, "History of Harbin," 262.

87 Ibid., 263.

88 These were, from the most to the least important, trade taxes (162,000 rubles), rental of city property (129,000 rubles), land and house taxes (126,800 rubles), fees from municipal slaughterhouse (72,700 rubles), vehicles tax (25,800 rubles), spirit taxes (50,000 rubles), and miscellaneous taxes (50,000 rubles). China: The Maritime Customs. Statistical Series No. 6 Decennial Reports, "Harbin Report, 1907-1911," in *Volume 1: Northern and Yangtze Ports* (Shanghai: Statistical Department of the Inspectorate General of Customs, Shanghai, 1913), 6.

89 Bakich, "History of Harbin," 258.

CHAPTER 3: THE CHINESE EASTERN RAILWAY

1 Wang, a Yale University engineering graduate, had extensive experience with railways across China. He was appointed to the position of CER president in 1920. *Who's Who in China* (Shanghai: China Weekly Review, 1930), 408.

2 George Hanson to American Ambassdor, NARA, RG 59, M316, File 871.77 3306, 15 December 1923.

3 Thomas Lahusen, "A Place Called Harbin: Reflections on a Centennial," *China Quarterly* 154 (June 1998): 185. Some contemporary Chinese have proposed this date, not the date of the CER concession's foundation, as the city's true birth date, a proposal that speaks to the fact that Harbin's troubled origins have still not been settled.

4   H.S. Brunnert and V.V. Hagelstrom, *Present Day Political Organization of China* (Shanghai: Kelly and Walsh, 1912), 386.

5   Brunnert and Hagelstrom, *Present Day Political Organization,* 389.

6   Rosemary K.I. Quested, *"Matey" Imperialists? The Tsarist Russians in Manchuria, 1895-1917* (Hong Kong: University of Hong Kong, 1982), 181.

7   Ibid., 185.

8   Ibid.

9   Shing Chang Tao, *International Controversies over the Chinese Eastern Railway* (Shanghai: Commercial Press, 1936), Chapter 5.

10 "China Complains to Britain," *New York Times* (New York), 14 February 1909.

11 "Russia Insists on Taxes," *New York Times* (New York), 8 August 1909.

12 Fred Fisher, to American Secretary of State, 2 July 1909, NARA, RG 59, M862, Roll 367.29, File 1292.

13 Ibid.

14 Prince of Ch'ing [Qing] to Mr. H.P Fletcher, 4 December 1909, translated, NARA, RG 59, M862, Roll 367, File 367.1313, 6 December 1909.

15 The Chinese note also referred to the 1905 Treaty of Portsmouth, in which Russia promised to "restore entirely and completely to the exclusive administration of China all portions of Manchuria." Prince of Ch'ing to Mr. Fletcher, 4.

16 Gavan McCormack, *Chang Tso-lin in Northeast China, 1911-1928: China, Japan, and the Manchurian Idea* (Stanford, CA: Stanford University Press, 1997).

17 Translation from *Novosti zhizni,* NARA, RG 59, M316, File 861.00/963, 1910-29, 28 October 1917.

18 Thomas Lahusen, "Silver Screens and Lost Empires, or, 'Where the Russians Used to Live,'" unpublished paper, author's collection, 5. Riutin later escaped from Harbin after the Harbin Council was defeated by the Chinese, allegedly dressed as a women. He became a prominent member of the Communist Party in Russia and was shot by Stalin in 1937. Thanks to Olga Bakich for this information.

19 Zhang Nanzhao, "Memoirs," in Dongchui shangbao [Northern Frontier Business Association], *Haerbin zhinan* [Guide to Harbin] vol. 1 (Harbin, 1922), 7.

20 Tang Zhongmin, *Haerbin shizhi: gongan sifa xingzheng* [Harbin City Records: Public Security and Legal Administration] (Harbin: Heilongjiang People's Publishing House, 1996).

21 Letter from American Ambassador to Secretary of State, 17 December 1917, NARA, RG 59, M316, Roll 11, File 861.00/963.

22 "Anarchy in Harbin," *Japan Chronicle* (Tokyo), 13 December 1917, 832.

23 Zhang, "Memoirs," 7.

24 Ibid.

25 Ibid.

26 Ibid., 8.

27 Ibid., 9.

28 Ibid., 10.

29 Ibid.

30 Police in the Region of the Chinese Eastern Railway, NARA, RG 59, M316, Roll.158, File 861.77/3593, 6 March 1924.

31 Zhang, "Memoirs," 10.

32 Ibid., 13

33 According to Bakich the second version of his death is correct. Thanks to O. Bakich and see Telegram from the Japanese Military Mission, 29 June 1920, NARA, RG 59, Roll 150, M316 861.77/1769, 19 April 1920. The telegram referred to him as the "Jewish Bolshevik Tcherniavsky." See copy of telegram to

Commander in Chief Oi, Vladivostok from General Issizaki, Harbin, 15 August 1920, NARA, RG 59, M316, Roll 150, File 861.77/1769, 19 April 1920.

34 Information from the Japanese Military Mission, NARA, RG 59, Roll 150, M316 861.77/1769, 19 April 1920. While the Bolshevik Party was blocked in elections to the Russian National Assembly, the Harbin party elected three men, one Socialist and two Communists. On 24 June 1918, there was a big Bolshevik Party meeting in Harbin.

35 Zhang, "Memoirs," 13.

36 Inter-Allied Commision Head John Stevens to US Secretary of State, NARA, RG 59, Roll 150, M316 861.77/1023, 16 August 1919.

37 Doc 188, Consul Sly to Mr. Alston, 13 June 1920, in United Kingdom, Foreign Office, *BDFA* E.2, *China Annual Reports: January 1919 to December 1920*, vol. 23 (Bethesda, MD: University Publications of America, 1994), 221.

38 Li Shuxiao, ed., *Haerbin lishi biannian: 1896-1949* [Chronology of Harbin history: 1846-1949] (Harbin: People's Publishing House, 1986), 96.

39 Doc 188, Consul Sly to Mr. Alston, 13 June 1920, in United Kingdom, Foreign Office.

40 Consul Jenkins to US Secretary of State, NARA, RG 59, Roll 316, M316 861.77/1377, 18 February 1920.

41 Li, ed., *Haerbin lishi biannian, 1896-1949*, 97.

42 "Chinese Proclamation in Harbin," *Japan Chronicle* (Tokyo), 25 March 1920, 362; Doc 262, Mr. Clive to Earl Curzon, 18 August 1920, in United Kingdom, Foreign Office, *BDFA* E.2, *China Annual Reports, January 1919 to December 1920*, vol. 23 (Bethesda, MD: University Publications of America, 1994), 292.

43 Ibid.

44 Dongchui Shangbao, "Letters and Telegrams Concerning the Takeover of the Courts," *Haerbin zhinan* vol. 2, 9-42.

45 Dr. John Ferguson, "Report on the CER," NARA, RG 59, M316, Roll 150, File 861.77/1919, 25 October 1920.

46 Ibid.

47 Cui Wei, "Settling Relations between the Temporary Nanjing Government and China's Minorities," *Nanjing jihui kexue* [Social Sciences in Nanjing] 2 (February 2003): 52-55; Wen-Djang Chu, *The Moslem Rebellion in Northwest China, 1862-1878: A Study of Government Minority Policy* (Paris: n.p., 1966); Zuoshan Yang, "A Discussion of Republican Period Frontier Ethnic Policy," *Guyuan shixuebao (shehui kexueban)* [Journal of the Guyuan Teachers College (Social Sciences)] 21, 5 (2000): 43-47.

48 "An Interview between One of Our Reporters and Mr. Sun Sheng Wu of the High Administrators Office," *Harbin Dawning* (Harbin), 8 March 1923, translated, NARA, RG 59, M316, Roll 153, File 861.77/3056, 23 March 1923.

49 Ronald Stanley Suleski, "Regional Development in Manchuria: Immigrant Laborers and Provincial Officials in the 1920s," *Modern China* 4, 4 (1978): 419-34.

50 Harbin Municipal Council Members, NARA, RG 59, M329, Roll 100, File 893.102H/379, 1 September 1922.

51 Harbin Yearbook Society, *Haerbin nianjian 1994* [Harbin yearbook 1994] (Harbin: Harbin Yearbook Society, 1994), 54.

52 "An Interview between One of Our Reporters and Mr. Sun Sheng Wu," NARA, RG 59, M329, Roll 100, File 893.102H/379, 11 September 1922.

53 "Autonomy for the Railway Zone," *Zaria* (Harbin), 26 September 1923, NARA, RG 59, M316, Roll 153, File 861.77/3249, 19 October 1923.

54 *Administrativnoe uctpoictvo severnoi Man'chzhuriia* [The Administration of Northern Manchuria] (Harbin, 1926), 14.

55 "A Man Worth Watching," *Harbin Daily News* (Harbin), 9 May 1923, Enclosure 1, Dispatch 1232, NARA, RG 59, M316, Roll 153, File 861.77/3108, 11 May 1923.

56 "Zhu Qinglan heads Refugee Society," *Jilin shengbao* [Jilin provincial reports], 11 March 1923, File 2254, Jilin Provincial Archives. General Zhu also contributed to the construction of Harbin's Confucian temple and new Chinese middle school. He was an active Chinese patriot and protector of the Russian community.

57 Doc. 80, Consul General Philips to Sir R. Macleay, United Kingdom, Foreign Office, *BDFA* E.2, *China Annual Reports: November 1925-June 1926*, vol. 30, (Bethesda, MD: University Publications of America, 1994), 125.

58 E.Kh. Nilus, "Istoricheskii obzor Kitaiskoi vostochnoi xheleznoi dorogi, 1896-1923" [Historical survey of the Chinese Eastern Railway, 1896-1923], unpublished manuscript, 1923, Hoover Institution on War, Revolution and Peace, 40.

59 "The Executive Committee Should Be Fundamentally Changed," *Binjiang shibao* (Harbin), 30 May 1922.

CHAPTER 4: SECURING THE SPECIAL DISTRICT

1 Olive Gilbreath, "Where Yellow Rules White," *Harper's Magazine*, February 1929, 367.

2 Igor Mitrofanov, *The Lands and Land Administration of the Chinese Eastern Railway Company, and the Incident of August 1st 1923* (Harbin, n.d.), 2.

3 China: The Maritime Customs. Statistical Series No. 6 Decennial Reports, "Harbin Report, 1907-1911," in vol. 1: *Northern and Yangtze Ports* (Shanghai: Statistical Department of the Inspectorate General of Customs, Shanghai, 1913), 6; Tang Zhongmin, ed., *Harbin shizhi: Gongan sifa xingzheng* [Harbin city records: Public security and legal administration] (Harbin: Heilongjiang People's Publishing House, 1996), 31.

4 Harbin Consul to US Ambassador, NARA, RG 59, M316, Roll 99, File 893.102/H/317, 28 November 1915, 7.

5 Tang Zhongmin, *Haerbin shizhi*, 309.

6 Consul Fisher to US Secretary of State, NARA, RG 59, M862, Roll 367,File 1906-10, 21 July 1909.

7 Doc 13, Memorandum respecting Northern Manchuria, in United Kingdom, Foreign Office, *BDFA* E.2, *China Annual Reports: September 1928-June 1929*, vol. 36 (Bethesda, MD: University Publications of America, 1994), 25.

8 In his memoir, which was written in the 1920s in the context of increased debate over the illegal interpretation of the original 1898 agreement, Horvath felt the need to explain why the Russians had extended policing powers far beyond those needed for ordinary railway protection. Khorvat, memoirs, Chapter 3, p. 11, Hoover Institution on War, Revolution and Peace.

9 Green to US Secretary of State, NARA, RG 59, M316, Roll 99, File 893.102/291, 8 June 1910, 10; Fisher to Assistant Secretary of State, NARA, RG 59, M862, Roll 366,File 1906-10, 24 February 1908.

10 "State of Anarchy Found at Harbin," *New York Times* (New York), 19 April 1908.

11 Zhang Nanzhao, "Memoirs," in Dongchui shangbao [Northern Frontier Business Association], *Haerbin zhinan* [Guide to Harbin], vol. 1 (Harbin, 1922), 10.

12 Ibid.

13 Ibid.

14 Ibid., 12

15 Ibid.

16 Ibid.; "Interview with General Wen Ying-Hsing," NARA, RG 59, M316, Roll 158, File 861.77/3718, 13 October 1924.

17 "Interview with General Wen Ying-Hsing."

18 General Chu and the CER, NARA, RG 59, M316, Roll 158, File 861.77/2980, 6 January 1923.

19 Letter from John Stevens to American Consul, NARA, RG 59, M316, Roll 316, File 861.77/1430, 16 March 1920.

20 Dongchui shangbao, "Railway Police Regulations, 25 December 1920," *Haerbin zhinan* vol. 2, 125-27.

21 Letter from John Stevens to American Consul, NARA, RG 59, M316, Roll 316, File 861.77/1430, 16 March 1920.

22 "Journey of the American Minister to Harbin and over the CER," NARA, RG 59, M316, File 861.77 3233, 25 September 1923, 7.

23 "The Internal Situation of the CER Police," *Binjiang shibao* (Harbin), 22 June 1923.

24 Report from Harbin, NARA, RG 59, M316, Roll 153, File 861.77/2988, June 1922; Letter from John Stevens to American Consul, NARA, RG 59, M316, Roll 316, File 861.77/1430, 16 March 1920.

25 "Russians Ask for Employment as Railway Police," *Binjiang shibao* (Harbin), 1921.

26 It was a much larger force than was employed by comparable railways. In England the norm for railway security was one railway guard for every fourteen employees; on the CER there were thirty-six hundred police and guards for eighty-five hundred employees. "What the Russian Papers Say," *Harbin Daily News*, NARA, RG 59, M316, Roll 158, File 861.77/3730, 28 November 1924.

27 Doc 242, Consul Grant Jones to Sir M. Lapson, 27 October 1927, in United Kingdom, Foreign Office, *BDFA* E.2, *China Annual Reports: June 1927-December 1927*, vol. 33 (Bethesda, MD: University Publications of America, 1994), 368.

28 South Manchurian Railway, *Report on Progress in Manchuria, 1907-1928* (Dalian: SMR Publishing House, 1929).

29 Report from Harbin, NARA, RG 59, M316, Roll 153, File 861.77/2988, June 1922.

30 Toa-Keizai Chosakyoku [East-Asiatic Economic Investigation Bureau], *The Manchurian Yearbook, 1932-33* (Tokyo, 1932), 49.

31 China: The Maritime Customs.

32 Report from Harbin, NARA, RG 59, M316, Roll 153, File 861.77/2988, June 1922; Letter from US Embassy Peking to Washington, NARA, RG 59, M316, Roll 151, File 861.77/2197, 5 July 1921.

33 Report from Harbin, NARA, RG 59, M316, Roll 153, File 861.77/2988, June 1922; Municipal Contributions, NARA, RG 59, M316, Roll 153, File 861.77/3070, 15 March 1922.

34 "Interview with General Wen Ying-Hsing," NARA, RG 59, M316, Roll 158, File 861.77/3718, 13 October 1924.

35 Memorandum on the Problem of Chinese Taxes in the CER Zone, NARA, RG 59, M316, Roll 153, File 861.77/3344, 2 January 1924.

36 The Situation of the Russians in the CER Zone, NARA, RG 59, M316, Roll 153, File 861.77/3231, 22 September 1923.

37 The Sino-Soviet co-administration was established in 1924 as a means of removing the last vestiges of the CER's Russian colonial administrative policy. It is examined in more detail in chapter four.

38 "What the Russian Papers Say," *Harbin Daily News*, NARA, RG 59, M316, Roll 158, File 861.77/3730, 28 November 1924.

39 "To Make Room for Soviet Officers," *Manchuria Daily News* (Dalian), 2 March 1925.

40 "Interview with General Wen Ying-Hsing," NARA, RG 59, M316, Roll 158, File 861.77/3718, 13 October 1924.

41 "Interview with General Wen Ying-Hsing," NARA, RG 59, M316, Roll 158, File 861.77/3718, 13 October 1924; NARA, RG 59, M316, Roll 154, File 861.77/2747, 30 January 1925.

42 "Interview with Mr. W.H. Donald," NARA, RG 59, M316, Roll 150, File 861.77/1572, 28 April 1920; Consul Jenkins to Secretary of Stste, NARA, RG 59, M316, Roll 150, File 861.77/1454, 8 April 1920.

43 "Home by Siberia," *Japan Chronicle* (Tokyo), 28 April 1927, 479.

44 "No Russian Policemen," *Binjiang shibao* (Harbin), 1 April 1921.

45 "Russian Police Statistics," *Binjiang shibao* (Harbin), 7 July 1923.

46 Doc 80, Consul Philips to Sir R. Macleay, 3 December 1925, in United Kingdom, Foreign Office, *BDFA* E.2, *China Annual Reports: November 1925-June 1926*, vol. 30 (Bethesda, MD: University Publications of America, 1994), 125.

47 Memorandum du Comité des Représentants des Institutions Judiciaires à Harbin, NARA, RG 59, M329, Roll 92, File 893.04/1, 2 April 1921.

48 Harbin Consul to Secretary of State, NARA, RG 59, M316, Roll 152, File 861.77/2598, 7 June 1922.

49 "Police Schools in the Special District," *Binjiang shibao* (Harbin), 12 October 1922; "Russian and Chinese Police to Study Each Other's Language," *Binjiang shibao* (Harbin), 29 August 1922; "The Graduation of the Railway Police," *Binjiang shibao* (Harbin), 22 September 1922.

50 "Graduation Speech for the 2nd Class of the CER Police School," *Binjiang shibao* (Harbin), 29 October 1922.

51 This put a lie to the claim that the signals were only to extract money from foreigners for the benefit of the Chinese. "Russians Have Monopoly over Signal Lamp," *Binjiang shibao* (Harbin), 13 September 1921.

52 N.S. Zakharova, *Guide for Homeowners* (Harbin: Zaria Press, 1927).

53 "Police Procedures," *Peking and Tientsin Times*, 23 January 1924, enclosed in NARA, RG 59, M329, Roll 100, File 861.102/H/437, 11 February 1924; Report on Article in *Special Police Weekly*, NARA, RG 59, M329, Roll 100, File 861.102/H/421, 28 November 1923.

54 "News from Harbin," *Manchuria Daily News* (Dalian), 31 January 1929.

55 "Harbin Police to Port Arthur," *Manchuria Daily News* (Dalian), 7 April 1924.

56 "Railway Police Get New Russian Officer," *Binjiang shibao* (Harbin), 30 June 1922; "Russian Police Fined," *Binjiang shibao* (Harbin), 23 March 1923.

57 Consul Sly to Me. Alston, 13 June 1920, in United Kingdom, Foreign Office, *BDFA* E.2, *China Annual Reports: January 1919-December 1920*, vol. 23 (Bethesda, MD: University Publications of America, 1994), 229.

58 Maurice Hindus, "Manchuria: Boom Land of the Orient," *Asia* 28, 8 (1928): 626.

59 Harbin's police could also be called out for dog-killing duty, as they were in 1928, when reports of ten dog attacks came in from the suburbs. "Harbin Infested with Homeless Dogs," *Manchuria Daily News* (Harbin), 30 October 1928.

60 "Newspapers in Harbin," *Japan Chronicle* (Tokyo), 27 July 1922, 133.

61 His petition was refused. "News from Harbin," *Manchuria Daily News* (Dalian), 29 January 1929.

62 Russian papers attempted to get around censorship laws by publishing special issues with no page numbers. "Regulations for Special Editions of Russian newspapers," *Binjiang shibao*, 30 February 1927.

63 "Communist Literature in Harbin," *Japan Chronicle* (Tokyo), 24 April 1930, 414.

64 "Russian Infighting in the Special District," *Binjiang shibao* (Harbin), 6 September 1923.

65 Administration of Justice in Chinese and Extraterritorial Courts in China, NARA, RG 59, M329, Roll 92, File 893.041/40, 31 May 1923, 3.

66 "Chinese Authorities in Harbin on the Side of Decency," *Manchuria Daily News* (Dalian), 20 August 1929.

67 Shuxias Li, ed., *Haerbin lishi biannian: 1896-1949* [Chronology of Harbin history: 1846-1949] (Harbin: People's Publishing House, 1986), 113.

68 "Special District Almost Bans Cinemas," *Binjiang shibao* (Harbin), 23 August 1923.

69 "The Harbin Temporary Self-Governing Committee and the Supervisory Prices and Taxation Committee Joint Meetings," in *Haerbin tebie shizheng baoshi* [Report on the Harbin Special City: City Government] (Harbin, 1931), 88.

70   J.B. Powell, "Sidelights on Harbin," *China Weekly Review* (Shanghai), 19 October 1929; "The Russian Traffic Police," *Binjiang shibao* (Harbin), 8 June 1927.

71   "Special District Police Inspect Drivers," *Binjiang shibao* (Harbin), 14 July 1927; Li, *Haerbin lishi biannian*, 113; "Automobile Census in China," *Chinese Economic Review* 157, 23 February 1924.

72   There were guides called *provodniaki* who made their living illegally guiding refugees across the border. Yaacov Liberman, *My China: Jewish Life in the Orient, 1900-1950* (Jerusalem: Gefen, 1998), 23.

73   "The Licensing of Russian Immigrants," *Binjiang shibao* (Harbin), 7 April 1921.

74   "Protect Russian Immigrants," *Binjiang shibao* (Harbin), 9 November 1922.

75   Passengers who were heading south from the Special District had always been checked, but after 1920 passengers headed east and west were also checked. Consul Hanson to Peking, NARA, RG 59, M316, Roll 154, File 861.77/4061, 30 July 1926.

76   Act of Indictment, NARA, RG 59, M316, Roll 158, File 861.77/2861, 2 November 1922.

77   The police approached the Harbin Self-Governing Committee in 1926 for funds to feed and house destitute foreigners and Chinese found on the streets. The committee asked for a detailed report on numbers and promised to give aid. "The Harbin Temporary Self-Governing Committee and the Supervisory Prices and Taxation Committee Joint Meetings. Meeting Fifteen, May 18th, 1926. Case Eleven," *Haerbin tebie shizheng baoshi* [Report on the Harbin Special City: City Government] (Harbin, 1931), 88; "Investigation of Russians without Passports in the Special District," *Binjiang shibao* (Harbin), 17 December 1925.

78   S.T. Tepnavskii, *Ves' Kharbin* [All Harbin] (Harbin: CER Publishing House, 1923), 53.

79   "Passport Application," *Jilin sheng baogao* [Jilin provincial reports], Jilin Provinicial Archives, File 2625.1, 30 May 1924.

80   Gong Jianghong, *Harbinshizi minzheng qiaowu* [Harbin city government: Immigration] (Harbin: Heilongjiang People's Publishing House, 1994).

81   "Russian Resident Applications Are Numerous," *Binjiang shibao* (Harbin), 23 July 1923; "Russian Workers Registered by the 4th District Police," *Binjiang shibao* (Harbin), 23 August 1923; "The Special Police Cares for Russians," *Binjiang shibao* (Harbin), 12 November 1928; "Stateless Russians in the CER Concession," *Binjiang shibao* (Harbin), 13 June 1924; "The Special Police Cares for Russians."

82   "The Law to Limit Russian Passports," *Binjiang shibao* (Harbin), 1 January 1923.

83   "The Special Police Cares for Russians."

84   Thanks to Olga Bakich for this detail.

85   "Russians with Chinese Citizenship," *Binjiang shibao* (Harbin), 19 October 1924; "Registration of Russians in the Special District with Chinese Citizenship," *Binjiang shibao* (Harbin), 11 November 1925; Nina Federova's fictional account of a Russian émigré family living in Tianjin contains a description of an illegal border crossing back into Russia. Any number of guides took émigrés back and forth for 100 rubles. Nina Federova, *The Family* (New York: Little and Brown, 1940), 320.

86   *Jilin sheng baogao* [Jilin Provincial Reports], File 2625.1, 30 May 1924.

87   "To Prevent Russian Arms Falling in Bandit's Hands," *Binjiang shibao* (Harbin), 1 December 1925.

88   Meeting between Chu and Davtyan, NARA, RG 59, M316, Roll 154, File 893.77/3406, 17 March 1924.

89   "The Russian Police and the Last Events," *Zaria*, 8 October 1924, NARA, RG 59, M316, Roll 154, File 861.77/3722, 14 October 1924.

90   "White Russian Police Officers Naturalized," *Manchuria Daily News* (Dalian), 21 November 1930.

91   "Vigorous Control over White Russians in Harbin," *Manchuria Daily News* (Dalian), 6 March 1930.

92   "Police Regulations," *Russki Golos*, 9 March 1923, NARA, RG 59, M329, Roll 100, File 893.102/H/415, 14 March 1923.

93   "Special District Regulations for Russian Meeting," *Binjiang shibao* (Harbin), 10 October 1921; "Russian and Chinese Communists Dispersed by Police," *Manchuria Daily News* (Dalian), 14 March 1930; "October Revolution at Harbin," *Manchuria Daily News* (Dalian), 8 October 1930.

94 "News from Harbin," *Manchuria Daily News* (Dalian), 13 April 1929.

95 S. Hautenschlager, "Harbin, Center of a Greater Chinese Civilization," *Chinese Weekly Review* (Shanghai), 21 September 1929.

96 Mitrofanov, *The Lands and Land Administration*, 2.

97 "Agreement Regarding the Jurisdiction over Chinese Subjects in the Chinese Eastern Railway Zone. Kirin Province – May 19th/31st," in Mitrofanov, *The Lands and Land Administration*, 27.

98 "Agreement between the Chinese Eastern Railway and the Provincial Authorities of Kirin Regarding the Jurisdiction over Chinese Subjects in the Railway Zone – June 5th/18th 1901," in Mitrofanov, *The Lands and Land Administration*, 25.

99 Ibid.

100 "Agreement between the Chinese Eastern Railway and the Provincial Authorities of Heilungjiang – January 1st/14th 1902," Mitrofanov, *The Lands and Land Administration*, 9.

101 Khorvat, memoirs, Chapter 3, p. 18, Hoover Institution on War, Revolution and Peace.

102 Ibid., Chapter 7.18. Although there was a provision that cases that involved Chinese and Russian disagreement should be submitted to Chinese authorities in Jilin, Horvath, the first general manager, could not recall there ever having been such a disagreement.

103 That the order was placed under the highest code of secrecy demonstrates that the Russian government knew it was pushing the boundaries of the CER contract. F.B. Skvirsky, "Bor'ba Tsarskaia klik na KVzhd" [Struggle of the Czarist Clique on the CER]," *Manchurian Monitor* 9, (1930), 64. Although Skvirsky, who wrote for the CER-sponsored publication during the period of Soviet joint administration, was firmly anti-czarist, there is no reason to doubt the existence of the order itself or that Skvirsky had access to the relevant archives in Leningrad.

104 Skvirsky, "Bor'ba Tsarskaia klik na KVzhd," 45.

105 "Preliminary Russo-Chinese Arrangement Regarding Manchuria," in John MacMurray, *Treaties and Agreements with and Concerning China, 1894-1919*, vol. 1 (New York: Oxford University Press, 1921), 29.

106 Khorvat, memoirs, Chapter 3, p. 17, Hoover Institution on War, Revolution and Peace.

107 The open-door policy originally meant that all powers had equal access to economic activity within China. The concept was eventually broadened to mean that all foreigners had equal rights within the Chinese extraterritorial system. George Brown Rea, "Harbin: The Aftermath of Russia's Adventures," *Journal of the American Asiatic Association* 9, 4 (1909): 200.

108 China: The Maritime Customs, 10.

109 Khorvat, memoirs, Chapter 7, p. 18, Hoover Institution on War, Revolution and Peace.

110 Heilongjiang Provincial Historical Research Society, *Heilongjiang jindai lishi dashuji, 1840-1949* [Chronology of Heilongjiang contemporary history, 1840-1949] (Harbin: People's Publishing House, 1987), 16.

111 Ibid.

112 "Binjiang Daoyin Proclaims End to Extraterritoriality, 2 October 1920," in Dongchui shangbao, *Haerbin zhinan* vol. 2, 9.

113 There may actually have been two presidential decrees – one in September 1920 that announced the coming end of Russian extraterritoriality and another in October that constituted a formal announcement of the termination. Although I have found only the text of the October telegram, several Chinese sources mention an earlier, possibly secret, telegram in September.

114 Li, *Haerbin lishi biannian*, 102.

115 Dr. John Ferguson, "Report on the CER," NARA, RG 59, M316, Roll 150, File 861.77/1919, 25 October 1920.

116 "Binjiang Daoyin Proclaims End," 9.

117 Ibid.

118 "Suggestion of the Legal Department on the Takeover of the CER Legal Institution and the Temporary Legal System," 17 September 1920, in Dongchui shangbao, *Haerbin zhinan* vol. 2, 7.

119 "Telegram, Binjiang Legal Department to Bao Dujun, 30 September 1920," in Dongchui shangbao, *Haerbin zhinan* vol. 2, 8.

120 "Jilin Province Dujun Bao's Telegram," in Dongchui shangbao, *Haerbin zhinan* vol. 2, 6.

121 "Telegram, Binjiang Legal Department to Bao Dujun," 2 October 1920, vol. 2, chap. 2, 5.

122 Li, *Haerbin lishi biannian,* 103.

123 "Telegram, Zhang to the Binjiang Legal Department, 11 and 16 October 1920," in Dongchui shangbao, *Haerbin zhinan* vol. 2, 10, 12. China stopped paying the Russian Boxer indemnity on 1 July 1920. The cost of the courts would eventually be shared between Jilin, Heilongjiang, and the Special District, with 70,000 yuan coming from the Russian Boxer fund. "Special District Courts Ask for Funds," *Binjiang shibao,* 30 June 1922.

124 Li, *Haerbin lishi biannian,* 103.

125 "Telegram – Yin's Report on Taking over Russian Court Files and Appointment of Russian Member, 10 October 1920," in Dongchui shangbao, *Haerbin zhinan* vol. 2, 21.

126 Li, *Haerbin lishi biannian,* 103; "Telegram – Yin's Report," 22; "Rules Governing the Organization of the Special District of the Eastern Provinces," *Chinese Social and Political Science Review* 5a, 4 (1920): 310, article 8; Administration of Justice in Chinese and Extraterritorial Courts in China, NARA, RG 59, M329, Roll 92, File 893.041/40, 31 May 1923.

127 China: The Maritime Customs, 11; Yu-Chuan Chang, "The Chinese Judiciary," *Chinese Social Science and Political Science Review* 3, 1 (1918): 12; "Telegram, Legal Department to Jilin High Court, Approval of Russian Lawyers and Certification, 5 October 1920," in Dongchui shangbao, *Haerbin zhinan,* vol. 2, 62; "Special District Regulations on the Limits of the Procurator's Power"; "Telegram – Yin's Report."

128 "Provisional Regulations Governing the Appearance in Court of Lawyers of Countries Which Are Not Entitled to Consular Jurisdiction," *Chinese Social and Political Science Review* 5a, 4 (1920): 319. The Special District was perhaps too generous in the certification of Russian lawyers. It was reported that because of the difficult economic situation, many unemployed persons, both Chinese and Russian, were passing themselves off as lawyers. In response, the names of all approved lawyers, Chinese and Russian, were posted outside the court houses, and the Binjiang and Special District courts were required to exchange lists of registered lawyers. "The Special District Legal Department on Russian and Chinese Lawyers Advertising (Blowing Their Own Trumpet), 26 February 1921," in Dongchui shangbao, *Haerbin zhinan* vol. 2, 66.

129 "Telegram, Legal Department to Jilin High Court, Approval of Russian Lawyers and Certification, 5 October 1920," in Dongchui shangbao, *Haerbin zhinan* vol. 2, 62; "Secret Telegram, Other Countries with Consular Jurisdiction Have the Right to Bring Cases Forward, 28 December 1920," in Dongchui shangbao, *Haerbin zhinan* vol. 2, 63; Li, *Haerbin lishi biannian,* 105. The use of terms for non-Chinese is interesting, for it demonstrates that Chinese administrators distinguished between Russians, who had legitimate claims on residence in the Special District, and other foreigners. Russians were referred to as immigrants *(imin)* or Russian immigrants *(emin, eqiao).* Other foreigners were referred to as foreigners *(waiguo)* or designated by their citizenship.

130 "Legal Department Regulation on Judges Communicating with Lawyers or Living with Them, 31 February 1920," in Dongchui shangbao, *Haerbin zhinan* vol. 2, 64.

131 China: The Maritime Customs, 10.

132 S.T. Tepnavskii, "Temporary Regulations for Foreign Lawyers," *Ves' Kharbin* [All Harbin] (Harbin: CER Publishing House, 1923), 90; "Russian Lawyers Form Association," *Binjiang shibao* (Harbin), 12 October 1922.

133 "Regulations for Foreign Advisors of the Special District Legal Department, October 1920," in Dong-chui shangbao, *Haerbin zhinan* vol. 2, 32.

134 China: The Maritime Customs, 11.

135 "Regulations Governing the Committee," 314, article 1.

136 "Special District Regulations for the Foreign Consultants and Advisors, 15 November 1920," in Dong-chui shangbao, *Haerbin zhinan* vol. 2, 35; "Telegram – Yin's Report," 22.

137 "Special District Office, Translators Regulations, July 1921," in Dongchui shangbao, *Haerbin zhinan*, vol. 2, 57. Translating Chinese into Russian took more time – hence the price difference. "Special District Office, Translators Regulations," 57.

138 "Telegram Binjiang Legal Department to Bao Dujun, 2 October 1920," in Dongchui shangbao, *Haerbin zhinan*, vol.2, 11.; "The Legal Department Decrees That the Collection of Case Document Fees Should Be According to the Rules of the Department, 26 March 1921," in Dongchui shangbao, *Haerbin zhinan*, vol.2, 65.

139 "The Legal Department Decrees That the Collection of Case Document Fees Should Be According to the Rules of the Department, 26 March 1921," in Dongchui shangbao, *Haerbin zhinan* vol. 2, 65.

140 Ibid.

141 "Memorandum du Comité des Représentants des Institutions Judiciaires à Harbin," NARA, RG 59, Roll 92, M329 893.04/1, 2 April 1921.

142 "Special District Office in Charge of Old Russian Cases, March 1921," in Dongchui shangbao, *Haerbin zhinan*, vol.2, 39.

143 Ibid., 39; "Order No. 7 Concerning the Establishment of the Special District Office for the Review of Unresolved Russian Cases," *Dongfang zazhi* [The Eastern Miscellany] 18.6, 2 March 1921, 128.

144 China: The Maritime Customs, 11.

145 Doc 100, Wai-Chao Pu to Doyen of Diplomatic Corps Peking, 22 October 1920, in United Kingdom, Foreign Office, *BDFA* E.2, *China Annual Reports: January 1921-May 1921*, vol. 24 (Bethesda, MD: University Publications of America, 1994), 76.

146 "Russians Like to Sue," *Binjiang shibao* (Harbin), 27 August 1928.

147 "Russian Property Needs to Be Registered," *Binjiang shibao* (Harbin), 17 July 1921; China: The Maritime Customs, 221.

148 Mao Hong, "Haerbin zhong e renmin shenghuo zhuangkuang" [Harbin's Russian and Chinese citizens' lifestyles compared], *Shishi Yuebao* [China Monthly] 1, 2 (1929): 115-23.

149 "The Harbin Special City Supervisory Committee Meetings: Meeting Eight, 18 June 1927, Case One," in *Haerbin tebie shizheng baoshi* [Report on the Harbin Special City: City Government] (Harbin, 1931), 88.

150 Doc 100, Wai-Chao pu to Doyen of Diplomatic Corps Peking, 22 October 1920, in United Kingdom, Foreign Office, *BDFA* E.2, *China Annual Reports: January 1921-May 1921*, vol. 24, (Bethesda, MD: University Publications of America, 1994), 76. The most successful of these were the notaries. Within two years, thirty-five Chinese notaries were listed in Harbin's directory.

151 "The Special Area Court Regulations, September 1920," in Dongchui shangbao, *Haerbin zhinan*, vol. 2, 30. China's first modern legal code had been published in 1912, and it was revised and translated into Russian in 1920. It preserved the civil code of the last dynasty. By contrast, criminal law was based on European criminal law. G.I. Gerts, "Ten Years as an Advocate to the Chinese Courts," unpublished manuscript, Bakhmeteff Archive, Rare Book and Manuscript Library, Columbia University, New York; China: The Maritime Customs, 221.

152 Harold Scott Quigley, "Extraterritoriality in China," *American Journal of International Law* 20, 1 (1926): 65.

153 "Telegram, Sun Dujun to Special District and Beijing Legal Departments, 5 October 1920," 62; "Reply, Special District Legal Office to Sun, October 6th, 1920"; "Telegram, Special District Legal Office to Sun Dujun, December 22nd, 1920," in Dongchui shangbao, *Haerbin zhinan*, vol. 2, 63.

154 "The Career of Special District Judge Li Lanzhou," in Dongchui shangbao, *Haerbin zhinan,* vol. 8, 43; "Russian People Grateful to Li Jia'ao," *Binjiang shibao* (Harbin), 28 February 1922. The loyalty owed to Li was demonstrated after his resignation in 1923, which was described as forced because of his interest in politics. "Chinese and Russian court employees resigned in protest," *Haerbin lishi biannian, 1896-1949* [Chronology of Harbin], ed. Li Shuxiao (Harbin: Harbin Peoples Publishing House, 1986), 101.

155 Administration of Justice in Chinese and Extraterritorial Courts in China, NARA, RG 59, M329, Roll 92, File 93.041/40, 31 May 1923, 26; *Who's Who in China* (Shanghai: China Weekly Review, 1930).

156 Administration of Justice in Chinese and Extraterritorial Courts in China, NARA, RG 59, M329, Roll 92, File 893.041/40, 31 May 1923, 4, 12, 15, 18. The consul intimates that bribery was common, although he does not provide any evidence.

157 Ibid., 25.

158 "The Special Chinese Courts in the CER Zone," translated and enclosed with a letter from Douglas Jenkins, American Consul to American Secreaty of State, NARA, RG 59, M329, Roll 92, File 893.041/25, 11 January 1922.

159 A. Novitskii, "The Fourth Anniversary of the Chinese Court," NARA, RG 59, M316, Roll 158, File 861.77/3915, 3 October 1924.

160 "Do-It-Yourself Temporary Russian Lawsuits Suspended," *Binjiang shibao* (Harbin), 26 February 1922.

161 "Russian Legal Documents," *Binjiang shibao* (Harbin), 9 September 1922.

162 G.I. Gerts, "Ten Years as an Advocate to the Chinese Courts," 4.

163 These cases were found in consular records and newspapers. The actual court records are in Harbin's municipal archives, which were closed in the late 1990s.

164 Administration of Justice in Extraterritorial Courts in Harbin, NARA, RG 59, M329, Roll 92, File 893.041/46, 14 June 1923, and "Protection for Lawless Russians," *Binjiang shibao* (Harbin), 30 August 1921.

165 "Justice in Chinese Courts," *Harbin Daily News,* 29 July 1923, NARA, RG 59, M329, Roll 92, File 893.041/51, 2 August 1923.

166 "Notes from Harbin," *Manchuria Daily News* (Dalian), 7 January 1929.

167 Eighty people were detained during the raid; however, forty-two of them were consulate employees who claimed diplomatic immunity and were expelled from China. That representatives from twelve different CER stations and the three most important unions were arrested was a testament to the extent of the Russian Communist Party's influence in the district. "Report of the Police Headquarters to the Civil Administrator of the Special Area of the Eastern Provinces," in Harbin Observer, *Protsess 38: Stenogramma protsessa 38 sovetskikh grazhdan, arestovannykh pri nalete 27 maia 1929 g. na Sovetskoe Konsyl'stvo v g. Kharbine, ORVP* [Process of the 38: Stenographic report of the process of the 38 Soviet Citizens arrested during the raid on the Soviet Consulate General in Harbin on 27 May 1929] (Harbin: Harbin Observer, 1929), 1-43.

168 Two months later, on 5 July, the Soviet director of the CER, Chuvmarenko, was found dead in his home. It was speculated that he was in liaison with the Chinese board members and may have tipped off the police regarding the alleged meeting at the consulate. "CER Director Assassinated," *Manchuria Daily News* (Dalian), 5 July 1929.

169 Zhang Guichen, Procurator of the High Court of the Special District, "Circumstances and Motives of the Case," in Harbin Observer, *Protsess 38.*

170 J.B. Powell, "The Trial of the Thirty-Eight Soviet Prisoners," *China Weekly Review,* 26 October 1929.

171 Ibid. Certainly the principle source, *Process of the 38,* is biased. It was published by the *Harbin Observer,* an English-language newspaper, and registered to an English national, B. Hayton Fleet, who was said to be symphathetic to the USSR. According to the book's preface the trials "as a matter of fact were nothing but a detective story." "Preface," in Harbin Observer, *Protsess 38.*

172 The photographs are clear enough that the original Russian could be read. The documents that were intact included a "Plan for Summer Work," which co-ordinated the political activities of several CER unions (illegal according to the 1924 Sino-Soviet agreement); plans to do political outreach work among sympathetic Chinese; several telegrams to Moscow, including one that detailed how to search out and hide weapons in the Special District; and plans to destabilize the Zhang regime by advancing monetary and military aid to another northern warlord. "Circumstances of the Case," in Harbin Observer, *Protsess 38*. Opinion was divided as to whether the documents were fake. Chinese supporters said it was impossible to fake the level of detail in the documents. Supporters of the Soviet citizens said they were planted by a émigré Russian agent of the Chinese police. Powell, "The Trial of the Thirty-Eight Soviet Prisoners."

173 Report of the Procurator, vol. 1, 166. Letter No. 4977, dated 15 August 1929, in Harbin Observer, *Protsess 38*, 203.

174 *Protsess 38* gave the Soviet version of events, which cast doubt on the Chinese administration and the Special District courts. The account was published by an English national with close political ties to the Soviet Union (see Powell, "The Trial of the Thirty-Eight Soviet Prisoners"). Perhaps because of extraterritoriality, the publisher was able to escape Special District censorship laws. Certainly, J.B. Powell believed that the Soviets were guilty and that the trial had been fair. By contrast, the *China Weekly* was generally sympathetic to the Special District. The Special District, with assistance from Zhang Xueliang and the Nanjing government, published its own version, lavishly illustrated with photos of the prisoners and partially burned documents in Russian, English, and Chinese.

175 For more on the reformist impulse in Republican Chinese penal reform see Frank Dikotter, *Crime, Punishment and the Prison in Modern China* (London: Hurst and Company, 2002).

176 Harbin's prison, with a capacity of five hundred, was the largest and employed one prison head, one assistant, one bookkeeper, two male secretaries, one female secretary, four head guards, twenty-six male guards, two female guards, four janitorial staff, one doctor, and one pharmacist. "The Takeover of the Court System, Including Prisons," in Dongchui shangbao, *Haerbin zhinan* vol. 2, 9; Gerts, "My Ten Years as an Advocate in the Russian Courts," 3.

177 Minutes of the meeting of the Harbin Technical Board, NARA, M569, RG 59, File 861.77 2197, 5 July 1921.

178 "Vice-Director Zhang to the Head of the Special District Legal Department, 16 October 1920," in Dongchui shangbao, *Haerbin zhinan* vol. 2, 10; George Hanson to Secretary of State, 24 March 1924, NARA, RG 59, M569 861.77 1222; Harry Frank, *Wandering in Northern Manchuria* (New York: Century Publishers, 1923), 97; "The Takeover of the Court system, Including Prisons," in Dongchui shangbo, *Haerbin zhinan*, vol. 2, 9; "The Special Area Courts Prepare to Take Over Prisons," in Dongchui shangbao, *Haerbin zhinan* vol. 2, 31; Tepnavskii, *Ves' Kharbin*, 1926, 90.

179 Tang Zhongmin, ed., "History of Harbin's Police," in *Harbin shizhi*, 32; Gerts, "My Ten Years as an Advocate," 3.

180 Doc 188, Consul Sly to Mr. Alston, 13 June 1920, in United Kingdom, Foreign Office, *BDFA* E.2, *China Annual Reports: January 1919-December 1920*, vol. 23 (Bethesda, MD: University Publications of America, 1994), 229; "History of Legal Rights in the Special Zone," *Binjiang shibao* (Harbin), 23 July 1925.

181 George Hanson to Secretary of State, 31 May 1923, in "The Administration of Justice in Chinese and Extraterritoriality in China," NARA, RG 59, M529, File 893.041/40, 9.

182 Ibid.

183 Ibid.

184 J.B. Powell, "The Soviet Prisoners at Harbin," *China Weekly Review*, 28 September 1929.

185 Powell's story, originally written for the *Chicago Tribune* (whose readership presumably had little stake in the maintenance of foreign privilege in China), has no tone of moral indignation at the detainment of thousands of whites by Chinese authorities.

186 Powell, "The Soviet Prisoners at Harbin."

187 Doc 188, Consul Sly to Mr. Alston, 13 June 1920, in United Kingdom, Foreign Office, 228; "Administration of Justice in Chinese and Extreterritorial Courts in China," NARA, RG 59, M329, Roll 92, File 893.041/40, 31 May 1923, 6.

188 Doc 188, Consul Sly to Mr. Alston, 13 June 1920, in United Kingdom, Foreign Office.

189 Chinese members of the assembly, NARA, RG 59, M329 Roll 100, File 893.102/H/411, 27 February 1923.

190 Gilbreath, "Where Yellow Rules White," 316, 368.

191 H.W.K. "Extraterritoriality and Harbin," *Manchuria Daily News,* 13 May 1926. The identity of the author is unknown.

192 "Extraterritoriality Commission," *Manchuria Daily News* (Dalian), 11 June 1926.

193 "Glaring Breach of US Extraterritorial Rights in Harbin Chinese City," *China Weekly Review* (Shanghai), 12 October 1929.

194 Detention of American by Chinese Police, George Hanson to Jacob Schurman, NARA, RG 59, M329, Roll 100, File 861.012/H/360.5, 5 May 1922.

195 "Police Vent Hatred on Foreign Victims," *Harbin Daily News* (Harbin), 31 October 1923, NARA, RG59, M316, Roll 158,File 861.77/3393, 6 March 1924; "What the Russian Papers Say," *Harbin Daily News* (Harbin), 1 November 1923, NARA, RG59, M316, Roll 158, File 861.77/3289, 24 November 1924.

196 Harbin Consul to Secretary of State, NARA, RG 59, M329, Roll 92, File 893.10/75, 14 March 1924.

197 "Anti-Foreign Attitude" *Russian Daily News,* 17 August 1923; NARA, RG 59, M329, Roll 98, File 893.10/21, 17 August 1923. Because this was printed in the *Russian Daily News,* a foreign publication noted for showing hostility toward the Special District, the actual circumstances may have been different.

198 "Police Attack," *Russian Daily News,* 25 August 1923, NARA, RG 59, M329, Roll 98, File 893.10/33, 29 August 1923.

199 "Echo Investigation Finished," *Harbin Daily News,* 16 July 1924, NARA, RG 59, M316, Roll 154, File 861.77/3635, 4 August 1924.

200 "Further Details of the 'Echo' Outrage," *Harbin Daily News,* NARA, RG 59, M369, Roll 154, File 861.77/3622, 14 July 1924.

201 "Echo Investigation Finished," *Harbin Daily News,* n.d., NARA, RG 59, M369, Roll 158 861.77/3635, 4 August 1924.

202 "The Echo Outrage," *Zaria* (Harbin), n.d., NARA, RG 59, M369, Roll 158, File 861.77/3622, 14 July 1924.

203 *Jilin sheng baogao* [Jilin Provincial Reports], File 2616.6, 20 June 1924; File 2635.1, 22 June 1924; and File 2635.1, 12 June 1924.

204 "Attack on Russian Women," *Harbin Daily News,* 24 March 1924, NARA, RG 59, M329, Roll 98, File 893.10/78, 24 March 1924.

205 *Jilin sheng baogao* [Jilin Provincial Reports], File 2645.1, 24 June 1924; File 2861.3, 27 March 1925; and File 438.10, 22 September 1930.

206 Tang Zhongmin, *Harbin shizhi,* 325.

207 "Robbers and Their Rich Booty," *Manchuria Daily News* (Dalian), 15 November 1927.

208 "The Difference between the Lifestyles of Russians Past and Present," *Binjiang shibao* (Harbin), 20 April 1921.

209 Tang Zhongmin, *Harbin shizhi,* 32.

210 "Notes from Harbin," *Manchuria Daily News* (Dalian), 14 January 1929.

CHAPTER 5: EXPERIMENTS IN CO-ADMINISTERING THE CHINESE EASTERN RAILWAY

1 Chin-Chun Wang, "The Chinese Eastern Railway Question," *Chinese Students Monthly* 22, 2 (1926): 58.

2 The Railway Zone, NARA, RG 59, M316, Roll 151, File 861.77/2059, 4 April 1921, 4-6.

3 C. Walter Young, *International Relations of Manchuria* (Chicago: University of Chicago Press, 1929), 155.

4 Foreign Policy Association, "The Chinese Eastern Railway," *Foreign Policy Association Information Service*, vol. 1: *1925-1926* (New York: Kraus Reprint, 1967), 5.

5 "The Railway Zone," 398.

6 The CER's high rates resulted in a thriving Chinese cart trade. From 1908 to 1913 the cart trade increased by 250 percent, while the trade eastward to Vladivostok, assisted by advantageous rates, only increased 150 percent. Economic Bureau of the Chinese Eastern Railway, *North Manchuria and the Chinese Eastern Railway* (Harbin: Chinese Eastern Railway Printing Office, 1924), 401.

7 Ibid.

8 In addition, the soya bean market collapsed: beans that at the beginning of 1920 had been thirty-one to thirty-eight pounds sterling per ton on the London market were twenty-three to twenty-four pounds sterling by July and eleven pounds per ton by February 1911. Economic Bureau of the Chinese Eastern Railway, *North Manchuria*, 404-5.

9 A.A. Neopihanoff, "The Development of North Manchuria," *Chinese Economic Journal* 2, 3 (1928): 264-65.

10 Economic Bureau of the Chinese Eastern Railway, *North Manchuria*, 407.

11 "Chinese Doing Good Work on the C.E.R. Railway," *Peking Leader*, 5 April 1921, Enclosure 1 in Dispatch 1053, 19 April 1921, NARA, RG 59, Roll 151, M316 861.77/2113.

12 Economic Bureau of the Chinese Eastern Railway, *North Manchuria*, 410, 412, 421, 430.

13 Economic Bureau of the Chinese Eastern Railway, *The Chinese Eastern Railway and Its Zone* (Harbin: Chinese Eastern Railway Printing Office, 1923), 31. For more on the Ostroumoff administration's *mission civilisatrice*, see Chapter 3.

14 This made control of the CER a prize for all parties: émigré Russians, Soviet Russians, and Chinese. China: The Maritime Customs. Statistical Series No. 6 Decennial Reports, "Harbin, 1922-31," in vol. 1: *Northern and Yangtze Ports* (Shanghai: Statistical Department of the Inspectorate General of Customs, Shanghai, 1933), 1.

15 Economic Bureau of the Chinese Eastern Railway, *North Manchuria*, 398.

16 Ibid., 400.

17 Ibid., 398.

18 Doc. 28, General Chang-Huan-Hsiang [sic] to General Chang-Tso-lin [sic], 11 September 1920, United Kingdom, Foreign Office, *BDFA* E.2, *China Annual Reports: January 1921 to May 1921*, vol. 24 (Bethesda, MD: University Publications of America, 1994), 21.

19 My thanks to Ronald Suleski, who pointed out that Zhang Zuolin's period of maximum administrative efficiency came before his expensive national aspirations to reunite China under his control.

20 K.K. Kawakami, "The Russo-Chinese Conflict in Manchuria," *Foreign Affairs* 8 (October 1929–July 1930), 62.

21 "CER Workers," *Echo*, 19 January 1926, translated, NARA, RG 59, Roll 154, M316 File 861.77/3974, 22 January 1926.

22 "The Agitation of the CER White Party," *Binjiang shibao* (Harbin), 24 June 1923; "Railway Workers Listen to Imperialism," *Binjiang shibao* (Harbin), 5 April 1923.

23 "The Question of the CER Russians' Unfairness to Remaining Chinese Residents," *Binjiang shibao* (Harbin), 5 May 1923.

24 "The Problem of Russian and Chinese Language," *Binjiang shibao* (Harbin), 10 June 1923. The article noted the activities of the Manchurian Research Society, supported by the CER, which were conducted primarily in Russian.

25 At that time, the Russians, buttressed with the sense that their culture was superior, reacted to these accusations with the charge that the Chinese were being overly sensitive and nationalistic. In the new millennium, the problem of dominant culture, identity, and language in what we may now call a postcolonial context is all too familiar. Witness the ongoing debate over the use of English in Quebec, the attempt to marginalize Russians and their language in the Baltic States, the resurgence of minority languages and identities in the European Union, and the debate over the use of Spanish in the United States.

26 List of Conflicts on the CER, NARA, RG 59, M316, Roll 154, File 861.77/3680, 8 September 1924.

27 Chinese and the Railroad, NARA, RG 59, M316, Roll 154, File 861.77/3447, 25 April 1924. From the source, "arrest," in this case, meant an investigation. Presumably, before 1920, Chinese fatalities on the railroad did not warrant an investigation or even a comment.

28 "Two Jubilees," *Novosti zhizni,* n.d., translated and included as Enclosure 1 with Dispatch 1294, 29 May 1923, in NARA, RG 59, M316, Roll 153, File 861.77/3121, 29 May 1923.

29 There was also a short English language history.

30 Olga Bakich, "Émigré Identity: The Case of Harbin," *South Atlantic Quarterly* 99, 1 (2000): 57.

31 "Twenty-Fifth Anniversary of the Chinese Eastern Railway," *Russian Daily News,* 7 June 1923, Enclosure 1 with Dispatch 1335, 8 June 1923, NARA, RG 59, M316, Roll 153, File 861.77/3133.

32 "The Harbin Municipal Council is neither a Chinese funded nor administered institution. It is a political and economic organization of the residents of Harbin. In as much as Russians form the majority of Harbin residents, the Russian language was made the official language of the city," *Novosti zhizni,* 25 March 1926, translated and enclosed in NARA, Rg 59, M329, Roll 100, File 892.102H/466, 1 April 1926.

33 Ostroumoff to Stevens, 24 January 1924, NARA, RG 59, Roll 154, 861.77/3411, 3 March 1924.

34 Ostroumoff to Stevens, 24 January 1924. The conflict was certainly over treaty rights, but given the willingness of the Chinese board members to work with the Russians in 1920 and Zhang Zuolin's support for Ostroumoff, the general manager could be taken to task for failing to reach a settlement with the Chinese. However, there is evidence that Ostroumoff was also in contact with the Soviets. Perhaps he was trying to play both sides.

35 Bruce Elleman, *Diplomacy and Deception: The Secret History of Sino-Soviet Diplomatic Relations, 1917-1927* (Armonk, NY: M.E. Sharpe, 1997), 121. Elleman's description of Soviet double-dealing supports his argument that the Soviet Union was not interested in normal relations with China but wished to regain all czarist privileges and influence the course of Chinese politics.

36 Peter Tang, *Russian and Soviet Policy in Manchuria and Outer Mongolia, 1911-1931* (Durham, NC: Duke University Press, 1959); Sarah C.M. Paine, *Imperial Rivals: China, Russia and Their Disputed Frontiers* (Armonk, NY: M.E. Sharpe, 1996); and Elleman, *Diplomacy and Deception.* Peter Tang's work focuses on diplomatic history and exposing the myth of Soviet friendship. Although he is inspired by Chinese nationalism, Tang demonstrates why the Chinese regional government in the northeast reacted so negatively to the USSR. Sarah Paine's and Bruce Elleman's books develop Tang's thesis that the policy the Soviet Union pursued in the Chinese northeast was much like its czarist predecessor's – aggressive and imperialistic.

37 George Hanson to the Secretary of State, 19 January 1929, "China's Obligations under the Washington Conference," Dispatch 1889, NARA, RG 59, M316, Roll 156, File 861.77/CER/8, 9.

38 Young, *International Relations of Manchuria,* Appendix G, "Official Texts of the Sino-Russian Agreements of 1924," 285.

39 Ibid.

40 Wang, "The Chinese Eastern Railway Question," 61.

41 The Soviets stalled and created excuses for not calling the promised conferences. See Elleman, *Diplomacy of Deception,* for details.

42 "Agreement between the Government of the Autonomous Three Eastern Provinces of the Republic of China and the Government of the USSR, Shenyang, 20 September 1924," in Young, *International Relations in Manchuria*, 297.

43 Ibid., 298, article 10.

44 Translated Memorandum on the CER, NARA, RG 59, M316, Roll 154, File 861.77/3627, 29 July 1924.

45 Elleman, *Diplomacy and Deception*, 125.

46 Ibid., 115.

47 N.V. Borzov, "Raising the Flag," unpublished manuscript, Hoover Institution on War, Revolution and Peace, Borzov Papers, Roll 13, Box 13, Folder 7.

48 Wang was an engineering graduate of Yale University and had extensive experience with railways across China. *Who's Who in China* (Shanghai: China Weekly Review, 1930). Wang tended to absent himself during difficult periods. During the Land Department struggle, he moved to Station Man'chzhuriia, the most western part of the line, for two months. He is said to have suffered from nervous exhaustion. Given the stress of dealing with the Ostroumoff administration, this might have been true. Despite his propensity for falling ill at moments of administrative crisis, his contemporaries credited him with being a good administrator.

49 Harry Kingman, *Effects of Chinese Nationalism upon Manchurian Railway Developments* (Berkeley: University of California Press, 1932), 62.

50 "Interview with General Wen Ying-Hsing," NARA, RG 59, M316, Roll 158, File 861.77/3718, 13 October 1924.

51 "CER Director Shot for Being a Red Agent," *Manchuria Daily News* (Dalian), 6 January 1927.

52 General Yang Cho discusses railway affairs, NARA, RG 59, Roll 154, M316, File 861.77/3656, 3 September 1924. My thanks to Olga Bakich for further details.

53 Memorandum, NARA, RG 59, M316 Roll 154, File 861.77/4099, 7 October 1926.

54 Mao Hong, "Haerbin zhong e renmin shenghuo zhuangkuang" [Harbin's Russian and Chinese citizens' lifestyles compared] *Shishi yuebao* [China Monthly] 1, 2 (1929): 116.

55 George Hanson to Secretary of State, 19 April 1928, in NARA, RG 59, M316, Roll 154, File 816.77/4157.

56 Consul Hanson, Report on the Land Department, NARA, RG 59, M316, File 871.77 5165, 20 July 1923.

57 Doc 1242, Consul Sly to Sir M. Lapson, in United Kingdom, Foreign Office, *BDFA* E.2, *China Annual Reports: June 1927-December 1927*, vol. 33 (Bethesda, MD: University Publications of America, 1994), 368.

58 *Harbin Daily News*, NARA, RG 59, M316, Roll 154,File 861.77/3725, 16 October 1924.

59 "To Make Room for Soviet Officers," *Manchuria Daily News* (Dalian), 2 March 1925.

60 Thanks to Olga Bakich for this information.

61 "Arrest of Ostroumoff," *Peking and Tientsin Times*, 6 October 1924, enclosure in NARA, RG 59, M 316, Roll 154, File 861.77/3715, 17 October 1924.

62 "CER Workers," *Echo*, 19 January 1926, translated, NARA, RG 59, M316 Roll 154, File 861.77/3974, 22 January 1926.

63 "CER Board Meeting," *Zaria*, 10 October 1924 translated, NARA, RG 59, 316, Roll 154, File 861.77/3713, 13 October 1924.

64 "8th District Dispute,"NARA, RG 59, M316, Roll 154, File 861.77/3838, 14 February 1925.

65 Doc 1242, Consul Sly to Sir M. Lapson, 368. The American consul speculated that the Soviets had achieved their objective of flushing out the neutrals by forcing the Harbin Russians to declare themselves.

66 CER under Soviet Administration, NARA, RG 59, M316, Roll 154, File 861.77/3872, 15 April 1925.

67 *Harbin Daily News*, enclosed in NARA, RG 59, M316, Roll 154, File 861.77/3873, 15 April 1925.

68 "White workers on CER," *Tribuna*, 21 April 1925, translated, NARA, RG 59, M316, Roll 154, File 861.77/3875, 26 April 1925.

69 Ibid.
70 Interview with General Chu, NARA, RG 59, M316, Roll 154, File 861.77/4043, 19 April 1926.
71 Ivanov was recalled by the Soviet government in 1926, presumably for his mishandling of the citizenship issue and the conflict over troop transportation in the Special District. He died in a Soviet labour camp in the 1930s. Thanks to O. Bakich for this information.
72 Doc 168, Consul Jones to Sir M. Lapson, in United Kingdom, Foreign Office, *BDFA* E.2, *China Annual Reports: June 1927-December 1927*, vol. 33 (Bethesda, MD: University Publications of America, 1994,) 368.
73 Zhang Xueliang was the son of Zhang Zuolin. He took over after his father was assassinated by Japanese agents in 1928.
74 Harbin Consul, Report for November 1-20, NARA, RG 59, M316, Roll 155, File 861.77/Chinese Eastern/ 3, 29 December 1928.
75 "Wholesale Dismissal of CER Servants," *Manchuria Daily News* (Dalian), 7 February 1929.
76 "Hunger Striker Eating Again," *Manchuria Daily News* (Dalian), 17 November 1927.
77 "200 Ex 'White' Russian Employees on Hunger Strike," *Manchuria Daily News* (Dalian), 5 October 1927; "Hunger Striker Eating Again."
78 Report from Harbin, NARA, RG 59, M329, File 861.77, Roll 82, 22 July 1929.

CHAPTER 6: MANCHURIAN LANDLORDS

1 David Wolff, *To the Harbin Station: The Liberal Alternative in Russian Manchuria, 1989-1914* (Stanford, CA: Stanford University Press, 1999), 28.
2 Maurice Baring, *With Russians in Manchuria* (London: Methuen and Co., 1905), 33.
3 E.Kh. Nilus, quoted in Wolff, *To the Harbin Station*, 28.
4 Igor Mitrofanov, "The Lands and Land Administration of the Chinese Eastern Railway Company, and the Incident of August 1st, 1923," (Harbin: n.d.), 11.
5 Wolff, *To the Harbin Station*, 28.
6 A Chinese source disagrees. According to this source, following the railway's construction, Russian authorities lobbied the Jilin Negotiation Bureau in Harbin to increase the lands held by the CER. It is speculated that Zhang was bribed to ensure his co-operation and that a private contract was signed between him and the assistant to the CER's head. However, both the Jilin and the Heilongjiang negotiation bureaus refused to honour the agreement. Both sides renegotiated, and the Chinese and Russians signed another agreement in 1904 that extended the land owned by the CER. The land was divided into three types: cultivated, wasteland, and swamp. Both sides agreed that the CER would never again ask for an extension to its lands. There is, however, no other evidence to substantiate the Chinese claim of an illegal extension of the concession zone. See "Jilin and Heilongjiang Negotiation Bureaus," in Dongchui shangbao [Northern Frontier Business Association], *Haerbin zhinan* [Guide to Harbin], vol. 2 (Harbin, 1922), 117.
7 Mitrofanov, *The Lands and Land Administration*, 4.
8 Consul Green on the Harbin Municipal Council, NARA, RG 59, M316 File 893.102 291, 8 June 1910, 10.
9 My thanks to Ronald Suleski for pointing out the different worldviews held by the two sides. While the transportation infrastructures were justified by investors (often national governments) as apolitical modern development, local populations challenged the undertakings as colonial and imperialist. Throughout the twentieth century, there have been varying degrees of conflict over the rights of administration and ownership.
10 For Chinese acknowledgement of Harbin's Russian origins, see Mao Hong, "Haerbin zhong e renmin shenghuo zhuangkuang" [Harbin's Russian and Chinese citizens' lifestyles compared], *Shishi yuebao* [China Monthly] 1, 2 (1929): 115-23. See also Dongchui shangbao, *Haerbin zhinan*, Preface, and

Haerbin tebie shizheng baoshi [Report on the Harbin Special City: City Government] (Harbin, 1931), Chapter 1, Section 1. With the lessening of Communist influence and the re-emergence of a transnational regional identity, research is now appearing in China that acknowledges Russian contributions to the northeast. See Ding Lianglun, "A Survey of Harbin's Russian Community, 1917-1931," *Beifang wenwu* [Culture of the North] 61 (January 2000): 81-86.

11 Harbin Consul Fletcher to US Secretary of State, NARA, RG 59, M862, Roll 567, File 1292, 14 November 1909, Enclosure 1. In addition, see articles 1 through 5 of the 1909 municipal agreement for Harbin, which affirmed Chinese sovereignty.

12 Ibid.

13 Khorvat, *Memoirs,* chapter 7, 10, Hoover Institution on War, Revolution and Peace. The administrative functions of the CER Civil Department are explained in Chapter 3.

14 "Jilin and Heilongjiang Negotiation Bureaus," in Dongchui shangbao, *Haerbin zhinan,* vol. 2, 117.

15 George Brown Rea, "Harbin: The Aftermath of Russia's Adventures," *Journal of the American Asiatic Association* 9, 4 (1909): 199.

16 Report of the Inter-Allied Technical Board, 8 April 1921, NARA, RG 59, M316, File 861.77 2161, 3 May 1921; "CER Land," *Far Eastern Times,* 23 August 1923, NARA, RG 59, M316, File 861.77 3206, 29 August 1922.

17 Mitrofanov, *The Lands and Land Administration,* Part 3, "The Administration of the Concession Zone," 15-16.

18 Mitrofanov, "The Lands and Land Administration," Part 1, "History and Legal Basis, Operation of Lands," 5.

19 "The CER Company and the 1914 Anglo-Russian Agreement," in *Haerbin tebie shizheng baoshi,* 3.

20 "Outline of the CER Civil Department and Its Rules," in *Haerbin tebie shizheng baoshi,* 21.

21 The Chinese supervisory body of Hankou's former Russian concession set off a major scandal in 1921 when it attempted to sell off unoccupied land worth some 1.5 million taels. Russians and non-Russians objected, writing that the sale of lands to Chinese would result in a fall in their value. Harold S. Quigley, "Foreign Concessions in Chinese Hands," *Foreign Policy* 7, 1 (1928): 153. In fact, Harbin's land retained its value throughout the period of Chinese administration.

22 "The CER Russians Unfair to Remaining Chinese," *Binjiang shibao* (Harbin), 16 May 1923.

23 Mitrofanov, "The Lands and Land Administration," Part 3, "The Administration of the Concession Zone," 14.

24 "Report of the Sub-Committee for the Investigation of the Accounts of the CER," NARA, RG 59, M316, Roll 157, File 861.77 3073, 20 March 1923, 3.

25 Letter from President Wang to Russian Board Members, 20 July 1923, NARA, RG 59, M316, Roll 157, File 861.77 3183, 9 August 1923. Dr. Wang remained at Station Man'chzhuriia for several months, where he ignored the calls of Chinese elite, consuls, and Russians to deal with the land conflict. Perhaps because of his inactivity, Wang was soon replaced as CER president.

26 Consul Hanson: Report on the Land Department, NARA, RG 59, M316, Roll 157, File 871.77 3165, 20 July 1923.

27 The policy was well planned in advance. On 1 August the police forbade the publication of articles that criticized the takeover. All stories had to be submitted to the police station for review, a policy that was criticized by the Russian paper *Novosti zhizni.* "Chinese Seizure of the Land Department of the CER," letter from George Hanson to Jacob Schurman, 1 August 1923, NARA, RG 59, M316, Roll 157, File 861.77 3175, 2 August 1923, and "Chinese Attempt to Seize the Land Department of the CER," letter From George Hanson to Jacob Schurman, 7 August 1923, in NARA, RG 59, M316, Roll 152, File 861.77 3181, 23 August 1923.

28 "From the Central Administration of the Special Region of the Northeastern Provinces, July 29th, 1923," in N.S. Zakhvarova. *Spravochnik' domovladel'tsa* [Reference book for home owners] (Harbin: Zaria Press, 1927), 37.

29 "Proclamation 6, 29 July 1923," enclosure 2 in NARA, RG 59, M316, Roll 157, File 871.77 3175, 2 August 1923.

30 Letter from S. Ughet to Even Young, 2 August 1923, NARA, RG 59, M316, Roll 157, File 871.77 3176, 23 August 1923.

31 Chinese Seizure of the Land Department of the CER, letter from George Hanson to Jacob Schurman, 1 August 1923, NARA, RG 59, M316, Roll 157, File 871.77 3175, 2 August 1923.

32 Igor Saveliev, "Chinese Migration in Space and Time," in *Globalizing Chinese Migration: Trends in Europe and Asia,* ed. Pal Nyiri (Farnham, UK: Ashgate, 2002), 35-73; Frederic Coleman, *Japan Moves North: The Inside Story of the Struggle for Siberia* (London: Gassell and Company, 1918).

33 "Historical Day for the CER," *Zaria* (Harbin), 1 August 1923, NARA, RG 59, M 316, Roll 157, File 871.77 3175, 2 August 1923.

34 Chinese Seizure of the Land Department of the CER, NARA, RG 59, M316, Roll 157, File 871.77 3175, 2 August 1923.

35 Letter from the Harbin Consul to Jacob Schurman, American Ambassador to China, 1 August 1923, NARA, RG 59, M316, Roll 157, File 871.77 3175, 2 August 1923.

36 "Extracts from Minutes of Conference regarding the Land Department 6 August 1923," NARA, RG 59, M316, Roll 157, File 861.77 3216, 13 September 1923.

37 "CER Railway Lands Deadlock," *The North China Herald,* 19 January 1924, enclosure in NARA, RG 59, M316, Roll 157, File 871.77 3175, 28 January 1924.

38 "Memorandum on the events of the Land Conflict," in NARA, RG 59, M316, Roll 157, File 861.77, 15 November 1923.

39 "Chinese attempt to seize Land Department," letter from George Hanson to Jacob Schurman, 7 August 1923, NARA, RG 59, M316, Roll 152, File 861.77 3181, 23 August 1923.

40 "Looking for Trouble," *Peking and Tientsin Times,* enclosure 1 in NARA, RG 59, M316, Roll 15, File 861.77 3190, 14 August 1923; Letter from daoyin Tsai to George Hanson, 11 August 1923, enclosure 1, NARA, RG 59, M316, Roll 157, File 861.77 3191, 28 August 1923.

41 "Memorandum on the Lands Problem," enclosure 8 with dispatch 382 in NARA, RG 59, M316, Roll 15, File 861.77 3181, 7 August 1923; CER Land Department, enclosure 1 in NARA, RG 59, M316, Roll 15, File 861.77 3204, 28 August 1923.

42 Reports from CER Stations, NARA, RG 59, M316, Roll 152, File 861.77 3261, 1 November 1923.

43 CER Land Department, enclosure 1 in NARA, RG 59, M316, Roll 152, File 861.77 3204, 28 August 1923; Reports from CER Stations, NARA, RG 59, M316, Roll 152, File 861.77 3261, 1 November 1923; "Looking for Trouble," *Peking and Tientsin Times,* 7 August 1923, NARA, RG 59, M316, Roll 152, File 861.77 3190, 14 August 1923.

44 Reports from CER Stations, NARA, RG 59, M316, Roll 152, File 861.77 3261, 1 November 1923.

45 "The Land Bureau of the Special District, 8 November 1923," in Zakhvarova, *Spravochnik' domovladel'tsa,* 38.

46 Quigley, "Foreign Concessions," 153.

47 "Extracts from the Minutes of the Conference Regarding the Land Department Held on 6 August," NARA, RG 59, M316, Roll 152, File 861.77 3216, 15 September 1923.

48 "Mr. Gondatti Boasts," *Chen-Huan-Pao,* 14 October 1923, translated, NARA, RG 59, M316, Roll 152, File 861.77 3250, 19 October 1923.

49 "Women Attack the Land Department," *Zaria,* 1 July 1924, NARA, RG 59, M316, Roll 152, File 861.77 3540, 7 July 1924; Letter to the American Minister, Peking American Department of State, 24 April 1924, NARA RG 59, M316, Roll 152, File 861.77 3439, 20 April 1924.

50 "CER Legal Department," *Zaria,* 20 May 1924, translated, NARA, RG 59, M316, Roll 152, File 861.77 3488, 24 May 1924.

51 "What the Russian Papers Say," *Harbin Daily News*, 24 Janaury 1924, NARA, RG 59,M316, Roll 152, File 861.77 3343.

52 "Notice," 21 January 1926, in Zakhvarova, *Spravochnik' domovladel'tsa*, 44.

53 "Notice," 1 December 1924, in Zakhvarova, *Spravochnik' domovladel'tsa*, 40.

54 "CER Lands Deadlock," *North China Herald* (Tianjin), 19 January 1924.

55 Memorandum, NARA, RG 59, M316, Roll 152, File 861.72 3346, 1 February 1924, 1-6.

56 Ibid.

57 "The Supplementary Agreement," *Harbin Daily News*, 30 January 1924, NARA, RG 59, M316, Roll 152, File 861.77 3353, 2 February 1924.

58 Letter from British Consul, Harbin to London, 1 August 1924, United Kingdom, Foreign Office, *BDFA* E.2, *China Annual Reports: January 1924-December 1924*, vol. 20 (Bethesda, MD: University Publications of America, 1994,), 185.

59 "Telegraphic Reply from President Wang," *International*, 12 August 1923, translated and included in Enclosure 1, Dispatch 293, NARA, RG 59, M316, Roll 152, File 861.77 3191, 17 August 1923.

60 Ibid; "Notice," 11 February 1925, in Zakhvarova, *Spravochnik' domovladel'tsa*, 41.

61 CER Land Department, Enclosure 3, Dispatch 382, 2 August 1923, NARA, RG 59, M316, Roll 152, File 861.77 3181, 2 August 1923; "Looking for Trouble," *Peking and Tientsin Times*, 7 August 1923, Enclosure 1, Disptch 192, NARA, RG 59, M316, Roll 152, File 861.77 3190, 14 August 1923.

62 "The Various Bodies Met Wednesday Night in Connection with the Land Department Case," *International*, 10 August 1923 (translation), enclosure 3 in NARA, RG 59, M316, Roll 152, File 871.77 3193, 23 August 1923.

63 Telegram from the Special District to the Foreign Consuls, 21 August 1921, enclosure in Letter from George Hanson to US Secretary of State, NARA, RG 59, M316, Roll 152, File 861.77 3163, 31 August 1923.

64 "Land Department of the Chinese Eastern Railway," letter from Consul Charles Gauss, Shenyang, to Jacob Schurman, 23 August 1923, NARA, RG 59, M316, Roll 152, File 861.77 3196, 23 August 1923.

65 "Land Department of the Chinese Eastern Railway," letter from Charles Gauss to Jacob Schurman.

66 Journey of the American Minister to Harbin and over the CER, NARA, RG 59, M316, Roll 15, File 861.77 3233, 25 September 1923, 3.

67 Ibid., 4.

68 Ibid., 9.

69 Ibid., 6.

70 Ibid., 1-6, 10.

71 Ibid., 7.

72 "A Letter Addressed to the American Minister by the High Civil Administration," *Commerce*, 11 September 1923, translated, enclosure 3 in NARA, RG 59, M316, Roll 15, File 871.77 3218, 20 September 1924.

73 Journey of the American Minister, 30; "Land Department Employees Arrested," *Harbin Daily News*, 16 April 1924, enclosed in NARA, RG 59, M316, Roll 156, File 861.72 3435, 17 April 1924.

74 Ibid.

75 "Chinese Farmers at Anda Attack the Agricultural Experimental Station," *Sungari Daily News*, 29 April 1924, NARA, RG 59, M316, Roll 153, File 861.77 3459, 5 May 1924; Agricultural Experiment Station at Station Anda, NARA, RG 59, M316, Roll 153, 861.77 3071, 19 March 1923.

76 "Agricultural Experiment Station at Station Anda," NARA, RG 59, M316, Roll 153, File 861.77/3071, 19 March 1923.

77 Letter from Consul George Hanson to Jacob Schurman, 19 December 1923, NARA, RG 59,M316, Roll 156 File 871.77/3315, 24 December 1923.

78 Attacks at Station Anda, Consul Hanson to Jacob Schurman, enclosure in NARA, RG 59, Roll, File 861.77/3445, 25 April 1925.

79 Letter to the American Minister, Peking, 24 April 1924, NARA, RG 59, M316, Roll 153, File 861.77 3449, 1 May 1924.

80 Attacks at Station Anda, Consul Hanson to Jacob Schurman, enclosure in NARA, RG 59, M316, Roll 153, File 861.72 3445, 25 April 1925.

81 Letter to the American Minister, Peking, 24 April 1924; "New Troubles at Station Anda," *Russkii golos*, 23 April 1924, NARA, RG 59, M316, Roll 153, File 861 771 3445, 2 May 1924.

82 Journey of the American Minister, 11.

83 "Excerpts from the Harbin Russian Press," *Harbin Daily News* and *Russkii golos*, 14/15 April 1924, NARA, RG 59, M316, Roll 153, File 861.77 3439, 20 April 1924.

84 "A Sad Page," *Russkii golos*, 13 April 1924, NARA, RG 59, M316, Roll 153, File 861.77 3439, 20 April 1924.

85 Note, NARA, RG 59, M316, Roll 154, File 861.77 3506, 4 June 1924.

86 Letter from Ostroumoff to Stevens, 2 June 1924, NARA, RG 59, M316, Roll 154, File 861.77 3520, 15 June 1924.

87 The double-edged nature of Soviet policy in northern China in the 1920s – avowed imperialism combined with policies that affected local and regional Chinese sovereignty – is best explained in the work of Paine and Elleman. S.C.M. Paine, *Imperial Rivals: China, Russia, and Their Disputed Frontier* (Armonk, NY: M.E. Sharpe, 1996); Bruce Elleman, *Diplomacy and Deception: The Secret History of Sino-Soviet Diplomatic Relations, 1917-1927* (Armonk, NY: M.E. Sharpe, 1997).

88 "Looking for Trouble," *Peking and Tientsin Times*, 7 August 1923, NARA, RG 59, M316, Roll 157, File 861.77 3190, 14 August 1923; "L.M. Karahan's [sic] Declaration," *Zaria*, 16 August 1923, translated, Enclosure 7, Dispatch 393, NARA, RG 59, M316, Roll 157, File 861.77 3191, 17 August 1923.

89 Consul George Hanson to Peking, NARA, RG 59, M316, Roll 157, File 861.77 3619, 16 June 1924; Renewal of Consular Seats, NARA, RG 59, M316, Roll 157, File 861.77 3692, 30 September 1924; "The Land Question in the Railway Zone," *Harbin Dawning*, n.d., NARA, RG 59, M316, Roll 157, File 861.72 3865, 25 March 1925.

90 "Land Question in the Railway Zone," *Harbin Dawning*, 19 March 1925, translated, enclosed in NARA, RG 59, M316, Roll 157, File 861.77 3865, 25 March 1925.

91 Letter to the American Minister, Peking, American Department of State, 16 January 1925, NARA, RG 59, M316, Roll 154, File 861.77 3817, 16 January 1925.

92 "The Land Department Conflict Settled," *Zaria*, 15 February 1924, translated, NARA, RG 59, M316, Roll 157, File 861.77 3369, 18 February 1924.

93 Mao Hong, "Haerbin zhong e renmin shenghuo zhuangkuang," 18.

94 V.A. Kormazov, "Growth of the Population of Harbin and Fujiatian," *Manchurian Monitor* 7 (1930): 25.

95 Harbin Special City Bureau, "The Harbin Temporary Self-Governing Committee and the Supervisory of Prices and Taxation Committee Joint Meetings," *Haerbin tebie shizheng baoshi*, 88; "Notice 626," 12 July 1926, in Zakharova, *Spravochnik' domovladel'tsa*, 43, 44.

96 "Notices," 26 August 1925, in Zakharova, *Spravochnik' domovladel'tsa*, 43, 44.

97 "Notice," 5 September 1926 and 13 August 1926, in Zakharova, *Spravochnik' domovladel'tsa*, 43, 44.

98 "Notice," 10 July 1926, in Zakharova, *Spravochnik' domovladel'tsa*, 43, 44.

99 Harbin Special City Bureau, "The Harbin Temporary Self-Governing Committee," vol. 1, meetings 1-22 (March-August 1926), 88-156.

100 "New Land Regulations," *Manchuria Daily News*, 28 December 1927.

101 Ibid.

102 French Consul to Harbin Reynaud to French Minister to China Martel, 24 November 1928, Ministère des Affaires Etrangères, Archives Diplomatiques, Series E, Asie-oceanie, 1918-1940, Paris, France (Hereafter MAEAD), Archive Kharbine, March 1923-December 1928, vol. 226, 155.

103 Harbin Consulate, Memorandum, NARA, RG 59, M316, Roll 154, File 861.77/4099, 7 October 1926.

104 The Russians were not alone in identifying property control in China as the key to the maintenance of foreign privilege. Robert Bickers has shown that the English settler colony in Shanghai based its economic and political existence on land investment and real estate firms that controlled the settlements. As in Harbin, control over Shanghai's land and its incomes, which were derived from Chinese renters, was seen as the key to maintaining foreign privilege. As in Harbin, Chinese tenants in Shanghai also had no political voice. See Robert Bickers, "Shanghailanders: The Formation and Identity of the British Settler Community in Shanghai, 1843-1937," *Past and Present* 159 (May 1998): 161-211.

105 For the CER's Russian board members, politics was a divisive activity, best left to Socialists. In their opinion, they were directing, administering, and protecting an investment. In contrast, Chinese members perceived their Russian colleagues' belief as being essentially political, because, in Chinese opinion, the Russians were protecting a Russian investment for the exclusive benefit of Manchuria's Russian population. Thus, the two sides could not even settle on a common language to settle their dispute, because any compromise would undermine the other's claim to legitimacy.

106 "News from Harbin," *Manchuria Daily News* (Dalian), 8 April 1929; "Notes from Harbin," *Manchuria Daily News* (Dalian), 28 March 1929.

CHAPTER 7: WHOSE CITY IS THIS?

1 "Notes from Harbin," *Manchuria Daily News* (Dalian), 1 January 1926.

2 China: The Maritime Customs. Statistical Series No. 6 Decennial Reports, "Harbin Report, 1907-1911," in vol. 1: *Northern and Yangtze Ports* (Shanghai: Statistical Department of the Inspectorate General of Customs, Shanghai, 1913), 8.

3 Throughout the period of this study, Newtown and Pristan were administratively separate from Fujiadian. Only after the Japanese takeover in 1932 would the three areas be politically integrated. James Carter makes the interesting observation that foreign observers prior to 1920 tended to see Fujiadian as a separate entity. By the mid-1920s, however, they referred to it as part of Harbin, a practice that suggests the ongoing integration of the city. By the late 1920s, reports on the regional economy referred to the three areas as a single integrated unit. See China, Bureau of Industrial and Commercial Information, "Household Industries in Harbin," *Chinese Economic Bulletin* 15, 8 (August 1929): 92, and James Carter, *Creating a Chinese Harbin: Nationalism in an International City, 1916-1932* (Ithaca, NY: Cornell University Press, 2002) 25.

4 According to Carter, the population of Newton and Pristan was dominated by Europeans until after the Second World War. Carter, *Creating*, 20. See also Mao Hong, "Haerbin zhong e renmin shenghuo zhuangkuang" [Harbin's Russian and Chinese citizens' lifestyles compared], *Shishi yuebao* [China Monthly] 1, 2 (1929): 116.

5 Xin Peilin, "Ma Zhongjun shensheng" [A biographical sketch of Ma Zhongjun], *Harbin wenshi ziliao* [Harbin Cultural and Historical Materials] 6 (1985): 13. China, Bureau of Industrial and Commercial Information, "Household Industries in Harbin," 93. Ma's lifestyle was not considered odd for members of Harbin's Chinese elite.

6 Fred Fisher, American Consul General, Harbin, to the Secretary of State, 25 November 1906, National Archives and Records Administration, General Records of the Department of State, RG 59, Numerical File 1906-10, Case 4002.

7 Mao, "Harbin zhong-e renmin shenghuo zhuangkuang," 116. In 1929 there were 3,007 Japanese, 1,350 Koreans, 1,300 Jews, 590 Poles, 160 English, 150 French and Germans, 150 Latin Americans, 60 Italians, 50 Americans, 56 Turks, 50 Czechs, 30 Swedes, 30 Dutch, 9 Greeks, 8 Indians, 6 Hungarians, and 3 Belgians.

8 Ibid.

9   A measure of their success in Russia was Russian fears that the Chinese would eventually dominate the region, economically and demographically. By the early 1900s, there were three Chinese for every two Russians in the Russian Far East. The Russian government despaired of creating a Russian-dominated economy that could compete with its Chinese-run counterpart. Andrew Malozemoff, *Russian Far Eastern Policy, 1881-1904, with Special Emphasis on the Causes of the Russo-Japanese War* (Berkeley: University of California Press, 1959), 9.

10 Mao, "Haerbin zhong e renmin shenghuo zhuangkuang," 116, 119.

11 Simon Karlinsky, "Memoirs of Harbin," *Slavic Review* 48, 2 (1989): 285. My emphasis. The dialect existed as long as a large Russian population lived in the region.

12 Mao, "Harbin zhong e renmin shenghuo zhuangkuang," 116.

13 Ibid., 117.

14 Olga Bakich, "A Russian City in China: Harbin before 1917," *Canadian Slavonic Papers* 28, 2 (1986): 144.

15 Karlinsky, "Memoirs of Harbin," 285.

16 Olga Bakich, "Émigré Identity: The Case of Harbin," *South Atlantic Quarterly* 99, 1 (2000): 57.

17 See Michael Hamm, *The City in Late Imperial Russia* (Bloomington: Indiana University Press, 1986), and Vasilif V. Ushanoff, "Recollections of Life in the Russian Community in Manchuria and in Emigration," in *Russian Émigré Recollections: Life in Russia and California*, ed. Richard Pierce (Berkeley: University of California Press, 1986), 2.

18 "Regulations for the Autonomous City Council, 1912, Article One," in *Haerbin tebie shizheng baoshi* [Report on the Harbin Special City: City Government] (Harbin, 1931), 21.

19 "The Municipal Assembly and the Municipal Council," in *Haerbin tebie shizheng baoshi* vol. 1, 1.

20 China: The Maritime Customs. Statistical Series No. 6 Decennial Reports, "Harbin Report, 1907-1911, 6.

21 "Japanese Interests in Harbin," *Japan Chronicle Weekly Edition*, 13 July 1916, 53; Olga Bakich, "History of Harbin: The Establishment of the City Council," unpublished manuscript, Bakich private collection, 263.

22 Bakich, "History of Harbin," 264.

23 "In the City Council," *Kharbinskii den'* [Harbin Day], 19 February 1914.

24 Report from Harbin, NARA, RG 59, M329, Roll 99, File 893.102/312, 19 February 1915.

25 Mao, "Harbin zhong-e renmin shenghuo zhuangkuang," 616.

26 "Restoration of Foreign Concessions and Settlements," *Chinese Social and Political Science Review* 5a, 1-2 (1920): 146-52.

27 The activity around concession retrogression and municipal reform is striking, considering the disintegration of the national government. The issue touched on foreign privilege, which was one issue that the Chinese Foreign Ministry could safely pursue without touching on warlord interests. The interest in municipal politics at the local level speaks perhaps to the need, in the absence of a coherent national political project, to focus on reforms in local politics that the local community could control.

28 Toshi Go, "The Future of Foreign Concessions in China," *Pacific Affairs* 12, 4 (1939): 395.

29 David Strand, *Rickshaw Beijing: City People and Politics in the 1920s* (Berkeley: University of California Press, 1993), 179.

30 Li Shuxiao, ed., *Haerbin lishi biannian: 1896-1949* [Chronology of Harbin history: 1846-1949] (Harbin: People's Publishing House, 1986), 97s.

31 "Regulations for the Formation of Law Courts for the Special District," 31 October 1920, Enclosure 1, Dispatch 1358, NARA, RG 59, M329, Roll 92, File 893.041/11, 1 December 1922.

32 "The Railway Zone," NARA, RG 59, M316, Roll 151, File 861.77/2059, 19 April 1921, 5.

33 Ibid., 4.
34 Inter-Allied Technical Board, letter to Colonel Johnson, 8 April 1921, Enclosure 1, Dispatch 1238, NARA, RG 59, M316 Roll 151, File 861.72/2161, 3 May 1921; "The Railway Zone," NARA, RG 59, M316, Roll 151, File 861.77/2053, 19 April 1921.
35 After 1924 the new Soviet partners, rejecting spiritual and chemical opiates for their people, refused to continue funding the asylum and the church departments. The asylum was placed under the municipal administration, and the Russian Orthodox Church was left to its own devices but continued to receive a great deal of unofficial assistance from the Special District. According to the 1924 Shenyang and Beijing accords, the Chinese government was not only to cease protecting or funding the Russian Orthodox Church but also to turn all of the churches over to representatives of the Soviet Union. This did not happen in Manchuria, and there are several references to Zhang Zuolin's blocking any attempts to seize church property. The Shenyang government went so far as to prepare a standard form for each county (which every intendant would have been required to file) that listed the number of Russian Orthodox churches and their assets. There is not one instance where this occurred, however, and no forms were filed. The Russian Orthodox Church flourished in Manchuria, and churches continued to be built. As far as I can determine, the only institution in Harbin that could ask for free repair work from the municipality was the Russian Orthodox Church. Perhaps this was a policy established by the émigré-controlled municipal government and honoured by the new Chinese board after 1926. *Jilin shengbao* [Jilin provincial reports], 2368.3, 16 September 1924, and Blaine Chiasson, "How can we sing the Lord's song in a strange land? A Russian Baptist Mission in Harbin and Shanghai," unpublished paper. See also "The Harbin Temporary Self-Governing Committee and the Supervisory Prices and Taxation Committee Joint Meetings," in *Haerbin tebie shizheng baoshi* and Bruce A. Elleman, *Diplomacy and Deception: The Secret History of Sino-Soviet Diplomatic Relations, 1917-1927* (Armonk, NY: M.E. Sharpe, 1997).
36 "Mr. Tong Returns from Beijing," *Binjiang shibao* (Harbin), 9 September 1921.
37 China, "Regulations Governing Municipal Self-Government, 3 July 1921," in Commission on Extraterritoriality, *The Constitution and Supplementary Laws and Documents of the Republic of China*, trans. Commission on Extraterritoriality (Peking: Commission on Extraterritoriality, 1924), 150.
38 Ibid., 151, 152.
39 Ibid., 162.
40 China, "District Self-Government Law, 7 September 1919," in Commission on Extraterritoriality, *The Constitution and Supplementary Laws and Documents of the Republic of China*, trans. Commission on Extraterritoriality (Peking: Commission on Extraterritoriality, 1924), 129-47.
41 China, "Regulations Governing Municipal Self-Government, 3 July 1921," 149-74.
42 See Chapter 3, Note 59.
43 Editor, "The Extent of Russian Powerlessness in China," *Russkoe obozienie* 3 and 4 (March-April 1921): 150-51.
44 Translation of "The CER Interferes with the Municipal Administration in the Special District," from *Commerce of the Three Eastern Provinces,* enclosed in NARA, RG 59, M316, Roll 152, File 861.77/2901, 15 November 1922.
45 American Consul to French Consul, Harbin, n.d., MAEAD, General Dossier, 1921-24, vol. 430, 155.
46 Letter from Dong to Consuls, 12 February 1921, MAEAD, Archive Manchourie, 1918-22, vol. 12, 277.
47 S.T. Tepnavskii, *Ves' Kharbin* [All Harbin] (Harbin: CER Publishing House, 1923), 60. See Chapter 2 for more detail about pre-1920 municipal government in the concession.
48 Letter from the Department for Municipal Affairs of the Special Region to the CER Board, 25 May 1922, NARA, RG 59, M316, Roll 152, File 861.77/2624, 27 June 1922.

49 *Administrativnoe ustroistvo severnosi Man'chzhurii* [Administrative structure of northern Manchuria] (Harbin, 1926), 19.

50 "General Chu Ching-lan's Speech on Taking the Oath of Office," *Russian Daily News* (Harbin), 2 March 1923, Enclosure 1, Dispatch 91, NARA, RG 59, M316, Roll 153, File 861.77/3056, 23 March 1923.

51 Carter, *Creating a Chinese Harbin,* 222.

52 The 1986 *Haerbin lishi biannian: 1896-1949,* edited by Li Shuxiao, states that this "angered public opinion, both Chinese and Russian" (Li, 105). However, this observation may reflect post-1949 revisionism. Zhu Qinglan himself toasted Horvath's health at New Year's celebrations at the Railway Club in 1924. But perhaps this gesture was meant as an insult to the Soviet members of the CER board who were present. "Seeing the New Year in at Harbin," *North China Herald,* 14 January 1924, NARA, RG 59, M329, Roll 100, File 893.102H/435, 25 January 1924.

53 Carter, *Creating a Chinese Harbin,* 233.

54 R. Polchaninov, "A Short History of Harbin," unpublished manuscript, n.d., Hoover Institution on War, Revolution and Peace, Loukaskin Papers, Reel 12, Folder 2.

55 Li, *Haerbin lishi biannian,* 111-1; Municipal Contributions, NARA, RG 59, M316 Roll 153, File 861.77/3070, 15 March 1923; "An Interview between One of Our Reporters and Mr. Sun Sheng Wu of the High Administrators Office," *Harbin Dawning,* 8 March 1923, translated, NARA, RG 59, M316, Roll 153, File 861.77/3056, 23 March 1923.

56 Doc. 61, Consul Philip to Mr. Palairet, 12 March 1925, United Kingdom, Foreign Office, *BDFA* E.2, *China Annual Reports: January 1925 to October 1925,* vol. 24 (Bethessa MD: University Publications of America, 1994), 91.

57 Li, *Haerbin lishi biannian,* 113; "The City Government Collects Double Tax," *Binjiang shibao* (Harbin), 6 June 1924.

58 "The Right of Administration in the Region of the CER," Enclosure in NARA, RG 59, M316, Roll 153, File 861.77/3394, 6 March 1924, 9, 11, 13.

59 N.N. Bektjaschinsky, "The Municipality of the City of Harbin," *Manchurian Monitor* 5-7: 10-17 (1925): 13 [quote], 7, included in NARA, RG 59, M329 Roll 100, File 893.102H/459, 19 November 1925.

60 Memorandum from the Japanese Delegate to the Municipal Council to the Consular Corps, NARA, RG 59, Roll 100, M329 893.102H/458, 13 November 1924; "Russian Teachers to Be Hired," *Binjiang shibao,* 22 June 1922, and "Schools Programs Settled by General Ma," *Zaria,* translated and enclosed in NARA, RG 59, M316, Roll 154, File 861.77/3725, 16 October 1924.

61 "The Harbin Municipal Government of the Eve of Reforms," *Novosti zhizni,* 2 July 1924, NARA, RG 59, M329, Roll 100, File 893.102H/444, 7 July 1924; Letter from Delegate Jiang, in *Haerbin tebie shizheng baoshi,* vol. 1, 148.

62 Extracts from *Novosti zhizni,* 25 March 1926, and *Russkoe slovo,* 26 March 1926, translated and enclosed in NARA, RG 59, M329, Roll 100, File 892.102H/466, 1 April 1926.

63 "The Manifesto of [the] Language Issue of the Chinese Members of the Harbin Municipal Council," *The International,* 25 March 1925, translated and enclosed in NARA, RG 59, M329, Roll 100, File 893.102H/465.

64 "Making Things Lively, Continued," *Manchuria Daily News* (Dalian), 8 April 1926.

65 "Municipal Council Salaries," *Zaria,* 6 June 1923, enclosed in NARA, RG 59, M329, Roll 100, File 893.102H/418.5, 22 June 1923; *Zaria,* 12 June 1923, enclosed in NARA, RG 59, M329, Roll 100, File 893.102H/418.5, 22 June 1923; "The City's Affairs," *Russki Golos,* 15 December 1923, NARA, RG 59, M329, Roll 100, File 893.102H/425, 28 December 1923; "The Chinese Delegates' First Statement," in *Haerbin tebie shizheng baoshi* vol. 1, 149.

66 N.N. Bektjaschinsky, "The Municipality of the City of Harbin," *Manchurian Monitor* 5-7 (1925): 12, included in NARA, RG 59, M329, Roll 100, File 893.102H/459, 19 November 1925, 10; Harbin Public

Administration, *Kharbin: Itogi otsenochnoi perepisi po dannym' statisticheskogo oblsdovaniia, proizvodivshegosia s 15-go iunia po 1oe sentiabria 1923 g* [Harbin: List of total data from the statistical service from 15 June to 1 September 1923] (Harbin: CER Press, 1924), 7, 94.

67 George Hanson, American Consul, Harbin, to American Embassy, Beijing, 21 September 1922, NARA, RG 59, M329, Roll 100, File 893.102H/383, 21 September 1922

68 As of 1919, there had been twelve Chinese and three Japanese members in the Municipal Assembly. Annex to letter of 15 April 1921, French Consul Lefussier to the French Foreign Minister, MAEAD, Archive Mandchourie, 1918-22, vol. 12, 217-19.

69 Hanson, American Consul, Harbin, to American Embassy, Beijing, 21 September 1922, NARA, RG 59, M329, Roll 100, File 893.102H/383, 21 September 1922; "New Bloc," *Russian Daily News,* 16 January 1923, Enclosure 3, Dispatch 773, NARA, RG 59, Roll 100, M329, File 893.102H/399, 17 January 1923; "The Coming Election," *Russkii golos,* 6 October 1922, translated, NARA, RG 59, M329, Roll 100, File 893.102H/387, 27 October 1922.

70 "The Pretext Taken by the Assembly in Pressing Down the Chinese under Its Control," *International,* 22 October 1922, NARA, RG 59, M329, Roll 100, File 893.102H 388.

71 "Foreign Representation on the Municipal Council," *Russkii golos,* 14 September 1922, translated, NARA, RG 59, M329, Roll 100, File 893.102H/382, 16 September 1922.

72 "Letter from Mayor Tishenko to Harbin Consul," 24 September 1923, enclosed in NARA, RG 59, M329, Roll 100, File 893.102H/420.5, 27 September 1923.

73 Bektjaschinsky, "The Municipality of the City of Harbin," 4.

74 "The City Elections," *Russkii golos,* 27 August 1922, translated, NARA, RG 59, M329, Roll 100, File 893.102H/380, September 1922.

75 "Municipal Elections," *Zaria,* 17 July 1922, NARA, RG 59, M329, Roll 100, File 893.102H/360.5, 4 May 1922.

76 "Unusual Fiasco in Municipal Elections," *Zaria,* 18 December 1922, NARA, RG 59, M329, Roll 100, File 893.102H/399, 17 January 1923.

77 "Whom to Vote For," *Russkii golos,* 18 January 1923, translated, NARA, RG 59, M329, Roll 100, File 893.102/400, 19 January 1923.

78 "The Election," *Russian Daily News,* 23 January 1923, translated, NARA, RG 59, M329, Roll 100, File 893.102/404, 24 January 1923; "The Deadlock in the City Assembly," *Russian Daily News,* 23 February 1923, NARA, RG 59, M329, Roll 100, File 893.102/411, 27 February 1923. Tishenko was mayor from 1917 to 1926. Tishenko was a graduate of the Eastern Institute in Vladivostok, an institution that specialized in training Russian experts on the Far East. Two other graduates – Vladimir Spitsyn and Dobrolovskii – were prominent members of the Municipal Assembly. Spitsyn had edited a Chinese newspaper, the *Yuandongbao,* for the CER, and Dobrolovskii had worked as a Chinese, Korean, and Japanese language censor. Both men spoke Chinese.

79 "Municipality without a Head," *Zaria,* 2 February 1923, translated, NARA, RG 59, M329, Roll 100, File 893.102H/405, 5 February 1923; "Assemblymen's Meeting Results in Conflict," *Russian Daily News,* 22 February 1923, NARA, RG 59, M329, Roll 100, File 893.102H/411, 27 February 1923; "What the Russian Papers Say," *Russian Daily News,* 22 February 1923, NARA, RG 59, M329, Roll 100, File 893.102H/411, 27 February 1923.

80 "New Members for Town Council," *Russian Daily News,* 25 February 1923, Enclosure 2, Dispatch 958, NARA, RG 59, M329, Roll 100, File 893.102H/411, 27 February 1923.

81 Ibid.; Bektjaschinsky, "The Municipality of the City of Harbin," 11.

82 "Director Chu Zen's Secret Note," in *Haerbin tebie shizheng baoshi* vol. 1, 154.

83 Letter to the CER Board of Directors from the Municipal Bureau, 29 September 1923, translated from Russian, NARA, RG 59, M329, Roll 100, File 893.102H/422, 23 November 1923.

84 "Provisional Statute for Municipal Self-Regulation in the Cities and Settlements of the Special Area,"
    NARA, RG 59, M329, Roll 100, File 893.102H/443, 10 June 1924.
85 "Threat to the Municipal Administration," *Russkii golos,* 15 November 1923, translated, NARA, RG 59,
    M329, Roll 100, File 893.102H/422, 26 November 1923.
86 "A Threat to City Administration," *Russkii golos,* 8 December 1923, translated, NARA, RG 59, M329,
    Roll 100, File 893.102H/423, 20 December 1923.
87 Consul Reynaud to Minister Martel, 4 April 1925, MAEAD, Concessions Etranger, Dossier General
    Russes, 1923-29, vol. 348, 148.
88 "Seeing the New Year in at Harbin," *North China Herald,* 14 January 1924, NARA, RG 59, M329, Roll
    100, File 893.102H/435, 25 January 1924.
89 Conditions on the Municipal Council, NARA, RG 59, M329 Roll 100, File 893.102H/449, 18 December
    1925; "Soviets in Harbin Change Front," *Manchuria Daily News,* 13 March 1926.
90 "The Provisional Committee," in *Haerbin tebie shizheng baoshi,* vol. 1, 46.
91 "The Chinese Delegates' First Statement," in *Haerbin tebie shizheng baoshi,* vol. 1, 148. Zhang's
    report is undated but appears to have been made in late 1924 or 1925. See "Document from Zhang
    huan hsing," in *Haerbin tebie shizheng baoshi,* vol. 1, 154.
92 Commemoration of the Administration of Towns and Villages, December 1925, enclosure in NARA,
    RG 59, M329, Roll 100, File 893.102H/461, 10 February 1926.
93 "New Municipal Constitution," *Zaria,* 11 March 1926, NARA, RG 59, M329, Roll 100, File 893.102H/463,
    11 March 1926.
94 "Harbin Consular Representatives Protest," *Manchuria Daily News,* 6 April 1926.
95 "Harbin Municipal Council Dissolved," *Manchuria Daily News,* 23 March 1926; "Making Things
    Lively in Harbin," *Manchuria Daily News,* 7 April 1926.
96 E.Kh. Nilus, "Istorichheskii obzor Kitaiskoi vostochnoi xheleznoi dorogi, 1896-1923" [Historical sur-
    vey of the Chinese Eastern Railway, 1896-1923], unpublished manuscript, 1923, 40, Hoover Institution
    on War, Revolution and Peace.
97 Minutes of the meeting of the Harbin Consular Body, NARA, RG 59, Roll 100, M329 893.102H/469, 26
    April 1926. "5th Joint Meeting, 17 April 1926," 95; "9th Joint Meeting, 27 April 1926," 99; "22nd Joint
    Meeting, 26 June 1926," 117; "26th Joint Meeting, 27 July 1926," 120; "31st Joint Meeting, 29 July 1926,"
    123, in *Haerbin tebie shizheng baoshi.*
98 "Speech on the Official Opening of the Harbin Council," *Harbin Daily News,* 2 November 1926,
    NARA, RG 59, M329, Roll 100, File 893.102H/480, 14 January 1927.
99 Doc. 13, Memorandum respecting Northern Manchuria, part of enclosure dated 7 October 1928,
    United Kingdom, Foreign Office, *BDFA* E.2, *China Annual Reports: September 1928 to June 1929,* vol.
    36 (Bethesda, MD: University Publications of America, 1994), 35; "Second Manifesto of the Language
    Question," *International* 30, March 1926, NARA, RG 59, M329, Roll 100, File 893.102H/466, 1 April 1926.
100 "New Draft Municipal System," *Manchuria Daily News,* 17 July 1926.
101 "The Harbin Municipal Council Question," *Manchuria Daily News,* 9 July 1926.
102 "Harbin Self-Governing Regulations," *Binjiang shibao,* 18 July 1926, article 63; Harbin Franchise,
    NARA, RG 59, M329, Roll 100, File 893.102H/476, 2 October 1926. Previously the suburb Majiagou was
    not under the Harbin Municipal Government. Harbin Yearbook Society, *Haerbin nianjian 1994* [Har-
    bin yearbook 1994] (Harbin: Harbin Yearbook Society, 1994), 54; "Speech on the Official Opening of
    the Harbin Special Council," *Harbin Daily News,* 2 November 1925, NARA, RG 59, M329, Roll 100, File
    893.102H/ 480, 14 January 1927. Gilbreath wrote of Zhu: "If you rise early enough you may even see
    the Chinese mayor making his rounds. He is Buddhist and arises at six to see if the municipal plant
    is working." Gilbreath, "Where Yellow Rules White," 368.
103 J.B. Powell, "Sidelights on Harbin," *China Weekly Review,* 19 October 1929.

104 Report from Harbin, NARA, RG 59, M329, Roll 82, File 861.77, 25 March 1928.

105 "Fast Growing Harbin," *Manchuria Daily News,* 16 April 1929.

106 Monthly Report, Harbin, Consul George Hanson, NARA, RG 59, M329, Roll 82, File 861.77, 28 December 1928. See also J.B. Powell, "Manchuria Joins National Government," *China Weekly Review,* 5 January 1929; China: The Maritime Customs. Statistical Series No. 6 Decennial Reports, "Harbin, 1922-1933," in vol. 1: *Northern and Yangtze Ports* (Shanghai: Statistical Department of the Inspectorate General of Customs, Shanghai, 1933), 220.

107 Dain-houa Jao, *La loi municipal Chinoise du 20 mai 1930* [The Chinese Municipal Law of the 20th May, 1930] 1939 (Bordeaux, 1939), 33, 64.

108 "Chinese Authorities of Harbin on the Side of Decency," *Manchuria Daily News,* 20 August 1929.

109 "Taming of Harbin," *China Weekly Review,* 7 September 1929.

110 Mao, "Harbin zhong-e renmin shenghuo zhuangkuang," 621; "A Strange Incident in the Special District Park," *Binjiang shibao,* 27 August 1926.

111. "Russian Immigrants," *Binjiang shibao,* 4 April 1921.

112 "Municipal Notes," *Russkoe slovo,* 21 February 1932, 4, 5.

113 "5 February 1932," in United Kingdom, Foreign Office, *BDFA* E.2, *China Annual Reports: February 1929 to January 1932,* vol. 37 (Bethesda, MD: University Publications of America, 1994), 37.

114 Harbin Special District, *In Commemoration of the Inaugural State Celebrations in the Special District of Harbin, Special Area of the Eastern Provinces* (Harbin: CER Press, 1932), Hoover Institution on War, Revolution and Peace.

115 Harbin Observer, "Harbin Municipal Council," *Fleet's Directory of Manchurian Cities, 1934-35* (Harbin: Harbin Observer Press, 1935).

CHAPTER 8: MAKING RUSSIANS CHINESE

1   Olga Bakich, "Russian Education in Harbin," *Transactions of the Association of Russian-American Scholars in the USA* 26 (1994): 271.

2   Mao Hong, "Haerbin zhong e renmin shenghuo zhuangkuang" [Harbin's Russian and Chinese citizen's lifestyles compared], *Shishi yuebao* [China Monthly] 1, 2 (1929): 619.

3   Xin Peilin, "Ma Zhongjun shensheng" [A biographical sketch of Mr. Ma Zhongjun], *Harbin wenshi ziliao* [Harbin Cultural and Historical Materials] 6 (1985): 7; Adelaide Nichols, "Any Night at the Opera in Harbin," *New York Times,* 23 March 1923.

4   Bakich, "Russian Education in Harbin," 273; China: The Maritime Customs. Statistical Series No. 6 Decennial Reports, "Harbin, 1912-1921," in vol. 1: *Northern and Yangtze Ports* (Shanghai: Statistical Department of the Inspectorate General of Customs, Shanghai, 1924), 17-18; I.G. Baranov, "Prepodavanie kitaiskogo iazyka v russkoi nachal'noi i srednei shkole Osobogo Raiona Vostochnykh Provintsii" [The teaching of the Chinese language in Russian primary and secondary schools of the Special Area of the Eastern Province], *Manchurian Monitor* 7-8 (1929): 9; Harbin Schools, NARA, RG 59, M329, Roll 99, File 893.102 Harbin/276, 4 January 1910.

5   China: The Maritime Customs, 17-18.

6   Harbin Schools, NARA, RG 59, M329, Roll 99, File 883.102 Harbin/276, 4 January 1910.

7   S.T. Tepnavskii, "Temporary Regulations for Public Education," *Ves' Kharbin* [All Harbin] (Harbin: CER Publishing House, 1924), 93.

8   Gavan McCormack, *Chang Tso-lin in Northeast China* (Stanford, CA: Stanford University Press, 1977), Chapter 3; "Education in Kwangtung," *Manchuria Daily News,* 12 June 1924.

9   "CER School," *Peking and Tientsin Times,* 15 December 1923, enclosed in NARA, RG 59, M316 Roll 158, File 861.77/3322, 3 January 1924; Tepnavskii, "Education Section," *Ves' Kharbin,* 92; China: The Maritime Customs, 224. James Carter points out the importance of the architectural style of both Jilesi Temple and the Third Middle School for the project of making Harbin Chinese. See James

Carter, "A Tale of Two Temples: Nation, Region, and Religious Architecture in Harbin, 1928-1998," *South Atlantic Quarterly* 99, 1 (2000): 97-115.

10 Minutes of the meeting of the Technical Board, enclosure in NARA, RG 59, M329, Roll 150, File 861.77/2197, 5 July 1921, 22; CER Schools, Report by Consul Hanson, enclosure in NARA, RG 59, M316 Roll 158, File 861.77/3074, 21 March 1923; Tepnavskii, "Education Section," 93.

11 China: The Maritime Customs, 37-39, 228; Bakich, "Russian Education in Harbin," 273.

12 The Education Department's mandate covered primary schools, kindergartens, reading rooms, museums, libraries, religious establishments, schools for the blind and the deaf, professional schools, private schools subsidized by the city, and various educational courses. *Haerbin tebie shizheng baoshi* [Report on the Harbin Special City: City Government] (Harbin, 1931), Chapter 4.2.

13 Department of Public Education, Special District of the Northeastern Provinces, *Curriculum for Russian Secondary Schools in the Special District* (Harbin: CER Press, 1926).

14 "The Harbin Temporary Self-Governing Committee and the Supervisory Prices and Taxation Committee Joint Meetings," Meeting 6, 6 April 1926, Case 4; Meeting 9, 17 April 1926, Case 1; Meeting 14, 5 May 1926, Case 3; Meeting 20, 8 June 1926, Case 3; Meeting 22, 23 June 1926, Case 3; Meeting 14, 5 May 1926, Case 7, in *Haerbin tebie shizheng baoshi.*

15 Ibid., Meeting 14, 5 May 1926, Case 4; Meeting 23, 25 June 1926, Case 1 and 2; Meeting 26, 6 July 1926, Case 3 and 4. And Zhang Guanhuang, "Speech for the Foundation of City Autonomous Government, November 1st 1926," in *Haerbin tebie shizheng baoshi,* Chapter 4.2.

16 Doc. 61, Consul Philip to Mr. Palairet, 12 March 1925, United Kingdom, Foreign Office, *BDFA* E.2, *China Annual Reports: January 1925 to October 1925,* vol. 24 (Bethessa MD: University Publications of America, 1994), 91.

17 Tepnavskii, "Education Section," 92; "The Future of Russian Schools," *Novosti zhizni,* 31 October 1924, NARA, RG 59, M316, Roll 158, File 861.77/3775, 8 December 1924.

18 Doc. 61, Consul Philip to Mr. Palairet, 91.

19 Ibid. Ustrialov was a prominent émigré academic who decided that support for the USSR was necessary because the USSR represented Russia and national interests were more important than political interests. His rejection of émigré identity was seen as a betrayal by his fellow émigrés. See Bakich, "Russian Education in Harbin," 281.

20 "The Regular Paroxysm," *Russkii golos,* 28 February 1925, NARA, RG 59, M316, Roll 158, File 861.77/3862, 18 March 1925.

21 Howard Lee Haag, "Notes on the Harbin School System," unpublished, n.d., Sterling Memorial Library, Manuscripts and Archives, Yale University, Howard Lee Haag Papers, Box 4, Folder 92.

22 "Regarding the Questions of the Day," *Echo,* 2 September 1926, NARA, RG 59, M316, Roll 154, File 861.77/4073, 19 September 1926; D. Poliakov and B. Eltekov, "Zheleznodorozhnye shkoly dlia detei grazhdan SSSR" [Railway schools for the children of Soviet citizens], *Manchurian Monitor* 8 (1930): 33-43.

23 "The Future of Russian Schools," *Novosti zhizni,* 25 October 1924, NARA, RG 59, M316, Roll 158, File 861.77/3746, 5 November 1924.

24 "The Schools Question," *Tribuna,* 23 October 1924.

25 The Chinese authorities did insist that military drills taught to boys in Russian secondary schools under Chinese control be abolished. "Recovery of Educational Authority," *Manchuria Daily News,* 8 August 1926.

26 Chinese Flag raised in Harbin, enclosure 1 in NARA, RG 59, M316 Roll 154, File 861.774/4082, 22 September 1926.

27 Haag, "Notes on the Harbin School System"; French Consul, Chemin de fer l'est Chinois, 1926 Novembre, MAEAD, Dossier General Chemin de fer l'est Chinois, November 1926-August 1938, vol. 432, 110-13; "Why the CER Office Was Closed," *Manchuria Daily News,* 8 September 1926.

28 Doc. 36, Memorandum respecting Northern Manchuria, part of Enclosure dated 7 October 1928, United Kingdom, Foreign Office, *BDFA* E.2, *China Annual Reports: September 1928 to June 1929*, vol. 36 (Bethesda, MD: University Publications of America, 1994), 35; "Why the CER Office Was Closed," *Manchuria Daily News*, 8 September 1926; "CER Educational Office Ordered Closed," *Manchuria Daily News*, 27 August 1926.

29 Order Number 16, NARA, RG 59, M316, Roll 154, File 861.77/4081, 18 September 1926.

30 Chinese Flag raised in Harbin, enclosure 1 in NARA, RG 59, M316 Roll 154, File 861.774/4082, 22 September 1926.

31 "Regarding the Questions of the Day," *Echo*, 2 September 1926, NARA, RG 59, M316, Roll 154, File 861.77/4073, 19 September 1926.

32 "News from Harbin," *Manchuria Daily News*, 7 February 1929; "The Knotty Problem Solved," *Manchuria Daily News*, 5 October 1927; George Hanson to L. Mayer, Solution of the Sino-Russian Educational Problem, NARA, RG 59, M316, Roll 154, File 861.77/4146, 7 December 1927; "CER Education Office," *Manchuria Daily News*, 1 April 1927; "The Education Question," *Kung Pao*, 4 December 1927, NARA, RG 59, M316, Roll 154, File 861.77/4146, 7 December 1927.

33 *Who's Who in China* (Shanghai: China Weekly Review, 1930).

34 Chinese Flag raised in Harbin, enclosure 1 in NARA, RG 59, Roll 155, M329, File 861.77 CE/6, 31 December 1928.

35 "Chinese Influence Spreading in CER," *Manchuria Daily News*, 18 August 1927.

36 Report from Harbin, NARA, RG 59, Roll 82, M329, File 861.77, 27 April 1928.

37 Report from Harbin, NARA, Rg 59, Roll 82, M329, File 861.77, 28 December 1928.

38 "News from Harbin," *Manchuria Daily News*, 9 February 1929.

39 Report from Harbin, NARA, RG 59, Roll 82, M329, File 861.77, 25 February 1929.

40 "News from Harbin," *Manchuria Daily News*, 25 February 1929. This was part of an overall policy to make Chinese and Russian equal languages on and in the CER.

41 Report from Harbin, NARA, RG 59, Roll 82, M329, File 861.77, 25 August 1929.

42 Report from Harbin, NARA, RG 59, Roll 82, M329, File 861.77, 27 October 1929.

43 Letter to Harbin Consul Hanson from the Special District Education Bureau, 24 July 1929, enclosed in NARA, RG 59, Roll 155, M329, File 861.77 CE/332, 21 August 1929.

44 "Circumstances and Motives of the Case," in Harbin Observer, *Protsess 38: Stenogramma protsessa 38 sovetskikh grazhdan, arestovannykh pri nalete 27 maia 1929 g. na Sovetskoe Konsyl'stvo v g. Kharbine, ORVP* [Process of the 38: Stenographic report of the process of the 38 Soviet citizens arrested during the raid on the Soviet Consulate General in Harbin on 27 May 1929] (Harbin: Harbin Observer, 1929), 9.

45 Zhang Yuanrong, *Heilongjiang shengzhi jiaoyuzhi* [Heilongjiang provincial records: Administration] (Harbin: Heilongjiang People's Publishing House, 1996), 708. An article by D. Polakov and B. Eltekov written in 1930 puts a brave face on the Soviet reversal. The period between 1926 to 1929 is acknowledged as a period in which the Soviet schools came under increased Special District control. The 1929 crisis is not referred to, and the article consists primarily of charts and graphs comparing the square footage of schools with the numbers of Soviet students. The authors do congratulate the Special District's Education Department for creating an outdoor summer course designed to introduce students to real life. See D. Polakov and B. Eltekov "Railway Schools for the Children of Soviet Citizens," *Manchurian Monitor*, 8 (1930): 33-43.

46 F.B. Skvirsky, "Central Library of the CER," *Manchurian Monitor* 3 (1930): 1-4.

47 "The Executive Committee Should Be Fundamentally Changed," *Binjiang shibao* (Harbin), 30 June 1922; "Russian Women Establish School," *Binjiang shibao* (Harbin), 10 October 1922.

48 Baranov, "Prepodavanie kitaiskogo iazyka v russkoi nachal'noi i srednei shkole Osobogo Raiona Vostochnykh Provintsii," 8-13.

264 *Notes to pages 193-97*

49 Department of Public Education, Special District of the Northeastern Provinces, *Curriculum for Russian Secondary Schools*.

50 I.G. Baranov, "Prepodavanie kitaiskogo iazyka v russkoi nachal'noi i srednei shkole Osobogo Raiona Vostochnykh Provintsii," 10-11; "The Harbin Temporary Self-Governing Committee," Meeting 6, 6 April 1926, Case 4; I.G. Baranov, "Prepodavanie kitaiskogo iazyka v russkoi nachal'noi i srednei shkole Osobogo Raiona Vostochnykh Provintsii," 11.

51 I.G. Baranov, "Prepodavanie kitaiskogo iazyka v russkoi nachal'noi i srednei shkole Osobogo Raiona Vostochnykh Provintsii," 11.

52 V.I. Anders. Private High School. "Lapiken, Petr Petrovich: Diploma, 1927"; "Memo from V. Shkurkin," no date; V. Shkurkin, photos of staff and students of the CER Chinese Language Course, All Shkurkin Archive.

53 Carter, *Creating a Chinese Harbin*, 88.

54 "Russian Sports," *Binjiang shibao* (Harbin), 1922; Wang Lijiang, "Huiyi Haerbin tiyu" [Recalling Harbin physical education] *Harbin wenshi ziliao* [Harbin Cultural and Historical Materials], 2 (September 1983): 59-77.

55 Haag, "Notes on the Harbin School System"; Carter, *Creating a Chinese Harbin*, 198.

56 "The Donghua's Students' Assembly Six Resolutions Adopted Yesterday," *Binjiang shibao* (Harbin), 18 September 1926, translated by James Carter.

57 Wang, "Huiyi Haerbin tiyu," 59-77.

58 Bakich, "Russian Education in Harbin," 270.

59 Yutaka Otsuka, "Japan's Involvement with Higher Education in Manchuria: Some Lessons from an Imposed Educational Cooperation," unpublished paper, author's collection, Harbin Technical University History Department, *Harbin gongye daxue jianshi, 1920-1985* [History of Harbin Technical University, 1920-1985] (Harbin: Technical University Press, 1985). Although many did not graduate, most students found work.

60 "The Harbin Temporary Self-Governing Committee," Meeting 22, 22 June 1926, Case 7; Harbin Technical University History Department, *Harbin gongye daxue jianshi*. A degree from the institution was seen as essential for entrance into the CER. In 1926 the newly reorganized Harbin Municipal Council donated money and letters of introduction to the CER's Engineering Department to a Russian student and a Chinese student from the institute who had together won a model bridge construction contest.

61 The deanship was primarily a ceremonial position. In 1924 Zhu Qinglan was the dean. Harbin Technical University History Department, *Harbin gongye daxue jianshi*, 6.

62 Bakich, "Russian Education in Harbin," 279-80.

63 Ibid., 280.

64 Harbin Technical University History Department, *Harbin gongye daxue jianshi, 1920-1985* [History of Harbin Technical University, 1920-1985] (Harbin: Technical University Press, 1985), Introduction.

65 "Otchet o deiatel'nosti Obshchestva Izucheniia Man'chzhurskogo Kraia" [Report of the activities of the Manchurian Research Society], *Isvestiia obshchestva izucheniia Man'chzhurskogo kraia* [Review of the Manchurian Research Society] 7 (December 1928): 77; Obshchestva izucheniia Manchzurskogo kraia (hereafter OIMK), *Isvestiia obshchestva izucheniia Man'chzhurskogo kraia* [Review of the Manchurian Research Society](October 1926): 3-12; Olga Bakich, "Society for the Study of Manchuria," unpublished notes, Bakich private collection, 1.

66 OIMK, "The Manchuria Research Society: Its Aims, Organization and Activity," *Isvestiia obshchestva izucheniia Man'chzhurskogo kraia* [Review of the Manchurian Research Society] (October 1926): 7.

67 A.S. Lukashkin, "Muzei Severnoi Man'chzhurii v kharbine" [The Museum of northern Manchuria in Harbin], *Manchurian Monitor* 1 (1934): 184; A. Rachkovskii, "Shest' let" [Six years], *Isvestiia*

obshchestva izucheniia Man'chzhurskogo Kraia [Review of the Manchurian Research Society] 7
(December 1928): 3.

68 Ito Takeo, *Life along the South Manchurian Railway,* trans. Joshua Fogel (Armonk, NY: M.E. Sharpe, 1988), 8.

69 OIMK, "The Manchuria Research Society: Its Aims, Organization and Activity," 10; Rachkovskii, "Shest' let," 3.

70 OIMK, "The Manchuria Research Society: Its Aims, Organization and Activity," 9.

71 "The Problem of Russian and Chinese Language," *Binjiang shibao,* 10 June 1923. The article noted that the activities of the Manchurian Research Society, supported by the CER, were conducted primarily in Russian.

72 OIMK, "The Manchuria Research Society: Its Aims, Organization and Activity," 10.

73 "The City Advisory Committee, Meeting Sixty-Nine, October 18th, 1927," in *Haerbin tebie shizheng baoshi,* Chapter 4.1.

74 Lukashkin, "The Museum of Northern Manchuria in Harbin," 187.

75 Ibid.

76 "News from Harbin," *Manchuria Daily News,* 28 February 1929.

77 Lukashkin, "The Museum of Northern Manchuria in Harbin," 187.

78 E.A Baranovy and N.M. Baranovy, "Cultures in Contact," 201-10.

CHAPTER 9: CONCLUSION

1 Fraser Charlton, *The Geisha: Introduction and Synopsis,* http://www.staff.ncl.ac.uk/fraser.charlton/edmuscom/page28/page30/geisyn.html.

2 Letter to the editor of the *International,* 30 January 1924, NARA, General Records of the Department of State, RG 59, M316, Roll 153, File 861.77/3371, 1 February 1924.

3 In 1997 the former club was closed for repairs, but the lobby – which had been turned into a store and which had several dusty chandeliers and lots of faded gilt and elaborate plasterwork – gave a sense of its grandeur.

4 Adelaide Nichols, "Any Night at the Opera in Harbin," *New York Times,* 23 March 1923.

5 Unfortunately, I could find no further information on RABIS or why a Soviet theatre group was in Harbin in January 1924, five months before the Beijing-Soviet agreement and nine months before the Shenyang-Soviet agreement were signed. The author, Kruzenshtern-Peterets, insinuates that the performance and insult were an intentional bid to provoke the Chinese and embarrass the CER's émigré administration. Since the source incorrectly identifies one opera as *Turandot* and the date of the performance as the eve of the Sino-Russian agreement (which would not be signed for several months), it is impossible to accept her charges without further proof. However, they do raise some fascinating questions. Thanks to Olga Bakich and Carl Morey, Faculty of Music, University of Toronto, for their assistance. Iu. V. Kruzenshtern-Peterets, "Memoirs," *Russians in Asia* 4 (Autumn 1997): 124-209.

6 César Cui, *Fils du mandarin overture* (Miami, Florida: E.F. Kalmus, 1984). The opera is still popular in Russia, especially among children. Several Russian friends have spoken of it fondly, and one said it shaped her first images of China.

7 Kruzenshtern-Peterets, "Memoirs," 196.

8 Charleton, *Geisha.*

9 Kruzenshtern-Peterets, "Memoirs," 143.

10 "Propaganda of All Circles in Favor of the Banish [sic] of Ostroumoff," *Dawning,* 25 January 1924, translated from Chinese, NARA, RG 59, M316, Roll 153, File 861.77/3371, 1 February 1924.

11 American Consul George Hanson to American Ambassador Jacob Schurman, Beijing, 20 February 1924, NARA, RG 59, M316, Roll 153, File 861.77/3373, 20 February 1924.

12   Harbin Technical University History Department, *Harbin gongye daxue jianshi, 1920-1985* [History of Harbin Technical University, 1920-1985] (Harbin: Technical University Press, 1985).

13   "CER to Demand Guarantees against Demonstrations," *Harbin Daily News,* 22 February 1924, NARA, RG 59, M316 Roll 153, File 861.77/3376.

14   "Indecent Behaviour," *Russkii golos,* 23 February 1924, translated, NARA, RG 59, M316, Roll 153, File 861.77/3379, 29 February 1924.

15   "Demonstration of Interest and Solidarity," *Russkii golos,* 25 February 1924, NARA, RG 59, M316, Roll 153, File 861.77/3379, 29 February 1924.

16   "Proclamation Issued to Prohibit the Circulation of Rumors," 24 February 1924, NARA, RG 59, M316, Roll 153, File 861.77/3379, 29 February 1924.

17   See James Carter for his analysis of the dynamics of student protests in Harbin. James Hugh Carter, *Creating a Chinese Harbin: Nationalism in an International City, 1916-1932* (Ithaca, NY: Cornell University Press, 2002).

18   "Chinese Authorities Give Quieting Assurances," *Harbin Daily News,* 26 February 1924, NARA, RG 59, M316, Roll 153, File 861.77/3379, 29 February 1924.

19   See Rana Mitter, *The Manchurian Myth,* chapter 8.

20   The 1929 crisis has barely been researched because the event, which dominated world headlines for a month, was overshadowed by the growing Japanese threat in Manchuria. In the best account of the incident, Bruce Elleman argues that Soviet aggression was consistent with a two-faced Soviet policy in China. The Soviets assumed a special relationship with China based on a fictitious friendship between the nations and augmented the relationship by claiming to be looking out for the interests of the Chinese working class. Elleman claims the Soviets pursued an imperialist policy almost identical to that of czarist Russia: they used political propaganda to interfere in Chinese politics. The Chinese side of the dispute has not been explored, nor have there been attempts to untangle competing regional and national positions on the event.

21   "Why the CER Office Was Closed," *Manchuria Daily News,* 8 September 1926.

22   Although parity had been a goal of the 1924 agreement, the number of Russians working for the CER had increased. When Ivanov assumed control of the line in 1924, 10,853 ethnic Russians worked on the line; by the time of the 1929 crisis, Soviet citizens working on the line numbered 11,251. Harry Kingman, *Effects of Chinese Nationalism upon Manchurian Railway Developments* (Berkeley: University of California Press, 1932), 64.

23   "News from Harbin," *Manchuria Daily News,* 12 February 1929.

24   Doc. 38, Sir Arthur Chamberlain to Sir M. Lampson, 14 January 1929, United Kingdom, Foreign Office, *BDFA* E.2, *China Annual Reports: September 1928 to June 1929,* vol. 36 (Bethesda, MD: University Publications of America, 1994), 243; "Notes from China to the Powers Concerning the 1929 Incident," *Chinese Social Science and Political Science Review* 13, 4 (1929): 5-6; "CER Director Assassinated," *Manchuria Daily News,* 5 July 1929.

25   Mao Hong, "Haerbin zhong e renmin shenghuo zhuangkuang" [Harbin's Russian and Chinese citizens' lifestyles compared], *Shishi yuebao* [China Monthly] 1, 2 (1929): 119.

26   Doc. 38, Sir Arthur Chamberlain to Sir M. Lampson, 14 January 1929, United Kingdom, Foreign Office, 245 [quote], 248.

27   "CER Papers and Documents," *Manchuria Daily News,* 15 November 1929. Russian-speaking Chinese disagreed with Chinese graduates of American colleges who wanted to increase the use of English on the line. Report from Harbin, enclosure in NARA, RG 59, M316, Roll 155, File 861.77/Chinese Eastern/8, 19 January 1929.

28   "New Soviet Heads at Harbin," *Manchuria Daily News,* 27 December 1929.

29   Report from Harbin, enclosure in NARA, RG 59, M316, Roll 155, File 861.77/Chinese Eastern/9, 4 January 1929.

30 Rosemary K.I. Quested, *"Matey" Imperialists? The Tsarist Russians in Manchuria, 1895-1917* (Hong Kong: University of Hong Kong, 1982).

31 Amleto Vespa, *Secret Agent of Japan* (London: Victor Gollancz, 1938); Harry Frank, *Wandering in Northern Manchuria* (New York: Century Publishers, 1923); Maurice Baring, *With the Russians in Manchuria* (London: Methuen and Co., 1905).

32 Maurice Hindus, "Manchuria: Boom Land of the Orient," *Asia* 28, 8 (1928): 629.

33 Xiao Hong, *Market Street: A Chinese Woman in Harbin*, trans. Howard Goldblatt (Seattle: University of Washington Press, 1986).

34 Nina Fedorova, *The Family* (New York: Little and Brown, 1940).

35 We should not let our conception of the Sino-Russian border – formed during the long cold war between the two countries – shape our understanding of the border before the 1930s. What the archival and anecdotal evidence shows is that the border was porous – thousands of people crossing easily between the two countries. In the political imagination of both the Chinese and Russians, the border was either negligible or an annoyance.

36 Beginning in the 1800s, during the reign of Alexander III, there was a strong program of administrative, religious, and linguistic Russification of the empire's non-Russian areas. This brief and extremely unpopular policy (among Russians and non-Russians alike) was unsuccessful and remains an aberration in the longer trend of Russian colonial accommodation.

37 Nicholas Breyfogle, "Colonial Contact as Creation: Relations between Russian Settlers and the Peoples of Transcaucasia, 1830-1900," unpublished manuscript, author's collection.

38 Hindus, "Manchuria," 629.

39 Blaine Chiasson, "How Can We Sing the Lord's Song in a Strange Land? A Russian Baptist Mission in Harbin and Shanghai," paper presented at the Canadian Historical Association Meeting, Canadian Association of Learned Societies, St. John's Newfoundland, June 1998.

40 S. Hautenschlager, "Harbin, Center of a Greater Chinese Civilization," *Chinese Weekly Review*, 21 September 1929.

41 "On Citizenship," *Russkii golos*, 22 November 1924, translated in James Hugh Carter, "Symbolic Assaults: The Construction of Regional and National Identity in Harbin, 1928-1998," unpublished paper.

42 Nicholas V. Borzov, "Raising the Flag," unpublished manuscript, Hoover Institution on War, Revolution and Peace, Borzov Papers, Roll 13, Box 13, Folder 7.

43 Tsao Lien-en, "Travels in Manchuria," *China Journal* 7 (June 1930): 345.

Bibliography

ARCHIVAL SOURCES

Bakhmeteff Archive, Rare Book and Manuscript Library, Columbia University, New York
Gerts, G.I. "Ten Years as an Advocate in the Russian Courts."

Hoover Institution on War, Revolution and Peace, Stanford, California
Borzov Papers
Overview of the Dmitrii Leonidovich Khorvat Memoirs.
Loukaskin Papers
Nilus, E.Kh. "Istorichheskii obzor Kitaiskoi vostochnoi xheleznoi dorogi, 1896-1923" [Historical survey of the Chinese Eastern Railway, 1896-1923], 1923.

Jilin Provincial Archives, Changchun, Jilin Province
Jilin sheng baogao [Jilin Provincial Reports]

Ministère des Affaires Etrangères, Archives Diplomatiques, Series E, Asie-Oceanie (MAEAD), 1918-1940, Paris, France

Shkurkin Archive, San Pablo, California
Administrativnoe ustroistvo severnosi Man'chzhurii [Administrative structure of northern Manchuria]. Harbin: CER Press, 1926.
Anders, V.I. Private High School. "Lapiken, Petr Petrovich: Diploma, 1927."

"Memo from V. Shkurkin," no date.
Photos of staff and students of the CER Chinese Language Course.

Sterling Memorial Library, Manuscripts and Archives, Yale University, New Haven, Connecticut
Howard Lee Haag Papers

National Archives and Records Administration (NARA), Washington, DC
RG 59, General Records of the Department of State

NEWSPAPERS
Binjiang shibao [Binjiang News]
Chinese Economic Review
Chinese Weekly Review
Harbin Daily News
Japan Chronicle
Kharbinskii den' [Harbin Day]
Manchuria Daily News
New York Times
North China Herald
Peking and Tientsin Times
Peking Leader
Sungari Daily News
Zaria

CHINESE PRIMARY SOURCES
Haerbin tebie shizheng baoshi [Report on the Harbin Special City: City Government]. Harbin, 1931.

Dongchui shangbao [Northern Frontier Business Association]. *Haerbin zhinan* [Guide to Harbin]. 8 volumes. Harbin, 1922.

Mao Hong. "Haerbin zhong e renmin shenghuo zhuangkuang" [Harbin's Russian and Chinese citizens' lifestyles compared]. *Shishi yuebao* [China Monthly] 1, 2 (1929): 115-23.

"Order No. 7 Concerning the Establishment of the Special District Office for the Review of Unresolved Russian Lawsuits." *Dongfang zazhi* [Eastern Miscellany] 18, 6 (2 March 1921): 128-29.

Zhang Nanzhao, "Memoirs," in Dongchui shangbao [Northern Frontier Business Association], *Haerbin zhinan* [Guide to Harbin] (Harbin, 1922), 1:3.

Zhongdong tielu [The Chinese Eastern Railway]. Harbin: Heilongjiang Provincial Archive, 1986.

RUSSIAN PRIMARY SOURCES

Baranov, I.G. "Prepodavanie kitaiskogo iazyka v russkoi nachal'noi i srednei shkole Osobogo Raiona Vostochnykh Provintsii" [The teaching of the Chinese language in Russian primary and secondary schools of the Special Area of the Eastern Province]. *Manchurian Monitor* 7-8 (1929): 8-13.

Editor, "The Extent of Russian Powerlessness in China," *Russkoe obozienie* 3 and 4 (March-April 1921): 150-51.

Harbin Observer. *Protsess 38: Stenogramma protsessa 38 sovetskikh grazhdan, arestovannykh pri nalete 27 maia 1929 g. na Sovetskoe Konsyl'stvo v g. Kharbine, ORVP* [Process of the 38: Stenographic report of the process of the 38 Soviet citizens arrested during the raid on the Soviet Consulate General in Harbin on 27 May 1929]. Harbin: Harbin Observer, 1929.

Harbin Public Administration. *Kharbin': Itogi otsenochnoi perepisi po dannym' statisticheskogo oblsdovaniia, proizvodivshegosia s' 15-go iunia po 1-oe sentiabria 1923 g.* [Harbin: List of total data from the statistical service collected between 15 July and 1 September 1923]. Harbin: CER Press, 1924.

Kormazov, V.A. "Growth of the Population of Harbin and Fujiatian," *Manchurian Monitor* 7 (1930): 25-31.

Kruzenshtern-Peterets, Iu. V. "Memoirs." *Russians in Asia* 4 (Autumn 1997): 124-209.

Loukashkin, A.S. "Muzei Severnoi Man'chzhurii v kharbine" [The Museum of northern Manchuria in Harbin]. *Manchurian Monitor* 1 (1934): 183-87.

Obshchestva izucheniia Man'chzhurskogo kraia [OIMK]. "The Manchuria Research Society: Its Aims, Organization and Activity." *Isvestiia obshchestva izucheniia Man'chzhurskogo kraia* [Review of the Manchurian Research Society] (October 1926): 3-12.

–. "Otchet o deiatel'nosti Obshchestva Izucheniia Man'chzhurskogo Kraia" [Report of the activities of the Manchurian Research Society]. *Isvestiia obshchestva izucheniia Man'chzhurskogo Kraia* [Review of the Manchurian Research Society] 7 (December 1928): 75-107.

Poliakov, D., and Eltekov, B. "Zheleznodorozhnye shkoly dlia detei grazhdan SSSR" [Railway schools for the children of Soviet citizens]. *Manchurian Monitor* 8 (1930): 33-43.

Rachkovskii, A. "Shest' let" [Six years]. *Isvestiia obshchestva izucheniia Man'chzhurskogo Kraia* [Review of the Manchurian Research Society] 7 (December 1928): 3-7.

Skvirsky F.B. "Bor'ba Tsarskaia klik na KVzhd" [Struggle of the Czarist Clique on the CER]." *Manchurian Monitor* 9 (1930): 62-66.

Tepnavskii, S.T. *Ves' Kharbin* [All Harbin]. Harbin: CER Publishing House, 1923 and 1926.

Zakharova, N.S. *Spravochnik' domovladel'tsa* [Reference book for homeowners]. Harbin: Zaria Press, 1927.

WESTERN-LANGUAGE PRIMARY SOURCES (OTHER THAN RUSSIAN)

"Agreement between the Republic of China and the Union of Soviet Socialist Republic (and Annexes), Peiping 31 May 1924." *Chinese Social and Political Science Review* 8, 3 (1924): 220-33.

"Automobile Census in China." *Chinese Economic Review* 157 (February 1924): 4.

Bureau of Industrial and Commercial Information. "Household Industries in Harbin." *Chinese Economic Bulletin* 15, 8 (August 1929): 92-95.

"Chang Chih-Tung's Memorial of August 1895." In *China's Response to the West: A Documentary Survey, 1839-1923*, ed. Ssu-yu Teng and John Fairbank, 128-31. Cambridge, MA: Harvard University Press, 1982.

Chang, Yu-Chuan. "The Chinese Judiciary." *Chinese Social Science and Political Science Review* 3, 1 (1918): 70-71.

China. "District Self-Government Law, 7 September 1919." In *The Constitution and Supplementary Laws and Documents of the Republic of China*, trans. Commission on Extraterritoriality, 129-47. Peking: Commission on Extraterritoriality, 1924.

-. "Regulations Governing Municipal Self-Government, 3 July 1921." In *The Constitution and Supplementary Laws and Documents of the Republic of China*, trans. Commission on Extraterritoriality, 149-74. Peking: Commission on Extraterritoriality, 1924.

China: The Maritime Customs. Statistical Series No. 6 Decennial Reports, "Harbin Report, 1907-1911." In vol. 1: *Northern and Yangtze Ports*. Shanghai: Statistical Department of the Inspectorate General of Customs, 1913.

-. "Harbin, 1912-1921." In vol. 1: *Northern and Yangtze Ports*. Shanghai: Statistical Department of the Inspectorate General of Customs, 1924.

-. "Harbin Decennial Reports, 1922-1931." In vol. 1: *Northern and Yangtze Ports*. Shanghai: Statistical Department of the Inspectorate General of Customs, 1933.

Coville, Lillian Grosvenor. "Here in Manchuria." *National Geographic Magazine* 63 (January-June 1933): 233-56.

Department of Public Education, Special District of the Northeastern Provinces. *Curriculum for Russian Secondary Schools in the Special District*. Harbin: CER Press, 1926.

Economic Bureau of the Chinese Eastern Railway. *North Manchuria and the Chinese Eastern Railway*. Harbin: Chinese Eastern Railway Printing Office, 1924.

Frank, Harry. *Wandering in Northern China*. New York: Century Publishers, 1923.

Gilbreath, Olive. "Where Yellow Rules White." *Harper's Magazine*, February 1929, 367-74.

Glenny, Michael, and Norman Stone, eds. *The Other Russia: The Experience of Exile*. London: Faber and Faber, 1990.

Gong Jianghong. *Harbinshizi minzheng qiaowu* [Harbin city government: Immigration]. Harbin: Heilongjiang People's Publishing House, 1994.

Governments of China and Russia. "Preliminary Arrangement for the Municipal Organizations in the Zone of the Chinese Eastern Railway." *American Journal of International Law* 3, 4 (October 1909), 289-93.

Harbin Observer. *Fleet's Directory of Manchurian Cities, 1934-35*. Harbin: Harbin Observer Press, 1935.

Harbin Special District. *In Commemoration of the Inaugural State Celebrations in the Special District of Harbin, Special Area of the Eastern Provinces*. Harbin: CER Press, 1932. Hoover Institution on War, Revolution and Peace.

Hautenschlager, S. "Harbin, Center of a Greater Chinese Civilization." *Chinese Weekly Review*, 21 September 1929.

Hindus, Maurice. "Manchuria: Boom Land of the Orient." *Asia* 28, 8 (1928): 626-33.

Kawakami, K.K. "The Russo-Chinese Conflict in Manchuria." *Foreign Affairs* 8 (October 1929–July 1930): 52-68.

Kormazov, V.A. "Growth of the Population of Harbin and Fujiatian." *Manchurian Monitor* 7 (1930): 25-31.

"Liu K'un-I's Secret Proposal, July 1895." In *China's Response to the West: A Documentary Survey, 1839-1923*, ed. Ssu-yu Teng and John Fairbank, 127-28. Cambridge, MA: Harvard University Press, 1982.

MacMurray, John. *Treaties and Agreements with and Concerning China, 1894-1919*. Vol. 1. New York: Oxford University Press, 1921.

Mitrofanov, Igor. *The Lands and Land Administration of the Chinese Eastern Railway Company, and the Incident of August 1st 1923.*
Harbin n.p., n.d.

Neopihanoff, A.A. "The Development of North
Manchuria." *Chinese Economic Journal* 2,
3 (1928): 264-65.

"Notes from China to the Powers Concerning
the 1929 Incident," *Chinese Social Science
and Political Science Review* 13, 4 (1929): 5-6.

"Provisional Regulations Governing the
Appearance in Court of Lawyers of Coun-
tries Which Are Not Entitled to Consular
Jurisdiction." *Chinese Social Science and
Political Science Review* 5a, 4 (1920): 70-71.

Rea, George Brown. "Harbin: The Aftermath of
Russia's Adventures." *Journal of the American Asiatic Association* 9, 4 (1909): 199-204.

"Regulations Governing the Committee on the
Selection of Special Candidates for the Judi-
ciary." *Chinese Social Science and Political
Science Review* 5a, 4 (1920): 312-14.

"Restoration of Foreign Concessions and Settlements." *Chinese Social Science and Political
Science Review* 5a, 1-2 (1920): 146-52.

"Rules Governing the Organization of the Special District of the Eastern Provinces." *Chinese Social Science and Political Science
Review* 5a, 4 (1920): 309-11.

Simpich, Frederick. "Manchuria: Promised Land
of Asia." *National Geographic Magazine* 56,
4 (October 1929): 379-428.

Skvirsky, F.B. "Central Library of the CER."
Manchurian Monitor 3 (1930): 1-3.

Tsao, Lien-en. "Travels in Manchuria." *China
Journal* 7 (June 1930).

United Kingdom. Foreign Office. *British Docu-
ments on Foreign Affairs: Reports and Papers
from the Foreign Office Confidential Print.*
Series E, Part 2: Asia, 1914-1939: *China
Annual Reports.* 36 volumes. Bethesda, MD:
University Publications of America, 1994.

United States. Department of State. *Proposed
Establishment by the Chinese Eastern Rail-
way Company of a Municipality at Harbin.*
Washington, DC: 1910.

Ushanoff, Vasilif V. "Recollections of Life in the
Russian Community in Manchuria and in

Emigration." In *Russian Émigré Recollections:
Life in Russia and California,* Richard A.
Pierce, ed., 1-56. Berkeley: University of
California Press, 1986.

Wang, Chin-Chun. "The Chinese Eastern Railway Question." *Chinese Student Monthly* 22,
2 (1926): 51-63.

Who's Who in China. Shanghai: China Weekly
Review, 1930.

Young, C. Walter. *International Relations of
Manchuria.* Chicago: University of Chicago
Press, 1929.

SECONDARY SOURCES

Bakich, Olga. "City and Émigré Identity." Paper
presented at "Place, Space, and Identity:
Harbin and Manchuria in the First Half of
the Twentieth Century," University of
Toronto, 19-21 November 1988.

–. "Émigré Identity: The Case of Harbin." *South
Atlantic Quarterly* 99, 1 (2000): 51-73.

–. "History of Harbin: The Establishment of the
City Council." Unpublished manuscript.
Bakich Collection.

–. "A Russian City in China: Harbin before 1917."
Canadian Slavonic Papers 28, 2 (1986): 129-48.

–. "Russian Education in Harbin." *Transactions
of the Association of Russian-American
Scholars in the USA* 26 (1994): 269-94.

–. "Society for the Study of Manchuria." Unpublished notes. Bakich Collection.

Baranovy, E.A and N.M. "Cultures in Contact
and the Demise of Russian Harbin." *Transactions of the Association of Russian-
American Scholars in the USA* 26 (1994):
201-10.

Baring, Maurice. *With Russians in Manchuria.*
London: Methuen and Co., 1905.

Bektjaschinsky, N.N. "The Municipality of the
City of Harbin." *Manchuria Monitor* 5-7
(1925): 10-17.

Bickers, Robert. "Shanghailanders: The Formation and Identity of the British Settler Community in Shanghai, 1843-1937." *Past and
Present* 159 (May 1998): 161-211.

Breyfogel, Nicholas B. "Colonial Context as
Creation: Relations between Russian Settlers and the Peoples of the Transcaucasia,

1830-1900." Unpublished paper. Author's collection.

Brunnert, H.S., and V.V. Hagelstorm. *Present Day Political Organization of China*, trans. A. Beltchenko and E.E. Moran. Shanghai: Kelly and Walsh, 1912.

Buck, David. *Urban Change in China: Politics and Development in Tsinan, Shantung, 1890-1949*. Madison: University of Wisconsin Press, 1978.

Carter, James Hugh. *Creating a Chinese Harbin: Nationalism in an International City, 1916-1932*. Ithaca, NY: Cornell University Press, 2002.

– "Symbolic Assaults: The Construction of Regional and National Identity in Harbin, 1928-1998." Unpublished paper. Author's Collection.

– "A Tale of Two Temples: Nation, Region, and Religious Architecture in Harbin, 1928-1998." *South Atlantic Quarterly* 99, 1 (2000): 97-115.

Charlton, Fraser. *The Geisha: Introduction and Synopsis*. http://www.staff.ncl.ac.uk/fraser.charlton/edmuscom/page28/page30/geisyn.html.

Chiasson, Blaine, "How Can We Sing the Lord's Song in a Strange Land? A Russian Baptist Mission in Harbin and Shanghai." Unpublished paper. Author's collection.

Chu Wen-Djang. *The Moslem Rebellion in Northwest China, 1862-1878: A Study of Government Minority Policy*. Paris: n.p., 1966.

Coleman, Frederic. *Japan Moves North: The Inside Story of the Struggle for Siberia*. London: Gassell and Company, 1918.

Coleman, Maryruth. "Municipal Politics in Nationalist China: Nanjing, 1927-1937." PhD diss., Harvard University, 1984.

Cui, César. *Fils du mandarin overture*. Miami, FL: E.F. Kalmus, 1984.

Cui, Wei. "Settling Relations between the Temporary Nanjing Government and China's Minorities." *Nanjing jihui kexue* [Social Sciences in Nanjing] 2 (February 2003): 52-55.

Dikotter, Frank. *Crime, Punishment and the Prison in Modern China*. London: Hurst and Company, 2002.

Ding, Lianglun. "A Survey of Harbin's Russian Community, 1917-1931." *Beifang wenwu* [Culture of the North] 61 (January 2000): 81-86.

Duara, Prasenjit. "Transnationalism and the Predicament of Sovereignty: China, 1900-1945." *American Historical Review* 102, 4 (1997): 1030-51.

Economic Bureau of the Chinese Eastern Railway. *The Chinese Eastern Railway and Its Zone*. Harbin: Chinese Eastern Railway Printing Office, 1923.

–. *North Manchuria and the CER*. Harbin: Chinese Eastern Railway Printing Office, 1924.

Elleman, Bruce A. *Diplomacy and Deception: The Secret History of Sino-Soviet Diplomatic Relations, 1917-1927*. Armonk, NY: M.E. Sharpe, 1997.

–. "The Soviet Union's Secret Diplomacy Concerning the Chinese Eastern Railway." *Journal of Asian Studies* 52, 2 (1994): 459-86.

Esherick, Joseph. "Harvard on China: The Apologetics of Imperialism." *Bulletin of Concerned Asian Scholars* 4 (December 1972): 9-16.

Fairbank, John King. *Trade and Diplomacy on the China Coast: The Opening of the Treaty Ports, 1842-1854*. Stanford, CA: Stanford University Press, 1953.

Fedorova, Nina. *The Family*. New York: Little and Brown, 1940.

Foreign Policy Association. "The Chinese Eastern Railway." *Foreign Policy Association Information Service*, vol. 1, 1925-1926. New York: Kraus Reprint, 1967.

Gilbert, Rodney. *What's Wrong with China*. London: John Murray, 1927.

Go, Toshi. "The Future of Foreign Concessions in China," *Pacific Affairs* 12, 4 (1939): 394-99.

Gong Jianghong. *Harbinshizhi: Minzheng qiaowu* [Harbin City records: People's Government, Overseas Chinese Affairs]. Harbin: People's Publishing House, 1994.

Harbin Technical University History Department. *Harbin gongye daxue jianshi, 1920-1985* [History of Harbin Technical University, 1920-1985]. Harbin: Technical University Press, 1985.

Hamm, Michael, ed. *The City in Late Imperial Russia.* Bloomington: University of Indiana Press, 1986.

Harbin Yearbook Society. *Haerbin nianjian 1994* [Harbin yearbook 1994]. Harbin: Harbin Yearbook Society, 1994.

Heilongjiang Provincial Historical Research Society. *Heilongjiang jindai lishi dashuji, 1840-1949* [Chronology of Heilongjiang contemporary history, 1840-1949]. Harbin: People's Publishing House, 1987.

Henriot, Christian. *Shanghai, 1927-1937: Municipal Power, Locality and Modernization.* Berkeley: University of California Press, 1993.

Hong Xiao. *Market Street: A Chinese Woman in Harbin*, trans. Howard Goldblatt. Seattle: University of Washington Press, 1986.

Ito, Takeo. *Life along the South Manchurian Railway: The Memoirs of Ito Takeo*, trans. Joshua Fogel. Armonk, NY: M.E. Sharpe, 1988.

Jao, Dain-houa. *La loi municipale Chinoise du 20 mai 1930* [The Chinese municipal Law of 20 May 1930]. Bordeaux, 1939.

Karlinsky, Simon. "Memoirs of Harbin." *Slavic Review* 48, 2 (1989): 284-89.

Kingman, Harry L. *Effects of Chinese Nationalism upon Manchurian Railway Developments.* Berkeley: University of California Press, 1932.

Kong Jingwei. *Di-e dui haerbin yidai de jingji lueduo* [The economic plunder of Harbin by imperial Russia]. Harbin: Heilongjiang People's Publishing House, 1986.

Lahusen, Thomas. "A Place Called Harbin: Reflections on a Centennial." *China Quarterly* 154 (June 1998): 181-90.

–. "Silver Screens and Lost Empires, or, 'Where the Russians Used to Live.'" Unpublished paper. Author's collection.

Lensen, George Alexander. *Balance of Intrigue: International Rivalry in Korea and Manchuria, 1884-1899.* Tallahassee: University of Florida Press, 1982.

Li Shuxiao, ed. *Haerbin lishi biannian: 1896-1949* [Chronology of Harbin history: 1846-1949]. Harbin: People's Publishing House, 1986.

Li Xinggeng. *Feng yu fu ping: Eguo qiaomin zai zhongguo, 1917-1945* [Leaves in the storm: Russian refugees in China, 1917-1945]. Beijing: Central Publishing House, 1997.

Liberman, Yaacov. *My China: Jewish Life in the Orient, 1900-1950.* Jerusalem: Gefen, 1998.

Malozemoff, Andrew. *Russian Far Eastern Policy, 1881-1904, with Special Emphasis on the Causes of the Russo-Japanese War.* Berkeley: University of California Press, 1958.

McCormack, Gavan. *Chang Tso-lin in Northeast China, 1911-1928: China, Japan, and the Manchurian Idea.* Stanford, CA: Stanford University Press, 1977.

– "Manchukuo: Constructing the Past." *East Asian History* 2 (December 1991): 105-25.

McQuilkin, David K. "Soviet Attitudes towards China, 1919-1927," PhD diss., Kent State University, 1973.

Medvedeva, Yelena. "Good Neighbourliness (Sketches of Daily Life)." *Far Eastern Affairs*, 1, (1994): 65-74.

Melikhov, G.A. *Manch'zhuriia: Dalekaia i blizkaia* [Manchuria: Far and Near]. Moscow: Hauka, 1991.

Mitter, Rana. *The Manchurian Myth: Nationalism, Resistance, and Collaboration in Modern China.* Berkeley: University of California Press, 2000.

Murphey, Rhoads. "The Treaty Ports and China's Modernization." In *The Chinese City between Two Worlds*, ed. M. Elvin and G.W. Skinner, 17-72. Stanford, CA: Stanford University Press, 1974.

Myers, Ramon, and J. Metzger. "Sinological Shadows." *Washington Quarterly* 3, 2 (1998): 87-114.

Paine, Sarah C.M. *Imperial Rivals: China, Russia, and Their Disputed Frontier.* Armonk, NY: M.E. Sharpe, 1996.

Petrov, Viktor. "A Town on the Sungari." In *The Other Russia: The Experience of Exile*, ed. Michael Glenny and Norman Stone, 206-21. London: Faber and Faber, 1990.

Quested, Rosemary K.I. *"Matey" Imperialists? The Tsarist Russians in Northern Manchuria, 1895-1900.* Hong Kong: University of Hong Kong Press, 1982.

Quigley, Harold Scott. "Extraterritoriality in China." *American Journal of International Law* 20, 1 (1926): 46-68.

–. "Foreign Concessions in Chinese Hands." *Foreign Policy* 7, 1 (1928): 150-55.

Romanov, B.A. *Russia in Manchuria*, trans. Susan Mann Jones. Ann Arbor, MI: American Council of Learned Societies, 1952.

Saveliev, Igor. "Chinese Migration in Space and Time." In *Globalizing Chinese Migration: Trends in Europe and Asia*, ed. Pal Nyiri, 35-73. Great Britain: Ashgate, 2002.

Schimmelpenninck van der Oye, David. *Toward the Rising Sun: Russian Ideologies of Empire and the Path to War with Japan*. DeKalb: Northern Illinois University Press, 2001.

South Manchurian Railway. *Report on Progress in Manchuria, 1907-1928*. Dalian: SMR Publishing House, 1929.

Spedelow, Howard. "Conflict of Authority in South Manchuria: The Early Years of the Russian Leasehold, 1898-1900." PhD diss., Harvard University, 1982.

–. *Rickshaw Beijing: City People and Politics in the 1920s*. Berkeley: University of California Press, 1993.

Suleski, Ronald Stanley. *Civil Government in Warlord China: Tradition, Modernization and Manchuria*. New York: Peter Lang, 2002.

–. "Manchuria under Chang Tso-lin." PhD diss., University of Michigan, 1974.

–. "Regional Development in Manchuria: Immigrant Laborers and Provincial Officials in the 1920s." *Modern China* 4, 4 (1978): 419-34.

Sun, Zhengjia. "Looking at the Glorious Historical Culture of Harbin through Its Cultural Relics." In *The Making of a Chinese City: History and Historiography in Harbin*, ed. S. Clausen and Stig Thogersen, 12-16. Armonk NY: M.E. Sharpe, 1995.

Tang, Peter S.H. *Russian and Soviet Policy in Manchuria and Outer Mongolia, 1911-1931*. Durham, NC: Duke University Press, 1959.

Tang Zhongmin, ed. *Haerbin shizhi: gongan sifa xingzheng* [Harbin city records: Public security and legal administration]. Harbin: Heilongjiang People's Publishing House, 1996.

Tao, Shing Chang. *International Controversies over the Chinese Eastern Railway*. Shanghai: Commercial Press, 1936.

Teng, Ssu-yu, and John Fairbank, eds. *China's Response to the West: A Documentary Survey, 1839-1923*. Cambridge, MA: Harvard University Press, 1982.

Thurston, Robert. *Liberal City, Conservative State: Moscow and Russia's Urban Crisis, 1906-1914*. Oxford: Oxford University Press, 1987.

Toa-Keizai Chosakyoku [East-Asiatic Economic Investigation Bureau]. *The Manchurian Yearbook, 1932-33*. Tokyo, 1932.

Tsai, Jung-Fang. *Hong Kong in Chinese History: Community and Social Unrest in the British Colony, 1842-1913*. New York: Columbia University Press, 1993.

Vespa, Amleto. *Secret Agent of Japan*. London: Victor Gollancz, 1938.

Wang Lijiang. "Huyi Haerbin tiyu" [Recalling Harbin physical culture]. *Harbin wenshi ziliao* [Harbin Cultural and Historical Materials] 2 (September 1983): 59-77.

Wang Zhicheng. *Shanghai eqiao shi* [A history of the Russian émigré community in Shanghai]. Shanghai: Shanghai Branch of the Third Publishing House, 1993.

Wolff, David. *To the Harbin Station: The Liberal Alternative in Russian Manchuria, 1989-1914*. Stanford, CA: Stanford University Press, 1999.

Xin Peilin. "Ma Zhongjun shensheng" [A biographical sketch of Mr. Ma Zhongjun]. *Harbin wenshi ziliao* [Harbin Cultural and Historical Materials] 6 (1985): 1-22.

Yang, Zuoshan, "A Discussion of Republican Period Frontier Ethnic Policy." *Guyuan shixuebao (shehui kexueban)* [Journal of the Guyuan Teachers College (Social Sciences)] 21, 5 (2000): 43-47.

Yutaka, Otsuka. "Japan's Involvement with Higher Education in Manchuria: Some Historical Lessons from an Imposed Educational Cooperation." Unpublished paper. Author's collection.

Zhang, Chunlin. "The Foundation of the Harbin City Government." *Harbin Shijiu* [Harbin Historical Research] 9, (January 1989): 8-15.

–. "Haerbin tiebie shijian zhiyange" [The foundation and development of Harbin Special City]. *Harbin shizhi* [Harbin Historical Records] 3, 9 (1986): 20-25.

Zhang, Dongmin "Recollections on the Foundation of the Northern Section of the Party." *Beifang Luncong* [Northern Research] 4, (1981): 9-14.

Zhang Yuanrong. *Heilongjiang shengzhi jiaoyuzhi* [Heilongjiang provincial records: Administration]. Harbin: Heilongjiang People's Publishing House, 1996.

Index

Note: "(a)" after a page number indicates the appendix; "(f)," a figure; "(m)," a map, and "(t)," a table.

China: boundaries, 229n3; civil war, 8, 9, 230n25; legal code, 47-48, 71, 72, 75, 79, 84, 245n151; military, 41; open-door policy, 28, 32, 39, 42, 71, 73, 159, 242n107 (*see also* concession cities; extraterritoriality); policy of compromise, 3; Russian revolutions and, 74, 98-99, 159; Sino-British relations, 13-14; Sino-foreign relations, 4-5, 11, 12, 15, 36-37; Sino-Soviet relations, 195-96, 214-18, 250nn35-36, 268n20

China Weekly Review, 93, 246n174

Chinese Bank of Communication, 102

Chinese Communist Party (CCP), 85, 230n25, 246n172

Chinese Eastern Railway (CER), 17(m); administration, 6, 48, 63, 69-70, 100, 109-12, 118-19, 123-24, 216-17, 239n37, 250n41; board members, 23-24, 29, 32, 195, 233n25; board members, Chinese, 113, 116, 218; board members, émigré, 105, 167-68, 256n105; board members, Soviet, 115-16, 176; conflict within, 105-7, 117, 155-56; contracts, 11, 21-24, 35, 42, 58, 59, 99, 100, 129-30 (*see also* Beijing agreement (1924); Shenyang agreement (1924)); deterioration, 100-2, 138; directors, 63-64, 194-95, 246n168 (*see also specific directors*); employees, 101, 115-16, 117-18, 216-17, 217(t), 268n22; jubilee, 107-8, 203; and Land Bureau, 139; management principles, 111; nature and purpose, 16, 19-20, 21-24, 30-31, 38, 75, 100-4, 120-22, 136, 156, 199; and OIMK, 202-3; ownership, 23, 143, 149, 252n14; parity in management, 111-12; property archives, 129, 134, 144; Railway Club, 185-86, 209, 210(f), 211, 267n3; revenues, 22-23, 29, 102, 103, 124-25, 138, 144-45; route, 1, 20, 232n3; Soviet strategies, 112, 114, 196, 215-16; statutes, 24; unions, 85, 86, 114, 215, 246n172; veto power, 30, 32, 33, 157, 164

Chinese Eastern Railway (CER) concession, 17(m); Chinese presence, 37, 40-41; guards/police, 45-46, 47, 48, 58-59, 61-62, 63, 115, 239n26; judicial system, 25-26, 71-73, 242n102; martial law, 47; municipal government, 32-33, 34-35, 161-62, 163-65, 167-68, 235n73; vs other concessions, 42, 219, 229n4; and regional development, 94-95, 98, 102-3, 120, 140-41; Russian population, 36-37, 48, 137; schools, 184-85, 186-88; size, 121

Chinese Eastern Railway (CER) departments: Agricultural, 102-3; Civil, 29-30, 32-33, 160; Economic, 102; Education, 191, 193; Land, 66, 120-30, 131-32, 133-34, 146-47, 148-49, 252n6; Merchant Marine, 110

Chinese Eastern Railway (CER) zone. *See* Chinese Eastern Railway (CER) concession

Chinese elite: administrative decisions, 221-22; comprador class, 52, 54; and culture, 207, 208; and education, 185, 189; and émigré community, 9, 51, 99, 106, 147, 223-24; and good governance, 3; and Japanese occupation, 183; politics of, 14-15, 181-82; self-regulating society, 11; view of concessions, 136-37, 143, 149; views of OIMK, 206-7; worldview, 50, 197

Chinese Land Bureau. *See* Special District of the Three Eastern Provinces, Land Bureau

Chinese Municipal Bureau. *See* government, Chinese, Municipal Administration Bureau

Chinese-Soviet relations. *See* China, Sino-Soviet relations

Chuvmarenko, 246n168

citizenship: Chinese, 116-17, 118; laws, 224; Soviet, 157; views of, 69-70

Coleman, Maryruth, 12, 13

colonialism/colonization: CER and, 16, 103-4, 120-22, 136-37, 148-49; Chinese, 38-39, 126; and indigenous peoples, 185; Japanese, 149, 204-5; justification, 12, 28-29, 120-23; Russian, 2-3, 10, 18, 19-20, 38-39, 49, 101, 102, 137-38, 218-20; and Sino-foreign relations, 4-5, 36-37; Soviet, 99, 139, 268n20; strategies, 26-27, 35, 141-43, 201-8; studies of, 218-19

Commission on Extraterritoriality, 91-92

concession cities, 11-12, 12-13, 53, 149, 159, 229n4. *See also* Chinese Eastern Railway (CER) concession; *individual concession cities*

control: of CER, 29, 109-12, 160, 248n14, 250n41; of control institutions, 46-49, 74; of education, 168, 186-88, 189-90, 193, 199-208, 265n45; of land, 120, 147-49, 256n104; of municipal government, 33, 151-52, 159-60, 181-82; territorial, 24-25, 47, 73, 122

control institutions. *See specific institutions*

co-operation: China and Manchurian Russians, 219; Chinese and Russian police, 47, 48; regional and national, 50-51 crime, 73, 95-97

Cui, César, 209, 267n6

Dalian, 17(m), 24, 29, 101

Daowai. *See* Fujiadian

daoyin, 234n50. *See also specific daoyins*

Davtian, Yacov, 143, 226(a)

Deng Jiemin, 189

deportation/eviction: Chinese, 24, 155; Chinese
    Harbiners, 125, 126; Chinese leaseholders,
    120, 140, 141; convicted Soviets, 87, 195; crim-
    inals, 88; duties and, 70; Russian police, 48;
    Russian troops, 46

Ding Lianglun, 10

diplomatic bureaus, 41

Dong Shien, 32, 45-46, 52, 59-60, 74, 226(a),
    234n65; and municipal reform, 160, 161, 162,
    164, 165

Dongbei. *See* Manchuria

Dongsansheng. *See* Manchuria

dragomen. See judicial system, translators

Duara, Prasenjit, 15

education: budget, 188-90, 192; cross-cultural
    influences, 190, 191-92, 193-95, 196, 197, 198-99;
    curricula, 198, 218; importance, 184-85; lit-
    eracy rate, 205; of refugee children, 188; of
    Soviet children, 193-95

education system: budget, 194; CER schools,
    184-85, 186-87, 188-89, 192; émigré vs Soviet
    teachers, 196; institutes of higher education,
    59-61, 199-202, 266n59; middle vs high schools,
    186, 188, 196, 197; private schools, 184-85, 186-
    87, 189, 198; research institutes, 200-208 (*see
    also* Manchurian Research Society (*Obsh-
    chestva izucheniia Manchzurskogo Kraia*,
    OIMK)); Special District schools, 187, 188-89

educational reform, 189-91, 193, 194, 195-98;
    Russian resistance, 186

Educator, 66, 195

electoral system, 171, 173, 175, 177

Elleman, Bruce, 250n35

Eltekov, B., 265n45

émigré community: associations, 70; Chinese
    passports, 216; and security costs, 63; and
    Soviets, 69-70, 85, 112-13, 191-92, 195, 222;
    status, 53, 199, 224; and USSR, 264n19

Emshanov, Boris, 117, 226(a)

enfranchisement: Chinese, 32, 108; minorities,
    14; property owners, 34; regulations, 180,
    231n45; restrictions, 161, 175; vs voter turn-
    out, 158

extraterritoriality: abolition, 4, 5, 52-53, 73-74,
    91-92, 247n185; and censorship, 246n174;
    Commission on Extraterritoriality, 91-92;
    and education, 193; ideological foundation,
    56, 85, 221, 223; and judicial system, 71, 73;
    and municipal politics, 158-59, 258n27; open-
    door policy and, 242n107; property control
    and, 256n104; in question, 149; redefined,
    72-73, 242n103; Russian, 25-26, 48-49, 242n113;
    and sovereignty, 35, 130-31; upheld, 6

Fairbank, John King, 11-12

Far Eastern News, 66

Federova, Nina, 241n85

Ferguson, John, 74

Filipovich, 195, 226(a)

First World War, 159

foreign consuls: American, 32, 33, 45, 58-59, 68,
    91, 92-93, 113, 121-22, 135, 137-39, 167, 169-71,
    181; diplomatic immunity, 73, 246n167;
    French, 192; protection of foreign privilege,
    139, 147, 149, 170; resistance to administrative
    reform, 75, 80, 81-82, 89, 90-91; resistance to
    land reform, 129, 130-33, 134-39; resistance
    to municipal reform, 164-67, 180; resistance
    to Russian control, 31-32, 33, 73; Russian, 31,
    74; on security, 44-45, 47; Soviet, 70, 90; and
    Soviets, 90, 144

foreign privilege. *See* extraterritoriality

Fourth Division compromise, 194-96

France, 20, 21, 130-31, 147

Fu Guicheng, 178, 226(a)

Fu Xinnian. *See* Fu Guicheng

Fujiadian, 28, 58, 76, 92-93, 234n50; Binjiang
    County Office, 39; vs Harbin, 59

funding: education, 188-90, 192, 193-94, 200-
    202; prisons, 88; reorganized courts, 74,
    75, 76-79, 243n125; research institutes, 202,
    205; security forces, 62-64, 167; Soviet,
    258n35

Geisha, The, 209-10, 211

intermarriage, 7, 9, 189, 229n7

International, 136, 181

International Committee for Indigent Russians, 176

international law, 123

International Society for the Protection of Refugees, 54

Irkutsk High Court, 73

Ivanov, A.N., 226(a); and non-Soviets, 63-64, 112, 114-15, 116-17, 251n65, 268n22; new taxes, 144; recalled, 251n71

Japan, 43, 130-31; and CER, 28; Chinese elite and, 15; and Manchuria, 19-20, 147

Jehu, 4, 229n5

Jilin, 41; government, 63; Railway Bureau, 71; Railway Foreign Affairs Bureaus, 40-41

Jilin sheng baogao (Jilin Provincial Reports), 95

Jinan, 12

Jones, Sidney, 209

journalists, 90; Caucasian, 4, 229n7; Chinese, 9, 158; Japanese, 91, 151. *See also* press

judicial reform: costs, 74, 243n125; implementation, 74, 80-81, 86-87, 245n151; legal codes, 72-73, 79, 80, 81-82, 83; views of, 92

judicial system: bribery, 245n156; cases, 79, 84-85, 245n163 (*see also* trial of the thirty-eight); Chamber of Reconciliation, 80; Chinese judiciary, 80, 81-82, 83-84, 85; Chinese notaries, 80, 245n150; court procedure, 76-80; High Court, 75, 76; and land reform, 134-35; Public Safety Courts, 74; Russian influence, 77-78; Russian judiciary, 75-76, 82-83, 84, 86, 243n128; Russian legal consultants, 78; Supreme Court (Beijing), 76; translators, 78, 81, 83, 88, 244n137; views of, 81-84

Karakhan, Lev, 109, 143

Karlinsky, Simon, 155, 156

Khabarovsk, 17(m); conference, 8, 230n20

Kharbin. *See* Harbin

Kokovstov, V.N., 28

Koo, Wellington, 111

Korostovetz, J., 33

Kruzenshtern-Peterets, 267n5

Kuropatkin, Alexei N., 72

Lahusen, Thomas, 10-11

land: acquisition, 120-21, 147, 252n6; leasing, 123-24, 131-32, 133-34, 140-41, 146-47; regulations, 122-24; values, 125, 145, 253n21

land reform: and Chinese tolerance, 146-47; consular resistance, 129, 130-33, 134-39; implementation, 126, 128, 129, 141, 147-48; Soviet blocking, 144-45; views of, 136-37, 207

language education, 186; Chinese, 186, 188, 189, 197-98, 207; Russian, 184, 185, 188, 189

languages: of business, 179, 197; on CER, 268n27; of CER contract, 22, 23-24; in Harbin, 155, 257n11; of judicial system, 79; official, 108, 168-70, 175, 177, 216, 249n32; postcolonial context, 249n25

Lashevitch, 215, 227(a)

law: Chinese, 47-48, 71, 72, 75, 79; civil, 84; Guomindang, 181; international, 123; Russian, 72-73, 79

leaseholders, 120, 126, 134, 145-46

Li Hongzhang, 20, 227(a)

Li Jiaao, 52, 81, 83, 165, 189, 227(a), 245n154

Li Lanzhou. *See* Li Jiaao

Li Shuxiao, 259n52

Li Xiaogen, 227(a); CER director, 194-95; CER president, 183; comprador career, 52, 54, 81; and municipal government, 165, 170, 173-74, 178

Liaodong Peninsula, 17(m), 19, 20-21, 24-25

Liberman, Yaacov, 7-8

Liu Minshen, 174

Liuqin. *See* Riutin, Martem'ian Nikitich

Lüshun (Port Arthur), 17(m), 24, 65, 72

Ma Zhongjun, 227(a); creole elite, 154, 185-86, 212; and education, 168, 190, 209-10; and municipal politics, 52, 165, 172, 174-75

MacDonald, Claude, 28

Manchukuo, 149, 182-83

Manchuria, 17(m); battleground, 8; Chinese incorporation of, 38-39, 126; Chinese migration, 51-52; as Chinese state, 40; Chinese view of, 19, 251n40; as colonial frontier/crossroads, 224; development, 16, 43, 123; history, 205-6; names, 229n3; open-door

162; of municipal councils, 33; of railway
bureaus, 71-72; Russian, 27, 44, 58, 59, 74,
159, 238n8
press: Chinese, 9, 68, 86, 96, 105-6, 118, 133, 136-
37, 141, 181, 198-99, 206, 210; consular, 63, 89,
120; émigré, 141-42, 172, 173; foreign, 85, 86,
91-92, 118, 141, 212-13; Japanese, 170, 179(f), 196;
Russian, 63, 93-94, 95, 107-8, 120, 141, 169, 182-
83, 212-13, 253n27; Soviet, 118; treaty port, 5
Pristan, 125
propaganda: CER, 196; and Chinese takeovers,
132, 133; forbidden, 190-91; and religious
instruction, 191; in schools, 192, 194, 195;
suppressed, 215-16, 218
Pulandian Station, 24

Qing Empire, 19, 20, 38-39, 49-50. *See also* gov-
ernment, Qing
Qinghai Province, 49
Quested, Rosemary, 218
Quinzhou, 25

racial/cultural hierarchies, 7, 82, 207; in CER,
105-6; and enfranchisement, 158-59; and
hiring, 61-62, 112; and railway fatalities,
107, 249n27; and rent gouging, 125-26;
reversed, 3-5, 56; tension, 92-95; views of,
1, 205-6, 207
racism, 2; Caucasians, 89, 91; and extraterritoriality, 223; Russians, 64, 107-8, 173, 209, 223
railroad colonialism, 19
railway bureaus, 26, 40-41, 71-72
railway police. *See* Chinese Eastern Railway
(CER), guards/police
railway security. *See* Chinese Eastern Railway
(CER), guards/police
Rea, George, 73
Red Army. *See* Union of Soviet Socialist Republics (USSR), army
refugees *(nanmin)*, 10, 48, 68, 241n77; education
needs, 188; illegal, 69, 241n72, 241n85; registration, 69; vs veteran residents, 156
Republic of China, 73-74, 144. *See also* government, Chinese
rights: administrative, 123-24, 129-30, 134-35,
252n9; CER vs Chinese, 59-60; and duties,
162; extraterritorial, 93, 108-9, 123; human,
60; of minorities, 49-50; to parity, 126; of

Russians, 80; sovereign, 122-23; territorial,
128; treaty, 93, 249n34
rights-recovery movements, 52-53
Riutin, Martem'ian Nikitich, 44, 45, 46, 227(a),
236n18
Romanov, B.A., 8
Rudy, Yuly V., 216-18, 227(a)
Russia: consulate closed, 74; court advisors, 83,
84; Great Reforms, 34; imperial hierarchy,
29-30; imperial ideology, 19; imperial pretensions, 16, 18-19, 35-36, 269n36; municipal
regulations, 34; vs other foreign powers, 21;
revolutions, 30, 36, 74, 98-99, 159; Russian
Communist Party, 85, 246n167
Russian Daily News, 94, 143, 247n197
Russian elite, 99; attitudes toward Chinese, 9;
and Chinese neighbours, 208; constituents,
3; new purpose, 199-200, 205-6; view of
development, 107-8; worldview, 201-8
Russian Far East, 17(m), 18, 99, 257n9; occupation,
10; Soviet republic, 102
Russian Orthodox Church, 219-20, 258n35
Russian revolutions. *See* Russia, revolutions
Russkii golos (newspaper), 172
Russkoe slovo (newspaper), 169
Russo-Asiatic Bank. *See* Russo-Chinese Bank
Russo-Chinese Bank, 21-22, 100, 121, 232n14
Russo-Chinese Technical Institute, 108
Russo-Japanese War (1905), 27, 28; and Qing
Empire, 40

Savrassov, 193-94
Schurman, Jacob, 227(a)
security forces: Chinese Commercial Police,
46-47; Chinese police, 46-47; Chinese takeover, 44-55; divisions, 61; funding, 62-64;
Harbin vs Fujiadian, 70; hiring practices,
61-62; language schools, 60, 65; quality, 59;
Russian police, 58-60, 64; secret police, 58;
Sino-Russian police, 57-63, 64-67, 69-70;
Special District police, 64, 66-69, 92, 240n59;
training, 65. *See also* Chinese Eastern Railway (CER), guards/police
settler communities: in China, 10, 13-14; Chinese,
40, 44, 51-52, 154-55, 257n9; English, 256n104;
Russian, 5-6, 7, 10, 16, 69, 79-80, 104, 118, 155-
57 (*see also* Russian elite); in Russian Far
East, 18. *See also* refugees *(nanmin)*

community, 67; increased, 63; municipal, 30, 35, 235n88

Tibet, 49

Tishenko, Peter, 172, 174, 227(a), 261n78

Trans-Siberian Railway, 1, 16, 17(m), 18, 20, 99. *See also* Chinese Eastern Railway (CER)

Treaty of Aigun (1858), 18

Treaty of Peking (1860), 18

Treaty of Portsmouth (1905), 122-23, 236n15

Treaty of Shimonoseki (1895), 20

Treaty of Tientsin (1858), 71

treaty ports. *See* concession cities

trial of the thirty-eight, 85-88, 90-91, 246n174, 246nn167-68, 246nn171-72

Tribuna (newspaper), 66

Tsai, Jung-Fang, 14

Tumake, 47, 236n33

Union of Soviet Socialist Republics (USSR): army, 85-86, 87-88, 216, 250n25; Communist Party, 114; consulate, 86; double-dealing, 110-12, 250n35, 268n20; imperial presence, 221-22; and imperialism, 143; recognized, 70, 87; Sino-Soviet relations, 195-96, 214-18, 250nn35-36, 268n20; Soviet-Japanese relations, 112

United States, 21, 32

Ustrialov, Nikolai Vasil'evich, 191, 192, 228(a), 264n19

viceroy of the Far East, 28; power, 26-27

Vladivostok, 102, 110

Voiekov (Professor), 94-95

Wang, C.T., 92

Wang Jiabao, 81

Wang Jingchun, 38, 62, 75, 126, 135-36, 188, 228(a), 235n1, 250n48, 253n25

Wang Lijiang, 198, 199

Wang Zhicheng, 14, 231n43

Washington Naval Conference, 100-1, 129, 130-31

Wei Guozhong, 10-11

Wen Yingxing, 61, 63-64, 65, 228(a)

whites. *See* Caucasians

White Russians *(bai-E)*, 10. *See also* émigré community

Witte, Sergei, 18, 20, 31, 228(a), 234n61

Wolff, David, 14, 31, 120, 121

Yang Cho. *See* Yang Zhuo

Yang Zhuo *(aka* Yang Cho), 113, 228(a)

Yellow Peril, 1

Yuan Shikai, 43

Yugovich, Alexander, 108

Zaria (newspaper), 143, 193-94

Zhang Guo. *See* Zhang Guochen

Zhang Guochen, 194-95, 196

Zhang Huanxiang, 228(a); and education reform, 193; head of CER guards, 48, 54, 61; and judicial reform, 86-87; and land reform, 128, 131, 133, 136, 147-48; and municipal reform, 176-77, 178, 179(f), 180; and refugees, 68; and Soviets, 104-5; Special District head, 86

Zhang Nanzhao, 44, 45-46, 47, 228(a)

Zhang Qinghui, 54, 183, 228(a)

Zhang Xueliang, 87, 117, 195, 215, 216, 228(a), 246n174, 251n73

Zhang Yiping, 75

Zhang Zuolin, 228(a); assassinated, 251n73; and CER, 63-64, 104-5, 112, 113, 116-17; and CER Land Department, 126, 127-28; and church property, 258n35; Colonization and Development Plan, 52; and decolonization, 147-48; and education, 187-88, 190; and foreign consuls, 136; and land commission, 131; and municipal government, 177; and national and regional governments, 63; and opera scandal, 213; power, 42-44, 50-52, 66, 249n19; and Russians, 9, 69, 74; and Shurman, 139; and Special District, 222; and Special District administration, 51-52, 53-54; support for Ostroumoff, 249n34; and USSR, 111-12, 143, 144

Zhengyang, 125-26

Zhu Chen, 180, 262n102

Zhu Qinglan, 228(a); and land reform, 126, 129, 134-35, 141, 144-45; and municipal government, 165, 176, 262n102; and opera scandal demonstrations, 213; and Russian community, 54, 258n56; and Soviets, 114, 117, 259n52, 266n61; Special District head, 53-54, 93-94

zone of alienation *(polosa otchuzhdeniia). See* Chinese Eastern Railway (CER) concession

Zongli Yamen. *See* government, Qing

Printed and bound in Canada by Friesens

Set in News Gothic and Walbaum by Artegraphica Design Co. Ltd.

Copy editor: Lesley Erickson

Proofreader: Dianne Tiefensee

Indexer: Dianne Tiefensee